A Companion to Wagner's Parsifal

Studies in German Literature, Linguistics, and Culture

Edited by James Hardin
(*South Carolina*)

Camden House Companion Volumes

The Camden House Companions provide well-informed and up-to-date critical commentary on the most significant aspects of major works, periods, or literary figures. The Companions may be read profitably by the reader with a general interest in the subject. For the benefit of student and scholar, quotations are provided in the original language.

A Companion to Wagner's *Parsifal*

Edited by
William Kinderman
and Katherine R. Syer

CAMDEN HOUSE

First published 2005
by Camden House

Camden House is an imprint of Boydell & Brewer Inc.
668 Mt. Hope Avenue, Rochester, NY 14620, USA
www.camden-house.com
and of Boydell & Brewer Limited
PO Box 9, Woodbridge, Suffolk IP12 3DF, UK
www.boydell.co.uk

ISBN: 1–57113–237–6

Library of Congress Cataloging-in-Publication Data

A companion to Wagner's Parsifal / edited by William Kinderman and
Katherine R. Syer.
  p. cm. — (Studies in German literature, linguistics, and culture)
(Camden House companion volumes)
  Includes bibliographical references and index.
  ISBN 1–57113–237–6 (hardcover : alk. paper)
  1. Wagner, Richard, 1813–1883. Parsifal.   I. Kinderman, William.
II. Syer, Katherine Rae, 1967–   III. Series.   IV. Series: Studies in
German literature, linguistics, and culture (Unnumbered)

ML410.W17C66 2005
782.1–dc22

                                                        2005001139

A catalogue record for this title is available from the British Library.

This publication is printed on acid-free paper.
Printed in the United States of America.

Contents

I. The Text: Sources and Symbols

II. The Music: Evolution, Structure, Aesthetics

III. Reception and Interpretation

Illustrations

Acknowledgments

THIS BOOK HAS BENEFITED FROM the support of many individuals and several institutions. The Research Board of the University of Illinois at Urbana-Champaign generously provided funds for editorial support, the acquisition of illustrations, and the creation of the music examples, which were produced by Bradley Decker. Erik Horak-Hult offered valuable assistance with the preparation of the typescript. The editors are especially grateful to the staff of the Nationalarchiv der Richard-Wagner-Stiftung in Bayreuth, and especially to Günter Fischer, Gudrun Föttinger, Peter Emmerich, and the director, Dr. Sven Friedrich, who provided access to Wagner's manuscripts as well as to relevant photographs. Archival research for chapter 4 was sponsored by the Social Sciences and Humanities Research Council of Canada. The following persons provided especially generous assistance with illustrative material and valuable information: Dr. Nike Wagner; Tony Palmer; Udo Schmidt, Steingräber & Söhne, Bayreuth; Dr. Hella Bartnig, Bayerische Staatsoper, Munich; Christina Fallara, ArenaPAL; Brian Mitchell, Houston Grand Opera; Barbara Neumann, Hamburgische Staatsoper. We also thank Jim Hardin for his personal interest in this publication, and Jim Walker for his care in seeing the project through to completion. *Parsifal* is not easily and widely loved but is an engrossing work that raises complex and urgent issues. For their compassionate understanding, unwitting or otherwise, a final note of thanks goes to Daniel, Anna, and Marie.

Introduction: The Challenge of Wagner's *Parsifal*

William Kinderman

MORE THAN ALMOST ANY OTHER WORK, Wagner's *Parsifal* merits
reevaluation. The literature on it, although quite extensive, is often
unbalanced and contradictory. To an unusual degree, commentators have
promoted perspectives on the work that conform to divergent assumptions
and preconceptions. Such polarization has been encouraged by the contro-
versies that continue to surround Wagner, and especially by the religious
aura of *Parsifal*. Michael Tanner has observed: "Difficult as it is to believe,
Parsifal, Wagner's work of peace and conciliation, has been and remains
the subject of even more bitter contention than any of his other works."[1]
More recently, Dieter Borchmeyer has claimed: "As a rule, artists who
were violently controversial in their own day sooner or later achieve classic
status, no longer sparking dissent . . . Wagner's works, together with his
artistic personality, continue to provoke disagreement and militate against
their becoming classics."[2]

In his essay "Religion and Art" of 1880 Wagner wrote that

> da, wo die Religion künstlich wird, der Kunst es vorbehalten sei, den
> Kern der Religion zu retten, indem sie die mythischen Symbole, welche
> die erstere im eigentlichen Sinne als wahr geglaubt wissen will, ihrem
> sinnbildlichen Werte nach erfaßt, um durch ideale Darstellung derselben
> die in ihnen verborgene tiefe Wahrheit erkennen zu lassen.[3]

> [When religion becomes artificial, it remains for art to rescue the essence
> of religion by perceiving its mythical symbols — which religion would
> have us believe to be the literal truth — according to their figurative
> value, enabling us to see their profound, hidden truth through idealized
> representation.][4]

---

[1] *Wagner* (Princeton: Princeton UP, 1996), 184.

[2] *Drama and the World of Richard Wagner* (Princeton and Oxford: Princeton
UP, 2003), vii.

[3] Richard Wagner, *Sämtliche Schriften und Dichtungen*, vol. 10 (Leipzig: Breitkopf
und Härtel, 1912–14), 14.

[4] All translations are by the author unless otherwise noted.

As this statement indicates, Wagner was not interested in glorifying orthodox religion through art. Although he assimilates many Christian elements in *Parsifal,* the name "Christus" never appears, and some aspects of the work draw on pagan and Buddhist traditions. Wagner rejected assertions from both followers and opponents that Parsifal was a reflection of Jesus Christ; he stressed instead that Parsifal was not free of sin, and was at most a saint.[5] The work is far from a straightforward exemplification of Christian doctrine, and Nietzsche's comment that "Wagner . . . sank plötzlich, hülflos und zerbrochen, vor dem christlichen Kreuze nieder . . . " (Wagner . . . sank down suddenly, helpless and broken, before the Christian cross), is misleading.[6] Wagner's main source for the text, the thirteenth-century epic poem by Wolfram von Eschenbach (1170–1220), shows deep piety but scant evidence of formal religion. Here, as elsewhere, Wagner was not subservient to a single religious framework in his shaping of the text and music. On the other hand, the highly tensional relation of this artwork to religious issues rewards detailed attention.[7]

---

[5] A point emphasized by Geoffrey Skelton in *Wagner in Thought and Practice* (Portland, Oregon: Amadeus, 1992), 198. Wagner stressed the "Sündenlosigkeit" ("sinlessness") of Christ, and, according to Cosima Wagner's diary entry from 12 May 1879, claimed that "Alle anderen Stifter und Heilige, wie z.B. Buddha, beginnen mit der Sünde und gelangen dann zur Heiligkeit, Christus aber kann nicht sündigen." (All other religious founders and holy persons, like Buddha, begin with sin and progress toward holiness, but Christ is incapable of sin.) Cosima Wagner, *Cosima Wagner: Die Tagebücher,* 2 vols., ed. Martin Gregor-Dellin and Dietrich Mack (Munich and Zurich: Piper, 1982; hereafter *CT*), 2:348. On 20 October 1878, Cosima quotes Wagner as rejecting Hans von Wolzogen's view of Parsifal as an embodiment of the savior, saying "'Ich habe an den Heiland dabei gar nicht gedacht.'" (I didn't think at all of the savior in that respect; *CT* 2:205).

[6] This comment appears in the 1886 preface to the second volume of *Menschliches, Allzumenschliches* (*Human, All Too Human*), section 3 (*Nietzsche Werke: Kritische Gesamtausgabe,* ed. Giorgio Colli and Mazzino Montinari, IV:3 (Berlin: Walter de Gruyter, 1967), 6). A discussion of the break between Wagner and Nietzsche centering on Nietzsche's response to the *Parsifal* poem, which he received in January 1878, and the first publication that spring of *Menschliches, Allzumenschliches* is found in Ernest Newman, *The Life of Richard Wagner,* vol. 4 (New York: Knopf, 1946), 587–91. The account of this conflict in Curt von Westernhagen, *Wagner: A Biography,* trans. by Mary Whittall (Cambridge: Cambridge UP, 1978), 533–38, while containing some valid points, is slanted against Nietzsche and should be balanced against the very different assessment in Joachim Köhler, *Nietzsche and Wagner: A Lesson in Subjugation,* trans. Ronald Taylor (New Haven and London: Yale UP, 1998), 127–38.

[7] A contribution in this vein is Ulrike Kienzle's analysis of Wagner's "religious atheism" against the background of Schopenhauer's philosophy of the will. See Kienzle's *Das Weltüberwindungswerk: Wagners "Parsifal"* (Laaber: Laaber, 1992), especially 54–68, and her chapter in the present volume.

Reassessment of this "Bühnenweihfestspiel" (stage consecration festival play), as Wagner designated it, can best be undertaken if we view *Parsifal* in the broad context of his evolving career. In many ways it is his culminating work, a project that displays points of connection to every one of his major preceding operas and music dramas. The idea of redemption, which looms so large in *Parsifal,* had of course preoccupied Wagner ever since *The Flying Dutchman,* an opera completed forty years earlier. The direct mythic precursor, on the other hand, is *Lohengrin,* the last of his German Romantic operas and the work completed immediately before his long period of political exile in Switzerland, which started in 1849. The origins of *Parsifal* go back to this period, and notably to the summer of 1845, when, as Wagner relates in his autobiography, he studied Wolfram's *Parzival* while on vacation at the resort spa Marienbad in Bohemia.[8] (This spelling of the name [Parzival] was used by Wagner throughout the early phases in the genesis of the project.) Decades passed before the work gradually took shape. His thoughts returned to *Parzival* during the 1850s, in connection with his labors on *Tristan und Isolde.* The first surviving prose draft for what became *Parsifal* dates from 1865, but the complete text was finished only in 1877 and the music written mainly between 1877 and 1879, with the full score finished in January 1882, thirteen months before Wagner's death.

This "letzte Karte" (last card; *CT* 2:718), as Wagner once described *Parsifal,* thus underwent a genesis even more protracted than that of the *Ring* cycle, and became a final work that manifests his ripest and most advanced style. *Parsifal* also stands apart in that it is the only work whose music Wagner conceived with the unique acoustics of the Bayreuth *Festspielhaus* in mind. The first Bayreuth Festival took place in the summer of 1876, with performances of the cycle *Der Ring des Nibelungen,* but the huge resulting deficit placed future performances in jeopardy. The renewal of the Festival with the "stage consecration festival play" *Parsifal* in 1882 placed the enterprise on a sound footing for the first time, enabling it to prosper after Wagner's death. For a generation thereafter, performances of *Parsifal* were virtually confined to Bayreuth. Only with the so-called "*Parsifal* theft" to New York in 1903 and the formal expiry of copyright ten years later was this monopoly broken. On January 1, 1914, just eight months before the outbreak of the First World War, the exclusive claim of Bayreuth officially expired, and in that year a flood of *Parsifal* performances took place in many of the world's leading opera houses.[9]

---

[8] Richard Wagner, *My Life,* trans. Andrew Gray (New York: Da Capo, 1992), 302.

[9] The first of these performances, in Barcelona, actually began as early as December 31, 1913. Nora Eckert explores the juxtaposition of these events in her recent book *Parsifal 1914* (Hamburg: Europäische Verlagsanstalt, 2003).

Since that time, two world wars and the appalling consequences of the Hitler regime have affected the reception of Wagner's works. The most detailed analytical study of *Parsifal* appeared in 1933, the year Hitler came to power in Germany, and its author, Alfred Lorenz, was aligned with the National Socialist cause.[10] Since then, Lorenz's confident claim to have uncovered the "secret of form" in Wagner's music by segmenting its vast continuities into symmetrical forms has been met by widespread skepticism, as found in the writings of scholars such as Carl Dahlhaus and Anthony Newcomb,[11] as well as by attempts to approach the issue of large-scale form on a somewhat different basis.[12] Yet these differences pale next to the wildly divergent views of *Parsifal* advanced by other commentators. For instance, Robert Gutman describes it as a "*pasticcio* of freakish elements — at first glance a seemingly serene and ample frieze whose figures under closer examination reveal themselves as grotesques, moving puppet-like before backgrounds realized in a strange discontinuous perspective" and finds it "amazing that *Parsifal* was ever considered a Christian work,"[13] whereas Lucy Beckett finds that "The Good Friday scene is the most moving of all modern celebrations of, precisely, 'the world as created without the poet's intervention'" and that "The Grail in *Parsifal* . . . demands to be taken in its full Christian sense as the perpetually renewed chalice of the Last Supper which represents Christ's continuing presence among men."[14]

---

[10] This book, *Der musikalische Aufbau von Richard Wagners "Parsifal"* (Berlin: Max Hesses Verlag, 1933), is the fourth volume of the series *Das Geheimnis der Form bei Richard Wagner,* which includes studies of *Tristan und Isolde, Die Meistersinger,* and the *Ring.* In his study *Analysing Wagner's Operas: Alfred Lorenz and German National Ideology* (Rochester: Boydell & Brewer, 1998), Stephen McClatchie seeks to show how Lorenz's work acted as a "musical metaphor" for German nationalist ideology during the Nazi era. Lorenz also contributed an essay on *Parsifal* to the *Bayreuther Festspielführer 1933,* ed. Otto Strobel, a volume that opens with an enthusiastic double tribute to Wagner, fifty years after his death, and to Hitler, the new chancellor of Germany.
[11] See especially Newcomb, "The Birth of Music out of the Spirit of Drama," *19th-Century Music* 5 (1981): 38–66, who offers an overview of the post-war debate in German scholarship over the work of Lorenz.
[12] In this regard see the chapter "Analytical Positions" in Warren Darcy, *Wagner's "Das Rheingold"* (Oxford: Clarendon, 1993), 45–58, and my review of Darcy's book in *Music Theory Spectrum* 19 (1997): 81–86.
[13] *Richard Wagner: The Man, his Mind, and his Music* (New York: Knopf, 1968), 432, 439.
[14] *Richard Wagner: Parsifal* (Cambridge: Cambridge UP, 1981), 148, 140. A comparable interpretation is contained in Heinrich Reinhardt, *Parsifal: Studien zur Erfassung des Problemhorizonts von Richard Wagners letztem Drama* (Straubing: Donau, 1979).

A fresh approach to interpretation properly begins with Wagner's original engagement with the *Parzival* myth, which surely even predated his
summer vacation at Marienbad. In view of the considerable fame of Wolfram's *Parzival* and Wagner's early familiarity with this poet, it seems
unlikely that he came to know *Parzival* only in 1845. This was presumably
not the time of his initial acquaintance but rather the occasion when Wagner
first took time to study the poem in detail.[15] As early as 1840, while leading
a struggling existence in Paris, he had met Gottfried Engelbert Anders, a
curiously isolated German scholar from the Rhineland who was employed as
a librarian at the Bibliothèque Royale.[16] Although otherwise impoverished,
Anders owned a fine collection of books and possessed a keen bibliographic
knowledge in the field of music.[17] Through Anders, Wagner formed a last-
ing friendship with the Prussian philologist Samuel Lehrs, which he
describes in his autobiography as "einem der schönsten Freundschaftsver-
hältnisse meines Lebens" (one of the most beautiful friendships of my
life).[18] Lehrs was the younger brother of a noted literary scholar from
Königsberg, and he showed Wagner stimulating sources on medieval saga
material, contained in part in the 1838 *Jahresheft der Königsberger Deutschen
Gesellschaft* (*Proceedings of the German Society of Königsberg*). Wagner's
study of these sources soon bore fruit. Through Lehrs, he first came into
contact with the material for the Wartburg singing contest so important to
Tannhäuser, including the text in the original language, which, as Wagner
put it, "zeigte [er] mir doch das deutsche Mittelalter in einer prägnanten
Farbe, von welcher ich bis dahin keine Ahnung erhalten hatte" (indeed

---

[15] Beckett, in *Richard Wagner: Parsifal*, 1, writes that "Wagner first read Wolfram
von Eschenbach's *Parzifal* in the summer of 1845", but Wagner states merely, "I
had therefore chosen my summer reading with care," not that the work was unfamiliar to him. Wagner's personal library at Dresden included copies of editions and
translations of *Parzival* by Lachmann (1833), Simrock (1842), and "San Marte,"
or Albert Schulz (1836), as has been documented by Curt von Westernhagen
in his book *Richard Wagners Dresdener Bibliothek 1842 bis 1849* (Wiesbaden:
F. A. Brockhaus, 1966).

[16] "Anders" was a pseudonym, meaning "unlike" or "different," conveying a self-
image that Wagner too would have shared, particularly during his time in Paris.

[17] Following the appearance of Anton Schindler's flawed *Biographie von Ludwig
van Beethoven* in 1840, Anders and Wagner planned to write a Beethoven book in
two volumes, and Wagner submitted a proposal to three German publishers, none
of whom embraced the project.

[18] Wagner's account of his acquaintance with Anders and Lehrs is found in his
autobiography, *Mein Leben* (Munich: Paul List Verlag, 1963), 203–5; in English as
My Life, trans. Andrew Gray, ed. Mary Whittall (New York: Da Capo Press, 1992),
170–71. Quotation from 205; 171. Although the autobiography is not always reliable, there seems no reason to question this part of his account.

showed me the German Middle Ages in a significant coloring I had not yet dreamed of). In turn, the historical figure of Wolfram von Eschenbach became a major character in *Tannhäuser.* Furthermore, the same book with the Wartburg poem also contained "ein kritisches Referat über das Gedicht vom *Lohengrin,* und zwar mit ausführlicher Mitteilung des Hauptinhalts dieses breitschweifigen Epos (a critique of the poem *Lohengrin,* together with a lengthy narrative of the principal contents of this rambling epic).[19]

One source led to another in Wagner's diligent reading. The *Lohengrin* saga material is closely bound up with *Parzival,* and the conclusion of Wolfram's *Parzival* poem contains the account of the *Lohengrin* legend that formed the basis for that opera. In the mythic sources, Lohengrin is the eldest son of Parzival, and succeeds him as King of the Grail. In the last act of Wagner's opera, at the climax of Lohengrin's narrative in response to Elsa's having asked the forbidden question about his origins, Lohengrin reveals this suppressed information to the assembled populace:

> Nun hört, wie ich verbot'ner Frage lohne!
> Vom Gral ward ich zu euch daher gesandt:
> Mein Vater Parzival trägt seine Krone,—
> Sein Ritter ich — bin Lohengrin genannt.

> [Now hear how I reward the forbidden question:
> I was sent to you from the Grail;
> my father, Parzival, wears its crown.
> I am his knight, Lohengrin.]

Hence Wagner's composition of *Lohengrin* itself served as preparation for his final work. Through his prolonged engagement with Wolfram's poem and treatment of related material in *Lohengrin,* Wagner was already poised to contemplate *Parzival* as a serious operatic subject by the time of his period of exile in the 1850s. Yet the process of envisioning the work unfolded slowly. Wagner had to greatly condense the contents of the medieval epics on which he drew. While reshaping the saga material, he was influenced not only by the colorful array of incidents and by the narrative and language of these sources, but also by other, overriding qualities of the original poems that helped shape his own basic conception.

The most impressive of all the medieval epics that captured Wagner's attention were surely Wolfram's *Parzival* and Gottfried von Strassburg's *Tristan.*[20] In Gottfried's masterpiece, the depiction of Tristan as a musical

---

[19] *My Life,* 213.

[20] For studies of these works, see *A Companion to Wolfram's Parzival,* ed. Will Hasty (Columbia, SC: Camden House, 1999), and *A Companion to Gottfried von Strassburg's "Tristan,"* ed. Will Hasty (Rochester: Camden House, 2003).

artist rather than as merely a knight, as well as the musical abilities of his pupil Isolde, must have fascinated Wagner.[21] And although their musical endeavors are not mentioned as such in Wagner's narrative text, the full-blooded *musical* conception of *Tristan und Isolde* represents a logical outcome of Gottfried's distinctive treatment, conjoined with the emphasis on music as a revelation of inner reality that Wagner found articulated in the philosophy of Arthur Schopenhauer.

Wolfram von Eschenbach's story focuses on the quest for an ideal and goal for aspiration higher than knighthood; the inability of individuals to choose the right path is reflected in the key notion of "zwivel" (related to "Zweifel" or "doubt" in modern German). Some passages taken over by Wagner from Wolfram show Parzival at first unable to find the right path, as when he fails to show compassion by asking a question of the ailing Grail King Anfortas.[22] In Wolfram's version, it is Anfortas who informs Parzival of the death of his mother, Herzeloyde, and who forgives him his sins, reminding him of the importance of humility. Another common theme is the love of one's fellow creatures, which begins to dawn on Wolfram's Parzival when he weeps over the death of birds slain by his arrows. Wagner incorporates this moment into the killing of the swan, and deepens the quality of humility into compassion. This compassion (*Mitleid*) eventually broadens in its scope as Parzival becomes an instrument of higher spiritual forces.

It is revealing to consider other affinities between *Lohengrin* and *Parsifal,* the two Wagnerian works associated with the Grail legend. These affinities extend to aspects of the textual and musical treatment, as well as to the larger dramatic structure. One obvious point of contact is the role of the swan. The otherworldly Grail Knight Lohengrin approaches and departs from the action with the swan, and the special importance of the creature is unveiled at the conclusion, as the swan is transformed into Gottfried, Elsa's long-lost brother. A venerable mythic symbol, the swan would later assume signal importance for Wagner's indispensable patron, King Ludwig II (1845–86) of Bavaria, himself descended from an Order

---

[21] For a discussion of these attributes, see Will Hasty, "Performances of Love: Tristan and Isolde at Court," in *A Companion to Gottfried von Strassburg's "Tristan,"* ed. Will Hasty, 159–81, esp. 167–72.

[22] Wagner's sources used the spelling Anfortas, which he followed until he wrote the complete poem of *Parsifal* in 1877, when he changed it to Amfortas. Parzival's failure to intervene by posing a question at the Grail Temple results in the wounded king being condemned to continued agony and grief, as is emphasized in Wolfram's *Parzival* and also in Chrétien de Troyes's *Perceval.* In this regard, see among other studies the recent book *The Holy Grail: Imagination and Belief* by Richard Barber (Cambridge, MA: Harvard UP, 2004), esp. 20–21, 78.

of Swan Knights, as is reflected in the names of his castles Hohenschwan-gau and Neuschwanstein. Ultimately, Ludwig's fascination with Lohengrin as divine Swan Knight grew into an unhealthy obsession: at Linderhof (yet another of his castles) the king indulged in rides in a swan-boat in a private subterranean grotto adorned by scenes from Wagner's operas.

In *Parsifal*, the swan symbol from *Lohengrin* is turned on its head dramatically, with the naïve hero appearing as a swan killer, committing the shocking "murder" of the sacred bird in a realm of the Grail. The logic of this treatment rests in the character development of Parsifal, whose role as a "pure fool," who gains knowledge through compassion had been foretold. When his misdeed is pointed out to him, Parsifal demonstrates his capacity for compassion for the first time and discards his bow and arrow. The act of killing the swan is dramatically significant, and in act 3, when Parsifal returns years later to the realm of the Grail, Gurnemanz recognizes him as "the one who once killed the swan."

An intriguing connection exists between the musical motive employed in the passage beginning "Mein lieber Schwan!" in act 1 of *Lohengrin* and the same idea employed at the slaying of the swan in act 1 of *Parsifal*. Wagner reinterprets the preexisting motive with considerable subtlety, especially when Gurnemanz describes the graceful flight of the swan before it was struck by Parsifal's arrow. The delicate textures of this passage surpass the version in *Lohengrin* and match well to the text, with its references to the circling motion of the swan over the lake. Other motivic affinities exist between these works. The music heard when Gurnemanz describes the descent of the heavenly heralds to Titurel is quite similar, in its descending stepwise contour and dotted rhythm, to the soft descending theme heard near the end of the *Lohengrin* prelude, beginning eighteen bars from the conclusion. In this instance, the kinship is not created by a quotation but rather is an outcome of stylistic and symbolic procedures that reach beyond the level of an individual work. The passage in *Lohengrin* clearly has a symbolic import similar to the more concentrated "heavenly descent" in Gurnemanz's narrative.

There are also parallels in the dramatic construction of *Lohengrin* and *Parsifal* on the largest scale. In both works, the outer acts are most concerned with ritualistic events, whereas the middle act is dominated by darker, ominous characters. In both cases, the key event in the opening act is the astonishing arrival of an external agent. The dramatic problems that these agents need to solve differ considerably. Although Parsifal's first visit to the Grail is unsuccessful, it nevertheless launches him on his gradual path toward maturity and enlightenment. Lohengrin's arrival, on the other hand, is a quick fix to the dramatic problem — a solution that will not withstand the vicissitudes of real life, of human doubt and fallibility.

Of all Wagner's dramas, *Lohengrin* is the most tragic. The other-worldly character of the hero, and his dependence on Elsa's blind faith, prove no match for the shrewd and dishonest manipulations of Ortrud. The straightforwardness of Lohengrin and the innocent gullibility of Elsa are bound to be undone. Psychologically, the most penetrating character is Ortrud, whose bitter hatred has deep roots in an opposing ideological outlook that scornfully denies the existence of a monotheistic god. "Gottes Kraft? Ha, ha!" (Heavenly powers? Ha, ha!) she exclaims in her galvanizing response to the despairing Frederick von Telramund in act 2. The character of Ortrud invites comparison to Shakespeare's Lady Macbeth or Iago. Her "Credo" in act 2, in which she invokes the pagan gods in wild exultation to grant her vengeance, foreshadows the demonic confession of Verdi's Jago in his *Otello*.

In this context it is striking to observe the many musical and dramatic affinities that exist between Ortrud in *Lohengrin* and Klingsor and Kundry in *Parsifal*. There can be little doubt but that Wagner, when he initially fashioned the dramatic scenario for *Parsifal* in prose sketches in the 1850s and 1860s, must have envisioned prominent aspects of the music in a general way. What *Lohengrin* offered, in particular, was a framework in which the dark chromaticism of a distinctive minor key could serve as the vehicle for a corrosive, manipulative force. Ortrud's associative tonality of F♯ minor is especially predominant at the outset of act 2. In *Parsifal*, it is act 2 that is set away from the realm of the Grail, in Klingsor's Magic Castle, and Klingsor's associated tonality of B minor (itself closely related to F♯ minor) serves as the framing key for the act as a whole.

The scornful laughter of Ortrud corresponds to Kundry's mocking laughter, which, in its original incarnation as mockery of the Redeemer on the cross, resulted in her curse. The symbol of scornful laughter is developed further in *Parsifal,* and one of the main musical motives for Kundry is evocative of her laughter. Another point of contact is the dramatic function of Klingsor as the opponent of the Grail Knights, one who through magic and cunning has already damaged the Grail Order and who is intent upon its complete destruction. Ortrud's analogous role in *Lohengrin* offered a preexisting framework, and Wagner was probably conscious of not wanting to come too close to his earlier setting in composing the music to *Parsifal*. The broader family resemblance of Ortrud's music to the Klingsor-Kundry realm emerges if we compare the beginning of act 2 of *Lohengrin* to several passages in *Parsifal*. Notable in this regard is the chromatic motive that is associated with Kundry's deathly sleep but also with her attempted seduction of Parsifal. This musical idea is often described as the "Magic" motive (*Zaubermotiv*) in recognition of the influence of Klingsor, but Wagner once aptly described its character at Kundry's kiss as "Ein Augenblick dämonischen Versenkens . . . worin das tragische, wie Gift sich schlängelnde Motiv der Liebessehnsucht vernichtend wirkt" (a moment of demonic possession . . . in which the tragic, serpentine motive of love's desire acts destructively, like poison).[23] Here, as elsewhere, a single motive in Wagner takes on a range of dramatic meanings. It is this "serpentine motive of love's desire" that bears a tangible similarity to the haunting repeated phrase with cellos and bassoons heard at the outset of act 2 in *Lohengrin*. The winding contour, exposed dissonant tritones, and other shared features of these musical ideas point to a deeper dramatic affinity. In context, the obsessive patterning and heightened dissonance of such motives convey a sense of ill intent and destructive potential.

Soon after completing *Lohengrin*, Wagner fled Saxony and eventually found political refuge in Zurich, Switzerland. For several years, he was primarily occupied with various prose writings and with the gigantic cycle *Der Ring des Nibelungen*. However, for an extended period during the ensuing genesis of his following work, *Tristan und Isolde*, the character of Parzival surfaced again, as Wagner reflected upon dramatic parallels between the final act of *Tristan* and the *Parsifal* drama. As he put it in retrospect, "Dieser an der empfangenen Wunde siechende und nicht sterben könnende Tristan identifizierte sich in mir nämlich mit dem Anfortas im Gral-Roman" (The picture of Tristan languishing, yet unable to die of his wound, identified itself in my mind with Anfortas in the Romance of the Grail).[24] This identification dates from 1855, and is recorded in a notebook from that year.[25] Four years later, in May 1859, Wagner writes in a similar vein to Mathilde Wesendonk describing the figure of Anfortas as "mein Tristan des dritten Aktes mit einer undenklichen Steigerung" (my Tristan of the third act with an inconceivable intensification).[26] Later in the same letter he writes:

> Und noch dazu hat's mit dem Parzival eine Schwierigkeit mehr. Er ist unerläßlich nötig als der ersehnte Erlöser des Anfortas: soll Anfortas aber in das wahre, ihm gebührende Licht gestellt werden, so wird er von so ungeheuer tragischem Interesse, daß es fast mehr als schwer wird, ein zweites Hauptinteresse gegen ihn aufkommen zu lassen, und doch müßte dieses Hauptinteresse sich dem Parzival zuwenden, wenn er nicht als kalt lassender Deus ex machina eben nur schließlich hinzutreten sollte.

> [And yet there is still another difficulty with the character of Parzival: he is absolutely indispensable as the chosen redeemer of Anfortas: but should Anfortas be shown in a true, revealing light, he will be of such enormous

---

[23] See the entry in Cosima Wagner's diary dated 3 June 1878. This passage is cited in Richard Wagner, *Sämtliche Werke*, vol. 30, ed. M. Geck and E. Voss (Mainz: Schott, 1970), 33.

[24] Wagner, *Mein Leben*, 594.

[25] Richard Wagner, *Sämtliche Werke*, 30:12.

[26] Wolfgang Golther, ed., *Richard Wagner an Mathilde Wesendonk: Tagebuchblätter und Briefe 1853–1871* (Berlin: Alexander Duncker Verlag, 1910), 207.

tragic interest that it will be more than difficult to create another main interest against him, and yet this principal interest must be centered in Parzival if he is not to appear at the end as a cold deus ex machina.][27]

How then did Wagner successfully create "another main interest" in the character of Parsifal? Here his assimilation of the thought of Schopenhauer during the 1850s was pivotal. Seen as "durch Mitleid wissend, der reine Tor" (knowing through compassion, the pure fool), Parsifal could be treated initially as a raw youth at the outset of a long path toward enlightenment. Consequently, Wagner's *Parsifal* may be understood as a special type of *Bildungsroman,* with the education of the hero prolonged over the course of the drama. The guiding concept has a Schopenhauerian cast, involving an overcoming of the *principium individuationis* through an attainment of mastery over the individual will. In Schopenhauer's *The World as Will and Representation,* which Wagner read and re-read many times, starting in 1854, the principle is described as follows:

> Schon die Heiligkeit, welche jeder rein moralischen Handlung anhängt, beruht darauf, daß eine solche im letzten Grunde aus der unmittelbaren Erkenntnis der numerischen Identität des inneren Wesens alles Lebenden entspringt. Diese Identität ist aber eigentlich nur im Zustande der Verneinung des Willens (Nirwana) vorhanden, da seine Bejahung (Sansara) die Erscheinung desselben in der Vielheit zur Form hat. Bejahung des Willens zum Leben, Erscheinungwelt, Diversität aller Wesen, Individualität, Egoismus, Haß, Bosheit entspringen aus *einer* Wurzel, und ebenso anderseits Welt des Dinges an sich, Identität aller Wesen, Gerechtigkeit, Menschenliebe, Verneinung des Willens zum Leben. Wenn nun, wie ich genugsam gezeigt habe, schon die moralischen Tugenden aus dem Innewerden jener Identität aller Wesen entstehen, diese aber nicht in der Erscheinung, sondern nur im Dinge an sich, in der Wurzel aller Wesen liegt, so ist die tugendhafte Handlung ein momentaner Durchgang durch den Punkt, zu welchem die bleibende Rückkehr die Verneinung des Willens zum Leben ist.

> [The holiness attaching to every purely moral action rests on the fact that ultimately such action springs from the immediate knowledge of the numerical identity of the inner nature of all living things. But this identity is really present only in the state of denial of the will (Nirvana), as the affirmation of the will (Samsara) has for its form the phenomenal appearance of this in plurality and multiplicity. Affirmation of the will-to-live, the phenomenal world, diversity of all beings, individuality, egoism, hatred, wickedness, all spring from *one* root. Now, as I have sufficiently shown, moral virtues spring from an awareness of that identity of all beings; this, however, lies not in the phenomenon, but in the thing-in-itself, in the root of all beings. If this is the case, then the virtuous action

---

[27] *Richard Wagner an Mathilde Wesendonk,* 210.

is a momentary passing through the point, the permanent return to which is the denial of the will-to-live.][28]

Hence it is a decisive shift away from egoistic affirmation of the self in the phenomenal world that represents progress toward enlightenment. The hero's distance from this goal is made clear in the early stages of the action. Parsifal's very first words, "Gewiss! Im Fluge treff' ich, was fliegt!" (Of course! In flight I shoot everything that flies!) convey a sheer abandonment to the chase, with complete lack of concern for the creatures who fall victim to the hunt. In similar unthinking obliviousness, he fails to contemplate the consequences of his absence from his mother, Herzeleide (Heart's Sorrow), causing her death. Moreover, when Kundry tells of Herzeleide's death, Parsifal loses all control, and throttles her. "Schon wieder Gewalt!" (Violence again!), exclaims Gurnemanz.

Wagner's greatest difficulty was determining how Parsifal's further psychological progress could be adequately motivated in dramatic terms. Since a prose sketch allegedly made by Wagner in 1857 has not survived, we are somewhat at a disadvantage in judging his plans for *Parsifal* from this period. Houston Stewart Chamberlain claimed in his 1886 essay "Notes sur *Parsifal*" in the *Revue wagnérienne* that the sketch outlined a drama in three acts, containing scenes familiar from the completed work as well as fragments of musical motives.[29] To judge from the extant sources, however, it seems certain that some crucial aspects of the drama still remained undeveloped.

Around this time Wagner made a musical sketch for Parzival as wanderer seeking the Grail, an idea presumably identical with "Parzival's refrain" as mentioned in an earlier notebook entry from 1855. The relationship between *Tristan und Isolde* and *Parzival* fascinated Wagner, and his notion of introducing the character of Parzival into the third act of *Tristan* provides the context for this musical sketch. The theme is in the key of E major, and was ultimately replaced by Tristan's vision of Isolde, in the same key, as Robert Bailey has observed.[30] Although this musical idea was originally intended for *Tristan,* and not *Parsifal,* it bears a family resemblance to the complex of themes for the Grail in the later work, and belongs, broadly considered, to the genesis of the music for *Parsifal.* Nevertheless, Wagner's initial fixation on Parzival as wanderer seeking the

---

[28] Arthur Schopenhauer, *Die Welt als Wille und Vorstellung*, ed. Heinrich Schmidt (Leipzig: Alfred Kröner Verlag, 1911), 2:338; in English: *The World as Will and Representation*, trans. E. F. J. Payne (New York: Dover, 1966), 2:609–10.

[29] "Notes sur Parsifal," *Revue wagnérienne* 7 (1886): 220–26; here, 222.

[30] See Robert Bailey, "The Genesis of 'Tristan und Isolde' and a Study of the Sketches and Drafts for the First Act" (PhD diss., Princeton, 1969), 30–31. A transcription of this sketch is found in chapter 4 of the present volume.

Grail was somewhat downplayed when he worked out the details of the drama. There was to be no independent episode devoted to Parsifal's prolonged and tortuous return to the Grail. Instead, Wagner concentrated his depiction of this journey in the music of the prelude to act 3 and in the corresponding parts of Parsifal's narrative later in that act. Nevertheless, it is striking that Wagner repeatedly turned to the "Dresden Amen" motive, with its stepwise rising contour, when he conceived music associated with an arduous pilgrimage. The last act of *Tannhäuser* and the musical sketch for "Parzival's refrain" both use variants of this figure, which is absorbed as well into the so-called Grail motive in *Parsifal* and employed in the prelude to act 3 to signal Parsifal's eventual approach to the Grail realm, after his path has been blocked by Kundry's curse.

A crucial missing ingredient in Wagner's evolving dramatic scenario in the 1850s was that character who would serve to connect Amfortas and Parsifal, while motivating the downfall of the one and triumph of the other. This was of course Kundry, a fascinating amalgam who absorbs content from several of Eschenbach's characters. These include "Cundrie la sorcière," a Grail messenger of mysterious and sinister aspect; Orgeluse, a seductress held in the power of the sorcerer Clinschor; and Parsifal's cousin Sigune, a melancholy maiden and penitent. These three characters serve as models for Wagner's Kundry in each of the three acts.[31] Wagner's Kundry as a bringer of news (*Kunde*) also borrows from Eschenbach's character Trevrizent, an old knight who also served as one model for Gurnemanz. Yet there are dimensions of Kundry that have no basis in Eschenbach's *Parzival,* and her dramatic relationship to Parsifal rewards close attention.

Kundry also reflects aspects of the character of the young woman Sawitri in Wagner's unfinished Buddhist drama *Die Sieger* (The Victors), from 1856. The plot of *Die Sieger* centers on the relation of sensuous and godly love, of Eros and Agapē. In a previous incarnation, the beautiful Sawitri had spurned, with mocking laughter, a Brahmin's son. She passionately loves the chaste young man Ananda, but is influenced by the Buddha to renounce him when she is admitted into the Buddha's community. The notion of Kundry's many incarnations and her divided existence between the Grail and Klingsor suggests a connection to this unfinished project.[32]

More suggestive still is an important letter Wagner wrote to Mathilde Wesendonk from Paris at the beginning of August in 1860. Following

---

[31] Cf. Beckett, *Richard Wagner: Parsifal,* 10; and Wolfgang Golther, *Parzifal und der Gral in der Dichtung des Mittelalters und der Neuzeit* (Stuttgart: J. B. Metzler, 1925), 359–60.

[32] A recent discussion of related issues is contained in Bernd Zegowitz, *Richard Wagners unvertonte Opern* (Frankfurt am Main: Peter Lang, 2000), 257–71.

a discussion of the transmigration of souls related to *Parzival, Lohengrin,* and *Die Sieger,* Wagner turns to a detailed analysis of the character of Kundry in the *Parzival* drama, a passage that needs to be quoted at length:

Viel ist wieder der "Parzival" in mir wach gewesen; ich sehe immer mehr und heller darin; wenn alles einmal ganz reif in mir ist, muß die Ausführung dieser Dichtung ein unerhörter Genuß für mich werden . . . Sagte ich Ihnen schon einmal, daß die fabelhaft wilde Gralsbotin ein und dasselbe Wesen mit dem verführerischen Weibe des zweiten Aktes sein soll? Seitdem mir dies aufgegangen, ist mir fast alles an diesem Stoffe klar geworden. Dies wunderbar grauenhafte Geschöpf, welches den Gralsrittern mit unermüdlichem Eifer sklavenhaft dient, die unerhörten Aufträge vollzieht, in einem Winkel liegt und nur harrt, bis sie etwas Ungemeines, Mühvolles zu verrichten hat, — verschwindet zuzeiten ganz, man weiß nicht wie und wohin?

Dann plötzlich trifft man sie einmal wieder, furchtbar erschöpft, elend, bleich und grauenhaft: aber von neuem unermüdlich, wie eine Hündin dem heiligen Grale dienend, vor dessen Rittern sie eine Heimlich Verachtung blicken läßt: ihr Auge scheint immer den Rechten zu suchen, — sie täuschte sich schon — fand ihn aber nicht. Aber was sie sucht, das weiß sie eben nicht: es ist nur Instinkt.

Als Parzival, der Dumme, ins Land kommt, kann sie den Blick nicht von ihm abwenden: Wunderbares muß in ihr vorgehen; sie weiß es nicht, aber sie heftet sich an ihn. Ihm graust es — aber auch ihn zieht es an: er versteht nichts . . . — Dieses Weib ist in einer unsäglichen Unruhe und Erregung: der alte Knappe hat das früher an ihr bemerkt, zu Zeiten, ehe sie kurz darauf verschwand. Diesmal ist ihr Zustand auf das höchste gespannt. Was geht in ihr vor? Hat sie Grauen vor einer abermaligen Flucht, möchte sie ihr enthoben sein? Hofft sie — ganz enden zu können? Was hofft sie von Parzival? Offenbar heftet sie einen unerhörten Anspruch an ihn? — Aber alles ist dunkel und finster: kein Wissen, nur Drang, Dämmern? — In einem Winkel gelauert wohnt sie der qualvollen Szene des Amfortas bei: sie blickt mit wunderbarem Forschen (sphinxartig) auf Parzival. Der — ist auch dumm, begreift nichts, staunt — schweigt. Er wird hinausgestoßen. Die Gralsbotin sinkt kreischend zusammen; dann ist sie verschwunden. (Sie muß wieder wandern.)

Nun raten Sie, wer das wunderbar zauberische Weib ist, die Parzifal in dem seltsamen Schlosse findet, wohin sein ritterlicher Wut ihn führt? Raten Sie, was da vorgeht, und wie da alles wird. Heute sage ich Ihnen nicht mehr![33]

[Parzival has become much more alive in me; I see it more and more, and more clearly; once my ideas come to fruition, the execution of this poem will be an unheard-of pleasure for me . . . Did I tell you already that the

---

[33] *Richard Wagner an Mathilde Wesendonk,* 243–44.

legendary wild messenger of the Grail should be one and the same being as the seductive woman of the second act? Almost everything about this material became clear to me once I realized this. This wonderfully haggard creature, who serves the Grail Knights with inexhaustible eagerness, performing the most unheard-of tasks, lies in a corner, and just waits, until she has something extraordinary and difficult to do — sometimes disappearing totally for a time, so that one knows not how and where?

Then suddenly one encounters her again, terribly exhausted, wretched, pale and grim: but again she is indefatigable, serving like a dog the Holy Grail, toward whose knights she signals a secret disdain: her eye seems always to seek the right one — she has failed before, and not found him. But what she is seeking, she doesn't exactly know: it is only instinct. —

When Parzival arrives, the stupid one, she can't take her eyes off him: something wonderful must take place in her; she doesn't know it, but she is bound to him. He dreads it — but it also fascinates him: he understands nothing . . . — This woman is in an unspeakable state of disquiet and agitation: the old knight had noticed that about her at times, shortly before she vanished. This time her state is at the highest point of tension. What takes place in her? Does she fear some age-old curse, does she yearn to be freed from it? Does she hope — to finally end it? What does she hope from Parzival? Clearly she has some extraordinary expectation of him? — But everything is dark and obscure: no knowledge, just compulsion, twilight? — Huddled in a corner she witnesses the torturous scene with Amfortas: she looks with wonderful penetration (sphinx-like) at Parzival. He — is also dumb, understands nothing, stares — is silent. He is thrown out. The messenger of the Grail sinks down groaning; then she disappears. (She must continue her wandering.)

Now, can you guess who the wonderful magical woman is whom Parsifal finds in the strange castle to which his knightly courage has let him? You imagine what happens there, and how all of that will be. Today I'll tell you no more! —]

What stands out here is Wagner's inquiry into the existential state of Kundry — her deeper, hidden motivations, hopes, and fears.[34] One detail of his description suggests a new line of interpretation: the description of Kundry's "sphinx-like" regard of the "pure fool," Parzival.[35] A sphinx is a mysterious compound being — part human, part animal. The character of Kundry, as we have seen, is also a compound of characters drawn from Eschenbach's *Parzival*. Inasmuch as she consists of a complex amalgam of

---

[34] One consequence of this focus on Kundry's complex psychology is the rich array of gestural directions for this character in the score.

[35] Kundry's contemplation of Parzival was to have occurred in the Grail Temple, where, in the finished work, she is no longer present; yet her strange fascination with Parzival is clearly reflected in the first half of the act as we know it.

conflicting character types, Kundry does seem mysteriously "sphinx-like." Yet that in itself sheds but little new light on her character.

More revealing is the context that springs to mind from Kundry's "sphinx-like" aspect. The classic tale of the sphinx is Sophocles' play *Oedipus*, and a crucial encounter in that famous work is the confrontation of Oedipus with the sphinx. In other words, it is not just the bare analogy of Kundry with the sphinx that deserves attention here, but the *entire* relationship of Oedipus to the sphinx. For Parsifal displays some Oedipus-like traits, as Wagner must have been keenly aware. Parsifal's mother-fixation is signaled at once in his music in act 1, when Herzeleide's theme is played while Gurnemanz poses questions about Parsifal's name and background, none of which he can answer. Kundry's seduction attempt in act 2 relies heavily on her assuming the role of mother, and her kiss is "a last mother's greeting" as well as a "first kiss of love." The seduction scene derives much power from this incest motive. In Sophocles' play, by comparison, Oedipus actually commits incest, marrying his mother after killing his father.

A sphinx is a creature that guards gates and cemeteries, a dangerous opponent who devours victims who fail to answer the riddles she poses. Kundry too is capable of posing uncomfortable questions, even to her self-castrated master Klingsor, whom she torments with the biting retort: "Are you chaste?" The famous question of the sphinx, "What goes on four feet in the morning, on two at midday, on three in the evening?" is correctly answered, "man," by Oedipus. Yet, as Wagner claims in the long commentary on *Oedipus* in his treatise *Oper und Drama* of 1851, Oedipus failed to assert his humanity when he put out his own eyes in response to the social taboos he had violated. In so acting, he followed the sphinx into oblivion. Wagner demands instead that "*wir* haben dieses Rätsel zu lösen, und zwar dadurch, daß wir die Unwillkür des Individuums aus der Gesellschaft, deren höchster, immer erneuernder und belebender Reichtum sie ist, selbst rechtfertigen" (*we* must solve this riddle, and precisely by justifying the emancipation from society of the individual, its highest and always renewable and vital treasure).[36]

In the long history of this "Symbol gleichsam des Symbolischen selber" (symbol of the symbolic itself), in Hegel's words,[37] it is rare for a commentator to probe the soul of the sphinx-like protagonist, as Wagner

---

[36] Richard Wagner, *Oper und Drama*, ed. Klaus Kropfinger (Stuttgart: Reclam, 1984), 192.

[37] Hegel, *Aesthetik, Sämtliche Werke*, vol. 12, ed. Hermann Glockner (Stuttgart: Fromanns, 1949–63), 480; in English: *Aesthetics*, trans. T. M. Knox (Oxford: Oxford UP, 1975), 360. For a comprehensive survey of the symbol of the sphinx in cultural history, see Willis Regier, *Book of the Sphinx* (Lincoln and London: U of Nebraska P, 2004).

does. This unusual perspective helped him to fill out the dramatic psychology of *Parsifal* in unprecedented fashion, moving far beyond Wolfram von Eschenbach. The timeless, primeval aspect of Kundry, who had already been discovered by the Grail founder, Titurel, and whose incarnations included Herodias and Gundryggia, belongs to this symbolic context, as does the suggestion, in act 1, of her possessing animalistic features. (The squires accuse her of being a beast, to which she replies "Are the animals not sacred here?") The notion of another kind of compound being — part human and part flora — is developed in the Flowermaidens of act 2, whose leader and supreme embodiment is Kundry.[38] Yet most significant is the mysterious deepening of the encounter between Parsifal and Kundry in act 2. Her electrifying call "Parsifal, hier weile!" (Parsifal, linger here!) — the first time the hero's name is heard — bears comparison with a god's summoning of Oedipus "from many sides at once: 'Ho Oedipus, Thou Oedipus, why are we tarrying?'"[39] As a major threshold event in Parsifal's character development, Kundry's kiss occupies a central dramatic position. Her seduction attempt is the most formidable of all Parsifal's psychological challenges on his path toward the role of redeemer: its success would doom him. A normal human being should be unable to resist her, to see beyond the sensuous entanglement of Klingsor's magic realm. Parsifal's compassion for Amfortas enables him to resist Kundry, whereby the sphinx riddle of Kundry's seduction is answered by Schopenhauerian renunciation, ultimately setting her free from her curse. Herein lies the cause for her keen fascination with Parsifal in act 1: she instinctively yearns for the end to her servitude to Klingsor. In Sophocles' drama, Oedipus follows the sphinx to the abyss. Parsifal, by contrast, offers to his sphinx-like companion a release from her bondage and a promise of salvation.[40]

When Wagner wrote to Mathilde Wesendonk in August 1860, he was occupied with the revision of *Tannhäuser* for Paris. This revision involved his writing new text and music for the Venusberg scene, in which

---

[38] Kundry's relation to the Flowermaidens is made clear in the music toward the end of act 2, where she reverts to the Flowermaidens' music after the failure of the seduction has become evident.

[39] From *Oedipus Coloneus*, 1615–17, as cited in the chapter "Woman as the Temptress" in Joseph Campbell, *The Hero with a Thousand Faces* (Princeton: Princeton UP, 1972), 122.

[40] Interesting in this context is Robert A. Davis's recent suggestion that Parsifal's refusal of Kundry's embrace involves a "renunciation of the Oedipal symbolic order with its fatalistic account of split subjectivity and the dualism of spirit and flesh." ("The Truth Ineffably Divine: The Loss and Recovery of the Sacred in Richard Wagner's *Parsifal*," in *Voicing the Ineffable: Musical Representations of Religious Experience,* ed. Siglind Bruhn (Hillsdale, NY: Pendragon, 2002), 118).

Tannhäuser resolves to leave the garden of delights, despite Venus's efforts to block his departure. The contrast between ascetic spirituality and sensuality, Elisabeth and Venus, the Wartburg and the Venusberg, remains a stark dichotomy in *Tannhäuser*. It seems hardly coincidental that the ripening of his ideas for Kundry occurred around the time he wrote these additions to *Tannhäuser* for the Paris production. In *Parsifal*, the enigmatic figure of Kundry allows for a bridging of these opposing realms in what is probably the most symbolically rich character in all Wagner's works.

The ensuing years were the most turbulent and stressful of Wagner's life, and the fulfillment of his artistic goals must often have seemed remote. However, in 1864 the timely intervention of "Parzival" (Wagner's nickname for King Ludwig II) rescued his career, and it was at the urging of the king that Wagner wrote out an extremely detailed prose draft of *Parzival* in August 1865. This draft was written into the "brown book," the diary that Wagner began using shortly after the beginning of his relationship with his future wife Cosima von Bülow. On August 31 Wagner sent a copy of the draft to Ludwig II, who offered thanks a few days later in a highly exaggerated tone to his "worshipped, holy friend!"

For the most part, this prose draft resembles the finished work closely. In certain respects, it is even more detailed than the text of the completed poem. A conspicuously undeveloped section is Amfortas's lament in act 1, yet Parsifal's reexamination of this scene after Kundry's kiss in act 2 is richly elaborated. This suggests that in devising the text for Amfortas's lament, Wagner was guided by the later episode in which Parsifal's insight, which remained private and mute in the Temple Scene, becomes fully articulate. Sandra Corse relates this dramatic framework to the duality of the Apollonian and Dionysian in Nietzsche's book *Die Geburt der Tragödie* of 1872, seeing "the primordial pain externalized in *Parsifal* as Amfortas's wound, which the character of Parsifal enters into sympathetic relationship with, [as] a contradiction within a unity, the inevitable irruption of the Dionysian into the priests' dream of Apollonian order." Unlike the Knights, Parsifal is the "pagan observer who sees the literal blood rather than ignoring its obvious, material meaning . . . as the priests do"; his "stubborn refusal to see [the] religious significance [of the Grail] helps him later to have the insight that it, along with everything else in the world of the knights, is just representation."[41]

In the prose draft, unlike in Wolfram's version, the Grail is identified with the cup that received the blood of the redeemer.[42] The companion

[41] *Operatic Subjects: the Evolution of Self in Modern Opera* (Madison and Teaneck: Fairleigh Dickinson UP, 2000), 73, 72.

[42] In Wolfram von Eschenbach's *Parzival*, the Grail is a precious stone that gives nourishment to the Grail Knights.

piece to the Grail is the holy spear, but Wagner was uncertain how to handle the lance in his draft, and wrote out two different interpretations, asking Cosima "which is better?"[43] The difference lay in whether or not the spear was to have been given originally to the Knights of the Grail. In the version finally adopted by Wagner, the spear was bequeathed together with the Grail, but was lost to Klingsor after Amfortas carried it recklessly into combat against the sorcerer. This version has the advantage of showing how Amfortas's aggressive misuse of the spear permits both its loss to Klingsor and Amfortas's own wounding by the very instrument that had pierced the redeemer.

Ultimately, it is the spear itself, in Parsifal's hands, that will heal Amfortas's wound. In Wagner's prose draft, the closing scene of act 3 was envisioned quite differently than in the completed work. One difference consists in the more active role of Amfortas: after his healing by Parsifal, he helps lift the Grail from its shrine. Even more remarkable is the temporary revival of the dead Titurel in the draft, who momentarily stirs in his coffin. This unsettled nature of the conclusion of *Parsifal* during its genesis is striking in view of the approaches of modern opera directors, who have explored a variety of possibilities for the end of the drama, often departing from Wagner's stage directions.

One major stage in Wagner's evolving engagement with *Parsifal* during the period up to 1877 remains:[44] his use of preexisting musical material in connection with the central dramatic idea of the Grail. In devising the music for the Grail, which is for the most part harmonically stable and diatonic, Wagner drew heavily on musical materials with sacred associations. The most obvious of these is the "Dresden Amen" motive, which stems from Johann Gottlieb Naumann, Wagner's predecessor as court *Kapellmeister* at Dresden in the late eighteenth century. Mendelssohn had used the "Dresden Amen" in his "Reformation" Symphony in D minor, op. 107, of 1830. For Mendelssohn, as for Karl Loewe and Ludwig Spohr, the "Dresden Amen" is emblematic of Catholic church music.[45] In *Parsifal*, this traditional musical motive, which features the interval of a stepwise rising fourth (or fifth), is incorporated into the second part of the Grail motive. In turn, the prominent rising contour of the "Dresden Amen" is neatly complemented by the so-called Faith motive, which inverts this

---

[43] Joachim Bergfeld, *Richard Wagner: Das braune Buch: Tagebuchaufzeichnungen 1865 bis 1882* (Zurich: Atlantis, 1975), 76. The prose draft is found on pages 53–70.

[44] A detailed discussion of the evolution of the music, based on Wagner's numerous sketches and drafts, is offered in chapter 4 of the present volume.

[45] See R. Larry Todd, "Mendelssohn," in *The Nineteenth-Century Symphony*, ed. D. Kern Holoman (New York: Schirmer, 1997), 86.

intervallic shape, emphasizing a stepwise descent of a fourth. These two motives are often heard in conjunction with one another, and together with the opening Last Supper or Communion theme and its composite motives they form the most important body of music associated with the Grail in *Parsifal.*

The Communion theme heard at the very beginning of the work displays considerable complexity in its structural and expressive components, consisting as it does of a synthesis of several motives, each of which is capable of detachment and independent development. The beginning of the Communion theme, with its suspended rise through the notes of the tonic triad followed by another ascending step to the sixth scale degree, was also adapted by Wagner from a preexisting source — a rather obscure choral work composed by his father-in-law, Franz Liszt. In this instance, as with the Grail motive, the original context and associations of the music were clearly instrumental in drawing Wagner's attention. The connection is important yet unfamiliar in writings about *Parsifal,* so we shall describe it here in some detail.

The story begins on New Year's Eve of 1868 with a meeting between Liszt and the American poet Henry Wadsworth Longfellow. Liszt had become an abbé and was then living at the monastery of Santa Francesca Romana in Rome. Longfellow met Liszt that evening in the company of the American painter George Healy, who captured the occasion in a fine oil portrait of the composer that now hangs at the former Longfellow residence in Cambridge, Massachusetts.[46] Healy recalled:

> The Abbé himself came down to greet us, a Roman candlestick held aloft to light the way. His characteristic head, with its long, iron-grey hair, sharply etched features, and penetrating black eyes, and his tall, slim figure shrouded in priestly vestments produced so impressive a picture that Longfellow let out an involuntary whisper: "Mr. Healy, you must paint that for me!"[47]

The warmth of this personal encounter between Longfellow and Liszt was reflected in further meetings in early January 1869, gatherings that included Liszt's longtime companion Princess Carolyne Sayn-Wittgenstein and the poet's sister, Alice Longfellow, who wrote enthusiastic reports about Liszt's extraordinary piano playing. An outcome of these encounters was that Liszt soon regarded Longfellow's verse with an eye to a musical setting. The work in question was a German translation of

---

[46] See Alan Walker, *Franz Liszt* (New York: Knopf, 1996), 3:168, and the reproduction of the painting on p. 167.

[47] G. P. A. Healy, *Reminiscences of a Portrait Painter* (Chicago: 1894), 219–21, cited in Alan Walker, *Franz Liszt,* vol. 3, *The Final Years 1861–1886* (New York: Knopf, 1996), 167–68.

Longfellow's famous poem *The Golden Legend*. Five years later, in 1874, the collaboration bore fruit in the form of Liszt's cantata *The Bells of Strasburg Cathedral*, for orchestra, chorus, and baritone soloist.[48]

On its completion, Liszt sent a copy of the cantata to Wagner and Cosima, and she recorded its arrival in her diary on January 28, 1875. Cosima wrote that it was "sehr effektvoll gemacht, uns aber so fremd" (written very effectively, but so alien to us), yet subsequent events reveal its impact on Wagner. The triggering event was a joint concert by Liszt and Wagner in Budapest on March 10, 1875. The concert had been brought about by Hans Richter, who was conductor of the Budapest National Theater and who had been chosen by Wagner to conduct the first performances of the *Ring* cycle at the first Bayreuth Festival in 1876. The idea was to raise funds for Bayreuth, and the program accordingly included excerpts from the *Ring*, conducted by the composer. Another work on the program was *The Bells of Strasburg Cathedral*, conducted by Liszt himself.

Liszt's cantata clearly engaged Wagner's attention in the immediately ensuing period, when he turned to the sustained composition of the music for *Parsifal* in 1877. Evidence of the connection is provided by the shared rising contour of the motive that dominates the prelude to Liszt's cantata, with its association to the single Latin word "Excelsior!" and the head of the Communion theme in Wagner's *Parsifal* (exx. 1a and 1b).

Example 1a: Liszt, Excelsior! *Prelude*

Example 1b: Wagner, Prelude to Parsifal

---

[48] Liszt's cantata was first published as *Die Glocken des Strassburger Münsters* with a text in German and English and a dedication to Longfellow (Leipzig: J. Schuberth & Co., 1875).

It is notable in this regard that the earliest preserved sketch for this theme in *Parsifal*, as shown in ex. 4.3 of chapter 4 of the present volume, shows a more striking resemblance to the "Excelsior!" idea, since the fourth note of the motive is placed on a downbeat, as in Liszt's work. There are reports of Wagner acknowledging his borrowing or even his "theft" of this motive from Liszt, and although the details remain obscure, it seems that Liszt was aware of Wagner's assimilation of the "Excelsior!" motive into *Parsifal* by the time he visited Bayreuth in April 1878.[49] By then, the first act of *Parsifal* was complete in Wagner's drafts. The common ground between Liszt's "Excelsior!" prelude and Wagner's *Parsifal* is significant, and illuminates not only details of compositional genesis but also features of the expressive meaning and musical symbolism of these works.

As Arthur Marget pointed out,[50] it was surely the poetic intention stemming from Longfellow's work that fascinated Liszt and Wagner, and that helps explain their enthusiasm for the notion of "Excelsior!" Longfellow presumably explained his idea to Liszt at Rome, and elsewhere he specified his poetic intention as follows:

> This was no more than to display, in a series of pictures, the life of a man of genius, resisting all temptations, laying aside all fears, heedless of all warnings, and pressing right on to accomplish his purpose. His motto is Excelsior — "higher." He passes through the Alpine village — through the rough, cold paths of the world — where the peasants cannot understand him, and where his watchword is in an "unknown tongue." He disregards the happiness of domestic peace and sees the glaciers — his fate — before him. He disregards the warning of the old man's wisdom and all the fascinations of woman's love. He answers to all, "Higher yet!" The monks of St. Bernard are the representatives of religious forms and ceremonies, and with their oft-repeated prayer mingles the sound of his voice, telling them there is something higher than forms and ceremonies. Filled with these aspirations, he perishes; without having reached the perfection he longed for; and the voice heard in the air is the promise of immortality and progress ever upward.[51]

---

[49] See in this regard Arthur W. Marget's article "Liszt and *Parsifal*," *Music Review* 14 (1953): 107–24, especially 108 and note 8. There is a reference in Cosima Wagner's diary from December 28, 1877 to the effect that Wagner "sah noch die 'Glocken v. Strassburg' des Vaters sich an, um zu sehen, ob er kein '*Plagiat*' begeht" (looked again at father's "Glocken v. Strassburg" to see whether there was "plagiarism"), although this was during his work on the Transformation music of act I with its use of the motive of the bells. (*CT* 1:1100). Commentators on *Parsifal* have often paid insufficient attention to the influence of Liszt on Wagner.

[50] "Liszt and *Parsifal*," *Music Review* 14 (1953): 107–24.

[51] Longfellow's *Complete Poetical Works*, 19, cited in Marget, "Liszt and *Parsifal*," 120.

The notion of "ever upward" — the proverbial "Blick nach oben" as a symbol for unceasing striving — lends itself well to the spiritual aspiration associated with the Grail, and an ascension in pitch through the notes of the triad to the sixth degree becomes a musical counterpart to this idea. At the same time, in *Parsifal*, the initially unharmonized line, with its suspended rhythm and avoidance of stress on the downbeat, evokes the aura of Gregorian chant — an impression conveyed again toward the framing close of the Communion theme. Wagner also evokes Gregorian intonations in another prominent thematic idea associated with the Grail: the rising whole step and third of the first phrase of the Grail motive, immediately preceding the "Dresden Amen." Liszt had used these inflections too, in various works, and is supposed to have said that "these are intervals well known to us," adding that "these are *catholic* intonations, which I myself did not invent either."[52]

Apart from this specific affinity between the "Excelsior" motive and the Communion theme, there is a broader expressive duality that deserves attention. Longfellow's *Spire of Strasburg Cathedral* in his *Golden Legend* and Liszt's *Bells of Strasburg Cathedral* both center on a conflict between evil and good, as the forces of Lucifer, bent on destroying the cathedral, are confounded by spiritual powers invested in part in the church bells. One likely point of connection here rests in the role of the temple bells in *Parsifal*, but another even more fundamental affinity lies in Liszt's penchant for devising music that reflects the competing influences from both opposing realms. This type of duality appears in various compositions by Liszt, but the "Faust" Symphony springs particularly to mind. Since Mephistopheles is "der Geist, der stets verneint" (the spirit who always negates, in Goethe's words, Liszt withholds original music material from his realm, and instead fills up the final movement of the symphony, entitled "Mephistopheles" and marked "ironico," with parodistic distortions of themes drawn from the opening "Faust" movement.

Wagner, for his part, follows a parallel procedure in devising certain of the motives and themes in *Parsifal*. Hence the "serpentine" motive associated with Kundry's seduction involves a kind of chromatic distortion of the basic shape of the Communion theme, whereas the bleak "Öde" (wasteland) motive heard in act 3 when Gurnemanz describes the desolation of the Grail community is a compressed, dissonant version of the motive of

---

[52] This report stems from August Göllerich's book *Franz Liszt* from 1908, as cited in Marget, "Liszt and *Parsifal*," 112. As these examples show, Egon Voss is mistaken in stating that "Wagner avoids in striking fashion a connection with traditional church music." See "Wagners 'Parsifal' — das Spiel von der Macht der Schuldgefühle," in *Richard Wagner: Parsifal; Texte, Materialien, Kommentare* (Reinbek bei Hamburg: Rowohlt, 1984), 16.

the Temple Bells. In these instances, Wagner allows a basic intervallic shape to assume different and even antithetical meanings, depending upon whether the thematic contour manifests a consonant diatonic stability, or if that shape is distorted through dissonant chromaticism. The special richness of the *Parsifal* music depends crucially on such configurations that reflect the powerful oppositional forces at work in the drama.[53]

The sense of a collective redemption at the conclusion of *Parsifal* has provoked debate and sometimes denunciation; Arnold Whittall writes that "the apparent conviction of its integrative resolution is the most disturbing thing about it."[54] On the other hand, Dieter Borchmeyer has recently argued that Amfortas's replacement by Parsifal involves a cyclical return or restitution, but not "the prospect of a wholly new world." In Borchmeyer's view, "Parsifal sees himself not as the instigator of redemption but as its agent."[55] It is true that Wagner refrains from presenting Parsifal in a priestly role, and apart from illustrating the prophesied correct path through his capacity for compassion and avoidance of aggression, Parsifal's deed seems to consist in a restoration of the threatened Grail and not in the foundation of some new order. Nevertheless, the reunification of spear and Grail stands for a symbolic integration of male and female principles,[56] and a qualitatively new situation arises at the conclusion for Kundry, who is as ancient and archetypal as any of the characters in the drama.

Clues to Wagner's intentions at the pivotal moment of Kundry's death are found in reports from witnesses at the 1882 rehearsals at Bayreuth. According to Heinrich Porges, Wagner associated Kundry's earlier gaze at Parsifal as Grail King sustained by "Mitleids höchste Kraft" (the highest

---

[53] An author sensitive to such expressive polarities based on a single underlying configuration is Kurt Overhoff, whose study *Richard Wagners Parsifal* (Lindau im Bodensee: Werk-Verlag KG Franz Perneder, 1949) surely exerted influence on the 1951 Bayreuth staging of the work by his pupil, Wieland Wagner. For his discussion of the polarity of the Communion theme and the "serpentine" motive, which he terms the motives of "Gottesliebe" (divine love) and "Triebliebe" (compulsive desire), see pp. 89–91, and his book *Die Musikdramen Richard Wagners* (Salzburg: Verlagsbuchhandlung Anton Pustet, 1967), 361–63.

[54] "Wagner and Real Life," *The Musical Times* 137 (June 1996): 9.

[55] *Drama and the World of Richard Wagner*, 239, 240.

[56] Recent interpretations of this aspect include Kurt Hübner, *Die Wahrheit des Mythos* (Munich: C. H. Beck, 1985), 390–92; Eckhard Roch, *Psychodrama: Richard Wagner im Symbol* (Stuttgart and Weimar, 1995), 401; and Sven Friedrich, *Richard Wagner — Deutung und Wirkung* (Würzburg: Königshausen & Neumann, 2004), 39–41. For Jean-Jacques Nattiez, the character of Parsifal himself becomes "the symbolic embodiment of an angelic androgyny, proclaiming a new civilization and culture." *Wagner Androgyne: A Study in Interpretation,* trans. Stewart Spencer (Princeton: Princeton UP, 1993), 170.

power of compassion) with her discovery of him whom she has sought, "von Welt zu Welt" (from world to world).[57] Kundry's curse, and her subsequent bondage to Klingsor, stemmed from her mocking laughter at the Redeemer on the cross; it is this original encounter for which she has sought absolution "from world to world," as her narrative to Parsifal in act 2 makes clear. Accordingly, it seems that it is not simply Parsifal himself with whom she is to be reconciled at the conclusion, but with that undisclosed redeemer of whom Parsifal is the representative or agent. The final words in the chorus "Erlösung dem Erlöser!" (the Redeemer redeemed!) not only confirm the fulfillment of the prophecy but also recall and resolve the distressed cry from the undisclosed realm that had led Parsifal to Monsalvat and which is quoted by him after Kundry's kiss: "Erlöse, rette mich, aus schuldbefleckten Händen!" (Redeem, rescue me from hands sullied by guilt!). Parsifal's capacity for Schopenhauerian compassion allows for a selfless identification with the Other, creating a kind of transparency whereby the *principium individuationis* is negated and the boundaries between separate beings are overcome.

Thus, for Kundry, Parsifal creates a bridge to that other sphere, the realm of the undisclosed redeemer. Regarded in this way, Kundry's death at the end of *Parsifal* stands for her disappearance from the level of the visible action to another, metaphysical level, not so unlike Isolde's seemingly inexplicable death at the end of *Tristan und Isolde*, when she joins Tristan in the realm of Night.[58] The music heard at this juncture, marked by a crescendo at the shift from a major triad to a minor chord a third lower, corresponds to passages in each of the preceding acts associated with the revelation of the Grail: when Amfortas sets down the Grail in act 1, and at Parsifal's words "das Heilsgefäß" (the healing cup) after Kundry's kiss in act 2. According to Julius Kniese, Wagner asked for the curtain to begin to close three measures earlier than is indicated in the printed score, at this A-minor chord that marks Kundry's death; this gesture could reinforce the sense of her departure to another realm.[59] Moreover, Kundry's definitive release from the

---

[57] Heinrich Porges entered Wagner's comments at the rehearsals into a vocal score, which is held at the Wagner-Archiv at Bayreuth. At the passage in question, he writes "Kundry mit dem Ausdruck der Verklärung im Angesicht: 'Das ist der, den du gesucht hast von Welt zu Welt.' " See Richard Wagner, *Sämtliche Werke* 30:226.

[58] Nevertheless, the dramatic emphasis is quite different from that in *Tristan und Isolde,* and some will feel, as Joseph Chytry puts it, that "there are good reasons for finding distasteful a redemption of woman which, to be blunt, first renders her dumb and then liquidates her." *The Aesthetic State: A Quest in Modern German Thought* (Berkeley and Los Angeles: U of C Press, 1989), 309.

[59] Kniese's comment is as follows: "NB. Der Vorhang müßte hier fallen, an der Wendung nach a-moll." (NB. The curtain really ought to fall here, at the key change to A minor.) See Richard Wagner, *Sämtliche Werke* 30:228.

cycle of reincarnations removes her once and for all from Klingsor's grip, diminishing his sway. To McGlathery's proposal, in his chapter in this volume, that Kundry, having become Mary Magdalene, dies of a broken heart, we may suggest another possibility: she does indeed become a spiritual bride, but in a noumenal realm beyond outward appearances. Controversy about the ending of *Parsifal* will continue, but this assessment of the situation seems consistent with Wagner's known intentions as well as with his penchant for providing large-scale resolutions within the drama, such as Parsifal's healing of Amfortas's wound with the same weapon that smote him.

During afternoon coffee on April 29, 1879, after having recently completed the music of *Parsifal* in his drafts, Wagner told Cosima: "Eigentlich hätte Siegfried Parsifal werden sollen und Wotan erlösen, auf seinen Streifzügen auf den leidenden Wotan (für Amfortas) treffen — aber es fehlte der Vorbote, und so mußte das wohl so bleiben." (*CT* 2, 339; Siegfried ought really to have become Parsifal and redeemed Wotan; he should have encountered the suffering Wotan (in place of Amfortas) in the course of his wanderings — but there was no augury for it, and so it had to remain as it is). While viewing *Parsifal* as a fifth installment of the *Ring* cycle that evades the resignation of *Götterdämmerung*, commentators such as Hans Küng and Udo Bermbach part company over the religious implications of the closing utopian vision.[60] Yet in the music, at least, Wagner's strategy of creating an analogue for desire in the long-deferred resolution of harmonies and themes accords to the character of Parsifal a facilitating role that clearly transcends that of a "cold deus ex machina."[61] His reopening of the shrine can be understood as reclaiming subjectivity not merely as rationality but as a newly integrated state of feeling,[62] rejecting both the ascetic dogmatism of the Grail Knights and the manipulative egoism of Klingsor. The closing music then becomes the primary means of conveying this enhanced integration as a communal experience.

---

[60] Bermbach, *Der Wahn des Gesamtkunstwerks: Richard Wagners politisch-ästhetische Utopie* (Frankfurt am Main: Fischer, 1994), 311; Küng, "Was kommt nach der Götterdämmerung? Über Untergang und Erlösung im Spätwerk Richard Wagners," in *Programmhefte der Bayreuther Festspiele: Parsifal* (1989), 49. Also see Küng's centenary essay "Wagner's *Parsifal*: A Theology for Our Time," originally published in the Bayreuth *Programmheft* for the 1982 production and reissued in revised form in the *Michigan Quarterly Review* 23 (1984), 311–33.

[61] The role Wagner was afraid he might fall into — see the quote earlier in this chapter from Wagner, *Richard Wagner an Mathilde Wesendonk*, 210.

[62] See in this regard Sandra Corse, "*Parsifal*, Wagner, Nietzsche, and the Modern Subject," *Theatre Journal* 46 (1994): 98, 109.

I. The Text: Sources and Symbols

1: Medievalism and Metaphysics: The Literary Background of *Parsifal**

Mary A. Cicora

A S A FINAL WORK, *Parsifal* represents the culmination of Wagner's various philological interests and the creative tendencies that were present
in his previous projects. Among these are the use of source material from
the Germanic past; a liberal use, freely changing and selecting what he
needed. The medieval material provided him with a vehicle by means of
which he could portray problems of the nineteenth century. Thus in Wagner's works one encounters the paradox of medieval subject matter
employed as a vehicle for expressing problems of his time; as Peter Wapnewski points out, one does not find a medieval world, but mythical timelessness.[1] This chapter will investigate how Wagner transformed the
medieval world of chivalry portrayed in his major source for *Parsifal*,
Wolfram von Eschenbach's *Parzival*, into a nineteenth-century musical-
dramatic depiction of Schopenhauerian metaphysics.

The Genesis of Wagner's Parsifal Plan

Like many of Wagner's other works, *Parsifal* resulted from a philological
plan that spanned many years and that clearly indicates the interrelationship
of his works, an aspect of his creative output that Wagner himself often
commented upon.[2] The literary works that Wagner read in Marienbad

---

* Special thanks to R. T. Carr, Paul G. Foster, and Thomas Grey for help in
assembling research materials for this chapter.

[1] On Wagner's use of his medieval source material, see Peter Wapnewski, "Mitt-
ler des Mittelalters," in *Tristan der Held Richard Wagners* (Berlin: Severin und
Siedler, 1981), 33–63; and Volker Mertens, "Richard Wagner und das Mittelalter,"
in *Richard-Wagner-Handbuch,* ed. Ulrich Müller and Peter Wapnewski, 19–59
(Stuttgart: Kröner, 1986). A detailed older study of the topic is Wolfgang Golther's
Parzival und der Gral in der Dichtung des Mittelalters und der Neuzeit (Stuttgart:
J. B. Metzler, 1925).

[2] On the genesis of the plan and the Good Friday inspiration, see Peter
Wapnewski, *Der traurige Gott: Richard Wagner in seinen Helden* (Munich: Beck,

during the summer of 1845 provided him with the subject matter for many of his later dramas. In Paris several years earlier, when his friend Samuel Lehrs had loaned him some medieval works, specifically the *Wartburgkrieg* with Lukas's annotations and the anonymous poem *Lohengrin,* a new world had been opened up for him, as he described in his autobiography *Mein Leben.* Through these works, Wagner had become acquainted with the Grail legend for the first time, and the medieval world had a decisive impact on him. This was the beginning of his lifelong fascination with medieval literature that resulted in its use as raw material for his own works.

In 1843, Wagner had been appointed Hofkapellmeister in Dresden, and the reading that he did in the ensuing years proved decisive for his later dramatic production. In his autobiographical *Mein Leben,* Wagner recounts that when vacationing in Marienbad during the summer of 1845, he took with him works of Wolfram and the medieval fragment about Lohengrin as reading material. He narrates,

> Ich hatte mir vorgenommen, mich der gemächlichsten Lebensweise, wie sie andrerseits für die sehr aufregende Kur unerlässlich ist, hinzugeben. Sorgsam hatte ich mir die Lektüre hierzu mitgenommen: die Gedichte *Wolfram von Eschenbachs* in den Bearbeitungen von *Simrock* und *San Marte,* damit im Zusammenhange das anonyme Epos vom *"Lohengrin"* mit der grossen Einleitung von *Görres.* Mit dem Buche unter dem Arm vergrub ich mich in die nahen Waldungen, um am Bache gelagert mit *Titurel* und *Parzival* in dem fremdartigen und doch so innig traulichen Gedichte *Wolframs* mich zu unterhalten.[3]

> [I resolved to indulge myself in the most comfortable lifestyle, which is actually essential when enduring a rigorous course of treatment. So I took along reading material that would suit this purpose: the poetry of Wolfram von Eschenbach in the editions by Simrock and San Marte, and with that the great anonymous epic poem *Lohengrin* with the introduction by Görres. With the book under my arm I secluded myself in the nearby woodlands, to amuse myself with *Titurel* and *Parzival* while relaxing

---

1978; Deutscher Taschenbuch Verlag, 1982), 201–13; "Die Oper Richard Wagners als Dichtung," in Müller and Wapnewski, *Richard-Wagner-Handbuch,* 331–46; and Ulrich Müller, "Parzival und Parsifal: Vom Roman Wolframs von Eschenbach und vom Musikdrama Richard Wagners," in *Sprache-Text-Geschichte,* ed. Peter K. Stein et al., Göppingen Arbeiten zur Germanistik, no. 304 (Göppingen: Kümmerle, 1980), 479–502. I have based my discussion substantially on these sources; more specific references will be given when needed.

[3] Richard Wagner, *Mein Leben,* ed. Martin Gregor-Dellin (Munich: Paul List, 1963; Goldmann/Schott, 1983), 315.

by the brook, and occupying myself with the strange and yet so very familiar poetry of Wolfram.][4]

Peter Wapnewski has determined that these works were translations of the medieval originals. The *Parzival* translation of San Marte (Albert Schutz) first appeared in 1836, and his *Titurel* translation in 1841. Karl Simrock's annotated translations of both works appeared in 1842.[5] Wagner was aided in his research by Gervinus's literary history, which he also read that summer; Ursula Schulze comments on the role that Gervinus[6] played in awakening and cultivating the literary-historical consciousness of nineteenth-century intellectuals.[7] The reading that Wagner did in Marienbad thus established the foundation for all of his later works except for the *Ring* and *Tristan* — *Lohengrin*, *Meistersinger*, and *Parsifal*.

The Grail legend obviously spans Wagner's output, providing the scholar with apparent links between *Lohengrin* and *Parsifal*. The earlier Grail opera is based on an episode told at the end of Wolfram's *Parzival*, when the narrator outlines how Parzival's son frees Elsa and makes her promise not to ask his name. Though *Parsifal* was not to be completed for many years to come, the connections between Wagner's *Parsifal* and *Lohengrin* are made explicit in the Grail narrative of the earlier opera, in which the title character identifies himself as Parzival's son, and tells of the Grail and the Grail Knights of Monsalvat. Wagner also saw a clear association between Parsifal and Tristan in this early stage of his Grail legend research. In his autobiography, he reports that in 1854 he had considered including Parsifal as a character in *Tristan und Isolde*, his idea being to have Parsifal enter in the third act and, while on his way to the Grail Temple seeking the Grail, encounter the wounded Tristan on his sickbed.[8] Though later abandoned, the idea clearly shows, as his autobiography explicitly indicates, a "mythical" identification of Amfortas, the wounded and tormented Grail King, with the third-act Tristan. In theorizing about why

---

[4] All translations are my own, unless otherwise noted.

[5] Wapnewski, *Der traurige Gott*, 205.

[6] Georg Gottfried Gervinus's *Geschichte der poetischen Nationalliteratur der Deutschen*, consisting of five volumes, had first appeared between 1835 and 1840.

[7] Ursula Schulze, "Stationen der Parzival-Rezeption: Strukturveränderung und ihre Folgen," in *Mittelalter-Rezeption: Ein Symposium,* ed. Peter Wapnewski (Stuttgart: Metzler, 1986), 555–80, here cited from 558–59. All subsequent references to Schulze will be to this article.

[8] In a notebook containing a sketch for *Tristan,* Wagner also had Parzival appear. See Richard Wagner, *Dokumente zur Entstehung und ersten Aufführung des Bühnenweihfestspiels "Parsifal,"* ed. Martin Geck and Egon Voss, vol. 30 of Wagner, *Sämtliche Werke* (Mainz: Schott, 1970), 12. Subsequent references to this volume will be cited in the text using the abbreviation "*DEAP*" and the page numbers.

Wagner abandoned this plan, Wapnewski explains that despite the analogous situation of Tristan and Amfortas, it was not feasible, because Parsifal would have contrasted too strongly with Tristan, and the two figures would have represented an antithesis that Wagner, at this stage of his life, could not resolve. In some ways, the two works are based on different conceptions entirely. *Parsifal* represented, Wapnewski writes, Wagner's farewell to the total self-abandonment that *Tristan* stood for.[9]

Scholars frequently comment upon other parallels between *Parsifal* and Wagner's previous works. The late work obviously contains many variations of figures and themes present in Wagner's earlier dramas. Parsifal, as a naive young lad, is obviously a counterpart of Siegfried and Walther von Stolzing. Both Amfortas and Wotan, moreover, are "fallen," corrupt rulers of their respective realms, and Alberich and Klingsor represent the evil brought about by renouncing love for power. Kundry and Klingsor's realm, with its seductive Flowermaidens, resembles the Venusberg and its sinful pleasures.

In his autobiography, Wagner recounts having received the inspiration for *Parsifal* and having written the first prose sketch for the work in April 1857. Though an entry in the "annals" of his "brown book" substantiates the veracity of 1857 as the year of the conception of the project,[10] the autobiographical report is the subject of critical controversy, as the date mentioned in the passage as Good Friday was not the date on which that day fell that year, according to the calendar. In *Mein Leben*, Wagner wrote:

> Nun brach auch schönes Frühlingswetter herein; am Karfreitag erwachte ich zum ersten Male in diesem Hause bei vollem Sonnenschein: das Gärtchen war ergrünt, die Vögel sangen, und endlich konnte ich mich auf die Zinne des Häuschens setzen, um der langersehnten verheißungsvollen Stille mich zu erfreuen. Hiervon erfüllt, sagte ich mir plötzlich, dass heute ja "Karfreitag" sei, und entsann mich, wie bedeutungsvoll diese Mahnung mir schon einmal in *Wolframs Parzival* aufgefallen war. Seit jenem Aufenthalte in *Marienbad*, wo ich die *"Meistersinger"* und *"Lohengrin"* konzipierte, hatte ich mich nie wieder mit jenem Gedichte beschäftigt; jetzt trat sein idealer Gehalt in überwältigender Form an mich heran, und von dem Karfreitags-Gedanken aus konzipierte ich schnell ein ganzes Drama, welches ich, in drei Akte geteilt, sofort mit wenigen Zügen flüchtig skizzierte.[11]

> [We started having beautiful spring weather. On Good Friday I awoke in this house for the first time to bright sunshine: the garden was blooming,

---

[9] Wapnewski, *Tristan der Held Richard Wagners*, 173–74.

[10] Joachim Bergfeld, ed., *Richard Wagner: Das braune Buch: Tagebuchaufzeichnungen 1865 bis 1882* (Zurich: Atlantis, 1975), 127.

[11] Wagner, *Mein Leben*, 561.

the birds were singing, and finally I could sit on the battlements of the house and enjoy the promising stillness. Filled with this feeling, I suddenly said to myself that today was "Good Friday," and recalled the significance this reminder had had for me once before, in Wolfram's *Parzival*. I had not dealt with that poem since my vacation in Marienbad, where I conceived *Meistersinger* and *Lohengrin;* now its ideal content emerged overwhelmingly before me, and working from the thought of Good Friday I quickly conceived an entire drama, which I divided into three acts and immediately sketched out with a few broad strokes.]

Peter Wapnewski resolves the factual discrepancy of the dates concerned by interpreting Wagner's explanations in a metaphorical sense, as stating an analogy rather than a fact. Wapnewski theorizes that Wagner concocted a stylized pose, a myth, and "staged" the inspiration, which is based on a merely psychological reality. It was, he hypothesizes, a manipulation, a legend. In other words, Wagner's statements can be taken as merely descriptive, that is, it was as though it were Good Friday.

An entry in Cosima's diaries substantiates this theory. On April 22, 1879, Cosima reported:

> R. gedachte heute des Eindruckes, welcher ihm den Karfreitags-Zauber eingegeben; er lacht, und "eigentlich alles bei den Haaren herbeigezogen wie meine Liebschaften, denn es war kein Karfreitag, nichts, nur eine hübsche Stimmung in der Natur, von welcher ich mir sagte: So müßte es sein am Karfreitag," habe er gedacht.[12]

> [Today R. remembered the impression that had inspired in him the magic of Good Friday; he laughed and said, "Actually it wasn't meant seriously, because it was not Good Friday, not at all, nature just had such a beautiful mood that I said to myself: This is how it must have been on Good Friday," he had thought.]

In this manner, Wagner clearly acknowledged that the story of his Good Friday inspiration for *Parsifal* was not factual reality, but an analogy. According to Wapnewski, Good Friday, for Wagner, represented the idea of redemption, which was, after all, a major theme of Wagner's works.

The prose sketch in question has been lost. Wagner wrote the first surviving prose sketch in August 1865 in his "brown book."[13] The second prose sketch dates from January/February 1877. The first version of the dramatic text was written March/April 1877. The second version was undated. Schott published the dramatic text in Mainz in December of 1877. The progress of the work is well documented in Wagner's letters

---

[12] *CT* 2:335.
[13] Bergfeld, *Das braune Buch,* 53–70.

and notebooks, and in Cosima's diaries. These sources also provide valuable statements about Wagner's thoughts concerning the project, the special problems that it posed and how he solved them, and at least hints at, if not clear statements of, his intended meanings. These documents contain much material useful to the critic concerned with the genesis and the interpretation of the work. The influence of his past reading is unmistakable; at the same time, though, Wagner had his own aims in writing *Parsifal,* and ideas about the legend that differed vastly from the source materials and went far beyond the worlds portrayed in any of them.

The Nature of Wagner's Medieval Source Material

Wagner is generally acknowledged as having done more than any other artist to popularize medieval literature and archaic legends in his modern age. Although Wagner used works of the Germanic past, and was a major factor in helping to popularize them in the nineteenth century, he never intended his works as mere straightforward dramatizations of his medieval sources. Rather, he made radical changes in them to tailor them to his own historical age and contemporary circumstances. His *Parsifal,* accordingly, differs from the medieval Grail romances in drastic ways. Those who criticize Wagner for his eclectic use of traditional goods need to consider that this is also in a way how Wolfram proceeded with his own source for *Parzival,* the work *Li Contes del Graal* of Chrétien de Troyes, a fragmentary work that scholars date between 1180 and 1190.[14] Wolfram follows his source unmistakably but also inexactly, making important changes. In *Parzival,* Wolfram uses his French sources and the current medieval conventions in a new and complex way. In fact, he mentions Chrétien only once in his *Parzival,* toward the end, when he criticizes Chrétien for failing to report the story properly. To complicate matters of derivation, he also refers to a mysterious Kyot as his source, who is the subject of much critical controversy, quite possibly a fictitious entity whose function is to ironicize the medieval convention of citing authority.

Parzival was written roughly around the year 1210 by Wolfram von Eschenbach, a member of the knightly class, and consists of 25,000

---

[14] On the medieval Grail romances, and Wolfram's *Parzival* in particular, I have consulted and am basing the following general information on these works: Helmut de Boor, *Die höfische Literatur: Vorbereitung, Blüte, Ausklang 1170–1250,* vol. 2 of *Geschichte der deutschen Literatur von den Anfängen bis zur Gegenwart,* by Helmut de Boor and Richard Newald (Munich: Beck, 1953), 63–67, 90–114; and Joachim Bumke, *Wolfram von Eschenbach,* 7th rev. ed., Sammlung Metzler 36 (Stuttgart: Metzler, 1997).

rhymed verses in thirty-line segments. It is a highly complex work, and depicts Parzival's gradual progression as he learns about the world: that is, courtly society, the knightly code of chivalry, and God. For purposes of comparison with Wagner's work, a short summary, though admittedly inadequate, will prove nevertheless instructive. The first books of Wolfram's romance tell the prehistory of the main story. They deal with Parzival's father Gahmuret and his mother Herzeloyde. As a young boy, Parzival has rudimentary ideas about good versus evil, and God, and wants to learn about knighthood. His inability to discern between knights and deities leads him to ask a passing group of knights if they are God. He follows them, and runs away from his mother, who raised him sheltered from knights to avoid the perils that caused the death of his father. She has dressed him in fool's clothing so he will be beaten and sent back to her.

Parzival arrives at the court of King Arthur, and on the way there kills his cousin Ither and dons his red armor, which thus becomes his knightly costume. At Arthur's court, though, Parzival demonstrates that he has never learned how to behave properly in courtly society. He must learn the forms and customs of knightly existence while attaining a proper relationship with God. At Pelrapeire he frees Queen Condwiramurs and marries her. Later he encounters an old knight, Gurnemanz, who instructs him on chivalry. Upon entering the Grail Castle at Munsalvaesche, he watches the ceremony of the Grail. The king, Anfortas, suffers from a wound, yet Parzival does not inquire as to why the Grail King is ailing, as he has been taught not to ask inappropriate questions. During the ceremony, a lance is placed on Anfortas's wound in hopes of relieving the pain. Parzival spends a restless night in the Grail Castle; the next morning, it is empty, and he leaves.

He enters Arthur's court once more, but this time, the Grail messenger, Cundrie, arrives and reproaches him for not asking about Anfortas's ailment, and expels him from courtly society for this. Parzival feels he has been abandoned by God, and resolves to seek and find the Grail. He disappears from the latter part of the romance, for as he seeks the Grail, Gawan has departed from Arthur's court on new adventures. In these Gawan books, Parzival occasionally appears anonymously. Book 9 tells of Parzival's religious conversion. The basics of the Grail Realm are revealed when the hermit Trevrizent, whom Parzival encounters, teaches him about the Grail and his lineage; Parzifal himself is descended from the Grail family. Trevrizent explains to Parzival that the present Grail King has been wounded and tells of the circumstances surrounding the injury. The romance also contains various adventures that seem to have very little direct relation to Parzival, but rather narrate the exploits of Gawan, a model of chivalry and knightly conduct. Upon reentering the Grail Castle, Parzival asks the redeeming question of compassion and thus cures Anfortas's wound and attains the post of Grail King.

Parzival proceeds through a vast series of adventures, repeated encounters, revealed identities, and narratives that tell the prehistory and impart ontological information in pieces that gradually accumulate to form a rich, complex tapestry. It is full of varied verbal repetition and parallels, and contains many figures, events, and details. Ulrich Müller theorizes that Wolfram wanted to amuse his audience, and *Parzival* appears to have been very popular.[15] We have roughly seventy-five manuscripts and fragments of it. Despite its complexity, the crux of the story is very simple; it consists of Parzival's development from fool to Grail King. However, Wolfram's *Parzival* does not have a linear plot, since the Gawan books comprise about a third of the romance, and Parzival's story is masterfully interwoven with that of Gawan. The romance is, though, clearly a literary expression of the medieval worldview, and for this reason the main forces of the Middle Ages are evident in this work. They consist of family, the ties of blood relationship; the knightly status, the code of chivalry; courtly love (minne); and religion.

Wolfram has, nevertheless, decisively changed and significantly deepened the traditional structure of medieval knightly romance. The usual progress of the hero of a traditional Arthurian romance is termed by scholars the "Doppelweg," because it demonstrates a dual path.[16] In the first part of a typical romance, the medieval hero undergoes a limited character development and achieves some sort of illusive success. A catastrophe ensues, and he is found guilty of some fault or failing. He must therefore rectify the situation, expiate his guilt or make good on the omission, and accomplish something. Then he will be found worthy of being reintegrated into courtly society and joining the Round Table. Schulze argues that with the modern elimination of the "Doppelweg," the Parzival legend is fundamentally altered, for the structure that gives symbolic significance to the progress of the protagonist is removed, and in the process the protagonist is free to convey new ideological significance that is not specifically medieval.

Wolfram has already loosened the traditional structures that he was working with, for he demonstrated in *Parzival* that chivalry as an ideal was in itself not enough for him. King Arthur is much more than an individual literary figure; rather, he is the center of courtly society, and represents the entire chivalric worldview, the basic elements of which are adventure, honor, and courtly love. Gawan is the ideal Arthurian knight. Accordingly, Wolfram juxtaposes the Grail Castle with the King Arthur's court, and the Grail Realm and the Arthurian realm clearly comment upon each other. The Arthurian world lacks the religious perspective of the Grail Realm.

---

[15] Müller, "Parzival und Parsifal," 484–85.
[16] Schulze, 556–57.

Parzival's development is not complete once he has reached the Arthurian realm; he must also attain the Grail. The Arthurian knights represent the world of chivalry; Trevrizent teaches Parzival about God, and Wolfram's ideal type of chivalric existence is indeed the knight of God. The Grail requires humility and sacrifice, service of God. For Wolfram, God was the means to love and redemption.

With the pieces that he extracted from Wolfram's romance, Wagner would make even more radical alterations to these basic medieval elements and structures. Despite apparent similarities of plot, details, and characters, the drama that resulted from Wagner's reading is a radically altered version of the basic outline of Wolfram's romance and a very different work of art. Wagner was, like Wolfram, religious in a private, unconventional manner, one that resisted identification with organized religion or a particular faith or church. Both preferred to practice an individual piety, and questioned organized religion and learned theology. However, each of the two works under discussion here expresses its respective epoch, fulfilling the intentions of its creator while illustrating his particular *Weltanschauung*.

Wagner vs. Wolfram: From Medieval Romance to Stage Consecration Festival Play

Wagner's *Parsifal* represents a distinctively modern interpretation of the Parzival legend. The basic outline of Wagner's drama is the same as that of previous Grail tradition. The symmetrical nature of the drama is established by Parsifal's two visits to the Grail Temple, in the first and the third acts. As in Wolfram's work, Wagner's Parsifal must somehow cure the Grail King, who is ailing from a wound that seems to defy all attempts at healing. In order for Parsifal to do this, it is essential that he undergo a process of development or arrive at some insight into himself and the world in which he lives. He sees a ceremony and has no idea what is going on; later he understands. Wagner, however, had his own ideas about what the Parzival legend signified.

Some of the characters resemble their namesakes in obvious ways, through a similarity of name or dramatic function. The title character is clearly a modern counterpart of the medieval fool turned Grail King. Amfortas is clearly modeled after the ailing medieval Grail King Anfortas. Klingsor's magic garden is a vital, sensual, nineteenth-century version of Schastel Marveile, and the Flowermaidens musical-dramatic counterparts of the four hundred maidens whom the medieval magician holds captive. In other cases, the character derivation is more complex. Wagner's Gurnemanz, for instance, is a composite of two figures: Wolfram's Gurnemanz, the knight who instructs Parzival in chivalry, and the hermit

Trevrizent, from whom Parzival receives a theology lesson and absolution on Good Friday. Kundry is the most complex figure of the drama, being compounded from several figures that Wagner found in Wolfram's romance: Sigune, who tells Parzival his name and seems to know all about him as well as impart information of all kinds; Orgeluse, the object of the King's illicit and disastrous love-adventure; and Cundrie, the ugly and out-spoken messenger of the Grail, who is also a sorceress.[17]

Other brief details offer glimpses of the medieval source through flash-backs or seemingly minor mentions. Though entirely absent from the onstage drama, Herzeleide and Gamuret as well as their stories are clearly derived from Wolfram's romance. Their names resemble those of their pro-totypes, and the story of how Parsifal's father died in a knightly battle, how his mother thus sheltered him from knightly existence to protect him, and perished out of sorrow at her son's departure, are all details that Wagner took from the romance. In the first act of the drama, when Gurnemanz asks Parsifal where he got his bow and arrows from, he tells of how he fol-lowed the group of knights and wanted to become like them, as though he had read his script in the medieval romance that was the source of his story. Other minor elements of Wagner's drama offer glimpses into the source. Kundry's balsam from Arabia is reminiscent of the exotic episodes of Wol-fram's *Parzival* and the elaborate medieval concoctions of substances that are applied in a futile attempt to cure Anfortas's wound.

Gurnemanz's mention of the blood on the snowy white feathers of the swan that Parsifal shoots down upon his entrance onstage may be inspired by the episode in *Parzival* in which a transfixed Parzival sinks deep into thoughts of Condwiramurs when he has a vision of drops of blood in the snow. Gurnemanz mentions that the "snowy feathers" of the bird are flecked with blood by Parsifal's misdeed. Kundry's laughter quite possibly echoes that of Cunneware, who, in fairy tale manner, is fated not to laugh unless she sees the most worthy knight, and then laughs as Parzival leaves Arthur's court, thus expressing his exceptional nature and foreshadowing his eventual exaltation and elevation to the post of Grail King. Parsifal's misdeed of killing the swan, which he commits upon his entrance into the Grail Realm, is probably inspired by a mention of young Parzival shooting birds.

Wagner's Grail Realm also resembles Wolfram's in several important ways. Aside from skipping a generation in the succession of rulers and hav-ing Amfortas descending directly from Titurel and not from the intermedi-ary Frimutel, as in his source, the chain of succession is the same in Wagner's *Parsifal* and Wolfram's *Parzival*. Moreover, the basic ontology

---

[17] On Kundry, see Wapnewski, *Der traurige Gott*, 230–41.

of the Grail Realm is also similar. In both works, the Grail is guarded by a group of knights who are summoned to it and go forth into the world on adventures at its command. Wagner obviously based the story of the founding of the Grail Realm on his source. There are similarities between what Gurnemanz tells Parsifal in the first act and what Trevrizent narrates. Trevrizent gives Parzival a more detailed version of what Lohengrin and Gurnemanz relate to their onstage and offstage audience about how the Grail was brought to earth by a host of angels. Lohengrin even includes Trevrizent's detail about the wafer placed annually on the Grail by a dove that descends every year on Good Friday, replenishing its power. According to Gurnemanz, one cannot seek the Grail; it summons those chosen individuals to itself.

The changes that Wagner made in the legendary configuration and details were part of a far-reaching difference in conception. Wagner gives a new interpretation of the Grail legend based on Schopenhauer's pessimistic worldview, which states that the inevitable pain of earthly existence is the result of the clash of individual entities that are just differing manifestations of the world-will, the vital force that can only be stilled by renunciation. Accordingly, redemption consists in a negation of the will that manifests itself, in particular, through the sexual drive. Wagner's *Parsifal* is based on a very different value system from one found in any medieval work. It portrays the conflict between sensuality and salvation, and is, as mentioned, a musical-dramatic document of Wagner's fascination with the philosophy of Arthur Schopenhauer, whose work had influenced his thinking beginning in the mid-1850s. Thus, in Wagner's version of the Parzival legend, King Arthur has been dethroned by Arthur Schopenhauer.

A survey of some basic parameters indicates the vast difference in worldview in the two works. In Wolfram's romance, time is an important structural element that the author deliberately used to craft his narrative. Scholars have determined that the time structure is carefully worked out, as is evident in the characters' lives and the successions of generations, for instance. Trevrizent points out the significance of the liturgical calendar. Time has cosmic as well as religious dimensions, as it is also determined by the positions and rotations of the planets. In Wolfram's cosmos, the positions of Mars, Jupiter, and Saturn profoundly influence human lives, and *Parzival* is full of astrological symbolism that scholars have analyzed extensively. Cundrie's announcements, for example, are full of astrological details. Space, too, is an important dimension of Wolfram's romance. The geography of the Grail Realm is appropriately mysterious. It seems to exist, but at the same time, the Grail Realm and the Grail Castle do not seem real. However, many other names mentioned in the work are real, and the episodes take place in widely varied geographical locales. The romance spans three continents: Europe, Asia, and Africa. The work is full of actual geographical names, such as Arabia, Persia, and Syria; rivers such as the

Tigris and the Euphrates; and European countries including Norway, Denmark, and England.[18]

In Wagner's drama, however, both time and space have disintegrated and metaphysically merged. Wagner's mythical world is new indeed. The succession of generations has yielded to a surreal simultaneity, with Titurel alive in the grave. Furthermore, though the work supposedly takes place in medieval Spain, the entire drama, encompassing both the Grail Realm and beyond, exists at one further remove from the real world. Peter Wapnewski comments that whereas in Wolfram's romance Parzival is reintegrated into the standard time frame on Good Friday, Wagner's work takes place in a realm of timelessness, and Wagner takes Parsifal out of the usual time scheme entirely.[19] Wagner's libretti clearly demonstrate that he liked to experiment with philosophical concepts, using them, too, like his dramatic source materials, in new ways. Accordingly, in Wagner's musical-dramatic Grail Realm, as Gurnemanz remarks to Parsifal during the glorious first-act Transformation music, time turns into space.

In his notebooks, letters, and prose tracts, Wagner wrote extensively about the source material that he used for his dramas. In these commentaries, he also did not hesitate to specify what he felt this raw material lacked, and how his own versions improved on these legends in important ways. What is relevant for the understanding of his dramas is how he intended his work to differ from his sources. He had his own purposes, and expounded upon them at elaborate length. In the case of *Parsifal*, we have a lengthy letter to Mathilde Wesendonk (dating from May 29/30, 1859) outlining what Wagner felt were the faults of Wolfram's *Parzival*. The medieval romance was obviously unsuitable for stage presentation due to its epic scale: Wagner's first task was to condense and simplify the panoramic scope of the action. Thus he streamlined the action, locales, cast of characters, and plot. Both Wolfram's Parzival and Wagner's Parsifal are, Wapnewski writes, predestined to cure the Grail King. In both works, this predestination must merely unfold itself. But whereas Wolfram shows a gradual character development in the title figure, Wagner's Parsifal undergoes sudden, more drastic and abrupt changes. According to Wapnewski, the audience sees him in three stations: the fool, the cosmically clear-sighted one, and the redeemer.[20] The plot of Wagner's drama consists of the simple redemption of a sufferer by a chosen one: the action demonstrates the failure and eventual success of

---

[18] On time and space, see Bumke, *Wolfram von Eschenbach*, 140–43; on the Grail Kingdom, see Henry Kratz, *Wolfram von Eschenbach's "Parzival": An Attempt at a Total Evaluation* (Bern: Francke, 1973), 415–35.

[19] Wapnewski, *Der traurige Gott*, 211–13.

[20] Wapnewski, *Der traurige Gott*, 227.

this redemption.[21] In this manner, Wagner imposed onto the mass of material a basic unity that he felt Wolfram's *Parzival* lacked.

Much to the chagrin of medievalists, Wagner claims in his letter to Mathilde Wesendonk that Wolfram did not really understand the legend:

> Er hängt Begebnis an Begebnis an Begebnis, Abenteuer an Abenteuer, gibt mit dem Gralsmotiv kuriose und seltsame Vorgänge und Bilder, tappt herum und läßt dem ernst gewordenen die Frage, was er denn eigentlich wollte? Woraus er antworten muß, ja, das weiss ich eigentlich selbst nicht mehr wie der Pfaffe sein Christentum, das er ja auch am Meßaltar aufspielt, ohne zu wissen, um was es sich dabei handelt. — Es ist nicht anders. Wolfram ist eine durchaus unreife Erscheinung, woran allerdings wohl großenteils sein barbarisches, gänzlich konfuses, zwischen dem alten Christentum und der neueren Staatenwirtschaft schwebendes Zeitalter schuld. In dieser Zeit konnte nichts fertig werden; Tiefe des Dichters geht sogleich in wesenloser Phantasterei unter. (*DEAP*, 15)

> [He strings one event after another, one adventure after the next, associates curious and strange happenings and imagery with the Grail, gropes around and provokes any serious person to wonder just what exactly he really wants — to which he must answer that he himself doesn't really know this any more than the priest who practices his Christianity at the altar really knows what it is all about. — That is how it is. Wolfram is without a doubt an immature phenomenon, and surely the age in which he lived, which was barbaric and thoroughly confused, and vacillated between Christianity and the modern state system, is to a great extent to blame for this. Nothing could possibly come to fruition in that period; any depth that a poet had would be lost immediately in insubstantial fantasizing.]

In his excursions into folklore theory, Wagner usually acknowledged the historical relativity of how various kinds of raw material appeared in different ages, depending on the different historical circumstances. And so he "pardons" Wolfram for his literary and artistic failings, excusing him with the view that he could do no better. Thus Wagner cannot but mercifully concede that what he considered the deficiencies of Wolfram's work were only the inevitable results of the poverty-stricken age in which the medieval poet lived.

As Ulrich Müller observes, Wagner was, on the one hand, fascinated by Wolfram's romance, but on the other reduced the multifaceted work to a few main ideas, formulating his own interpretation of the legend. Thus he criticized Wolfram for failing to narrate (in the Middle Ages) the version of the Parzival legend that Wagner (from his nineteenth-century perspective)

---

[21] Wapnewski, *Der traurige Gott*, 231.

felt should be written.[22] He radically reduced Wolfram's huge cast of characters to a manageable number, in some cases by combining several of them into a composite character, or, as in most cases, disposing of them entirely. Gawan is relegated to a mere mention; the story of the title character's parents became an offstage pre-curtain feature. Wagner's *Parsifal* consists of a small group of basic scenes played out in a limited number of locales. Not only were the displays of chivalry virtually unstageable, but they were, for Wagner's purposes, irrelevant. The action of Wagner's drama is internalized to a greater extent than that of Wolfram's romance: adventure has been replaced by stasis. Whereas Wolfram's main purpose in writing *Parzival* was entertainment, Wagner had other more exalted ends that he wished to achieve with his works.

According to Carl Dahlhaus, *Parsifal* as a sacred drama is in many respects a paradoxical work. The title figure is a passive hero, and the decisive deed that forms the turning point or "peripeteia" of the drama is actually a renunciation. The outer action, Dahlhaus writes, is merely the occasion for an inner recognition. Parsifal does not act; rather, he finds himself in reacting to Kundry. The drama is actually epic, for it consists largely of narratives, such as those of Gurnemanz.[23] The stasis of the drama is also evident in its affinity to ritual and tableau. Besides tending to narrative, the language of the text is epic and ceremonial, and it frequently consists of verbal pronouncements that are repeated. Appropriately, the culmination of the drama is the fulfillment of an oracular prophecy that is ritually repeated throughout the drama by means of leitmotivs.[24]

Volker Mertens designates Wagner's *Parsifal* as a "Mysterienspiel," with the "mystery" at the root of this "mystery play" being that of the suffering of earthly existence, which can be relieved by insight into its cause. Mertens writes that Parsifal's triumph is a moral and spiritual one.[25] Chivalry and religiosity have become, in Wagner's work, metaphysics. The medieval Parzival of Wolfram attains his knightly red armor through the bitter irony of having killed a blood relation, Ither; Wagner's Parsifal is openly chided for the sin of killing an innocent swan, as the animals in the Grail Realm are sacred. A worldview that comprised alchemy and a medieval universe has been replaced by one that has as its ordering factor a reinterpretation of Christianity through the lens of Schopenhauerian philosophy to the end of the regeneration of modern

---

[22] Müller, "Parzival und Parsifal," 492.

[23] Carl Dahlhaus, *Richard Wagners Musikdramen* (Velber: Friedrich Verlag, 1971), 144–48.

[24] Dahlhaus, *Richard Wagners Musikdramen*, 148–50.

[25] Mertens, "Richard Wagner und das Mittelalter," 50–55.

THE LITERARY BACKGROUND OF *PARSIFAL* ◆ 43

society through a Buddhist brand of universal compassion with all living creatures.

Scholars find *Parsifal* a mythical work, primarily because of the universal nature of the religious insights that are presented in the drama.[26] Ursula Schulze designates Wagner's work "Parzival as redeemer" and argues that it represents a watershed in the modern reception and reinterpretation of the figure of Parzival. The elimination of Gawan and his adventures to a mere mention signifies much more than condensation for dramatic purposes. Schulze finds that the Arthurian world has been eradicated from Wagner's drama. She points out that Wagner has also eliminated the Orient as a locale from his work, thereby reducing the multidimensionality of Wolfram's romance and focusing instead on the sacred Grail Realm, to which Wagner's Parsifal brings a kind of redemption quite different from the salvation that the medieval world knew. She describes Wagner's drama as the myth of redemption, with this salvation consisting of insight into the suffering of existence and the resultant knowledge that one can be saved only through the renunciation of the individual will.[27] Kundry's character displays a radically altered personality that differentiates her from her medieval prototypes. Besides resembling Cunneware, Sigune, Cundrie, and Orgeluse, she also has a more timeless, mythical dimension. Klingsor calls her by various names, designating her as a prototype of the sinful female and the seductive woman, "Urteufelin," the primal temptress, Eve. In the Good Friday scene, she is a Mary Magdalene figure.

In Wagner's work, details about Parsifal's past are revealed to him, mainly by Kundry, and these exert an important psychological impact on Parsifal. Wolfram's Parzival witnesses and participates in knightly adventures; in order to attain the position of Grail King, Wagner's Parsifal must undergo an internal journey. Gurnemanz's narration of the convoluted prehistory of the onstage action is particularly significant because it functions as a prompt for Parsifal's psychological revelation. The internal is more important than the external. Medieval knightly adventure has stopped; the highest ideal is the renunciation of the will. Wagner's task of unifying his drama consisted not only of eliminating superfluous adventure, but also of interrelating the central episodes, objects, and figures with each other in an intricate way. Wolfram's additive narrative technique has become a tangled web of mirrorings. The complex genealogies highlighted

---

[26] On the mythical nature of *Parsifal*, see, for instance, Friedrich Oberkogler, *Parsifal: Der Zukunftsweg des Menschen in Richard Wagners Musikdramen* (Stuttgart: Verlag Freies Geistesleben, 1983).

[27] For the main part of her argument about Wagner's *Parsifal*, see Schulze, 557–60.

in the romance have been replaced by complex and at times sordid causal interrelationships of the characters and events portrayed. The duality of the Arthurian world and the Grail Realm that Wolfram presents has become, in Wagner's *Parsifal,* the juxtaposition of the Grail Realm and Klingsor's realm, which has directly or indirectly caused the loss of the sacred spear and the wound of Amfortas and thus of the entire realm.

Wagner's plan also dictated a reinterpretation of the Grail and the spear, as well as a resultant shift of emphasis from the title character to the Grail King. A redefinition of the Grail and the spear, the two central symbols of his drama, was very important to the composer and had widespread ramifications. Wagner criticizes Wolfram for choosing, as he explained in his letter to Mathilde Wesendonk, the most insignificant interpretation of the Grail from among all of those that were available to him. According to Wagner, Wolfram chose the most trivial among all of the various meanings that the Grail assumed in these legends. Wagner substantiates his claim with a lengthy explanation based on his own folklore research and his amateur philological investigations, in which he discusses the various legendary depictions of the Grail.

In Wolfram's *Parzival,* the Grail is a precious stone that gives out food and drink like a marvelous cornucopia. It chooses and calls the knights deemed worthy to serve it by naming them through inscriptions that appear on it. Wolfram's Grail does have some religious associations, including the wafer placed upon it on Good Friday and the "neutral angels" who, according to Trevrizent's theology, cared for it after the fall of Lucifer and brought it to earth. However, the basic definition of the Grail that Wolfram used simply did not suffice for Wagner. Whereas the Grail was in Chrétien's version a shallow bowl adorned with jewels, in most of the remaining Grail tradition, representative of which are the works of Robert de Boron, the Christian significance of the Grail is used, and this is the interpretation that Wagner preferred. According to Wagner, the Grail was the cup that Christ drank from at the Last Supper, and in which Joseph of Arimathia caught His blood as He was crucified.[28] Gurnemanz makes this explicit in his first-act narrative.

Similarly, Wagner uses a religious interpretation of the spear, an object that he correctly perceived as problematic in Wolfram's *Parzival.* Trevrizent explains to Parzival that Anfortas went into battle in the service of Orgeluse, and in doing so did not act according to the virtue of humility. While pursuing this adventure, he was wounded in the scrotum by a poisoned lance

---

[28] On the Grail in the traditional legend, see Bumke, 107–13; on Wolfram's version of the Grail, see Sidney Johnson, "Doing his own thing: Wolfram's Grail," in *A Companion to Wolfram's "Parzival"*, ed. Will Hasty (Columbia, SC: Camden House, 1999), 77–95.

wielded by a pagan who had been trying to win the Grail by force. A physician had removed the spearhead from the wound, from which the King never fully recovered. The wound is explicitly commented upon as God's punishment for the King's misconduct, just as Wagner makes the wound of Amfortas a sign of the Grail King's weakness. Anfortas, in serving the beautiful and haughty Orgeluse, embarked on an adventure not befitting the elevated status of the medieval Grail King, who is not allowed to marry any woman except for the one that the Grail names for him. Anfortas clearly lacked Gawan's humility. But the significance of the lance in Wolfram's *Parzival* is a point of scholarly contention. It is not even clear in that work, some scholars argue, whether the spear featured in the Grail ritual, when the lance is heated and placed in the cold wound to help relieve the pain, is the same one that wounded Anfortas and that the physician extracted from the wound.[29]

In his drama, Wagner made clear the whereabouts and the significance of the spear that wounded and will eventually heal the Grail King. Furthermore, the spear in question is the lance of Longinus,[30] with which Amfortas, as well as Christ, has been wounded. Wagner has also, appropriately enough, changed the position of the wound. His nineteenth-century Grail King has been wounded in the side, obviously a dramatic repetition, with significant and appropriate variation, of the side wound of the Passion. In fact, the dramatic figures expound at length about the symbolic significance of the wound from which Amfortas is suffering. Just as Gurnemanz makes Wagner's interpretation of the Grail and the spear explicit in his first-act narrative, Amfortas, too, is painfully aware of their significance, as he expresses his agony in the temple scene of the first act. Furthermore, he knows very well the resultant implications of his wound. As a necessary result of the general schema he had sketched, Wagner shifted the dramatic center from the title character to the wounded Grail King. In Wagner's drama, Parsifal exists in relation to Amfortas.[31]

Amfortas's suffering has acquired new psychological significance that the wound of Wolfram's Grail King lacked. In his letter to Mathilde Wesendonk, cited earlier, Wagner wrote:

> Genau betrachtet ist Anfortas der Mittelpunkt und Hauptgegenstand. Das ist denn nun keine üble Geschichte das. Denken Sie um des Himmels willen, was da los ist! Mir wurde das plötzlich schrecklich klar: es ist mein Tristan des dritten Aktes mit einer undenklichen Steigerung. Die

---

[29] On the lance in Wolfram's *Parzival*, see Kratz, *Wolfram von Eschenbach's "Parzival,"* 594.

[30] According to tradition, the name of the soldier who according to the Gospel of St. John wounded Christ on the cross with his lance.

[31] On the figure of Amfortas, see Wapnewski, *Der traurige Gott*, 213–29.

Speerwunde, und wohl noch eine andre — im Herzen, kennt der Arme in seinen fürchterlichen Schmerzen keine andre Sehnsucht, als die zu sterben; dies höchste Labsal zu gewinnen, verlangt es ihn immer wieder nach dem Anblick des Grals, ob der ihm wenigstens die Wunden schlösse, denn Alles Andre ist ja unvermögend, nichts — nichts vermag zu helfen: — aber der Gral gibt ihm immer nur das Eine wieder, eben daß er nicht sterben kann; gerade sein Anblick vermehrt aber nur seine Qualen, indem er ihnen noch Unsterblichkeit gibt. Der Gral ist nun, nach meiner Auffassung, die Trinkschale des Abendmahles, in welcher Joseph von Arimathia das Blut des Heilands am Kreuze auffing. Welche furchtbare Bedeutung gewinnt nun hier das Verhältnis des Anfortas zu diesem Wunderkelch; er, mit derselben Wunde behaftet, die ihm der Speer eines Nebenbuhlers in einem leidenschaftlichen Liebesabenteuer geschlagen, — er muß zu seiner einzigen Labung sich nach dem Segen des Blutes sehnen, das einst aus der gleichen Speerwunde des Heilands floß, als dieser, Weltentsagend, Welterlösend, Weltleidend am Kreuze schmachtete! Blut um Blut, Wunde um Wunde — aber hier und dort, welche Kluft zwischen diesem Blute, dieser Wunde! (*DEAP*, 14–15)

[If you look at it closely, Anfortas is the main character and the center of interest. That's not a bad story. Just think, for heaven's sake, what is going on there! Suddenly it became frightfully clear to me: he is my Tristan of the third act, only unimaginably more intense. He has a spear wound, and also another wound in his heart. In his terrible pain the poor man can long for nothing else but death; to attain this supreme comfort he yearns for the sight of the Grail, in the hopes that it can close the wound; nothing else matters to him, and nothing can help. But the Grail just prevents him from dying; gazing upon the Grail only prolongs his torment by granting him immortality. The Grail is, according to my understanding of it, the cup from which Christ drank at the Last Supper, and in which Joseph of Arimathia caught the blood of the Savior on the cross. What a dreadful meaning the relation of Anfortas to this miraculous cup now assumes; he who is suffering from the same wound, which the spear of a rival inflicted upon him in a passionate love-adventure — he must long for the blessing of the blood that once flowed from the spear wound of the Savior on the cross, as He was renouncing the world, redeeming the world, and suffering for the world! Blood against blood, wound against wound — but what a difference between them!]

Amfortas is suffering primarily from the torment of being wounded by the same spear that pierced Christ's side. The medieval emphasis on blood relation and inheritance, family ties, and the tangled web of family relationships contained in Wolfram's *Parzival* is transformed into Amfortas's miserable inheritance (wehvolles Erbe) of needing to uncover the Grail, thus increasing his own physical and spiritual suffering. The dual wounds of Amfortas, the one in his side and the one in his heart, can be considered representative of the physical and the psychological, and, by extension, the dual nature of the work in which Amfortas exists, the medieval and the modern aspects of the character and the music-drama in which he plays a role.

The character of Amfortas thus acquires a new significance by his participation in the Christ typology. Wagner elevates Amfortas's dramatic as well as symbolic significance. The analogy to the third-act Tristan is clear. Both suffer with no relief in sight. But the suffering of Wagner's Grail King has a new depth, an added dimension that the pain of Wolfram's Anfortas lacked. Though Trevrizent does explicitly point out Anfortas's lack of humility, and interprets the king's wound as punishment for his indiscretion, Wagner's Amfortas is suffering a kind of psychological torment of which the medieval Grail King shows no symptoms. The nineteenth-century Grail King is caught in a paradoxical situation. He longs for the Grail to relieve the pain, but uncovering the Grail only prolongs his torment, because it prevents him from dying, and death would be a release from his suffering. By its very nature and effects, the Grail denies him this release.

His illness has additional complications. The position of the wound, the circumstances under which it was incurred, and the implications of his post as Grail King all cause him more anguish. Wapnewski discusses Amfortas as a Christ-figure, a role he certainly seems a candidate for, as he was wounded in the side with the same spear that pierced Christ. But Amfortas, as Wapnewski points out, partakes of the Christ typology in a negative way. The analogy is also one of antithesis. Amfortas's anguished lament in the first-act scene in the Grail Temple clearly shows that he is suffering more from the wound in his heart than from the physical wound. Wagner continues the passage from which I cited earlier by explaining that performing the Grail ceremony becomes a torment for Amfortas. He wants to die, but cannot, and his role as Grail King is a constant reminder of his own sinfulness and his unworthiness to play this part.

Amfortas is suffering the torment of being wounded by the same spear that pierced Christ's side. One might consider Amfortas's physical wound an external sign of his inner "fall." To accentuate the sinfulness of Amfortas, Wagner revised the story of how the wound was incurred. An entry in his "brown book" clearly indicates that he thought hard about how to handle the motive of the spear.[32] Wagner pondered how the spear, which belonged in the Grail Temple with the Grail, could be used as a weapon against the Grail King. The spear, he decided, should be stolen from Amfortas during his fateful excursion. When Amfortas, much too boldly (as Gurnemanz describes the action) took the spear into battle against Klingsor, and was seduced by Kundry, Klingsor stole the spear from him

---

[32] See Bergfeld, *Das braune Buch*, 75–76. On the motive of the spear, see also Wapnewski, *Der traurige Gott*, 221–23.

and stabbed him in the side. Thus, a transgression of pride and arrogance caused him to be wounded. Wapnewski points out that in Wolfram's work, Anfortas is not a tragic but rather an epic figure, [33] and neither Wolfram nor Chrétien portrays his suffering to any extent. In Wagner's work, however, Amfortas is indeed tragic.

The Christological imagery is clear and extensive; the parallels and contradictions are manifold. Christ was innocent, and suffered for sinners. Amfortas is, as he himself points out, the only sinner among the sinless. The discrepancy between what he is supposed to be, as Grail King, and what he really is causes him pain. Christ died to save sinners. Amfortas wants to die to save himself, but not others. He would rather renounce life than gain eternal life. Whereas the wound of Christ was a sign of His innocence, Amfortas's wound indicates his sinfulness. Amfortas performed a sinful deed; Christ, who was sinless, took upon Himself the sins of mankind. Christ submitted to His Father's will. Amfortas rebels against his father. Christ saves all of humanity; Amfortas kills his father. Wapnewski points out that in the medieval source, the decisive sin is that of Parzival, whereas in Wagner's work, it is that of Amfortas.

In keeping with his basic schema, Wagner also revised the story of how the wound of the Grail King is healed, relating the suffering of Amfortas and the character progression of the title figure much more effectively than Wolfram, in his opinion. He disliked the motive of the redeeming question, and felt that Parzival's hatred of God also made little sense, as he wrote in the letter to Mathilde Wesendonk of May 29/30, 1859, cited above. He criticized the motive of the redeeming question for being tasteless. Similarly, Parzival's hatred of God was, Wagner thought, ridiculous and unmotivated. Wagner's solution was a sudden insight and the recovery of the spear to heal the wound. Wagner had no need for theology or the redeeming question. Therefore, Parsifal does not listen to long theological lessons such as Wolfram's Parzival hears from Trevrizent. No theological instruction instigates change in Wagner's Parsifal, but rather, he has a sudden insight, becoming cosmically clear-sighted by Kundry's kiss and experiencing a metaphysical revelation. The ritual of relieving the pain by putting the spear into the wound has been transformed, in the nineteenth-century musical-dramatic version, into Parsifal healing the wound by touching it with the regained spear. Thus there is an intricate interrelationship of the recovery of the spear and the healing of the wound. In Wolfram's *Parzival*, the narrator mentions that Parzival is the only knight who rejected and resisted Orgeluse. This detail obviously inspired Wagner to have Parsifal demonstrate his redeeming virtue by resisting Kundry.

---

[33] Wapnewski, *Der traurige Gott*, 150–56.

Kundry connects the two poles of the drama, and the two realms. In August 1860, Wagner wrote in a letter to Mathilde Wesendonk that he realized that the Grail messenger should be the same woman who seduced Amfortas (*DEAP*, 16–17). By making this woman a composite character with the appropriate double, split existence, Wagner's inspiration allowed him to further unify the drama. Not only does she travel far and wide geographically, but she also wanders from one existence to the next, through various reincarnations, unable to die, seeking Christ, whom she laughed at on the cross. Kundry's character is intertwined with that of Parsifal and she, like Amfortas, has a wound. She is suffering from a curse, and in a sudden outburst of self-revelation, she relates to Parsifal her cruel behavior to Christ on the cross. Her subsequent existence, she tells him, will be devoted to a search for the Redeemer whom she scorned. She believes that Parsifal is this same Savior, and that by seducing him, she can gain redemption. Parsifal's relation to Kundry demonstrates his growth. It is not enough when Parsifal attains compassion with Amfortas. In order for his development to be complete, he must suffer what Amfortas suffers, and in addition, he must accept and forgive Kundry.

Wagner masterfully accomplishes the correspondence of these dramatic events.[34] The spear was lost when Kundry seduced Amfortas; when Parsifal resists her, he regains the spear. Wolfram does not relate the fates of the redeemed one and the redeemer with Wagner's precision. Anfortas, as Wapnewski points out, serves more as an occasion for Parzival's elevation. In Wagner's work, however, there is a complementary relationship between Amfortas and Parsifal. The chosen one must be tested and withstand trials. The situation was thus contrived in which the redeemer is provoked to the same sin committed by the one who needs redemption. In Wolfram's romance, Parzival resists Orgeluse because of his marriage, that is, out of societal duty. In the second act of Wagner's work, when Parsifal rejects Kundry's attempt at seduction, he performs a denial of the will by renouncing sexuality, in keeping with Wagner's Schopenhauerian interpretation of the Grail legend. Parsifal must suffer what Amfortas suffers; in doing so, he regains the holy spear. In this way, Wagner's *Parsifal* seems to proceed through a complete determination of the dramatic action; the repeated oracular pronouncement that the "fool made wise through pity" will cure Amfortas gives the impression that the outcome has been predetermined.

Wagner has also tailored the figure of Klingsor to his own Schopenhauerian revision of Wolfram's basic schema.[35] In Wolfram's romance,

---

[34] Here again, I am following the argument of Wapnewski; cf. *Der traurige Gott*, 231–32.

[35] Cf. Wapnewski, *Der traurige Gott*, 243–46.

Clinschor was once a mighty duke and is descended from a family in Naples. He fell in love with Queen Iblis of Sicily and was caught in the act of adultery by her husband, King Ibert. As an appropriate punishment for the misdeed, Clinschor was castrated. He compensates for the deficiency by amassing power. He gains magical abilities. He proclaims that whoever withstands the adventure of Schastel Marveile will become ruler there. Gawan, who eventually accomplishes this feat, hears the story of Clinschor's past from King Arnive. In Wolfram's work, Clinschor provides a diversion from the main thread of action, which centers on Parzival. In Wagner's drama, however, Klingsor serves to illustrate the Schopenhauerian worldview. Wagner's magician attained magical powers through self-castration. In the first-act narrative in which he tells the prehistory of the onstage drama, Gurnemanz explains that Klingsor, unable to quiet the sinful urges within himself, resorted to a violent self-castration, thus employing external means to accomplish what is an inner state of peace. As a result, Klingsor is banished, and his resultant actions are taken in revenge. Wagner made him into the enemy of the Grail Realm and the ruler of the opposing realm. Wapnewski designates Klingsor an "anti-Amfortas," noting a parallel between Amfortas and Klingsor: both are rulers who have lost major abilities, and are thus dysfunctional.

In devising the plot in this way, to create his direct and complete determination of the dramatic action, Wagner has linked key incidents together in a decisive way. He was obviously inspired by the fact that in the source, Anfortas was wounded when battling in the service of Orgeluse. In Wagner's work, though, the Grail King's transgression has more dire results. Kundry's seduction of Amfortas coincides with the loss of the spear, just as Parzival's regaining of the spear happens when he rejects her attempted seduction, as an inevitable result of his heroism of renunciation. The spear can't hurt Parsifal once he has rejected Kundry's attempt at seduction, and hence there is a brilliant interconnection of Parsifal's rejection of Kundry and his regaining of the spear when the spear, hurled by Klingsor, hovers in the air over Parsifal's head at the end of the act. Thus Wagner effectively eliminates any need for the redeeming question, substituting for it the redeeming deed. The healing of the wound is the result of regaining the spear. In addition, the fact that Klingsor's realm crumbles when Parsifal makes the sign of the cross with the spear seems a clear indication that these realms are more inner states than outer places.[36]

---

[36] It is a misinterpretation of the work when modern productions do the "spear throw," as, for example, in the 1982 Götz Friedrich centennial production in Bayreuth. Parsifal regains the spear through a renunciation of the will, and thus he should be passive and bare his breast to the spear, which cannot hurt him once

Despite the presence of important Christian relics, rituals, terminology, and phraseology, *Parsifal* dramatically enacts a revision of Christianity. The ritual that the medieval Parzival witnesses in the Grail Castle is merely therapeutic. Its goal is to relieve the Grail King of some of his pain. In Wagner's *Parsifal*, the title character watches a "revisionist" Mass ceremony. The modern Grail ritual has obvious borrowings from the Catholic Mass, but these are in quotation marks. The commentary that is interspersed between these citations clearly demonstrates that Wagner's Grail Knights are celebrating a worldly religion. In Wagner's Grail ritual, no transubstantiation takes place. Wagner's knights change Christ's body back into bread, and His blood into wine. An entry in Cosima's diaries on September 26, 1877 clearly designates this as aiming toward a this-worldly religiosity: "Er spielt mir das Vorspiel in der Orchesterskizze vor! Lang andauernde Ergriffenheit — er spricht zu mir dann über diesen Zug des Grals-Mysterium, dass das Blut zu Wein wird, dadurch also wir gestärkt der Erde uns zuwenden dürfen, während die Wandlung des Weines in Blut uns von der Erde abzieht."[37] (He plays the prelude in the orchestra sketch to me. Emotion maintained for a long time — then he talks to me about this trait of the Grail mystery: that the blood becomes wine, so we, strengthened, can turn toward the earth, whereas the transformation of wine to blood draws us away from the earth.) In Wagner's religiosity, attention should be turned toward this world, whereas the traditional ceremony turns our attention away from this world to the next.

In the third act of *Parsifal*, when the title character returns to the Grail Realm with the sacred spear, the setting is Good Friday, as it is when, in Wolfram's romance, Parzival is prepared by Trevrizent to reenter the Grail Realm. However, Gurnemanz, the elderly mentor in Wagner's version of the Grail legend, gives a very different sermon to Parsifal, explaining that the day is not one of sorrow, but rather that nature rejoices at Christ's deed of redemption. This makes clear Wagner's worldly religiosity and revision of orthodox Christianity. The universal order displayed here is much different from that of the medieval romance. Gurnemanz corrects Parsifal when the latter says that nature is mourning on Good Friday, and explains that all of creation is rejoicing at the Savior's redeeming sacrifice. The external order into which Wolfram's Parzival is reintegrated is replaced in Wagner's *Parsifal* by a more internal one that renders the outer level

---

he has resisted Kundry. According to the stage direction, it pauses in the air over Parsifal's head. Thus it seems wrong when the tenor athletically catches the spear that is thrown by Klingsor. Ironically, it is a much more accurate depiction of Wagner's intention when the "spear throw" is "tricked."

[37] *CT* 1:1072.

almost insignificant. Christianity is not the only "mythological" system that Wagner uses in his religious drama; Wagner's *Parsifal* is the artistic result of a complex mythical syncretism. Besides elements of Christianity, it also contains basic concepts of Buddhism, such as Kundry's endless reincarnation.

Wagner's characters, moreover, have a psychological depth that is unlike anything in their medieval source material. The quasi-legendary nineteenth-century figures in this version of the Parzival legend are inwardly split and psychologically tormented in a specifically modern way. Hans Mayer writes that ambivalence is a main feature of *Parsifal*, and that it exemplifies a "dramaturgy of dialectic."[38] The characters mirror and shadow each other; they span the entire spectrum between good and evil, and in most cases, are neither and both. Amfortas's inner split is mirrored in Kundry's dual persona and her captivity by Klingsor. In fact, in the second act, she refers to her curse as her "wound." The maidens of the medieval castle Schastel Marveile, held captive by the magician, are freed by Gawan's deed of chivalric heroism; Kundry's release from her endless wandering from one existence to the next and from one persona to another is absolution, baptism by Parsifal, and death in front of the newly uncovered Grail.

Similarly, Titurel is anything but an exemplification of sanctity; rather, he provoked the dramatic action by haughtily rejecting Klingsor, who aspired to the status of Grail Knight, thus committing a sin of arrogance comparable to Amfortas's taking the sacred spear into battle and losing it. In revenge against the Grail Realm, Klingsor took to magic. As Wolfram uses the Grail Realm to show the insufficiencies and inadequacy of the standard Arthurian world of the romances of his knightly day and age, Wagner's work contains a blatant criticism of the main representatives of the Grail Realm that he depicts onstage. The character contrasts and juxtapositions significantly undermine the surface meanings, and thereby Wagner relativizes traditional values and standards as he portrays the Grail Realm in crisis. In this way Wagner's drama performs a revaluation of values. Ultimately, he wished to regenerate modern society through the use of art, and through the ultimate art form in particular, music-drama.

In his late essay "Religion und Kunst," along with its postscripts, Wagner presents his aesthetic program of using and reinterpreting traditional symbols so they can become symbols of essential truths. These treatises are often considered the theoretical counterparts of *Parsifal*, and one can understand the religious rituals that he stages in *Parsifal* in relation to

---

[38] Hans Mayer, "Anmerkungen zu Parsifal," in *Richard Wagner: Mitwelt und Nachwelt* (Stuttgart: Belser, 1978), 242–51.

these essays. The first-act ceremony in the Grail Temple is an altered version of the Catholic Mass, and Parsifal baptizes Kundry in the third act of the drama. Gurnemanz anoints Parsifal as king, and Kundry washes his feet and dries them with her hair. Through the impact of this work and its presentation upon the audience, Wagner aimed to contribute to a regeneration of modern society — a regeneration that, like that of the Grail Realm, would be achieved through an identification with Parsifal and through the acquisition of a universal compassion, gained through metaphysical insight into the unity of all creatures.

2: Erotic Love in Chrétien's *Perceval,* Wolfram's *Parzival,* and Wagner's *Parsifal*

James M. McGlathery

Introduction

SALVATION — OR REDEMPTION — being the dominant theme in Wagner's *Parsifal,* one might expect the opera to be about the means to its achievement. From the Christian standpoint, faith in God as Father, Son, and Holy Spirit is required for salvation. Wagner's young hero, however, seems less concerned with faith than with salvation or redemption. Indeed, he seems not to give much thought to the afterlife, seeking rather to be saved and redeemed in this life. He seeks redemption for not questioning the cause of Amfortas's suffering, and thereby showing a lack of compassion. In Christian terms, he has failed to live up to Jesus's teaching that we should love our neighbors as we love ourselves. Parsifal specifically seeks salvation from surrender to sexual seduction in the person of Kundry, a surrender associated in his mind with eternal damnation. In a truly Christian drama, loving one's neighbor would proceed from love of God and salvation from faith in God. These matters and related ones in Wagner's work lack that sort of clarity and simplicity.

The same can be said for Wolfram von Eschenbach's classic rendition of the Grail story in his medieval epic *Parzival.* There, indeed, the nature and degree of the hero's piety is in still greater doubt. Parzival's regret over having failed to ask about Anfortas's suffering is not so much a feeling of sinfulness as shame over having failed to live up to chivalric ideals. His goal is rather redeeming his honor than achieving redemption from sin. His aim is to become Grail King in spite of having missed that chance on the day appointed for him to heal Anfortas's wound by asking the fateful question. Faith does not seem to motivate Parzival's actions; on the contrary, misfortune moves him to doubt God's existence or to deny God his allegiance. Parzival, moreover, appears unconcerned about salvation.

The decidedly Christian atmosphere of Wagner's opera owes far more to Wolfram's source, the unfinished courtly romance *Perceval* by Chrétien de Troyes. Our last view of Perceval is his encounter with a group of knights and ladies returning from their Good Friday pilgrimage to a pious hermit. These pilgrims direct him to the hermit (6237–6519).[1] Through these encounters, Perceval's thoughts are turned toward faith in God and hope for redemption and salvation. Because Chrétien's epic remained unfinished, we do not know how Perceval was to reach his destiny of succeeding the Grail King or how the latter was to be delivered from his suffering.

Wagner's *Parsifal* deviates from its two principal medieval predecessors in important ways, among the most striking of which is its reduction of the role of women to a single figure, the seductress Kundry. Although, in Joseph Chytry's words, "*Parsifal* was primarily meant as Wagner's encomium to Agapē over Eros,"[2] the theme of seduction itself is a major innovation on Wagner's part. As we shall see, there are no seductresses in Wagner's medieval predecessors, although erotic attractions are certainly not lacking; quite the contrary. And not only in the depictions of courtly society, but in the Grail company, which abides by courtly decorum and demeanor, women are present and active in equal numbers with the men. In society and at the Grail castle, the noble women are beautiful and the knights handsome, as befits courtly romance. The lone exception is Cundrie herself, who serves as messenger at the Grail castle and is so ugly that one would wish to be able to say that she is beautiful. To compensate for her lack of beauty she dresses in the latest and finest fashions, whereas Wagner's Kundry has to hide her ravishing beauty in order to receive acceptance as servant to the knights of the Grail.

Wagner's Grail knights thus appear to have withdrawn radically into an all-male community. We do not hear even of any female servants at the Grail castle. Kundry is able to steal her way into their territory only by virtue of her knowledge of medicinal herbs and the knights' hope that she will be able to heal Amfortas's wound or at least lessen his suffering. Even so, she would not have been able to gain even that limited admittance had she presented herself in anything approaching the beauty she possesses. Women's presence for Wagner's knights carries the danger of succumbing to erotic desire; and it is resistance to the tug of desire on which the knights base their claim to purity and virtue. Even in her ugly, beast-like disguise Kundry arouses suspicion on the part of Gurnemanz's young charges, who in seeming error but with unerring instinct, suspect that

---

[1] Chrétien de Troyes, *Le Roman de Perceval ou le conte du Graal* (Geneva: Librairie Droz; Lille: Librairie Giard, 1956); in English: *Perceval: The Story of the Grail*, trans. Burten Raffel (New Haven and London: Yale UP, 1999). Passages will be identified in the text by line, e.g. (4401).

[2] *The Aesthetic State: A Quest in Modern German Thought* (Berkeley and London: U of California P, 1989), 308.

she is herself the seductress responsible for the wounding of Amfortas (1, 14–15).[3] We are left with the impression that the Grail company attracts, even seeks, novices of misogynist bent, young men whose visceral reaction to women is to see them as seductresses, as daughters of Eve.[4]

In *Parsifal*, Amfortas's father, Titurel, is the founder of the Grail community. As Gurnemanz explains to the young squires, Titurel was summoned by God to create the community. Apparently, Gurnemanz was not present at Titurel's reception of that call; indeed, the call evidently came in a vision experienced by Titurel alone (1, 17). In any event, Titurel seems to interpret his vocation as the founding not merely of a company of knights to defend the faith against the infidels on the southern boundaries of Christendom, but of an exclusively male company, with even the presence of women prohibited. Although the question is not raised in the opera, it does pose itself nonetheless: since Amfortas cannot have sprung full grown from Titurel's brow, who was his mother and what became of her? More important, if we assume that Titurel raised Amfortas in place of his mother, and since there seem to be no women at all at the Grail castle, Amfortas's fateful encounter with Kundry as a ravishing beauty on his first venture beyond the territory of the Grail castle must have been his first encounter with a woman since his early boyhood or infancy.

In Chrétien's Grail castle, by contrast, women have a prominent place. The sword that the Grail King presents to Perceval is a gift to the former from " 'That golden-haired girl, / Your beautiful niece,' " as the servant says to the Grail King (3146–47). Not only does Amfortas's counterpart here have a beautiful niece, but the Grail itself is carried by a member of the fairer sex: "And then two other servants / Entered, carrying golden / Candleholders worked / With enamel, They were wonderfully handsome / Boys . . . / . . . A girl / Entered with them, holding / A Grail-dish in both her hands / A beautiful girl, elegant / Extremely well dressed. / . . . / . . . Then another / Girl followed the first one, / Bearing a silver platter" (3213–32). Chrétien's Grail Knights clearly are accustomed to seeing beautiful girls, in contrast to the knights in Wagner's opera.

In Wolfram's *Parzival* the role of women in the Grail procession is greatly expanded. No fewer than two dozen beautiful women in dazzling

---

[3] Richard Wagner, *Parsifal: Ein Bühnenweihfestspiel in drei Aufzügen*, ed. Wilhelm Zentner (Stuttgart: Philipp Reclam, 1974). Further references to this source will be parenthetical, identified by act and page number, e.g. (2, 45).

[4] This dimension of *Parsifal* has been commented on by various authors. James Treadwell, in a chapter on "desire" in his recent book *Interpreting Wagner* (New Haven and London: Yale UP, 2003), 169, refers to "the opera's strenuous, almost maniacal insistence on chastity."

attire precede the one carrying the Grail. Here she has the title of Grail Queen and is the sister of the Grail King Anfortas, as one later learns. Her name, moreover, is Repanse de Joie, establishing an association between the Grail, joy, and female beauty. Purity is associated here not with male renunciation of desire but with female chastity and the accompanying absence of deceit (5:235, 25–30).[5] In Wolfram's telling, or, more precisely, as the hermit Trevrizent tells Parzival, the Grail King may marry, but only the wife appointed for him by God, as revealed in miraculous inscription on the Grail (9:478, 13–16).

Wolfram's Anfortas has thus not grown up in an exclusively male society, but has been exposed to beautiful women, who have an integral role in the ritual life of the Grail. While Wagner's Grail knights resemble monks in many respects, Wolfram's Grail company seems to combine elements of monastery and convent, with the important difference that the knights and ladies of Wolfram's Grail castle may leave to marry, as God (via inscriptions on the Grail) may ordain. No explanation is given in *Parzival* for the origin of the Grail company and Grail castle, though the earliest of the Grail kings of whom we learn is named Titurel. In this work, though, he is Anfortas's grandfather. Titurel's successor as Grail King was Frimutel, Anfortas's father. At Frimutel's death as a result of a joust, Anfortas, as his elder son, was summoned while still a boy to the Grail castle as Grail King (9:478, 1–7).

In Trevrizent's account to Parzival, with Anfortas's arrival at puberty he chose for himself a woman to whom he dedicated his service as a knight, and in so doing acted in a manner contrary to the commandment associated with the service of the Grail (9:478, 8–22). Anfortas is not presented to us as having been the victim of seduction or as having succumbed to it. He sought a woman's love in response to an adolescent awakening of sexual desire. As Trevrizent confesses to Parzival, much the same happened with him himself (9:495, 13–18). Despite Anfortas's loss of his father while still a boy and having perhaps left his mother already at that time to become Grail King, he remained in close touch with his family; his sister

---

[5] Wolfram von Eschenbach, *Parzifal*, ed. Walter Haug, Bibliothek des Mittelalters: Texte und Übersetzungen, vol. 8, nos. 1–2 (Frankfurt am Main: Deutscher Klassiker Verlag, 1994). Passages will be identified in the text by book, strophe, and verse, e.g. (9:480, 10–15). The secondary literature on Wolfram's *Parzival* is vast. The following three items provide a good overview, together with the detailed notes provided in the edition above: Joachim Bumke, *Wolfram von Eschenbach*, Sammlung Metzler: Realien zur Literatur, vol. 36, 8th ed. (Stuttgart: J. B. Metzler, 2004); Heinz Rupp, ed., *Wolfram von Eschenbach*, Wege der Forschung, vol. 57 (Darmstadt: Wissenschaftliche Buchgesellschaft, 1966); and Will Hasty, ed., *A Companion to Wolfram's Parzival* (Columbia, SC: Camden House, 1999).

had become Grail Queen and his brother Trevrizent had withdrawn to life nearby as a pious hermit after Anfortas's wounding, in order to seek God's rescue of his brother from his suffering (9:480, 10–15). The fourth of Frimutel's children is Parzival's dead mother Herzeloyde, so the Grail kingship remains a family matter, a dynasty as much as a holy order. In Wagner's opera, by contrast, Parsifal is not related to Amfortas, who apparently has no siblings or other family save for his father Titurel.

Sexual desire, as distinguished from fleshly lust, is not set in opposition to Christian piety in either Chrétien's *Perceval* or Wolfram's *Parzival* as it decidedly is in Wagner's *Parsifal*. Indeed, erotic passion is celebrated, especially in so far as it leads to marital fidelity, and is not censured except where it would lead to violation of God's commandments, such as those against adultery and covetousness.

Chrétien de Troyes's *Perceval*

Although Chrétien's Perceval sets out to learn about knighthood, not love, he almost immediately encounters a beautiful woman sleeping alone in a majestic tent in a clearing. While he displays no signs of awakening sexual desire, he is more than happy to be able to carry out what he interprets as his mother's parting advice to kiss the women he encounters (actually she talked about women allowing him a kiss as a reward for his service as a knight). He also knows how to kiss, by virtue of his having kissed or been kissed by his mother's chambermaids, since he tells the young woman he found sleeping that her mouth tastes better than theirs (725–28). More innocent than stealing kisses is his stealing of the ring on the young woman's finger (whereas his mother had said only that he should take a woman's ring if she offered it). This act has symbolic associations with stealing a woman's virtue, the more so in view of Perceval's having lain on top of the woman while bestowing his twenty kisses on her. His behavior is excused by his adolescent innocence of the sort of lust presumably at play in the abduction of the three girls by five knights that, with a distinct lack of interest, he had been hearing about from a group of knights who were pursuing the miscreants and seeking information from Perceval about them.

The encounter with the slumbering beauty in the tent turns Perceval's thoughts toward love, however unconsciously, judging from his notice of a beautiful young maiden after his ensuing arrival at King Arthur's court. He stops to greet her, she returns his greeting, and she then begins to laugh, evidently at the way he looks in the peasant attire his mother had dressed him in hoping it would put a quick end to his quest to become a knight. Instead of ridiculing him, though, the young lady declares that in time he will show himself to be the best knight in the world, a prophecy for which she receives a hard slap from Sir Kay, one of Arthur's knights; he had been taunted by the court fool with a foretelling that the girl would never laugh "until / She sees the man fated / To become the knight of all knights," an honor that Kay evidently wants her to bestow on him himself, not on some naive youth and seeming country bumpkin like Perceval (1057–62).

Perceval's sojourn with Gournement de Goort, during which the old knight instructs him in martial arts and other matters of proper chivalric conduct, does not do much to enlighten him about erotic desire. All Gournement has to say on that score is, "If you find a girl or woman, / Unmarried or married, deprived / Of assistance and counsel, provide it: / Women deserve our help, / If we know what ought to be done / And are able, ourselves, to do it" (1656–62). The old knight may have help of a sexual sort in mind in addition to other kinds of aid, but if so he can hardly expect a youth like Perceval to recognize that.

When Perceval immediately thereafter has just such a damsel in distress — indeed Gournement's beautiful niece Blanchefleur — climb into bed with him at her castle, however, he knows how to comfort her with kisses after pledging to go forth on the morrow to defeat the forces of her spurned suitor Clamadeu, who has laid siege to her castle. While not a seductress, Blanchefleur perhaps recognizes that coming to Perceval's bedside while the rest of Beaurepaire castle sleeps may help in winning his aid. At any rate she calls attention to the possibility that he might attribute her visit to erotic desire, saying " 'Oh noble knight, have mercy! / I pray you by God and His son, / Don't change your opinion of me / Because I've come to your bed. / Don't think me wild and foolish / And wicked because I'm wearing / Only my nightshirt, for in all / This world there's no one afflicted / With misery and sadness whose pain / And suffering can equal mine' " (1982–91). Though she is not exactly wild, foolish, or wicked, Blanchefleur does not reject Perceval's invitation to join him in bed: ' "If that's what you want,' she said, / 'That's what I'll do.' And as / He held her in his arms, he kissed her. / . . . / And she let him kiss her again, / Nor did his kisses displease her. / And then they spent the night / Lying together, mouth / To mouth, till morning came" (2057–66).

After Perceval's ensuing defeat of Clamadeu's steward, Blanchefleur is quick to reward him with love-making: "Then the mistress of the castle came, / Wonderfully pleased, and led him / Away to her private apartment / To rest and relax. And there / She gave him hugs and kisses, / And denied him nothing at all. / Instead of eating and drinking / They played at hugging and kissing / And murmuring words of endearment" (2356–64). To Blanchefleur's angry and sad dismay, after his defeat of Clamadeu and after a time spent in delight over his life with her, Perceval's "heart pulled him away, / Tugging in a different direction: / He remembered his mother, and the sight of her / Fainting and falling to the ground [as he rode off leaving her] / And more than anything else / In the world he longed to see her / Again. . . ." (2918–24).

The sojourn with Blanchefleur is the last erotic involvement of Perceval's that is reported, much less described. To be sure, he meets again the two young beauties he encountered on his first day away from home: the girl slumbering in the tent in the forest, and the girl at Arthur's court who laughed on being greeted by him (forerunners of Wolfram's Jeschute and Cunneware, respectively). The encounter with the girl from the tent shows Perceval's compassion, not passion. When he discovers who she is and why she is being punished by her beloved for presumed infidelity with Perceval, he succeeds in restoring her honor. After defeating her ragingly jealous beloved in a joust, Perceval declares to him, ". . . Knight, by God, / I'll have exactly as much / Mercy on you as you show / To your lady, who never deserved — / And I can swear it! — the terrible / Things you've made her endure" (3938–43). Similarly, after by defeating Kay in a joust he has avenged the slap that the girl at Arthur's court received from the latter, "Perceval greeted the girl / . . . / . . . and throwing his arms / Around her, gave her a hug / And said, 'My beauty, if you need / My service, remember, this / Is a knight who will never fail you.' / And the girl thanked him as she should" (4596–4603). In this reunion, too, there is much chivalry and little hint of passion.

Since Chrétien did not finish the poem, we do not know whether Perceval was to be reunited with Blanchefleur. Instead of finding his mother he comes upon the Grail castle, where he fails to ask the proper question about the lance and the Grail. Indeed, on leaving the castle he encounters one of his cousins (the forerunner of Wolfram's Sigune) who is grieving over her dead beloved. She informs him of his mother's death, caused by the grief of his leaving her. Chastising him for having failed to ask the questions, she claims, " 'Ah, how unlucky you are, / For had you asked those questions / You could have completely cured / The good king of all his wounds: / He would have become entirely / Whole, and ruled as he should' " (3585–90). To be sure, after learning of his mother's death Perceval's thoughts turn briefly to Blanchefleur, but only because of drops of blood in the snow from a goose wounded by a falcon: "Blood and snow so mixed together / Created a fresh color, / Just like his belovèd's face, / And as he stared he forgot / What he was doing and where / He was. The red stain / Against the white snow / Seemed just like her complexion. / The more he looked, the happier / He grew, seeing once / Again the exact color, / Of her beautiful face" (4199–4211). Once the trance-like state has passed we hear nothing further of his thoughts about Blanchefleur.

Perceval's later denunciation at King Arthur's court by an ugly young woman (forerunner of Wolfram's Cundrie) for having failed to ask about the Grail and the lance at the Fisher King's castle propels him to pursue chivalric adventure: "Until he knew / For whom the Grail had been borne / And until he'd found the bloody / Lance and understood / Why it bled"

(4736–40). He receives the answers to those two questions five years later from a pious hermit who reveals himself to be Perceval's uncle, brother both to his mother and to the father of the Fisher King. All we hear about those five years is "that Perceval / Had so completely lost / His memory he'd even forgotten / God. . . . / And he'd never entered a church / To adore God or His saints. / For five years he lived / Like this, but never gave up / Hunting chivalric adventure, / Engaging in the wildest exploits, / Savage and cruel and hard. / He hunted them, and found them, / And proved his courage over / And over . . ." (6218–32). At our last glance, then, Perceval has been restored by his uncle to faith in God: "And Perceval learned, once again, / That Our Lord had died that Friday, / Crucified high on the Cross. / He made his Easter communion / Humbly, in perfect simplicity" (6510–14). It seems logical to conclude that Perceval's path is leading him in the direction of Christian compassion, toward *caritas*, not *eros*.

As devoid of erotic passion as the Perceval story becomes, that void is more than filled by the adventures of Gawain that comprise all but a few hundred lines (Perceval's Easter sojourn with the hermit) of the second half of Chrétien's unfinished epic. To be sure, the focus here is on Gawain as the perfect knight, fulfilling the chivalric ideal, just as the Perceval story had come to be centered on his piety. Still, erotic love is shown as integral to that ideal. More important, Gawain's several encounters with women depict various aspects of erotic attraction between the sexes.

First, there is King Tibault's eldest daughter, who demands that her suitor Meliant prove his love by jousting with her father. Gawain rescues the situation by taking Tibault's place in the joust. The matter, including the emotions involved, is complicated by Meliant's having grown up as Tibault's foster son and his daughter's foster brother, so that the girl is in effect asking the brother to prove himself in combat with the man who has been father to them both. She desires the joust so that she can boast to her girl friends about her suitor's prowess as a knight. Yearning to see herself as the object of love on the part of a brave, handsome knight, she belittles Gawain, who has become the object of her younger sister's attention (5001–91). The younger sister, for her part, wants to show the older sister that she is not too young to have a champion herself. Gawain indulges her in that wish, not least because he is quite charmed with her, as is her father Tibault, who advises her and helps fulfill her chivalric role (5331–5496). Thus Chrétien depicts for us a broad range of erotically tinged tenderness between family members and family friends of the opposite sex.

Then, there is a teenage boy who sends Gawain to his sister with the message that she is to treat him just as she would her brother (5730–48). Gawain's escort changes the message he delivers to the sister (5793–5805), especially in saying, "Don't be reluctant to allow him / Whatever a man might want / . . ." (5801–02). Gawain's amorous advances follow, and the sister accepts them gladly because he is so handsome (5816–37). When a knight interrupts their encounter and denounces her for making love with the man who — unbeknownst to her until that moment — killed her father, her attraction to Gawain proves decisive. Instead of registering any revulsion, she arms Gawain, giving him a chessboard as his shield. She defends her behavior with Gawain to the crowd by saying, " 'My brother himself sent him / Here, and asked me to be his host, / And treat him with all the warmth / And affection I'd show my brother' " (5967–70). Since that affection included acceptance of Gawain's passion, there is room to think that she and her brother feel some erotic attraction to one another, as we perhaps already sensed when the brother ("a boy in his teens, and the loveliest / Boy in the world . . .") sent the handsome knight off to be entertained and comforted by the beautiful sister. She tells her attackers they are wrong to call her a slut, but she fights like a common woman: "And the girl picked up the chessmen / Lying on the floor and threw them / Angrily into their faces. Tucking up her skirt / And swearing like a fishwife, / She told them she'd kill them all, / If she could, before they killed her" (6001–07).

Finally, we have Gawain's adventures with "the girl staring at her mirror," (later identified for us as the "Proud Beauty of Logres," 6658–7371). Her haughtiness seems to be thinly veiled seductiveness: " 'Don't think I plan to let you / Cart me away on your horse. / I'm not some silly little girl / Who plays such games with you fellows, / Letting you lug me away / When you need to prove your knighthood' " (6705–10). Then after Gawain has done her bidding by fetching her palfrey: "She'd let her cloak and her kerchief / Fall to the ground, the better / To show off both her face / And her figure . . . / . . . / 'By God,' said the girl, 'you'll never / Be able to boast, wherever / You go, that you held me in your arms. / If your naked hand so much / As touched anything I wore, / Or brushed against my skin, / I'd be dishonored and stained. / What a misfortune if anyone / Knew or said you were actually / Able to touch my flesh! / I'd infinitely rather, believe me, / That here and now they cut / My skin and flesh to the bone!' " (6833–53).

After Gawain has suffered her taunts and humiliations and done all her bidding — and accomplished the seemingly impossible task by rescuing the 500 girls and knights at an enchanted castle (named the Rock of Champguin, 8818), among them his sister, mother, and grandmother (7372–8244) — he gains the humble submission of the haughty beauty, who explains her prior behavior as a wish to die at the hands of a man angered by her abuse of him: " 'After my original / Lover was taken by death, / Grief drove me insane, / And I spoke with such wild pride, / Such wicked, half-crazed folly, / That it made no difference to me / Who might suffer for my words. / Indeed, I did it all / Deliberately, hoping / I'd find someone so easily / Angered I'd drive him to distraction / And he'd cut me to little pieces: / For a long time I've wanted / To be dead. Now deal with me / However justice may require, / So girls, hearing my story, / Won't shame and slander knights' " (8948–64). We can take her at her word regarding her aim and motivation, yet she seemed to enjoy playing the seductive femme fatale and was perhaps too much attracted by Gawain's masculine appeal. It is to that erotic attraction that she surrenders in the end.

Wolfram von Eschenbach's *Parzival*

In Wolfram's *Parzival,* the adventures of Gawan are focused on erotic love even more than Gawain's were in Chrétien's *Perceval.* In Wolfram's telling, Obie doesn't insist that Meleans, her foster brother, joust with her father. She asks only that he spend five years proving his courage as a knight before she would consider his request (that she reward his service with her love) and that even that would be too soon. In his anger at her haughty mocking of him, Meleans reminds her that her father is his vassal (his father was a king, her father is a prince), to which she replies that she does not accept vassalage to anyone and is worthy of every crown that anyone has ever worn (7:345–47). Wolfram's narrator explains that Obie and Meleans loved one another very much. The latter's riding off in anger depressed and hurt her. Seeing any noble man was a thorn in her eye because she wanted Meleans to be the first among men. This is the reason for her belittling of Gawan, which leads to her little sister Obilot's claiming of him as her champion (7:365–66).

Gawan was already charmed by "small, sweet beautiful" Obilot, having overheard her defense of him in the face of her sister's scorn. When she comes to see him to ask him to be her champion, he thanks her for her support. He tells her that if ever there were a knight who experienced pangs of love for a lady as young as she, it would have to happen to him with her (7:368, 26–30). Obilot's response is a confused speech containing elements of what she evidently thinks she has heard from her governess: he shall now bear her name, become both a girl and a man, and be in reality she herself (7:369, 16–20). Gawan tells her he has pledged his honor not to fight until he has jousted with a challenger (Kingrimorcel) and that she needs to wait another five years before she will be ripe for love. But then, remembering that Parzival recommended to him that he trust more to women than to God, he promises to be her champion, making the galant excuse that she would be fighting the joust for him, and thus inferring that this would not break his promise not to fight (7:370, 8–30). Obilot's playmate Clauditte asks, after they have left Gawan, what token of love Obilot plans to give him, since they have only their dolls. Clauditte says Obilot could give him hers if they are prettier than her own (7:372, 15–19). Obilot instead offers Gawan the sleeve of a dress that her mother and father had made for her and that has touched her arm, and Clauditte then brings the sleeve to Gawan (7:375).

When Wolfram's young King Vergulaht sends Gawan to be entertained by his beautiful sister, so that he himself can continue hunting, he only tells the knight who accompanies Gawan to say to the sister, Queen Antikonie, that she should entertain Gawan. He says nothing about doing so as a sister would entertain a brother, as in Chrétien's epic. Nor does the knight then tell her that she should grant Gawan anything he desires. Instead, Wolfram lets it be simply a case of passion at first sight. It is Antikonie who offers to entertain Gawan as he may wish and who says that her brother has recommended him to her so warmly that she will give him a kiss, to which Gawan responds by saying that her lips are made for kissing. The kiss proves to be more than one between strangers and leads to Gawan's begging her for more. In response, she protests suggestively that she does not even know who he is, yet in just a few minutes he wants to possess her love completely. Gawan assures her that he is of noble standing equal to hers, and having heard that an eagle often catches an ostrich that is hungry, he reaches under her outer garment to touch her. Far from causing her to repulse him, his action awakens such mutual passion that they are on the verge of intercourse when they are interrupted by the knight who rushes in to denounce Gawan — erroneously — for having slain Antikonie's father and now for raping his daughter (8:402–07). Antikonie fights like a knight, felling the attackers with the stone chess pieces, better than the storekeepers' wives at mardi gras, the narrator comments. Gawan pauses during the battle to stare lustfully at her body, her mouth, her eyes, her nose. She is as slender as a hare on a spit, he thinks, so narrow is she between her hips and breasts, her body made for arousing sexual desire (8:409, 22–410, 12).

Gawan's subsequent adventures result from his falling in love at first sight with the beautiful duchess Orgeluse de Logrois. Contrary to her depiction in Chrétien's telling, she does not show off her body to him, nor is she looking in a mirror. She is a haughty, unattainable beauty. However, she does call attention to his infatuation with her, asking him how he happens to be in love with her, and why so many men throw lightning-like glances her way. Her mockery and scorn seem aimed at spurring his interest in her as the unattainable beloved. She must know by seeing how handsome he is that he would expect her to be equally attracted to him (10:508–10). Another allusion (10:512) to physical love consists of her not wanting to touch anything he has touched (in chivalric romance wearing a garment that the beloved has worn is an affirmation of sexual favor).

When Orgeluse abruptly departs, the ferryman's daughter Bene, a female character added by Wolfram, falls in love with Gawan at first sight.

Her father asked her to serve Gawan in a friendly fashion. She takes him up to a room and helps him out of his armor. Gawan remarks about the intimacy of that act, saying that if her father had not demanded it she would have been doing too much for him. She responds that in whatever way she serves him it is solely to gain his favor (10:549). Gawan asks her father to let him eat with the girl, to which the father says that this has not been previously allowed for fear that it might go to her head. However, in view of their indebtedness to Gawan for enriching them, he does not object, and asks Bene to fulfill all of Gawan's wishes (10:550). At bedtime her ermine coat is placed on Gawan's bed and her parents leave her alone with him as he prepares to retire. Wolfram's narrator remarks that Bene would have allowed any liberties Gawan wished to take, leaving that possibility somewhat open by adding that Gawan had to go to sleep, if he could that is (10:552). The next morning Bene goes to Gawan's bedside and sits on the carpet next to the bed. Her father finds her there, thinks that she is crying because Gawan has seduced or raped her, and tells her it was done in fun and that she will get over it. In reality, her tears spring from Gawan persistently asking about the beautiful women in the windows of the magical castle nearby, who distract him from his attention to her (11:554–55).

After heroic Gawan releases the castle from its evil spell, he looks at the beautiful young women who are attending him, and is reminded of Orgeluse, who affected him as no woman ever had (11:581–82). In his sleep, as his body strives to recover from its wounds, Orgeluse rules in his heart. This causes Wolfram's narrator to scold Lady Love for attacking a man when he is down and to reflect that all of Gawan's relatives, including Parzival and his father Gahmuret, were Lady Love's captives and servants (12:584–87). When Gawan then sees Orgeluse riding with a knight, as an image in the magical column that Klingsor had brought from India, he is overcome with passion, a man completely helpless against love's power (12:593). The ladies attending him fruitlessly beg him not to do battle with so formidable a knight in his weakened condition. Following his defeat of the knight, Orgeluse heaps scorn on him and mockingly accedes to his request that she accept his chivalric services, granting only that he may ride along with her and try to gain further renown (12:599). He is overjoyed and his are thoughts so centered on her that he does not feel the pain of his wounds (12:601, 1–6).

When Orgeluse says that he must fetch a wreath for her, he asks where he can steal the wreath that will cure his pierced heart. With this remark, he may be alluding to his yearning to possess her. Wolfram's narrator, at least, comments that Gawan should have thrown her down on her back and "taken the wreath" as has happened with many a beautiful woman in the meantime (12:601, 17–19). Orgeluse suggests that the quickest and bravest way to get to the tree where he will find the twig for her wreath is to spur his horse to leap over the Severn River at a place called the Perilous

Gorge, a feat with possible erotic overtones like a dangerous leap into bed (12:602). The tree belongs to King Gramoflans, who tells Gawan he killed Orgeluse's husband Cidegast, presumably in order to have her for himself; but once he became convinced that he could not win her love he fell in love with a young lady he has never met, Itonje, who unbeknownst to Gramoflans is one of Gawan's sisters.

Orgeluse tells Gawan that her treatment of him was nothing but a test of love, implicitly attributing the test to her grief over the loss of so worthy a beloved as her dear Cidegast (12:614). She promises to give him her love, but only once his wounds, and the hurt caused by her behavior, are healed. Orgeluse offers to accompany him to the Castle of Marvels, whereupon he lifts her up onto her horse, affording him the opportunity to embrace her (12:615). She confesses to Gawan that Anfortas was serving as her champion when he was wounded, jousting with Gramoflans, on whom she wished to be revenged for his having killed her Cidegast (12:616–17). Then she enlisted the aid of the sorcerer Klingsor, using the gifts from the Orient that Anfortas had given her, in hopes of luring Gramoflans to the magical castle and the adventures there that he surely would not have survived as Gawan has. She brags to Gawan that she has been able to enlist all the knights into her service once they laid eyes upon her, with the exception only of one, the Red Knight, that is, Parzival (12:618). When she offered him her love he said his wife (Condwiramurs) was more beautiful and he liked her better (12:619). After she has asked Gawan whether it diminishes the value of her love that she offered it to Parzival and he replies that it does not, their eyes become riveted on one another.

The narrator suggests that if Orgeluse had slept with Gawan that night at the magical castle it would have done him well. At least he slept better than the earlier night he spent there, when thoughts of her caused him so much pain, though this time too he dreamed of her and of love's combats (13:628). The following day, Gawan plays messenger of love between Gramoflans and his sister Itonje, and he also makes it possible for the hundreds of young men and women who had been under Klingsor's spell to see one another for the first time. The sexes were magically separated until his breaking of the spell, and now they eat, converse, and dance together (13:631–39).

Without yet knowing that Gawan is her grandson, Arnive suggests that in view of his wounds he should get to bed, and that Orgeluse might tuck him in and stay with him, adding that she will surely know how to take care of his needs (13:640). In the bedroom, Arnive assures Orgeluse that the knight's wounds have been bound up well enough that he would be ready for any combat, whereby the old woman clearly has intercourse on her mind (13:642). The narrator, for his part, after saying it is not proper to relate what goes on between the sexes in bed, tells us that that night Gawan found the right herb to cure all his suffering, a herb that was something brown between white things, meaning of course Orgeluse's genitalia (13:643–44).

When Gawan asks Arnive about the spell cast on the magical castle, she relates to him that Klingsor became a sorcerer after he was ordered emasculated by a king in Sicily who found him making love to the latter's wife. As Arnive puts it, they fixed him so that he could never give joy to a woman. Deprived of pleasure in love, Klingsor learned magical arts in order to rob people of joy (13:656–58). Gawan's role is just the opposite: he brings the joys of love to women and, by breaking Klingsor's spell, to the hundreds of young men and women imprisoned at the enchanted castle.

In the parts of Wolfram's poem where the focus is on its central figure Parzival, erotic love is likewise the dominant theme from start to finish. Herzeloyde's passion for Gahmuret, her loyalty in love, and her grief over his death are such that she withdraws into the forest with his son (3:116–17). Her love of Gahmuret makes her dread losing the son she has from him and motivates her effort to keep him ignorant of knighthood. But when that effort proves to be in vain, her fond memories of love with Gahmuret surely help inspire her advice to Parzival about women. She tells him that if he can win a woman's favor and her ring, he should do so, because it will free him from pain and suffering; he should kiss the woman and hold her tight, and if the woman is chaste and good it will bring him joy and happiness (3:127, 26–30; 128, 1–2).

When Parzival finds the beautiful duchess Jeschute slumbering on a bed in a tent in the forest, her lips are parted because she is dreaming desirously of love, making her that much more attractive to the narrator if not to the young innocent Parzival. He is attracted instead by the ring on Jeschute's finger, since his mother had spoken of winning a woman's ring. Remembering that he is supposed to kiss the woman and hold her tight, Parzival jumps on top of her, awakening her (3:130–31). Her husband Orilus's ensuing jealous rage is motivated not least because of her beauty, enhanced by her higher station as a king's daughter; Orilus declares that he will never warm himself in her white arms, will not eat or sleep with her, and will see that her red lips turn pale (3:136). In a subsequent aside, the narrator comments that if Parzival had inherited his father Gahmuret's ways with women he would have attacked the hill, meaning Jeschute's mons veneris, when he found her alone (3:139, 15–22).

After leaving Jeschute, Parzival comes upon Sigune with her dead beloved Schionatulander in her lap. From her he learns that his mother is Sigune's aunt, that his name is Parzival and means "right in two" because the death of his father broke his mother's heart. Sigune's grief is all the greater because Schionatulander's death was a result of her failing to surrender herself to him, a grief that expresses itself in her declaring that she loves him still as a corpse (3:140–41).

At Arthur's court Cunneware's smile upon seeing Parzival may be attributed to the peasant clothes in which his mother dressed him, but also to his handsomeness that shines through, because the narrator tells us that it has been foretold that she would not laugh until she saw the man whose fame was the greatest or was to become greatest (3:151). Then at Gournemans's castle young ladies, described as both chaste and bold, arrive perhaps on their own initiative to give the handsome young knight a bath. When Parzival fails to put the bath towel that they offer him around himself as he emerges from the bath they withdraw, not daring to stay but also, as the narrator suggests, perhaps stealing a glance to see if he had anything missing down below, women being very concerned about that matter (3:167). Gournemans offers Parzival his daughter Liase as wife, to gain him as replacement for the three sons he has lost, but despite her beauty the young knight declines, because his mind is on chivalric adventure. He says though that should he win honor as a knight then Gournemans should give Liase to him in marriage (3:177–79). Still, after leaving Gournemans, pangs of love inspired by thoughts of Liase, who treated him as a friend but did not grant him her love, pursue Parzival. He is a true son of his amorous father Gahmuret (4:179–80).

Parzival's aimless wandering brings him by chance to the castle of Condwiramurs, who is described as being of incomparable beauty, in whom he finds Liase again or indeed more than compensation for having left her behind (4:188; as Condwiramurs tells Parzival, Liase's father Gournemans is her mother's brother; 4:189–90). Sleepless because of the plight of her people, Condwiramurs goes that night to Parzival's bedside, seeking love, the narrator tells us, but not the sort that leads to a maiden having afterwards to be called a woman, but instead seeking friendly advice and aid (4:192). Precisely by claiming that nothing untoward passed between Condwiramurs and Parzival, the narrator calls attention to the erotic potential of her nocturnal visit to him; such is the comment that the bodily members that gladly reconcile themselves to each other are not allowed to find their way to one another, because both she and he are thinking of entirely other things (4:193, 2–14). Parzival offers to let her lie in his bed while he finds another place, but she says that if he is sufficiently in control of himself that he will not want to wrestle with her, she will lie down beside him; in doing so then, she cuddles up to him (4:194). She calls attention to her body in telling Parzival that she would rather commit suicide than be deflowered by her spurned suitor Calmidé who is laying siege to her castle; under the circumstances she thereby indicates to Parzival, albeit perhaps unconsciously, that she would be willing to be deflowered by him, with whom she is presently lying in bed (4:195).

After Parzival has defeated Condwiramurs' besieger, she embraces him, presses him firmly to herself (as his mother told him he should do with a woman who offered him her love), and swears that no man in the world will get her as his wife other than the one she is embracing (4:199). The first two nights they do not have intercourse, although she considers herself already no longer a virgin; only on the third night does he, a virgin himself, begin to feel desire for intercourse, a desire helped along by his memory that his mother told him to embrace a woman tightly who granted him her love and that Gournemans had told him that man and woman are completely as one. The narrator reports that they wove arms and legs together and he found the sweet, nearby place, so that the old custom that is ever new proved itself with the two of them and they both felt happy (4:202–03). After they have been married a while, Parzival begs leave to find out how his mother is doing, to spend a little time with her, and then to seek adventure; because Condwiramurs loves him so, she does not deny him his wish (4:223).

In the evening of Parzival's stay at the Grail castle, four radiantly beautiful women appear in the door to his bedroom just as the young men have finished undressing him. He dives under the covers on the bed, causing the women to beg teasingly that he might remain awake a while for them. They are bringing him wine and fruit, and are much taken with his handsomeness and youth. When the fourth of the young women, who is bearing fruits of paradise, kneels beside his bed, he bids her to sit down beside him on the bed. She teasingly protests that he should not turn her head with an invitation like that, otherwise he will not get served in the way that the lord of the castle has directed (5:243–44).

After leaving the castle and encountering Sigune, who is sitting in a linden tree with the embalmed corpse of her beloved Schionatulander in her lap, and from whom he learns about the questions he was supposed at ask at the castle, Parzival comes upon Jeschute, whom her jealous husband Orilus is punishing for her presumed infidelity. Her loveliness — rendered the more appealing by the poor state of her clothing, her tears that moisten her breasts, and her use of her hands and arms to try to cover her nakedness in the presence of Parzival, whom she has recognized instantly because he is after all the most handsome of men — awakens his compassion and motivates him to restore her honor in her husband's eyes (5:257–58). After the reconciliation effected by Parzival, Orilus and Jeschute bathe and rush from the tub to the bed, where she gets rid of her sorrow as her body well deserves, and in a tight embrace and well-practiced in the art of love they attain its greatest pleasure (5:273).

Parzival then fights two duels in succession — with Segramors and Keye — in a trance, imagining that he sees Condwiramurs in the three drops of blood in the snow. It takes a man of great experience in love, namely Parzival's cousin Gawan, to recognize the trance for what it is. He asks himself whether this man, whose identity he does not yet know, has come under love's spell, as he himself has, with the result that all his thinking has been conquered by love (6:301, 22–25).

Cundrie, when she arrives to denounce Parzival in the presence of Arthur's court, is not blind to the young knight's radiant handsomeness, to the point where we may suspect that the denunciation is motivated not only by compassion for Anfortas, but by her regret that her ugliness renders any chance of awakening passion for her in Parzival impossible. She hurls shame on his beauty and his masculinity, and says that while she is ugly in his eyes, she is not as ugly as he (6:315, 20–25). Then she goes on to say to him that there was never baseness as great in a man so hand-some (6:316, 18–19).

When Parzival takes leave of Arthur and his court in order to restore his honor, which Cundrie's denunciation has besmirched, he does not talk first of Anfortas's suffering but instead of what he left behind at the Grail castle and what robbed him of true happiness. He first exclaims how many beautiful women were there and only then speaks of the Grail, as the great-est of miracles, and of Anfortas waiting so helplessly, and about how little help to Anfortas his visit to the castle was (6:330, 23–30).

The erotic attraction between Cunneware and Parzival that had shown itself on his arrival as a naive youth the first time at Arthur's court manifests itself again as he prepares to leave to restore his honor and to seek the Grail. In what seems a sort of love quadrangle, Parzival has acceded to the wish of Clamidé, erstwhile spurned suitor of Parzival's wife Condwiramurs, that Parzival intercede with Cunneware on his behalf. Though she has agreed to become Clamidé's wife, she tells Parzival that she wants to serve him in any way she can, namely as his guardian spirit in combat. Calling him her friend, she tells him that if he is faced with a battle, may a woman — meaning herself — fight it for him and guide his hand; a woman, of whom he knows that she possesses a woman's purity and goodness; let her love be his protection (6:331, 25–332, 24). After she has helped him into his armor, he kisses the beautiful, virginal Cunneware, in a farewell full of pain between the two who loved one another so (6:333, 10–14).

On Parzival's third meeting with Sigune, he asks her in jest why she is wearing a ring, for he has heard that pious recluses should not partake of love relationships, to which she replies that she accords Schionatulander her love because he fought as her knight until he died in her service. She is wearing the ring as a token of engagement to him, to whom she was pre-vented by death from offering the love customary between men and women and which her virginal heart told her she should give to him (9:439, 9–440, 8).

In Wolfram's telling, unlike Chrétien's, the noble couple Parzival encounters on their way back from visiting the hermit Trevrizent have two beautiful daughters to whom the handsome young knight feels attracted; that the feeling is mutual is shown by the girls' efforts to have Parzival stay the night in their parents' tents nearby. Parzival is attracted particularly to the girls' full red lips, which befitting the holiness of the day, as the narrator tells us, are not parted in a sensual way, though the narrator asks himself whether if he tried to fetch a kiss from them as penance they would agree to accept that penitence, adding ambiguously that women will after all always be women (9:448, 27–450, 4).

When Bene, the radiantly beautiful daughter of the ferryman, arrives with King Gramoflans, the beloved of Gawan's youngest sister Itonje, to whom Bene is confidante in love, she finds Gawan beaten up after his combat with Parzival. Bene tightly embraces Gawan, whom she has chosen in place of the whole world as the crown of her happiness, and declares to him that the hand of whoever has done this to his beautiful body should be cursed (14:691, 27–692, 23; it is only at this point that Bene learns from Gramoflans that her beloved Gawan is Itonje's brother). Parzival is welcomed not only by Arthur's court, but by all the others who have gathered at Joflanze for the expected duel between Gawan and Gramoflans, who agree that Parzival deserves the highest fame, not least because of his incomparable handsomeness, such that all women would want him for their lover (14:700, 9–14).

Arthur's effort to intercede between Orgeluse and Gramoflans is helped by her having found a replacement for Cidegast in Gawan; his frequent embraces have enlivened her and diminished her anger at Gramoflans for having slain her husband (14:723, 1–10). The two uncles, Arthur and the King of Pont Tortois Brandelidelin, join forces to see that their niece, Itonje, demands of her beloved, Bandelidelin's nephew Gramoflans, that he not do battle with her brother Gawan. Arthur can be certain that this demand will succeed, now that through his efforts Itonje and Gramoflans have finally met and looked into one another's eyes (14:725, 1–16; 726, 23–727, 16). Confronted by the happiness in love of Itonje and Gramoflans, and of Gawan's mother and other sisters, who had been imprisoned by Klingsor's spell in the magical castle, Parzival longs for the embrace of Condwiramurs. His quest of the Grail has deprived him of her, and he declares that God does not want him to be happy (14:732–33).

After Parzival's joust with his Moorish half-brother Feirefiz he invites him to come with him to the encampment of Arthur's court, an invitation the half-brother accepts enthusiastically on hearing about the many beautiful women he will see there; as the narrator tells us, women were his life's fulfillment (15:753, 25–754, 7). Cundrie arrives to tell Parzival that an inscription on the Grail has appointed him Grail King, that Condwiramurs and his little son Lohengrin are to join him at the Grail castle, that the position of the planets likewise prophesy his good fortune, and that he has won peace for his soul and good fortune in life through his brave deeds and his endurance of care and woe (15:781–82). Cundrie also asks to be brought to Arnive and the others who were held captive by Klingsor, for in her capacity as Grail messenger when she came to Arthur's court five years before, it was not only to denounce and shame Parzival but to declare the need for liberation of those held captive at the magical castle (see 15:784).

When Parzival asks Anfortas, "What ails you, Uncle?," the latter is not only released from his suffering, he is restored to his former physical beauty, which indeed surpasses even that of Parzival and his father Gahmuret (16:795, 11–796, 16). On his way to be reunited with Condwiramurs at the spot where he saw the three drops of blood in the snow, occasioning his trance-like visions of her, Parzival stops by to see his uncle Trevrizent, to tell him that his brother Anfortas has been healed. The pious hermit tells Parzival in turn that although out of pity for the nephew's despair he lied to him about God's nature, by suggesting that the Grail could be won in combat, yet Parzival, through his unknowing defiance in attempting just that, has won from God the greatest of miracles, accession to the Grail kingship. Trevrizent adds that now as Grail King it is time for Parzival to devote himself instead to humility (16:798).

When Parzival then arrives at Condwiramurs' tent, she is asleep with only her shift on; she throws the blanket around herself and jumps out of bed to greet him (16:800, 28–801, 5). They are discreetly left alone in the tent, so that Condwiramurs can give him a replacement, the narrator says, with red and white (her red lips and white skin) for the sufferings of love he experienced there earlier in seeing the three drops of blood. In the course of the five years of their separation he had never engaged in love-making despite many offers, the narrator tells us, adding that he thinks that night Parzival devoted himself to love's pleasures until well into the morning (16:802, 1–10). On their way back to the Grail castle, Parzival, likely moved by his experience of true love with Condwiramurs, asks that they seek out the place where Sigune had withdrawn as a pious recluse with Schionatulander's embalmed corpse. There they discover her dead, kneeling at the side of his corpse. They place her corpse next to his, and close the grave (16:804, 21–805, 2).

When Anfortas and Parzival suggest to Feirefiz that he let himself be baptized so that he may see the Grail, which Titurel says is invisible to heathens, Feirefiz asks whether baptism will help him in love. Indeed, we may wonder whether the heathen half-brother's failure to see the Grail is because it is carried by Anfortas's overwhelmingly beautiful sister Repanse de Joie (he only has eyes for her). She is Parzival's and Feirefiz's aunt, of whom he has become passionately enamoured, making him forget his love for his wife Secundille back in the Orient. Repanse de Joie's physical beauty has been restored by Anfortas's miraculous recovery (16:811–814, 10). When Feirefiz invites Anfortas to return to the Orient with him, the latter declines, saying that he will now devote himself to humility as a knight serving the Grail and will no longer fight on behalf of women, though enmity toward women will never arise in him, for men derive great pleasure from them, though he himself enjoyed little of it (16:819, 16–820, 4).

The theme of erotic love in Wolfram's *Parzival* is underscored by the provision of the introductory account of the adventures of Parzival's father Gahmuret. When the Moorish queen Belacane lays eyes on Gahmuret she is seized by the pain of love. Her heart that had remained virginally under lock and key opened itself immediately whether she wanted or not, so lovely did he seem to her (1:23, 22–28). She is besieged by Isenhart's people because her virginity caused her to spur him on to greater deeds as her champion, as she relates to Gahmuret with regret (1:27, 1–12). On learning that Gahmuret has defeated the forces besieging her, Belacane goes to meet him, brings him to her apartments, helps him out of his armor, and takes him to bed, where she engages with him in sweet, exalted love (1:44, 25–30). In Gahmuret's note of farewell to her, when the longing for adventure has moved him to steal away, he tells her that if she had herself baptized she might still win him back. Belacane proves more than willing to do this right away, but he has already sailed away by the time she finds the note (1:56, 25–30). The narrator tells us that her joy in love thus found "a dry twig" as does the turtle dove out of true love when the beloved is gone (1:57, 10–14; note that the turtle dove later is the emblem of the company of the Grail).

When Gahmuret rides in and sees the Queen of Wales, Herzeloyde, at her window, the bare, booted leg that he has stretched out in front of him on his horse's neck all at once jerks, his torso bolts upright, and he is rendered like a falcon spotting prey (2:64, 1–10). As he is pausing to rest from the jousting tourney, a letter is given to him from Amphlise, queen of France — whom like Belacane he has loved and left — offering him her love and saying that she is more beautiful, more powerful, and better at love-making than the Queen of Wales (2:77, 13–18). Herzeloyde declares that Gahmuret is the winner of the day's jousting and goes to his tent to greet him, falling quite in love with him at this first meeting and experiencing virginal concern when he seats himself so close to her that she could take hold of him, pull him to her, and embrace him tightly (2:84, 2–7).

Because Gahmuret was the victor, even if only in the preliminary jousts that resulted in the tourney itself having to be called off because of his defeat of the others, Herzeloyde lays claim to his love, which makes him the man between three women: Amphlise, his first love, who rendered him a knight; his Moorish wife Belacane, and Herzeloyde (2:94, 1–95, 26). Once the judgment has been given that he belongs by virtue of the tourney to Herzeloyde, she leads him off to her bed, to the ending point of all grief the narrator says, where Gahmuret's sorrow was defeated and he was made alive again, as is supposed to happen with love. Herzeloyde loses her virginity, as the two don't spare their lips in kissing (2:100, 8–17). From that point he wore a shift of hers that she had worn next to her body over his chain mail so that when he returned from combat she could put it on again (2:101, 9–20).

In her grief after hearing of Gahmuret's death in the service of the Caliph of Babylon, Herzeloyde rejoices that in her womb she has the fruit of their love and in her breasts the milk to nourish it. Not caring if anyone is looking on, she tears her shift from her chest, repeatedly grabbing her breasts and pressing them to her mouth — a very womanly thing to do, the narrator comments. Squeezing milk from her breasts she exclaims that it is the product of true love and that were she not yet baptized the milk would be her baptismal water with which she would sprinkle herself, alone and in front of the others, and with which together with her tears she will express her grief over the loss of her beloved husband (2:110, 23–111, 14). When Parzival is born fourteen days later, Herzeloyde and the other ladies inspect his genitals, and his mother can't resist kissing him over and over and calling him her good son, dear son, beautiful son. She takes out her breasts and pushes the nipples into his mouth, as it seems to her that she is cradling Gahmuret again in her arms and she thinks about the Queen of Heaven having nursed Jesus at her breasts (2:113, 1–26).

In providing an ending to the Parzival and Gawan plots that was lacking in Chrétien's unfinished poem, Wolfram introduced a third hero, Parzival's moorish half-brother Feirefiz, a heathen with a burning passion for women. When Feirefiz converts from paganism to Christianity, it is so that he can wed the Grail Queen, Anfortas's sister Repanse de Joie, not in the least out of piety. Thus it is passion more than piety that triumphs in the end. Wolfram's addition of the story of Feirefiz's and Parzival's father Gahmuret to introduce the Parzival and Gawain adventures serves not only to explain Feirefiz's existence, but to show that the two half-brothers are sons of a great lover of women.

Wagner's *Parsifal*

While Wolfram expanded the number of characters he found in Chrétien's poem, and at the same time shifted the focus toward erotic passion, Wagner reduced the number in his operatic version of the material, not only in accord with generic differences between epic and drama, but also in keeping with his shift of focus to a pious dedication to chastity and asceticism.[6] Gawain's role, centered on chivalric romance, has of course been completely eliminated, as have those of Wolfram's Gahmuret and Feirefiz, with their similar focus on erotic passion as the prime mover. The women's roles,

---

[6] For a fuller discussion of the opera from the interpretive view offered here, see the chapter on *Parsifal* in James M. McGlathery, *Wagner's Operas and Desire*, North American Studies in German Literature 22 (New York: Peter Lang, 1998), 235–67.

too, have been eliminated except in so far as they have been combined in the figure of Kundry. In Wagner's version, Kundry is messenger of the Grail castle only in so far as she harbors an ambivalent desire to serve the Grail knights, while her irresistible temptation is instead to seduce them or at least cause them to surrender to seduction. Do Wagner's changes then add up to a glorification of celibate chastity as opposed to Wolfram's celebration of erotic passion?

Part of the answer to the question may be found in Wagner's handling of the role of the sorcerer Klingsor, who played no part whatever in Chrétien's poem and does not put in an actual appearance in Wolfram's version, whereas Wagner introduces him to us in person (2:31–35). As we remember, Wolfram's Klingsor was emasculated after being caught in adultery with the wife of a king; and out of rage that, as the narrator says, he has been fixed so that he can no longer give pleasure to a woman, he acts to deprive others of sexual pleasure by confining a large number of knights and ladies in a castle where he magically prevents any intimacy between the sexes. Quite the opposite with Wagner's Klingsor, as we learn from Gurnemanz's report to the Grail youths (1:17–18). He has emasculated himself in a vain effort to gain admission to the company of the Grail knights; and instead of employing his magic to separate the sexes, he uses beautiful young women to tempt the Grail knights to violate their dedication to celibacy. While Wolfram's Klingsor is embittered because he can no longer experience sexual arousal, Wagner's Klingsor is enraged because he was unable to control his sexual urges and, to do so, had to emasculate himself. However, Klingsor's sacrifice of his sexual organs fails to gain him admittance to the company of the Grail because as a result of the emasculation he is no longer able to experience arousal and therefore his celibacy is meaningless, since it does not represent a victory over temptation.

The changes Wagner makes in the nature of the Grail King's wound are equally basic. Wolfram's Anfortas was injured in a joust fought in the service of the proud beauty Orgeluse and the wound was from the poisoned point of a lance to his genitals, not only causing him excruciating pain, but also rendering him unable to engage in intercourse or, in all likelihood, to experience a desire to do so. Wagner's Amfortas was wounded in the side, not the genital area, and not in combat so much as while surrendering to the seductive appeal of Kundry, Klingsor's chief seductress, as we learn from Gurnemanz's account (1:16). While Amfortas's pain is such that he likely could hardly engage in intercourse, he does appear to be able to experience desire, even arousal; his suffering is as much spiritual as physical, unlike Wolfram's Anfortas, with whom it is more the latter than the former. Wagner's Grail King suffers most when he is called upon to celebrate Holy Communion, because to do so reminds him of his trespass against his commitment to celibacy and, indeed, so vividly that he feels the same rush of blood to his loins that he experienced when succumbing to seduction with Kundry. It is the reawakening of that sexual desire that causes the wound in his side to reopen (1:26).

As we have seen, in the cases of Klingsor and Amfortas Wagner has not abandoned the focus on erotic passion associated with these figures in Wolfram's telling. In the opera, however, erotic passion is celebrated in the negative; our attention is centered on the struggle against it. That this is so is obviously the case in Wagner's depiction of the title role and central figure. Unlike Perceval and Parzival in the medieval poems, Parsifal is not depicted so much as the great warrior, and certainly not as jousting to win the favor of a woman. His struggle is indeed against desire, his great triumph that over women's seductive wiles. His turn to piety comes as a result of his reaction to his first experience of being kissed by a woman in a sexual way. His great spiritual revelation and awakening is a clairvoyant perception of what has caused Amfortas's painful suffering: surrender to the allure of the beautiful woman who is kissing him himself at that very moment.

Whereas in the medieval versions Perceval/Parzival is given some minimal advice by his mother about how to relate to women, Wagner's Parsifal does not seem to have been told anything about the matter. When he encounters Klingsor's Flowermaidens, apparently the first women other than his mother (and Kundry in her servile disguise) he has ever met, he thinks they must be flowers, not women. When Kundry then begins her attempt to seduce him, she quickly recognizes that she will have to approach him in a maternal fashion, the role of son to mother being the only way of relating to women that is familiar to him. Indeed, she has to go to the extreme of portraying herself as his deceased mother's agent or virtual reincarnation, as the woman his mother destined for him (2:37–38).

By using this approach, Kundry arouses his grief over his mother's loss and his guilt over having caused her death by leaving her to seek adventure: she hopes that this will lead him to seek solace in her embrace. Tender thoughts about his mother are not likely the stuff to arouse him sexually, one would think; yet Kundry must believe there is no choice with the son of a widowed mother who so wished to keep him for herself as Herzeleide did. Thus, in a desperate attempt to turn his thoughts to sex, Kundry asks him whether his mother did not embrace him almost too passionately at times, for example when he had been missing and then turned up unharmed (2:42). When that doesn't work, she resorts to the yet more desperate attempt to arouse him by inviting him to imagine how hot the passion must have been when his father Gamuret and mother Herzeleide were engaging in intercourse, as at the time of his conception (2:43).

It is at this point in her attempt to seduce Parsifal that, impersonating his mother, Kundry plants her long passionate kiss on his lips. That he does not reject the kiss immediately suggests that he is indeed in a reverie about his deceased mother; when he then leaps up and cries out "Amfortas!" it soon becomes clear that Kundry has indeed succeeded in awakening sexual desire in him, desire that he experiences as sinful and associates — correctly — with Amfortas's bleeding wound that will not heal. Indeed, Amfortas's susceptibility to Kundry's seductive wiles, like Parsifal's, may have been owing not least to his inexperience with women, as Grail King, and to his apparent separation from his mother, which must have occurred at some point between his birth and arrival at manhood. In the figure of Parsifal, as in that of Klingsor, the power of erotic passion is not denied, but rather celebrated, if only again rather in the negative.

Since Kundry represents the most radical departure from her counterpart in the medieval poems, it is well to conclude discussion of erotic love in *Parsifal* with a return to consideration of Wagner's changes in her depiction. In Chrétien's *Perceval* and Wolfram's *Parzival,* Cundrie is not Klingsor's agent, but quite the contrary: the Grail company's messenger. This role is in effect what Wagner's seductress yearns for, with part of her being; Kundry's master Klingsor, after all, emasculated himself in a vain attempt to gain admission to the company of the Grail knights. As seductress, Kundry's medieval counterpart was not Cundrie but Orgeluse, the proud beauty who sought proof of the power of her riper, no longer virginal charms in men's eagerness to suffer humiliation and mortal danger out of passionate desire to possess her. It was Orgeluse of whom Wolfram's Anfortas became enamoured, thereby violating his calling as Grail King and suffering the poisoned wound that would not heal, and Orgeluse whose advances Wolfram's Parzival rejected before Gawan then wins her. To be sure, Orgeluse expresses regret in the end over her activities as femme fatale, but she does not do so out of piety; she is not torn between a passion to seduce and a yearning for purity as is Wagner's Kundry. Similarly, while the Grail messenger Cundrie displays wounded vanity in the fashionable way she dresses to hide her ugliness, she is not depicted as struggling between pride and humility.

Kundry's pride concerns the irresistibility of her charms. Until she meets up with Parsifal she has never met a man she could not seduce, at least as she tells it. Or rather, the only man who did not succumb to her charms was Jesus himself, who met her laughter with a gaze that bespoke compassion not desire, *caritas* not *eros.* Ever since, she tells Parsifal, she has been seeking vainly for a man who would respond to her that way, impervious to her seductive beauty and wiles (2:45–46). Klingsor has gained dominion over her because she cannot awaken desire in him; but he is no longer a man and thus cannot satisfy her yearning for a man whose purity is proof against her seductive wiles. The woman in her seeks to meet her master, much as Wolfram's Orgeluse surrenders to Gawan's mastering of every task she sets and each humiliation she prepares for him. Both Orgeluse and Kundry find the role of femme fatale attractive, but in the end they yearn to be defeated. In Orgeluse's case defeat actually is a victory, for her beauty has won for her a husband she can adore. Yet Kundry's defeat is a triumph, too, in so far as she becomes something like Parsifal's spiritual bride. His great triumph was not only to reject her seductive advances, but to rescue her from the compulsion to seduce. She can be Mary Magdalene to his Jesus.

It is clear, though, that Kundry expires in the end, at the moment when Parsifal performs the miraculous healing of Amfortas and fulfills his destiny to become Grail King (3:61). There is thus the possibility that she dies of a broken heart. Her aim had been to seduce Parsifal and thereby to destroy him, but his resistance to her seductive wiles made her want instead to possess him, as lover or wife. In any event, she is proven right when, her advances having been rejected, she declares to Parsifal, in effect, that his pathway will always lead him to her even as he is intent on finding Amfortas (cf. 2:48). For he encounters her at the very moment he comes upon the Grail company again. Her subsequent death suggests that her heart's desire is not to serve the Grail knights, even with Parsifal as Grail King, but rather to surrender herself to him as his beloved. Wagner's work may seem to be about caritas, but like the medieval epics it is a celebration of the power of eros, the force that enables Parsifal to experience sexual arousal with Kundry as Amfortas did and that brings Kundry to surrender her prideful sensuousness and yearn in vain to be Parsifal's love.

3: *Parsifal* and Religion: A Christian Music Drama?

Ulrike Kienzle

WAGNER'S *PARSIFAL* POSES A RIDDLE that is hard to solve. The sacred character of the work is beyond question; this is obvious as well from the music of this "Bühnenweihfestspiel" (stage consecration festival play). But what form of the sacred are we dealing with here? Wagner's turn to Christian mythology, upon which the imagery and the spiritual contents of *Parsifal* rest, is idiosyncratic and contradicts Christian dogma in many important ways. In the case of a religion of revelation that is almost two thousand years old, and that in the course of its history has assumed huge societal significance in the Western world and quite early canonized rigid articles of belief, are we allowed even to talk of "myth"? But how else can the action of *Parsifal* be understood, if not in the category of myth? Furthermore, as Wagner understood it, "myth" is a distinctive way of thinking that has its own logic and truth. It distinguishes itself from the rationality of philosophy through its use of images and the archetypical nature of its forms and characters; it differs from dogmatic religion by the freedom with which it undertakes to re-form and re-create traditional elements to revitalize them. The philosopher Hans Blumenberg coined the phrase "Arbeit am Mythos" (work on myth) to describe this process.[1]

The story of the Holy Grail is just such a mythology. The most significant literary versions of this myth were written in quick succession between the end of the twelfth and the thirteenth centuries: the verse epics of Chrétien de Troyes, Robert de Boron, Wolfram von Eschenbach, and Albrecht von Scharfenberg.[2] They combine elements taken from the Celtic legend of King Arthur with those derived from currents of Christian

---

[1] Hans Blumenberg, *Arbeit am Mythos* (Frankfurt am Main: Suhrkamp, 1979). See also the well-known introductory passage of Wagner's "Religion und Kunst" (1880), in *Sämtliche Schriften und Dichtungen* (Leipzig: Breitkopf und Härtel, 1907), 10:211. Hereafter this edition will be cited with the abbreviation "*SSD*."

[2] For a collection of the source materials that were important to Wagner, see Ulrich Müller, "Wer ist der Gral?" in Ulrich Müller and Oswald Panagl, *Ring und*

mysticism. In Chrétien's version, the Grail is a mysterious vessel that holds the Eucharistic host and gives life. In Robert de Boron's work, it is the chalice from which Christ and His apostles drank at the Last Supper. Wolfram von Eschenbach interprets the Grail as a marvelous stone with the mysterious name "lapsit exillis."[3] It was brought down to the earth by the fallen angels, and only individuals who have been baptized can gaze upon it. The Grail offers eternal life and mystical enlightenment. Only those who have been called to the Grail can experience its wonders, but even Parzival, whom it has summoned, fails to prove himself worthy of it at his first visit and is thrown out of the Grail castle.

These various versions of the Grail legend share a Christian origin insofar as they combine the symbolism of the Grail legend with liturgical elements of the Christian Eucharist. Furthermore, in Chrétien's poem, the turning point of Parzival's growth is associated with his experience of Good Friday. At the same time, however, these works also point far beyond the Christian tradition by also using cryptic symbolism of ancient sects, Orphic mysteries, or Oriental teachings — for example, the mysteries of the phoenix, symbolizing rebirth; hermetic or alchemical elements; and teachings of secret societies in Arabia that came to Europe via Spain. The path to the Grail is always a way of initiation. The Grail works of the High Middle Ages arose at a time of religious unrest, in the midst of many forces that were seeming to bring about a spiritual rebirth. Thus they represent a synthesis of various religious currents that stood apart from the organized church, which the Grail legend deliberately ignored.

This is precisely what intrigued Wagner about the Grail legend. He wrote his final music drama at a time when traditional religion had become hard to believe in, even for him. Wagner's relationship to Christianity was characterized by both critical distance and fascination. He was convinced that it was necessary to have some kind of religious orientation, but he rejected rigid dogmaticism. Beneath the canons and traditions of organized religion, however, he discovered a hidden layer of discarded secret philosophical and spiritual wisdom, which he wished to revitalize and make resound in his music. Therefore, *Parsifal* musically cites basic sacramental experiences: the celebration of the Eucharist, the washing of the feet, the sorrow of Good Friday, confession, and funeral rites. But Wagner releases

---

Gral: Texte, Kommentare und Interpretationen zu Richard Wagners "Der Ring des Nibelungen," "Tristan und Isolde," "Die Meistersinger von Nürnberg" und "Parsifal" (Würzburg: Königshausen & Neumann, 2002), 199–237.

[3] It is usually assumed that lapsit is a form of lapis, Latin for "stone." Possible suggestions for the meaning of the full phrase include "stone of exile" or "stone of death."

these traditional situations from the context of the church, and they become for him isolated elements upon which he could build a new interpretation or devise a different experience of spirituality. This is what has always disturbed devout Christians about *Parsifal;* individuals who lack strong religious beliefs, on the other hand, are annoyed by the allegedly superfluous "liturgischer Schutt" (liturgical garbage).[4]

To understand the ways in which *Parsifal* is and is not a Christian drama, we need to look beyond the images and symbols to seek out the core of Wagner's religiosity. That is not a simple task, and it requires both a philosophical and a musical analysis of the work. How did Wagner's relationship to Christianity change through the course of his life? Which philosophical currents influenced his thought? How did he revise his conception of *Parsifal* as a result of these influences? And how is this expressed in the music? As we undertake to answer these questions, we find we can solve the riddle of the overly familiar and at the same time so arcane religiosity of Wagner's final music drama.

Wagner's Relationship to Christianity

Although Wagner always considered himself a freethinker, his criticism was directed more at the institution of the church than at Christianity itself. Throughout his life he was fascinated by the person of Jesus of Nazareth and the sacrament of the Eucharist. If we can believe the autobiographical account that he gives in *Mein Leben,* Wagner experienced a kind of "ekstatischer Begeisterung" (ecstatic enthusiasm) at the sight of the cross, but then at his confirmation ceremony he took part in the Eucharist with total skepticism and found himself surprised by the "Schauer der Empfindung bei Darreichung und Empfang des Brotes und des Weines" (shudder that he felt upon receiving the bread and wine).[5] His monumental choral work *Das Liebesmahl der Apostel,* which was first performed in 1843 in the Frauenkirche in Dresden, does not call into question the belief of the apostles at the Pentecostal miracle and portrays the pouring forth of the Holy Spirit through a glorious orchestral passage that follows a long period of unaccompanied singing.[6]

---

[4] Paul-André Gaillard, "Der liturgische 'Schutt' im *Parsifal,*" in *Programmhefte der Bayreuther Festspiele 1965: "Parsifal,"* 38–46 (the program also contains the English translation of the article).

[5] Richard Wagner, *Mein Leben,* ed. Martin Gregor-Dellin (Munich: Paul List, 1976), 27; in English: *My Life,* trans. Andrew Gray (New York: Da Capo, 1992).

[6] See Winfried Kirsch, "Richard Wagners biblische Szene *Das Liebesmahl der Apostel,*" in *Geistliche Musik: Studien zu ihrer Geschichte und Funktion im 18.*

By contrast, the portrayal of religion and the church in his "Romantic operas" seems highly ambivalent. Here the turn toward religion, especially Catholicism, which most of the Romantics experienced, appears in a broken way. In *Tannhäuser*, the religiosity that Elisabeth puts into practice contrasts sharply with what is really represented by the church; Tannhäuser is denied absolution and salvation by the pope, that is, through the church, but he is redeemed through Elisabeth's mystical martyrdom, which finds an alternate outlet through prayer to the Blessed Virgin. The action of *Lohengrin* takes place at a time in which Christianity was highly unstable; in Brabant during the tenth century, the battle between "heathens" and Christians was raging strongly, and the figure of Ortrud embodies the pagan Germanic elements that were still very much alive despite the presence of Christianity. Lohengrin does not appear as an emissary of the church; rather he has been sent by the Grail, which, in opposition to the church, symbolizes a transcendent power that at the end of the opera is taken away from the onstage world. *Lohengrin* can be understood as a parable of the end of transcendence.[7]

Wagner had an answer to contemporary religious criticism, especially that of David Friedrich Strauss (1808–74), author of the famous *Das Leben Jesu* (1835–36), for whom the Christian tradition was nothing more than a mythology and thus was a collection of symbols, not of facts, and that of Ludwig Feuerbach (1804–72), for whom God was merely a projection of man.[8] In 1848, Wagner jotted down that Christianity was a necessary aberration of history. At the same time he was intensively studying the New Testament and wrote a sketch of huge five-act opera entitled *Jesus von Nazareth*. Here he undertakes a new interpretation of the Bible — Jesus preaches a worldly religion of commonality and communism, and he advocates freedom from law and thus liberation from the shackles of the state. In doing so, he teaches the overcoming of egotism, which is responsible for ills such as inequality, striving for possessions, hatred, and oppression.[9]

While sketching this utopia of social revolution, Wagner's synopsis at the same time opens up an unusual metaphysical perspective. Jesus does not

---

und 19. Jahrhundert, Hamburger Jahrbuch für Musikwissenschaft, vol. 8 (Laaber: Laaber, 1985), 157–84.

[7] See Ulrike Kienzle, "Der vertriebene Gott: Über Glaube und Zweifel in Wagners *Lohengrin*," in *Programmhefte der Bayreuther Festspiele 2001*, ed. Wolfgang Wagner, 82–108 (English translation also included).

[8] David Friedrich Strauss, *Das Leben Jesu* (Tübingen: C. F. Osiander, 1835–36); Ludwig Feuerbach, *Das Wesen des Christentums* (Leipzig: O. Wigand, 1841).

[9] Richard Wagner, *Jesus von Nazareth: Ein dichterischer Entwurf,* in *SSD* 11, 273–324.

proclaim a divine paradise; rather than promising mankind a life after death, he encourages insight into the transience of the individual and the voluntary surrender of one's own life, with death overcoming egotism. By consciously giving back everything that once was his, the individual attains a new kind of immortality that is no longer individual — he becomes part of the eternal stream of life. This principle is exemplified in the martyrdom of *Jesus of Nazareth*. He freely took death upon himself, to complete his teaching for his apostles and reveal the core of its meaning, thus granting them a new eternal life. This vision was obviously influenced by Ludwig Feuerbach's 1830 essay "Gedanken über Tod und Unsterblichkeit" (Thoughts on Death and Immortality), with which Wagner was acquainted in the 1830s (though he did not know the name of the author at the time).[10]

Wagner turned his attention away from *Jesus of Nazareth* to work on *Siegfrieds Tod*. Setting Christianity aside, he turned intensely towards Nordic mythology. The writings of Ludwig Feuerbach convinced Wagner of the necessity of having a worldly orientation. According to Wagner's invective against Christianity, which should be understood in the context of the Revolution of 1848–49 and his Zurich aesthetic writings, the church is an instrument of power and control. Religion is actually not needed anymore, Wagner thought, for it could be replaced by love of one's neighbor in the utopia of a free society. But in 1854, after the failure of the Revolution, Wagner, in exile in Switzerland, read Schopenhauer's *Die Welt als Wille und Vorstellung* (1819, rev. 1844).

Schopenhauer and India

Wagner described his becoming acquainted with Schopenhauer's pessimism as an experience of awakening.[11] The critique of knowledge put

---

[10] The first version of this essay appeared anonymously with the title "Todesgedanken." Evidently Wagner had become acquainted with Feuerbach's thinking through conversations with Samuel Lehrs in Paris. Wagner later read "Gedanken über Tod und Unsterblichkeit," as it appeared under Feuerbach's name in 1849; traces of this work can be found in *Tristan und Isolde*.

[11] For a more complete discussion, see my book *Das Weltüberwindungswerk: Wagners "Parsifal," ein szenisch-musikalisches Gleichnis der Philosophie Schopenhauers* (Laaber: Laaber, 1992). Discussions of Schopenhauer's impact on Wagner include Hartmut Reinhardt, "Wagner and Schopenhauer" in *Wagner Handbook,* ed. Ulrich Müller and Peter Wapnewski, trans. Erika and Martin Swales, translation ed. John Deathridge, 287–96 (Cambridge, MA: Harvard UP, 1992); and the chapter "Schopenhauer and Wagner" in Bryan Magee, *Schopenhauer* (Oxford: Clarendon,

forth by Immanuel Kant had aroused Wagner's interest when he encountered it, and it was on Kant's philosophy that Schopenhauer in turn built his thought. According to Kant, we cannot perceive things as they really are; the "thing in itself" (Ding an sich) is forever hidden from us. Instead we can experience phenomena only within the categories of our thinking — space, time, and causality. There is no alternative for us, except to view the world with our own eyes, hear it with our own ears, or feel it with our own hands. Thus the world is different for every individual, and therefore it becomes fragmented into a series of endless perspectives, with truth itself remaining hidden from us. "Die Welt ist meine Vorstellung" (The world is my representation) — this is the first sentence of Schopenhauer's most important work.[12]

Schopenhauer solves the problem of the philosophical separation of the "thing in itself" from its appearance by an act of radical introspection. We can experience our own selves in our dichotomy of corporality and self-consciousness. We can view the body just as we could any other object outside of ourselves. But our body causes self-consciousness, too, as it also has the force of will and desire. The will consists of that which is not given to our bodies as representation. This will to existence is, for Schopenhauer, the basic principle of the world. It is active in all things — stones, plants, animals, and mankind. They are the objectifications of this will, which is infinite and exists and works outside space, time, and causality. The will is identical in all natural phenomena. Therefore everything that exists is in a deeper sense a unity. With this concept Schopenhauer leaves the realm of discursive argumentation and abandons the discipline of philosophy in the strict sense, for he is actually talking of the path to a mystical experience. Schopenhauer's metaphysics of the will has features that would qualify it as a religion. According to its author it made religion redundant, at least for those well-versed in the field of philosophy.

A further characteristic of Schopenhauer's philosophy is its radical pessimism. This feature of his thought necessarily results from the theory that the one primal will, which transcends space and time, has been split into countless objectifications, which are subject to space and time. Schopenhauer describes space, time, and causality, the forms through which we experience our world, as the *principium individuationis*. If countless individuals want to live together at the same time and in the same place, a conflict arises. Strict animosity is the ruling force in this life, and one being will

---

1997), 350–402. Also see Magee's book *The Tristan Chord: Wagner and Philosophy* (New York: Henry Holt, 2002).

[12] Arthur Schopenhauer, *Die Welt als Wille und Vorstellung* (Zurich: Diogenes, 1977), 1:29. This edition of Schopenhauer's works is published in ten volumes.

inevitably eat the other one up — mankind eats animals and plants, animals eat each other, and all living beings are subject to the destructive forces of nature. Strife and extirpation happen all the time. The drive of each individual is an egotistical force. Each being wants to keep itself alive and destroys the life of the other so it can guarantee its own survival. Because all natural beings are in their innermost essence one and a unity, the will to life actually does battle with and destroys itself. For this basic reason, the world permanently consists of suffering, which perpetuates itself indefinitely, as the will continues to destroy itself in new objectifications.

A way to escape from this suffering, however, is offered by the negation of the will — that is, the ascetic life in poverty and chastity, which saints of all religions have led since ancient times. Schopenhauer considers religious ecstasy, of which the mystics speak, a new form of consciousness that is freed from serving the will. Then the individual will have the infinite freedom of not willing anymore. One acquires this new freedom through recognizing the identity of all life as a unity in being part of the general will, and through experiencing compassion with all that exists. For Schopenhauer, compassion is a spontaneous, physical feeling of empathy with the suffering of another being. The suffering of the other becomes as though it were my own, and one being merges with the other (as Schopenhauer writes, "auf irgend eine Weise mit ihm identificirt" [becoming somehow identical with it]), so that "jener gänzliche Unterschied zwischen mir und jedem Andern, auf welchem gerade mein Egoismus beruht, wenigstens in einem gewissen Grade aufgehoben" (that complete difference between me and every other, upon which my egotism is based, is at least somewhat eradicated).[13]

The phenomenon of compassion is nonsense as far as the will to exist is concerned, for compassion can actually squelch the will. When one considers it as an instrument of redemption from the suffering of the world, though, it assumes immense metaphysical significance. Compassion offers an end to violence and oppression, and through it suffering can be obliterated and transformed; it shows us a path to a utopia of peaceful coexistence of all living beings. Therefore Schopenhauer terms compassion "das große Mysterium der Ethik, ihr Urphänomen und de[n] Gränzstein, über welchen hinaus nur noch die metaphysische Spekulation einen Schritt wagen kann" (the great mystery of ethics, its primal phenomenon and the landmark beyond which only metaphysical speculation can dare to venture).[14]

---

[13] Arthur Schopenhauer, *Preisschrift über die Grundlage der Moral,* in the Zurich edition, 6:248.

[14] Schopenhauer, *Über die Grundlage der Moral,* 248.

This notion was decisive for Wagner. In letters to his musician friend, the revolutionary August Röckel (1814–76), as well as to Franz Liszt, and later Mathilde Wesendonk, Wagner never tires of referring to Schopenhauer. He abandons the thought of revolution and develops a new kind of political stance, devises a new aesthetic position, and thinks new thoughts about religion. *Tristan und Isolde, Die Meistersinger von Nürnberg,* and *Parsifal* all contain evidence of Schopenhauer's philosophy; his ethic of compassion is the cornerstone on which Wagner built the conception of *Parsifal.* In his later years Wagner developed from these inspirations his own ideas on modern society and regeneration. This is a general complex of ideas that foreshadows the increasing concern since the late twentieth century with ecology, endangered species, environmental protection, and pacifism, all of which deal with protecting others, whether other human beings or other species.[15]

Schopenhauer's metaphysics professes to account for the meaning of religions, which are reactions to the metaphysical need of mankind.[16] Schopenhauer values above all else the Indian religions Hinduism and Buddhism. Their foundation is the view that all existence consists fundamentally of suffering, and the resultant ethic is one of compassion. Schopenhauer also holds Christianity in high esteem, because it teaches the insubstantiality and frailty of existence in this world and considers compassionate love (Agapē) to be the highest worth. However, Schopenhauer makes a crucial shift of emphasis here: his philosophy is atheistic, and he could not conceive of how there could be one God who created the world. For Schopenhauer, the origin of the world is the will, an impersonal drive without goal. Of course, Buddhism is also an atheistic religion (the numerous gods of Buddhism are mortal beings). In the monotheistic religions, though, like Christianity, Judaism, and Islam, it is different. Schopenhauer rejects Judaism as an optimistic illusion (and here Wagner follows him unconditionally). When it comes to the other monotheistic religions, Schopenhauer broadens his conception of the divine. These religions proclaim, as far as he was concerned, not the strict truth, but rather they speak of transcendence in mythical images and symbols, in pious legends and stories. They therefore proclaim truth in the guise of a lie ("Wahrheit im Gewande der Lüge").[17]

---

[15] On this point, see the recent study *Wagner and the Romantic Hero* by Simon Williams (Cambridge: Cambridge UP, 2004), 133, which lists Wagner's identification of "causes of human decline that we find especially compelling today, including cruelty to animals, destruction of the environment, surrender to the mechanical power of society, and unlimited greed."

[16] Schopenhauer, *Die Welt als Wille und Vorstellung,* 2:186.

[17] See Alfred Schmidt, *Die Wahrheit im Gewande der Lüge: Schopenhauers Religionsphilosophie* (Munich: Piper, 1986).

This is where Wagner for the second time encountered the notion that religions are mythical and that the mythical images assume only a relative significance. This is why they can be re-formed and placed in new combinations. The process of artistic formation has always played a part in the transmission of traditional religious goods, and thus they are already a result of a creative process. This idea paved the way for the new interpretation of Christian sacraments in *Parsifal*.

According to Schopenhauer, the experience of art can also transform one's consciousness, at least temporarily. In aesthetic contemplation, one is freed from the state of willing, and enters the realm of eternal ideas. Music is granted a special place in Schopenhauer's aesthetic system; he considers music an immediate expression of the world-will. Thus music becomes a metaphysical tool. Wagner adopted this notion and devised an aesthetics of music drama in which music expresses philosophical truth *in abstracto*. Because this truth can still only be expressed indirectly and is virtually inaccessible to human consciousness, the action of his music dramas assumes the function of a sort of "translation" of philosophical contents into the language of sensual portrayal.[18]

After Wagner had read Schopenhauer, Christianity assumed a new dimension for him. Schopenhauer's atheism was attractive to Wagner, who held that there could not possibly be a personal God who was also the creator of the world. On the other hand, Wagner's interest centered on the figure of Jesus of Nazareth. At the same time, he became fascinated with the world of Indian mythology. Schopenhauer used the Indian term "Schleier der Maya" (veil of Maya) to describe the blindness shackling every living being that does not recognize its unity with other manifestations of the world-will; this is the pleasant illusion of beauty and well-being that living creatures can experience. To describe his ethics of compassion, Schopenhauer cites the *Upanishads* and Buddhist legends. He likens this continual creation and destruction of life to the Indian image of the transmigration of souls in the eternal cycle of "samsara," and he describes the release from the will with the concept of "nirvana."

Wagner followed Schopenhauer's bibliographical instructions and intensively studied these pieces of Indian lore. He read Eugene Burnouf's standard work *Introduction à la histoire du Buddhisme indien* (1844), and became acquainted with the "Mahayana" Buddhism of Northern India. In addition, he also read Carl Friedrich Köppen's 1857 essay "Die Religion des Buddha und ihre Entstehung," the verse epic *Mahabharata* in the larger work *Indische Sagen* of Adolf Holtzmann, the verse epic *Ramayana*,

---

[18] Wagner elaborated a Schopenhauerian philosophy of music in his essay "Beethoven," in *SSD* 9:61–126.

and much else.[19] His later work contains much evidence of this philosophical and religious-historical research. In 1854, the same year that he read Schopenhauer, Wagner conceived his first plans for *Tristan und Isolde*. A few years later, in 1857, he recalled having read *Parzival* by Wolfram von Eschenbach thirteen years earlier (the experience that had inspired him to write *Lohengrin*) and thought about writing another Grail drama. He evidently sketched out a prose summary that same year. Around the same time he was inspired by a Buddhist legend to devise *Die Sieger*, an Indian drama of redemption. He suddenly interrupted his work on the *Ring* tetralogy as the revolutionary ideas that had given rise to it yielded to his new philosophical orientation.

Parzival, Tristan, and *Die Sieger*

The original conception of *Parzival* (Wagner later changed the spelling of the name) arose in close relation to both *Tristan und Isolde* and his Buddhist drama *Die Sieger* (The Victors). But each of these three works portrays a different slant on religion: the metaphysical night of love in *Tristan und Isolde* cannot be identified with any standard religion, but rather resembles in many isolated formulations the "unworldly" mysticism expressed in Novalis's *Hymnen an die Nacht* (1800) while being an artistic counterpart to what Schopenhauer sought to express with the concept of "nirvana." In sharp contrast to this, in *Die Sieger*, Wagner portrays the

---

[19] Eugene Burnouf, *Introduction à la histoire du Buddhisme indien* (Paris: Imprimerie royale, 1844); Carl Friedrich Köppen, "Die Religion des Buddha und ihre Entstehung," in *Die Religion des Buddha*, 2 vols. (Berlin: Schneider, 1857–59); *Rama, ein indisches Gedicht nach Walmiki*, trans. Adolf Holtzmann (Karlsruhe: G. Holtzmann, 1843); *Ramayana, poeme sanscrit de Valmiki*, trans. Hippolyte Fauche, 9 vols. (Paris: A. Frank, 1854–58); Adolf Holtzmann, *Indische Sagen*, 2 vols. (Stuttgart: A. Krabbe, 1854). In the course of the years Wagner added many works of Indian literature to his library, and also the primary source texts of his operas in German and French translations. Of course, his understanding of India was not completely free of misunderstandings and misinterpretations. In the nineteenth century, Indology was still in its formative stages. On Wagner's reception of India and its influence on *Parsifal* and *Die Sieger*, see Carl Suneson, *Richard Wagner und die indische Geisteswelt* (Leiden and New York: E. J. Brill, 1989); Derrick Everett, "Parsifal under the Bodhi Tree," in *Wagner* 22 (2001): 67–92; Oswald Panagl, "Mitleidvoll Duldender, Heiltatvoll Wissender! *Parsifal*, Richard Wagner, und die indische Geisteswelt," in Müller and Panagl, *Ring und Gral*, 238–45; and in the same work, "Wege und Umwege eines musikdramatischen Entwurfs: *Die Sieger* und *Parsifal*," 246–60.

Buddhist religion of enlightenment and the ascetic mystical union of man and woman as equals. *Parsifal* stresses Christian elements: Wagner's alleged first inspiration is associated with an experience of Good Friday.[20] Of all the possible representations of the Grail that can be found in works of the Middle Ages, Wagner chose from the beginning the one laden with Christian significance — he follows Robert de Boron and regards the Grail as the cup from which Christ drank at the Last Supper, and in which Joseph of Arimathia caught the blood of Christ from the cross.[21] At the same time, however, Wagner's conception of *Parsifal* also contains Indian, and especially Buddhist traits, particularly in the ethic of compassion that it propounds. Another connection between these works is established by the fact that Wagner originally intended to have Parzival enter as a character in *Tristan und Isolde*, and, wandering onstage while seeking the Grail, meet the wounded Tristan on his sickbed.[22]

Wagner reacted to Schopenhauer's philosophy, particularly its theory of the ethical significance of religion, by combining three strands of mythology, each of which highlights a different kind of spirituality. In a letter to Franz Liszt, moreover, he adopts Schopenhauer's thesis that Christianity was not derived from Judaism; rather, Christianity grew from elements taken from Indian religions, which reached Israel via Egypt.[23] With the conception of *Parzival*, Wagner intended to create a synthesis of Christian and Indian religions on the basis of Schopenhauer's philosophy. This synthesis remained a constant element of the project until its completion.

From the evidence of Wagner's letters to and diary entries for Mathilde Wesendonk as well as his entries in his "brown book," we can follow the growth of the *Parzival* project. On October 1, 1858, Wagner explained to Mathilde Wesendonk why he felt more compassion with animals than with human beings — animals, which are actually in the

---

[20] *Mein Leben*, 561. The inspiration to work on *Parzival* did not actually happen on Good Friday, as Wagner originally claimed that it did. Yet one can suppose that the blooming of nature on a spring morning caused him to associate it with Good Friday, and even though that provides the "wrong" date, it establishes the connection between *Parzival* and Christianity.

[21] The first prose sketch has been lost. In his letter to Mathilde Wesendonk of May 29/30, 1859, Wagner clearly expresses the idea; see Richard Wagner, *Dokumente zur Entstehung und ersten Aufführung des Bühnenweihfestspiels "Parsifal,"* ed. Martin Geck and Egon Voss, vol. 30 of Wagner, *Sämtliche Werke* (Mainz: Schott, 1970), 15. This volume will be cited henceforth as *DEAP*.

[22] See especially Wagner's entry in a notebook reproduced in *DEAP*, 12.

[23] Schopenhauer, *Über die Grundlage der Moral*, 281; Wagner, letter to Franz Liszt of 7 June 1855, in Erich Kloss, ed., *Briefwechsel zwischen Wagner und Liszt* (Leipzig: Breitkopf und Härtel, 1910), 2:79.

deepest sense identical with human beings, must surrender to their sufferings, whereas philosophical insights enable human beings to rise above their sufferings. Mankind acquires the metaphysically significant task of finding, through resignation, a deep, "divine consolation" (einer tiefen, göttlichen Beruhigung) that has been denied to animals.

> Wenn daher dieses Leiden [that is, of the animal] einen Zweck haben kann, so ist dies einzig durch die Erweckung des Mitleidens im Menschen, der dadurch das verfehlte Dasein des Tieres in sich aufnimmt, und zum Erlöser der Welt wird, indem er überhaupt den Irrtum alles Daseins erkennt. (Diese Bedeutung wird Dir einmal aus dem dritten Akte des Parzival, am Karfreitagsmorgen, klar werden.) (*DEAP,* 14)[24]

> [If therefore this suffering of the animal can have a purpose, this can only be through the awakening of compassion in a human being, who takes upon himself the inadequate existence of the animal and becomes the redeemer of the world by recognizing the error of existence. (This meaning will become clear to you in the third act of *Parzival,* on the morning of Good Friday.)]

According to Schopenhauer, one should show compassion not only to fellow human beings, but to animals as well. This is clearly expressed by the Indian religions; but Christianity needs this corrective, he felt. Wagner follows Schopenhauer's thinking here. But how can a human being become, through compassion, "Erlöser der Welt" (redeemer of the world)? This question addresses the foundation of the conception of *Parzival.* Schopenhauer is convinced

> daß die ethische Bedeutsamkeit der Handlungen zugleich eine metaphysische, d.h. über die bloße Erscheinung der Dinge und somit auch über alle Möglichkeit der Erfahrung hinausreichende, demnach mit dem ganzen Daseyn der Welt und dem Loose der Menschen in engster Beziehung stehende seyn müsse.[25]

> [That the ethical significance of deeds also has a metaphysical aspect, that is, one that goes beyond the mere appearance of things and thus also reaches beyond all possibilities of experience, and for that reason must stand in the closest relation to the entire existence of the world and the fate of mankind.]

Every single deed affects the whole of existence. Just as every act of violence backfires against the doer, who is thus in the innermost sense one with his victim, so does every deed that is done out of love and compassion

---

[24] *DEAP,* 14.
[25] Schopenhauer, *Über die Grundlage der Moral,* 302.

also work on all that is, and it therefore allows the utopia of peaceful coexistence of all living creatures to become a reality for at least a moment or so. This is the Indian concept of "karma" with a positive twist.

The "Irrthum des Daseins" (error of existence), as Wagner sees it, consists in egotism, which just gives rise to more and more violence and suffering. In overcoming egotism, a human being can become a redeemer of the world. With this formulation, which combines the ethic of compassion with the events of Good Friday, the connection to Christianity is established. According to Christianity, Jesus of Nazareth is the sole redeemer of the world. He sacrificed His life by suffering in place of all of sinful mankind; that is, as far as Wagner was concerned, for all those who are caught up in egotism and thus already miserable. This was the core of Wagner's drama *Jesus von Nazareth*. In his last music drama, Wagner took up this notion once again and the Christian implications seem clear even if Christ himself is not named. Wagner revised, however, the doctrine accepted by the conventional wisdom of Christianity, by allowing human beings to become redeemers of the world, insofar as an individual can imitate Christ by putting compassionate love into practice. Christ is the prototype of the redeemer, its mythical archetype. The Good Friday scene of *Parzival* was intended to develop this idea. Because every individual represents the whole of existence, each individual can become, according to Schopenhauer, either Adam (fallen mankind) or Christ (the Redeemer).

Wagner explicates this dichotomy a few months later with the opposition of Anfortas and Parzival.[26] In a letter to Mathilde Wesendonk of May 29–30, 1859, he designates Anfortas as "Tristan des dritten Aktes mit einer undenklichen Steigerung" (Tristan of the third act with an inconceivable intensification).[27] This "potentiation" consists in being not only, like Tristan, subject to the desires of love as a "furchtbare Qual" (terrible torment),[28] but beyond that, Anfortas must painfully feel how inadequate he himself is when compared with the redeemer, who can in this context be

---

[26] Wagner follows his sources, particularly Wolfram von Eschenbach, in the spelling of the names in the early stages of his work. The most significant change that he later makes is the one that concerns the title figure: he adopts a fallacious etymology that he learned from Joseph von Görres and writes "Parsifal." The name was supposedly derived from the Persian and meant "the pure fool." See: Oswald Panagl, "Wie der Name, so die Art: Etymologisierende Wortspiele und individuelle Wesenszüge in Wagners *Parsifal*," in Müller and Panagl, *Ring und Gral*, 267.

[27] Wolfgang Golther, ed., *Richard Wagner an Mathilde Wesendonk: Tagebuchblätter und Briefe 1853–187* (Berlin: Alexander Duncker Verlag, 1910), 207.

[28] Wagner summarizes the meaning of *Tristan und Isolde* in this way in a letter to August Röckel of August 23, 1856. See Hanjo Kesting, ed., *Richard Wagner: Briefe* (Munich: Piper, 1983), 336.

identified with Christ. There exists some mystical association between Christ and Anfortas. As King of the Grail and its high priest who presides over the Grail ceremony, Anfortas is a representative of Christ; this identity is underscored by the fact that Anfortas was wounded in the same place as Christ (in his side), and, as Wagner will later make clear, with the same weapon that wounded Christ. But unlike Christ, who suffered to redeem the world (Wagner wrote that Christ "Weltentsagend, Welterlösend, Weltleidend am Kreuze schmachtete" [died on the cross renouncing, redeeming, and suffering for the world; *DEAP*, 15]), Anfortas has succumbed to his sensual desires and betrayed his divine mission. The will to existence expresses itself according to Schopenhauer most directly in Eros; in that way it propagates itself from one generation to the next, and thus egotism and suffering continue as well. Sensual lust is for Schopenhauer the quintessence of egotistical self-love. Therefore — Wagner continues — the Grail Knights live ascetically. For that reason, the "Liebesabenteuer" (lustful encounter) of Anfortas is no mere indiscretion that can be easily pardoned, but rather an act of pure egotism and thus a betrayal of Christ. He is a perverted Christ figure: he has failed in his task of becoming a redeemer of the world. None of the Grail works with which Wagner was acquainted contain such a connection between Christ and the Grail King.

In contrast, Parzival is predestined by his compassionate nature (Wagner wrote that he had a "ganzes sinniges, tief mitleidsvolles Naturell" [introspective, deeply compassionate nature]) to overcome egotism and become the true follower of Christ. To that end, though, he needs to undergo development, an "erhabenste Läuterung" (most sublime purification; *DEAP*, 16), as Wagner recognized early on in the project. This task presented him with a problem: he feared that the center of interest would be Anfortas, and not Parzival. In 1859 he evidently lacked a solution and a way of portraying the transformation from fool to redeemer. He found a model for this process in Indian works. But his intensive preoccupation with the world of India allowed another figure of the drama to emerge. In a letter to Mathilde Wesendonk from the beginning of August 1860 he talks about "die tiefsinnige Annahme der Seelenwanderung" (the profound idea of metempsychosis) and applies this to the conflict between Elsa and Lohengrin. Then he writes:

> Viel ist wieder der Parzival in mir wach gewesen; ich sehe immer mehr und heller darin . . . Sagte ich Ihnen schon einmal, dass die fabelhaft wilde Gralsbotin ein und dasselbe Wesen mit dem verführersischen Weibe des zweiten Aktes sein soll? Seitdem mir dies aufgegangen, ist mir fast alles an diesem Stoffe klar geworden.[29]

---

[29] Golther, *Richard Wagner an Mathilde Wesendonk*, 243.

[Parzival has come very much alive for me again, and I see it more and more, and more clearly now . . . Have I told you already that the fantastic, wild messenger of the Grail is to be one and the same being as the seductive woman of the second act? Almost everything in this story became clear to me once I realized this.]

Kundry exemplifies the Indian doctrine of metempsychosis, which Wagner learned about from Schopenhauer's works and his studies of Indian religions. Although Wagner centered his drama around the Christian sacrament of the Eucharist and the meaning of Good Friday in this Christian context, early on in the project he synthesized these elements of the plan with concepts taken from Indian religion.

A Synthesis of Religions: The Prose Sketch of 1865

That this synthesis is closely knit was proven five years later. In the course of a few days in August 1865, Wagner wrote out for King Ludwig II, in response to his sovereign request, a detailed prose draft of *Parzival*. This prose draft agrees in most main details with the finished work. The thoughts about Anfortas, Christ, and Kundry that the composer had expressed to Mathilde Wesendonk are echoed almost verbatim in this prose sketch. The main outlines of the plan are based on Schopenhauer's philosophy, while elements taken from Christian and Indian teachings provide the imagery, symbols, and mythological features from which Wagner built the dramatic action. The thoughts and impressions that had previously been scattered here and there in Wagner's various scribblings have now been combined to form a unified drama.

Wagner's interpretation of the Grail remained the same:

Der Gral ist die kristallene Trinkschale, aus welcher einst der Heiland beim letzten Abendmahl trank und seinen Jüngern zu trinken reichte: Joseph von Arimathia fing in ihr das Blut auf, welches aus der Speerwunde des Erlösers am Kreuze herabfloß.[30]

[The Grail is the crystal cup from which the Savior once drank at the Last Supper and that He handed to His apostles to drink from: in it Joseph of Arimathia caught the blood that flowed from the spear wound of the Redeemer on the cross.]

---

[30] Joachim Bergfeld, ed., *Richard Wagner: Das braune Buch: Tagebuchaufzeichnungen 1865 bis 1882* (Zurich: Atlantis, 1975), 53.

In his miniature summary of the history of the Grail order, Wagner follows the outlines of *Der jüngere Titurel* by Albrecht von Scharfenberg (ca. 1270–80). In this medieval version, Titurel — according to the source material a seemingly ageless boy who is not allowed to marry until he is four hundred years old — built the castle Montsalvatsch (or, as Wagner called it, Monsalvat) in northern Spain out of precious jewels according to an occult plan that he received from angels.

In the prose draft from 1865 the main characteristic of the Grail is that it gives life. "Den Tod bannt er von seinen Geweihten: wer das göttliche Gefäß erblickt, kann nicht sterben." (It banishes death from its devotees: he who gazes at the divine vessel cannot die).[31] This is consistent with the medieval sources, especially Wolfram von Eschenbach. Moreover, through "geheimnisvolle Schriftzeichen" (mysterious messages), the Grail sends its knights into the world to rescue innocent individuals who find themselves in distress. Wagner derived this, too, from Wolfram von Eschenbach. In Wagner's drama, the Grail also produces goods, just as it does in Wolfram's *Parzival,* though Wagner's Grail is not quite so outlandish as that of his source: after the daily ceremony of uncovering the Grail, the tables are, Wagner wrote, "mit Wein und Brot versehen" (supplied with wine and bread).[32]

More important, however, is how closely Wagner follows the liturgy of the Eucharist of the Catholic Church. In the spring of 1865, after the birth of Isolde von Bülow, his first daughter, Wagner held a series of conversations with the Catholic priest Petrus Hamp, in which he learned intensively about the doctrine of transubstantiation and the course of the Eucharistic celebration.[33] In doing so, he obviously had his Grail drama in mind. Wagner consciously sought to associate the ceremony in his drama with the Catholic Eucharistic celebration, at least in its outward form. Significantly enough, the transubstantiation in Wagner's drama happens very differently — bread and wine are not transformed into Christ's body and blood. Rather, the opposite occurs, and Christ's body is changed into bread and his blood into wine. Wagner emphasized the importance of his revision of the traditional doctrine.[34]

---

[31] Bergfeld, *Das braune Buch,* 53.

[32] Bergfeld, *Das braune Buch,* 61.

[33] Anton Hamp, *Ein Blick in die Geisteswerkstatt Richard Wagners: Von einem alten geistlichen Freunde des Meisters von Bayreuth zur Erinnerung an dessen Schwanengesang — den "Parzival"* (Berlin: A. Böhler, 1904).

[34] See the diary entries of Cosima Wagner of September 26, 1877. Cosima Wagner, *Die Tagebücher,* ed. Martin Gregor-Dellin and Dietrich Mack, 2 vols. (Munich and Zurich: Piper, 1976 (hereafter cited as CT), 1:1072; also Cosima's letter to Otto Eiser of February 20, 1878, cited with commentary by Dieter Borchmeyer in

The daily repetition of the last love-feast that Christ celebrated with his apostles is, for Wagner, not merely a ceremony of remembrance. Christ is actually present in the ceremony. This is proven by the fact that the blood of Christ, with which the chalice is filled and upon which the entire ceremony centers, is illuminated through a "blendenden Lichtstrahl" (blinding shaft of light) that descends from the dome of the Grail Temple. The blood in the Grail holds, according to ancient Christian sources, the "essence" or the soul of Christ. Its glowing is akin to a hierophantic revelation, with the Grail's contents assuming full symbolic value and giving eternal life.

The lightning bolt is an ancient symbol of the divine power revealing itself to mankind. This divine light descends from above, and comes down vertically onto the chalice, which is resting horizontally.[35] The intersection of the horizontal and the vertical makes the sign of the cross. This symbol ranges far beyond the realm of Christianity; in many ancient cultures, the cross is a symbol of the whole of existence; it ranges into the four corners of the heavens and unites heaven and earth, life and death. Its four endpoints stand for the four elements from which the material world is built. At the same time, Wagner's pictorial imagination conjures up the idea of procreation, which ancient texts also portray in a similar way — the divine lightning can be thought of as the vertical, phallic force, which makes the resting cup, the symbol of the feminine organs, glow and thus vitalizes them. In Indian mythology and art, the symbol of the cup can be found, represented by Yoni, the feminine womb of goddess Shakti. The masculine symbol is accordingly Lingam, the procreative force of her husband Shiva. This shows how the horizontal and the vertical can be united to form an image of completion. Schopenhauer uses these symbols repeatedly in his writings. The spear is a phallic symbol, but also at the same time an instrument of the martyrdom of the Passion as understood by Christianity, and as such it is closely associated with Christ. Only when the spear is regained, in Wagner's drama, can the relics be reunited and, because they complement each other, a state of perfection is then achieved.

The celebration of the Eucharist forms the Christian context in which the drama takes place. However, Wagner also made numerous borrowings

---

his chapter "Eigensinn und Sinnenteignung des Mythos: Wagners Wirkung im Widerspruch von Poesie und Politik," in *Zukunftsbilder: Richard Wagners Revolution und ihre Folgen in der Kunst und Politik,* ed. Hermann Danuser and Herfried Münkler, 184–85 (Schliengen: Edition Argus, 2002).

[35] Originally the Grail was not so much a goblet as a large, deep platter, upon which various foods were offered to the members of the high society. This is the way Helinand de Froidmont described the Grail in the thirteenth century. See: Müller and Panagl, *Ring und Gral*, 200. Wagner speaks of a "bowl" (Schale) and thereby emphasizes the flat, horizontal form of the vessel.

from Indian mythology in this drama as well. In his sketch, Wagner describes the forest of the holy Grail according to the model of the Indian vale of penitents: here the animals are sacred. The forest of the Grail is a place where mankind lives in peaceful coexistence with nature. The animals are tame, for they need not fear that they will be hunted and killed. But the idyll has its price; the Grail Knights must resist the "Verlockungen der Sinnenlust" (temptations of sensual pleasure). Wagner writes, "nur dem Keuschen offenbart sich die beseligende Macht des Heiligtumes" (the power of the holy place to spiritually edify its adherents reveals itself only to the chaste; *DEAP,* 68). Asceticism characterizes life in a Christian cloister as well; vegetarianism and kindness to animals are demonstrations of Indian religious piety. Anfortas and the Grail Knights have their dramatic foil in the former hermit Klingsor, who could not curb his sensual desires. His self-castration was his desperate attempt to remove the obstacles on the way to a life of sanctity and thus approach the community of the Grail Knights. He is rejected by Titurel for the reason "dass die Entsagung und Keuschheit aus innerster Seele fließen, nicht aber durch Verstümmelung erzwungen sein müsse" (that renunciation and innocence must flow from the innermost soul, and not be forced through mutilation.[36] With this formulation, Wagner transfers a key doctrine of Buddha, which he read during his indological research, to Titurel — Buddha took only healthy, virile young men into his circle of disciples, and tested their strength of will, which is the key ingredient of voluntary renunciation.[37] This is just what Klingsor does, though he has very different, contrary motives. Out of hatred and revenge for his rejection, he wants to destroy the Grail Knights by showing their weakness of will — which they demonstrate when they succumb to seduction. They surrender, one by one, including the Grail King, Anfortas, to the magic of the beautiful women whom he has held captive in his castle.

As a result of these actions, a dark shadow falls on the idealized existence of the Grail Knights. They seem chaste only as long as they do not encounter women. Their purity rests on the exclusion of women. Wagner consciously meant it this way, for in the medieval Grail sources that he used, for example in Wolfram, women are present, even though the knights are not allowed to marry as long as they live in the Grail community. In Wagner's Buddhist drama sketch *Die Sieger,* the goal of the action is the acceptance of women into the community of saints. For Wagner, the most important thing that Shakyamuni learns on his journey to total

---

[36] Bergfeld, *Das braune Buch,* 54.

[37] Wagner attributes this also to Christianity in his essay of 1881, "Heldentum und Christentum," *SSD* 10:279).

enlightenment is that women are spiritually equal to men. By making the Grail Knights of *Parsifal* into an exclusive men's club, Wagner evidently wanted to show the questionable nature of this kind of institution.

The influences from his Indian studies are particularly evident, to judge from Wagner's letter to Mathilde Wesendonk, in the various reincarnations of Kundry. In her wandering from one life to another, Wagner demonstrates the Indian "samsara." He writes,

> Kundry lebt ein unermeßliches Leben unter stets wechselnden Wiedergeburten, in Folge einer uralten Verwünschung, die sie, ähnlich dem "ewigen Juden," dazu verdammt, in neuen Gestalten das Leiden der Liebesverführung über die Männer zu bringen; Erlösung, Auflösung, gänzliches Erlöschen ist ihr nur verhießen, wenn einst ein reinster, blühendster Mann ihrer machtvollsten Verführung wiederstehen würde.[38]

> [Kundry lives an immeasurable life consisting of constantly varying rebirths, as the result of an ancient curse, which condemns her, like the "Eternal Jew," to bring the torment of seduction upon men; redemption, dissolution, total obliteration is promised to her only if the purest, most youthful man were to resist her most powerful seduction.]

That sounds like a summary of Schopenhauer's philosophy in the form of a mythical story. Kundry would be an embodiment of the will to existence, which is immortal and objectifies itself in one incarnation after another. The will is a blind power that longs to propagate itself and drive its incarnations to seek new lives, too. The reason for the perpetuation of this will is sexuality, the "Leiden der Liebesverführung" (sufferings of the enticement of love). Because life is, as far as Schopenhauer is concerned, fundamentally suffering, Wagner speaks of "einer uralten Verwünschung" (an ancient curse). In every embrace and every birth, new life arises, which is destined to more and more suffering. The will has no kind of intellectual insight. Neither does Kundry realize the connection between her suffering and the seductions that she performs, which bring her transitory pleasure. The will cannot negate itself or redeem itself. Only a philosopher or a saint can do this; in these individuals, however, the will can achieve self-consciousness and be redeemed. Wagner describes this with the image of the "reinsten, blühendsten Mannes" (purest, most youthful man), who resists the will to life and makes the conscious decision to live the life of asceticism. Ironically enough, the decision that goes against the will ultimately fulfills its longing for redemption from the cycle of rebirths. The concepts with which Wagner expresses Kundry's longing for release from her wanderings are "Erlösung, Auflösung, gänzliches Erlöschen" (redemption,

---

[38] Bergfeld, *Das braune Buch,* 62.

dissipation, total obliteration). These words aptly describe Schopenhauer's understanding of the Indian "nirvana." Wagner's conception of Kundry is probably the element of the drama that is at furthest remove from his basically Christian scenario: Kundry is a heathen.[39]

The second, less obvious, borrowing from Indian sources concerns the title figure. When he first conceived *Parzival,* Wagner was concerned that beside the highly dramatic conflict taking place with the character of Amfortas, the title figure could only pale in comparison and "[as a] kalt lassender Deus ex machina eben nur schließlich hinzutreten" (would leave the audience cold, appearing at the end only as a *deus ex machina*).[40] In the meantime, he studied Buddhism and its psychology of enlightenment so intensively that he could therefore portray Parzival's character development as the process of a gradual growth of consciousness. He thus models the path of his protagonist on the example of Buddha and the Indian "Bodhisattva."[41]

In "Mahayana" Buddhism, which Wagner became acquainted with through Burnouf, wisdom (prajna) and compassion (karuna) are the highest ethical values. These concepts can be found in the *Parzival* sketch of 1865, although they remain disconnected. The prophecy about Anfortas's cure is "mitleidend leidvoll wissend ein Tor wird dich erlösen" (a fool whose knowledge comes from suffering, through compassion, will redeem you). The Grail Knights ask, "Wer kann der sein, der nur 'durch Mitleiden leidet,' und ohne zu wissen weiser ist als andre?'" (Who can that be, who "suffers through compassion" and in his innocence is wiser than everyone else?).[42] The paradox is expressed differently here than in the final text of

---

[39] The Indian doctrine of the transmigration of souls is by no means a unified one. According to the "Vedanta," a system of Hindu instruction from the seventh century A.D., the core of the individual existence ("atman") remains intact throughout changing incarnations. In contrast, Buddhism as strictly understood acknowledges no constancy in the identity of an individual, but only a new recombination of the "dharmas," the primal substances of life that creates the consciousness. This theory was, however, for the most part unknown to Europe in the nineteenth century. Wagner himself originally understood the Buddhist doctrine of reincarnation to mean that each soul was reborn in the guise of another individual being to whom it had previously dealt suffering — until through a long process of purification it attained a state of being fully free of violence. See *Briefwechsel zwischen Wagner und Liszt,* 2:78–79. This does not apply to Kundry; in her case a basic conflict repeats itself in new and different incarnations.
[40] Letter to Mathilde Wesendonk of May 29/30, 1859, cited in *DEAP,* 16.
[41] See Derrick Everett's aforementioned essay, "Parsifal under the Bodhi Tree." My analysis follows his in many points.
[42] Bergfeld, *Das braune Buch,* 57.

1877. Later Wagner was to associate compassion and wisdom with each other. In the text that he set to music, the prophecy begins: "Durch Mitleid wissend, der reine Tor" (Knowing through compassion, the pure fool). This makes clear that the human being lacking wisdom attains highest wisdom through compassion with others. The later version formulates succinctly what was already present as the central idea of the action of *Parzival* even in the sketch of 1865 — intuitive enlightenment and supreme knowledge come through identification with a suffering individual.

This idea links Schopenhauer's philosophy, the Indian "Mahayana" Buddhism, and the standard medieval Grail legend that is tinged in a definitely Christian way. Like Prince Gautama, the later Buddha, so is Parzival in Wolfram's epic raised in a very sheltered existence. He does not experience war and power plays, suffering and death. Wagner must have thought about the resemblance of these two characters' past lives, for Parzival's childhood does play a role in his drama. Parzival and Prince Gautama are, moreover, both innocent, though for different reasons. Wolfram's Parzival simply lacks the necessary education; he is a fool because he does not know how to become a knight and behave as one. He does not even know about God. Gautama's ignorance has other motives. It is the "avidya" of the Buddhist literature and consists in a lack of philosophical knowledge. He is oblivious to the sufferings of existence. On his excursions, the prince encounters, one after the other, an old man, a sick man, and a dead man. The shock that this causes him leads to the first enlightenment of the future Buddha. He leaves the house in which he has been sheltered, his young wife, and his newborn son, to go through the world begging as a monk. He seeks the reasons for suffering and the ways to overcome it. Even the strictest ascetic penitential rituals fail to help him attain a deeper insight into this. Only in meditation under the Bodhi tree is he granted complete enlightenment. Before that happens, though, he withstands a series of tests — Mara, the demon of death, sends his beautiful daughters to him and tries to kill him with a discus. But Buddha will not let himself be seduced, and the weapon that is supposed to kill him falls to the ground like a dead leaf. Buddha demonstrates that he has withstood the trial with a significant gesture — he touches the ground with his right hand, and the earth shakes.

This is obviously the basic model for Parzival's enlightenment.[43] However, it undergoes some important modifications. Like the young Prince Gautama, Parzival is confronted along the way with suffering, age, and death as soon as he leaves the place where he spent his childhood. Following

---

[43] On the correspondences with Wagner's *Parsifal*, see in particular: Suneson, *Richard Wagner und die indische Geisteswelt*, 95–113; and Everett, "Parsifal under the Bodhi Tree."

his spontaneous impulse, Parzival kills a swan, oblivious to the ramifications of his deed. Gurnemans shows him the cruelty of this thoughtless violence. The rudimentary compassion that he feels for the swan is the first stirring of his later experience of all-encompassing compassion.[44] Kundry tells him of the death of his mother, but Parzival denies the reality of this death and grabs Kundry by the throat, acting to destroy the message by assaulting the messenger. He loses consciousness and with it the knowledge of what he needs to experience. In the Grail Castle he encounters old age in the character of Titurel, who is still alive in his grave. Parzival witnesses the suffering of Anfortas but does not understand what it means.

Parzival's encounters with age, suffering, and death are, like the analogous confrontations that Prince Gautama makes, insufficient to bring him his first level of enlightenment. He remains in a state of "avidya." He needs to experience another kind of basic phenomenon, one that did not play such a huge role in the story of the Buddha — sexuality. When the future Buddha goes forth into the world, he already has a wife and a child. Parsifal, in contrast, is still innocent when he enters the Grail Realm. Wagner felt that was very important. Parzival gains enlightenment by experiencing erotic desire for the first time in his life; this is why he must encounter beautiful women, and Kundry in particular. According to Schopenhauer, sexuality is the center of the will, and in Wagner's conception, Kundry is the embodiment of the will to existence, which perpetually longs for life through one incarnation after another. Through his seduction, Parzival experiences the world of the will. He penetrates the *principium individuationis* and experiences the identity of all beings as manifestations of the one will. At the same time, he realizes that life is fundamentally suffering. This insight is associated with his recollection of what he watched at the Grail ceremony. Now the lament of Anfortas has become Parzival's own: "er fühlt nach seinem Herzen; dort brennt ihn plötzlich die Wunde des Anfortas: er hört dessen Klagen aus seinem eigenen tiefsten Innern aufsteigen" (He grips his heart; there the wound of Anfortas is burning: he hears his lament rise up from within his own innermost being).[45]

The mystery of compassion, as Schopenhauer understands it, that is, the sudden identification with another's suffering, is dramatically portrayed here onstage. Parzival *is* the suffering Anfortas. Not only that: in the lament of Anfortas, he hears "die göttlichen Klagen über den Fall des Auserwählten; er vernimmt den Ruf des Heilands nach Befreiung des

---

[44] Similar episodes can be found in Wolfram's *Parzival* and also in Buddhist writings. Wagner reinterprets them according to Schopenhauer's philosophy as regret for the killing of animals. See Schopenhauer, *Grundlage der Moral*, 282.
[45] Bergfeld, *Das braune Buch*, 66.

Heiligtums aus der Pflege befleckter Hände" (the divine laments about the fall of the chosen one; he hears the cry of the Savior to free the sanctuary from being guarded by soiled hands). Christ is present not only in the ceremony of uncovering the Grail; he somehow becomes present in Anfortas himself. Anfortas suffers in three different ways; in each case Parzival shares his suffering. He suffers, first of all, from the physical pain of the wound, which Parzival now feels as his own. Second, he feels "die unsäglichen Qualen des Liebessehnens, die unheiligen Schauer des sündigen Verlangens" (the unspeakable torments of love, the profane shudder of sinful desire),[46] which Parzival also experiences through the attempted seduction by Kundry. Finally, he hears the lament of Christ at the betrayal of the Grail mystery, and Parzival hears this lament in himself, too.

Through the mystery of compassion, Christ, Anfortas, and Parzival merge together to form one single identity. This is a mystical experience, an enlightenment. His insight into the identity of all living creatures gives Parzival the strength to withstand Kundry's seduction. Not only does he gain wisdom through compassion; he also becomes, in the sense in which Wagner once described it to Mathilde Wesendonk, "Erlöser der Welt" (redeemer of the world; *DEAP*, 14). He reverses the failing of Anfortas and brings about a turning point for the entire drama. Therefore the spear that inflicted Anfortas's wound cannot harm Parzival. In the sketch of 1865, Parzival wrests the spear away from a knight. Only in a later version does the action at this point of the drama derive from Buddhist legends — Klingsor hurls the spear at Parsifal, just as Mara throws his deadly discus at the Buddha. And just as Buddha touches the earth (which then shakes) to show that he has withstood and triumphed through this trial, so does Parsifal swing the spear (in the final version of the text he even makes the sign of the cross with it) thereby destroying the magic castle, which stands for illusion, the "Schleier der Maja" (veil of Maja).

In contrast to the Buddha, however, Parzival must prove himself worthy of this newly acquired wisdom by withstanding a series of trials and tribulations. Whereas Shakyamuni needed to perform penitential tasks *before* his enlightenment under the Bodhi tree, Parsival undergoes a similar test *afterward*, until he finally finds his way back to the Grail Realm. He tells Gurnemans that he despaired of ever finding the way back; "durch Büßungen jeder Art habe er sich der Gnade auf den rechten Pfad geleitet zu werden, teilhaftig machen wollen; vergebens" (through all kinds of penitence he wanted to become worthy of the grace of being led upon the right path; but in vain).[47] Here a concept comes into play that

---

[46] Bergfeld, *Das braune Buch,* 66.
[47] Bergfeld, *Das braune Buch,* 68.

leads from the world of Indian mythology directly into that of Christianity: "Gnade" (grace). Redemption cannot be earned through one's own devices; rather it is freely granted through an act of grace. This concept of grace brings to mind Good Friday, which provided inspiration for *Parzival* — the loving compassion of Christ. His martyrdom can be felt as a blessing for all nature and mankind. That Parzival finds the way back to the Grail Realm is clearly an appropriate occurrence for Good Friday. Now Gurnemans and Kundry can wash the dust of his long wandering from him; or, in the terms of Indian mythology, the last remnants of the "karma" that he has acquired in one existence after another. It is highly significant that in his last transformation Parzival depends upon the help of the very individuals he will redeem, that is, Gurnemans as a representative of the suffering Grail Knights, and Kundry, whom Parzival has freed from a series of countless rebirths and the compulsion to perform seductions one after another. The redeemer and the redeemed form a mystical community and become one.

The prose sketch of 1865 ends with a mixture of Indian and Christian elements. Parzival's words before he heals Anfortas and assumes the task of uncovering the Grail are "stark ist der Zauber des Begehrenden, doch stärker der des Entsagenden" (strong is the magic of the one who desires, but even stronger is the magic of the one who renounces).[48] This is also a Buddhist formula. The dove that at the end of the drama descends from the dome of the Grail Temple and hovers over Parzival's head is a Judaic-Christian symbol. The dove that Noah sent forth from the ark returned with an olive branch in its beak to proclaim the end of the flood, the renewal of life, and the new covenant between God and mankind. In Wolfram von Eschenbach's version of the Grail legend, the dove is sent from God on a yearly basis on Good Friday to renew the power of the Grail by bringing a host and thereby strengthening the bond between God and the Grail Knights. The dove that floats down is generally understood as a symbol of the Holy Spirit, which Wagner also portrayed with a shaft of light.

Parsifal: A Drama about Christ

As we have seen, influences from the two religions that became important to Wagner after he read Schopenhauer for the first time seem to balance each other out in the prose sketch of 1865. Twelve years elapsed between the time he wrote down the first extant sketch and when he penned the text of the final drama. During this period he composed *Die Meistersinger*

[48] Bergfeld, *Das braune Buch,* 70.

von Nürnberg, finished *Der Ring des Nibelungen,* and built the Bayreuth Festspielhaus. Moreover, his religious standpoint changed in the meantime, moving closer to Christianity.

On October 28, 1873, Cosima Wagner wrote in her diary:

> Das Leiden Christus' erregt uns tiefer als das Mitleiden Buddha's, wir leiden mit und werden zu Buddhas, durch die Betrachtung. Christus will leiden, leidet und erlöst uns, Buddha schauet und bemitleidet, lehrt, wie wir zur Erlösung kommen. (*CT* 1:744)

> [The suffering of Christ moves us more deeply than the compassion of Buddha; we suffer with him and become Buddhas through observing it. Christ wants to suffer, He suffers and redeems us; Buddha observes and pities, and in doing so shows us how we can achieve redemption.]

This diary entry shows the shift of emphasis referred to above. Wagner explains the difference between Buddhism and Christianity with the polarities of suffering and compassion, redemption and dogma. For him, Buddhism is primarily a religion of knowledge. "Betrachtung," or knowing the world through philosophical reflection, leads one along the path toward redemption; as far as Wagner was concerned, that was the essence of Buddhism. The main feature of Buddhism is this kind of mediation. Buddha was a teacher, and not a martyr. In contrast, Christianity is a religion of universal redemption, which is a direct result of the vicarious suffering of Christ, who took this freely upon Himself. This was not a matter of philosophical knowledge, but rather a radical act of self-martyrdom unlike the suffering of the Buddha. From this time of his life onward, Wagner valued the suffering of Christ much more highly than the compassion of Buddha. In his late essay "Religion und Kunst" (1880), Wagner wrote that the religion of the Brahmans was a religion of wisdom, one for the initiated. The religion of Jesus Christ, in contrast, was intended for the poor in spirit.[49] This polarity became increasingly important for Wagner. How did this happen?

We can find one answer to this question in Wagner's reaction to the political events that took place after the Franco-Prussian War (1870–71). Like most of his contemporaries, Wagner took a nationalistic stance on the war and the subsequent founding of the Second Empire. A few years later, though, his enthusiasm was gone. Along with many others, Wagner had hoped that German unification would bring about a spiritual renewal — a politics of liberalism and social justice, combined with generous support for culture and the arts, which in times of political strife promised to bind the people together and grant the Germans a cultural identity. The Second

---

[49] Richard Wagner, "Religion und Kunst," in *SSD* 10:212.

Empire, though, was characterized by a materialistic and opportunistic way of thinking. The impoverishment of huge groups of workers, the rapid growth of cities, and an open show of militarism formed the sobering downside of the new political regime. Knowledge was valued as long as it was scientific and positivistic. Art had a merely representative function, and found little state support.

This strongly contradicted Wagner's philosophical orientation. The ethic of compassion, which had been so important to him ever since he had read Schopenhauer, meant little in a land where the survival of the fittest was the rule of life and had the highest societal worth, for this meant for Wagner, in Schopenhauerian terms, the brutal reign of the Will. Rationality was valued more highly than empathy. The utopia in which egotism would be overcome and mankind would live in peaceful coexistence with nature receded further and further into the distance.[50] Wagner's metaphysical view of life contrasted strongly with the materialistic worldview that his contemporaries held. Because of these circumstances, Wagner ascribed to a religion that he understood to be a protest against the ruling materialism. He juxtaposed the poverty and the suffering of Christ with the values of his contemporary society. Wagner never tired of emphasizing that every true religion, and especially Christianity, had acknowledged the insubstantiality and frailty of this world, and that this was the foundation upon which they were built.[51] He offered the radical pessimism of Schopenhauer as a counterbalance to the optimism of his contemporaries and he considered religion the only consolation that was possible in a world in which ruled "das Grauen der Natur, des ewigen Verschlingens" (the horror of nature, of eternal devouring; *CT* 1:940).

Wagner saw Western history as just a series of wars and other acts of violence — and these were also waged in the name of Christianity. Thus he rejected all organized forms of religion, because he felt they had been exploited as instruments of power. Instead, he considered the primal Christian teachings, which he found in Buddhism as well as in the secret societies of the Pythagoreans, to be pacifism and abstinence from eating meat. The readiness of mankind to wage war, the phenomenon of murder,

---

[50] It is beyond question that Wagner's own thinking was fraught with the ideological contradictions of his time; for example, he ascribed to the prevalent anti-Semitism of his day. For him, Judaism was an example of a religion of optimism, capitalism, and egotism; he held the judgmental and punishing God of the Old Testament responsible for this. On this topic, and for a discussion of Wagner's anti-Semitism in particular, see Wolf-Daniel Hartwich, "Religion und Kunst beim spätem Wagner: Zum Verhältnis von Ästhetik, Theologie und Anthropologie in den 'Regenerationsschriften,'" in *Jahrbuch der deutschen Schiller-Gesellschaft* 40 (1996): 297–323.

[51] See "Religion und Kunst," *SSD* 10:212.

and other acts of violence were, as far as Wagner was concerned, a logical consequence of the disregard that mankind shows toward animals in killing them for food. In contrast, Christ gave His apostles "als letztes höchstes Sühnungsopfer für alles sündhaft vergossene Blut und geschlachtete Fleisch dahin, und reichte dafür seinen Jüngern Wein und Brot zum täglichen Mahle" (wine and bread for the daily meal as the last and supreme reconciliatory sacrifice for all the blood that was sinfully shed and the flesh that was sinfully slaughtered).[52]

In his late writings, Wagner severely criticizes the failings of his contemporary society, for it had no religious piety or compassion toward suffering. Starving workers, and animals that are tortured in scientific experiments to forward the state of knowledge, throw a dark shadow on a society that is focused on profit and progress (which would be impeded, Wagner theorized, by religion). This is the stigma of a barbaric civilization. The "Anbetung der Leiden des Erlösers" (adoration of the sufferings of the Redeemer) cannot be expected any longer from such a society.[53] Therefore Wagner champions the teachings of Christ, for he felt that Christ's voluntary suffering overturned the reigning moral code and value system of the day. Wagner felt that only a religion of this kind could form the basis for possibly bringing about a renewal of society, and through that, an end to violence and egotism. The organized church was not a candidate for this: "Für mich ist das Christentum noch nicht in das Leben getreten, und wie die ersten Christen erwarte ich eine Wiederkunft von Christus" (As far as I'm concerned, Christianity has not entered the world yet, and just like the first Christians I await the second coming of Christ), Wagner once said to Cosima (CT 2:382). In this sense, Christianity is for Wagner a religion of the future, which is based on a redeeming event in the past, the life and works of Jesus of Nazareth.

Wagner observed with distress the "Absterben der Religion, die sich nur durch Verdummung des Volkes aufrecht erhält" (the dying away of religion, which maintains itself only through the stupidity of the common people), as he said to Cosima (CT 1:535). The contradiction consisted for him in the fact that modern science had made "den Gott-Schöpfer" (the Creator-God) more and more impossible.[54] With this, he also had no quarrel. Wagner had been an atheist a long time earlier, when he ascribed to Schopenhauer's concept of the will and could no longer believe in a

---

[52] "Religion und Kunst," SSD 10:230. On Wagner's philosophy of regeneration and its place in the contemporary context, see Hartwich, "Religion und Kunst beim späten Wagner."

[53] "Wollen wir hoffen?" SSD 10:123–24.

[54] "Publikum und Popularität," SSD 10:86.

loving and benevolent god who made the heavens and the earth.[55] Though he rejected the traditional understandings of god, he did not want to discard religion entirely. Wagner was well aware that Christianity could not exist without the concept of a god. "Es wäre schon der Mühe wert, den Begriff Gott festzustellen, aber wer sollte es tun" (It would certainly be worth the trouble to define the concept of god, but who would do it), he admitted to Cosima (*CT* 2:472). He did not trust this task to contemporary theologians. Thus he undertook intensive religious-historical studies, and read Meister Eckhart and Johannes Tauler, Luther and the *Deutsche Theologie*. He studied the *Christliche Mystik* of the writer Joseph Görres and the *Geschichte des Urchristentums* by the distinguished theologian August Friedrich Gfrörer.[56] All of these studies stand in close relation to his renewed interest in working on the *Parsifal* plan after 1875.

While undertaking these theological studies, he became particularly interested in the mystics, as the evidence in various diary entries by Cosima Wagner, including this one of September 23, 1875, reveals: "Abends öffnet R. Meister Eckhart, einige Sätze erfüllen uns ganz, Sehen und Hören, das Sehen das Wirken, dass man durch das Wissen zum Unwissen kommen muß — so tief — da fühle ich mich heimisch, sagt R." (In the evening R. opens Meister Eckhart, a few sentences impress us deeply, about seeing and hearing, that one must process through knowledge to innocence — so deep — there I feel at home, says R; *CT* 1:937). The complex way in which Meister Eckhart understood the deity appealed to Wagner — it harked back to the "negative theology" of Dionysius Areopagita, which sees the deity as a being that cannot be defined and exists above all but is at the same time insubstantial and can be described as "Nichts" (nothing).[57] According to Meister Eckhart, only through destruction of one's egotism can the soul find its way to God. "Wo die Kreatur endet, da beginnt Gott zu sein" (Where the creature ends, there God begins to be), he states in one of his sermons.[58] One can understand the paradox of coming "vom Wissen zum Unwissen" (from knowledge to innocence) in a similar way — to him who leaves egotism behind and forgets everything that he knows

---

[55] Numerous pieces of evidence substantiating this can be found in the late letters and essays as well as in Cosima's diaries.

[56] Joseph von Görres, *Die christliche Mystik*, 5 vols. (Regensburg: Manz, 1836–42); August Friedrich Gfrörer, *Geschichte des Urchristentums*, 3 vols., Stuttgart: E. Schweizerhart, 1838.

[57] On Wagner's Eckhart reception, see also Alan David Aberbach, *Wagner's Religious Ideas: A Spiritual Journey* (Lewiston, NY: E. Mellen Press, 1996), 194–203.

[58] Meister Eckhart, *Die deutschen Werke,* ed. Josef Quint (Stuttgart: W. Kohlhammer, 1936–76), 1:92, 7ff.

(and included is also forgetting God), is revealed the working of the divine will. Perhaps Wagner thought of Parzival here, the prototype of innocent mankind, who precisely because he is a fool and forgets himself, that is, his own ego, is predestined to resolve the conflict of the other human beings, who are caught up in their egotism and with themselves. Thus the fool can rise to higher knowledge because of his innocence. There can be no doubt that Wagner interpreted the medieval mystics in a Schopenhauerian way and saw in their teachings Schopenhauer's postulate of the negation of the will. "Das Schweigen aller Vorstellung bringt die beseligende Ruhe der Seele hervor, zu dieser Ruhe zu kommen ist Christus der Weg" (The silencing of all representation brings a blessed peace to the soul, and Christ is the way to achieve this rest), Wagner said to Cosima on October 27, 1873 (*CT* 1:744). This refers to Martin Luther, but Wagner's reading of Meister Eckhart and also his study of the Indian mystics have other connotations as well: the "Schweigen aller Vorstellung" (silencing of representation) is the first goal of Buddhist meditation.[59]

Wagner returned repeatedly to a philosophical understanding of God. He believed, "die Wahrheit zu sehen, nicht mehr den Schein der Dinge, macht den Gott aus" (God consists of seeing truth, and not just the appearance of things; *CT* 2:376). This obviously comes from an anthropological perspective. Thus Wagner does not conceive of the divinity of Christ literally in the sense that Christ is descended from the highest deity, who has created the world, but rather felt that Christ was solely human — but He was the perfect human being. Therein rested His divinity. Wagner also followed among other sources August Friedrich Gfrörer's comprehensive *Geschichte des Urchristentums,* which he read in 1874–75, and through which he became acquainted with Jewish mysticism and the Kabbala.[60] Gfrörer wrote:

> Ich verstehe unter Gottes Sohn nicht das metaphysische, menschlicher Erfahrung ferne liegende Wesen der hergebrachten Dogmatik, sondern ich bezeichne damit die sittliche und geistige Vollkommenheit, durch welche sich Christus von anderen Menschen unterscheidet.[61]

---

[59] In the later twentieth century the parallels between Meister Eckhart and far eastern mysticism were investigated more closely for the first time. See Shitsuteru Ueda, *Die Gottesgeburt in der Seele und der Durchbruch zur Gottheit* (Gütersloh: G. Mohn, 1965).

[60] See Wolf-Daniel Hartwich, "Jüdische Theosophie in Richard Wagners *Parsifal:* Vom christlichen Antisemitismus zur ästhetischen Kabbala," in *Richard Wagner und die Juden,* ed. Dieter Borchmeyer, Ami Maayani, and Susanne Vill (Stuttgart: Metzler, 2000), 103–22.

[61] Gfrörer, *Geschichte des Urchristentums,* pt. 3, 3.

[I understand God's son as not the metaphysical essence that traditional dogmatism teaches us lies far away from human experience, but rather I use this term to describe the ethical and spiritual perfection through which Christ distinguished Himself from other human beings.]

This is just what Wagner portrayed in his early sketch *Jesus von Nazareth*. Now his conception became more precise: the divinity of Christ is described here by Wagner as a capacity for conscious and voluntary suffering. Therein consisted for Wagner the highest stage of the development of mankind. Working on the basis of Schopenhauer's philosophy, Wagner thus redefines the divinity of Christ. In voluntary suffering, Christ attains

Freiheit durch Aufhebung des rastlos sich selbst widerstreitenden Willens. Der unerforschliche Urgrund dieses Willens, wie er in Zeit und Raum unmöglich aufzuweisen ist, wird uns nur in jener Aufhebung kund, wo er als Wollen der Erlösung göttlich erscheint.[62]

[Freedom through elimination of the will that restlessly strives against itself. The incomprehensible primal foundation of this will, which is impossible to designate in time and space, becomes known to us in this elimination, when, as the will to redemption, it then appears divine.]

Jesus of Nazareth overcomes egotism by consciously taking suffering upon himself. Thereby he succeeds in transcending the laws of nature. Wagner summarizes the unnatural and wondrous nature of this deed with the concept of the divine. For Wagner, Christ becomes the "Inbegriff des bewußt wollenden Leidens selbst . . . das als göttliches Mitleiden durch die ganze menschliche Gattung, als Urquell derselben, sich ergießt" (embodiment of consciously willed suffering . . . which pours forth as divine compassion through all mankind, as its first foundation).[63] The late mysticism of suffering that Wagner devised can only be understood against the background of Schopenhauer's philosophy. On the other hand, it becomes clear that Wagner valued voluntary suffering also as a conscious opposition to the contemporary belief in progress.

Within this framework of ideas, Wagner turned again to *Parzival* in 1875. Here is the introductory passage from his essay "Religion und Kunst" from 1880, when *Parsifal* was largely completed:

Man könnte sagen, daß da, wo die Religion künstlich wird, der Kunst es vorbehalten sei den Kern der Religion zu retten, indem sie die mythischen

---

[62] Richard Wagner, "Heldentum und Christentum," *SSD* 10:281.
[63] Richard Wagner, "Heldentum und Christentum," *SSD* 10:281.

Symbole, welche die erstere im eigentlichen Sinne als wahr geglaubt wissen will, ihrem sinnbildlichen Werthe nach erfaßt, um durch ideale Darstellung derselben die in ihnen verborgene tiefe Wahrheit erkennen zu lassen.[64]

[One could say that when religion has become artificial, it is the task of art to rescue the core of religion by using the mythical symbols, which religion wants us to believe in literally, as just symbols, to make the deep truth that is hidden in them evident through ideal presentation.]

Wagner's final drama is an attempt to rescue the core of religion by transforming it into art, and thereby through "work on myth" to reveal anew the message of Christianity that had in his view become corrupt. He wrote another prose sketch in 1877, as well as the text and much of the music of the first act; the score was finished in 1882. For the most part, Wagner retained the conception of 1865 while making a few important details more specific. In so doing, he oriented the entire action, more emphatically than in the earlier conception, upon an undisclosed redeemer, who is never named but who can be assumed to be Christ. He becomes the hidden center of the stage consecration festival play.

This new perspective is most clearly shown in the part of the drama connected with Kundry and her past. Wagner now links her ancient curse, which in the prose sketch was not described any more specifically, directly with the Passion. Kundry encountered the suffering Christ and laughed at Him. In the prose sketch, Wagner had compared Kundry with the "Eternal Jew" Ahasuerus, who was damned for a similar transgression to be unable to die. But only in the text of 1877 did Wagner for the first time expand upon this parallel. Kundry's restless wanderings now appear as a futile search for a reconciliation with Christ. This seemingly impossible event happens when she is baptized by Parsifal in the third act. In this way, Wagner uses another Christian sacrament in the action of the drama.

In addition, in the final text Wagner more strongly emphasizes another layer of meaning: the drama of the suffering Christ, the unredeemed redeemer. This idea can be found in the earlier sketch in a rudimentary form, but now it becomes associated with a new complex of notions that resulted from Wagner's study of early Christian and Gnostic sects. Christ's death on the cross exemplifies the mystery of compassion to its fullest extent. According to Wagner, there followed no resurrection and no ascension into heaven. Rather, Christ surrenders himself to mankind in the form of the relics that He leaves behind — the cup from which He and His apostles drank at the Last Supper, and the spear that inflicted the

---

[64] "Religion und Kunst," *SSD* 10:211.

wound in His side.[65] The religion of compassion, which Christ founded with the sacrament of the Eucharist and the Last Supper, was then passed from one generation to another by Christ's followers, who lived accordingly. Titurel, Amfortas, and Parsifal are followers of Christ. In failing at this mission and committing his transgression, Amfortas endangers the mission of salvation entrusted to him by Christ and His supreme deed of love. In his "Offenem Schreiben an Herrn Ernst von Weber" (Open letter to Mr. Ernst von Weber), in which he objects to the cruelty of experimenting on animals, Wagner outlines his understanding of Christianity as a religion of compassion and stresses that through the supreme sacrifice of Christ, all living beings can be sure to be redeemed as far as they look to Christ as the exemplar to imitate (*SSD* 10:200; 202). It was important to Wagner that mankind understand its mission as one of "Nachahmung" (imitation) of Christ and that redemption consists in this imitation of Christ. Rather than the almighty God of the Judaic-Christian tradition, Wagner chose as his deity the dependent, suffering god-man who laments the betrayal of a sacred mission. *Parsifal* is about a religion of compassion that is sorely in need of renewal. It is not hard to see this mythical story about an endangered Grail society as an appeal to Wagner's own contemporaries to acknowledge the primal message of Christianity and to gain some inspiration from it.

A comment that Wagner made to Cosima on February 27, 1880 shows that he considered his last music drama as a drama about Christ: "Nach Tisch . . . erzählt er uns seinen Stoff der 'Sieger' ergreifend wundervoll. Das würde er im hohen Alter schreiben, das würde sanfter sein als Parsifal, im Parsifal sei alles jäh, der Heiland am Kreuz, da sei alles blutig" (After dinner . . . he tells us about his *Sieger* in a wonderfully moving way. He says he will write it in his old age, it will be more subtle than *Parsifal,* in *Parsifal* everything is abrupt, the Savior on the cross, it is all bloody; *CT* 2:496). In the text of *Parsifal* one can find only traces of this lamenting and suffering god. The Grail Knights recall, in their liturgy, that Christ's blood was shed for the sins of the world; however, they remember that with joyful hearts. Gurnemanz also emphasizes in his explication of the meaning of Good Friday not the aspect of suffering but the element of redemption; he explicitly corrects Parsifal, who initially understands Good Friday as a day of lament. If the suffering Christ is present in the drama, He is there in suffering mankind: in the pain of Amfortas, in Kundry's restless wanderings, and in Parsifal's experience of the "Gottesklage" (lament of

---

[65] See Dieter Borchmeyer, "Erlösung und Apokatastasis: *Parsifal* und die Religion des späten Wagner," in Borchmeyer, *Richard Wagner: Ahasvers Wandlungen,* 311–12 (Frankfurt am Main: Insel, 2002).

god). His medium is fundamentally a language that goes beyond words: music.

The Sacred Music of *Parsifal*

In 1880, Wagner wrote in the *Bayreuther Blätter* that God is not found in heaven, but rather "im Innern der Menschenbrust" (in the innermost hearts of mankind), and that the German mystics felt this in their enlightenment (Wagner uses the term "leuchtend" [shining] to describe their realization). Because God has been driven from the modern world, Wagner writes, "ließ er uns zu seinem ewigen Andenken die Musik zurück" (He left behind music to remember Him by; *SSD* 10:30). On October 22, 1882, Wagner said to Cosima, obviously with *Parsifal* in mind, "Christus kann man nicht malen, aber in Tönen kann man ihn wiedergeben" (One cannot paint Christ, but one can express Him in music; *CT* 2:1029). While Wagner's stage consecration festival play clearly presents a text that invites a Christian interpretation, we can look to the music for expressive and rhetorical means that convey Christian ideas such as suffering and compassion. In the following interpretation, I have sought to show how the music can be regarded as embodying Christian ideas as Wagner understood them.

The sacred music of *Parsifal* draws on older traditions of church music and combines these with more advanced features of modern music — with a highly differentiated, psychologically motivated technique of leitmotivs, with the expanded capacity of the large orchestra to create lush sounds, and with the harmonic expressivity of *Tristan*. Traces of sacred music specific to Christianity are to be found throughout the score: in musical citations like the "Dresden Amen," for example, which sounds in the parallel sixths of the Grail motive. This was a part of the sacred liturgy; Felix Mendelssohn had used it in his Reformation Symphony. The polyphony of the Faith motive recalls traditions of baroque church music. The choruses of the Grail Knights in the first act employ stylistic features of classical vocal polyphony as it was used by Palestrina. The Buddhist aspects of the text recede therefore somewhat into the background, since there was no musical language with which Wagner could express them. (According to a statement of his, this was one of the reasons that he later gave up trying to set *Die Sieger* to music).[66]

Wagner's various ways of using spiritual music of the past brings to mind the original meaning of the word "religio": a sacred event that happened in

---

[66] See *CT* 2:659 (entry of 6 January 1881) and 1007 (entry of 27 September 1882).

114 ♦ Ulrike Kienzle

the past. With these referential musical features, the drama celebrates religion as cult and rite. The characteristics of modern music, by contrast, serve to express the psychological conflicts of the figures in the drama. It is no accident that the most conflicted and the most tormented characters are given the most advanced music: Kundry, Amfortas, and Klingsor.

The Communion Theme

Two basic musical ideas can be associated with Christ in *Parsifal:* the Communion theme and the lament of the Savior. The Communion theme, with which the work begins, is later, during the liturgy of the Grail ceremony, associated with the sacramental words "Nehmet hin meinen Leib, nehmet hin mein Blut, um unsrer Liebe willen" (Take of my body, take of my blood, for the sake of our love). It is presented as a citation, as if Christ himself is speaking. Wagner described this theme to King Ludwig II as "Liebe" (love), while referring to the three virtues faith, love, and hope, which he thought to be at the core of the Christian religion (*DEAP,* 45; *SSD* 12:347).

The structure of the theme is complex (see ex. 3.1). It consists of four parts that are organically connected with each other. The rising triad at the beginning (1) is a simple, universal, primal element of major and minor tonal music. The key of A♭ major has often been considered since the eighteenth century as the key of the mystical. Wagner seems to have built on these associations, especially in his use of A♭ major and minor in the music associated with the realm of night in *Tristan und Isolde.* As the Communion theme opens in A♭ major, the melodic rise to the sixth scale degree lends sensitivity to the theme, placing a certain harmonic emphasis on pitches belonging to the submediant triad of F minor. The second part of

* Note: B. designates comments by Wagner as recorded by Felix Mottl.

Example 3.1: Beginning of prelude, Act 1

the theme (2) emphasizes the seventh degree, G, and redefines this pitch as the dominant of C minor; this gives rise to a highly expressive, dark sound. This internal musical idea is later developed independently to express the agony of Amfortas. Hans von Wolzogen, who first systematized and explicated Wagner's so-called leitmotives, accordingly named it the *"Schmerzensfigur"* (Pain motive).[67] After this expressive inflection, the harmony returns to A♭ major. The next motivic element is a rising scale segment from A♭ to D♭ that often assumes — together with the following concluding portion of the theme — a dramatic association with the spear (3). The theme continues in a syncopated downward motion to B♭, and it concludes by floating onto the third, C. (4). If we already sense in these six measures that Wagner is attempting to convey the notion of suffering in the theme's central section, we may also feel that the concluding segment suggests a promising response or outcome to this suffering.

From this multi-faceted theme a wide net of musical relationships unfolds. The Communion theme is central to the music of *Parsifal*. Many leitmotivs relate to this theme or derive from it through fragmentation, variation, or contrast. The semantic dimension of the leitmotivs in *Parsifal* is multilayered and ambiguous. Through a process of combination and interweaving, different connections and meanings are constituted. In his last music drama, Wagner develops a compositional technique that could even be described as cabbalistic, insofar as he pervasively recombines melodic elements, with the result that everything ultimately seems to refer to everything else.[68] Such open-endedness lends to the work enigmatic

---

[67] Hans von Wolzogen, *Thematischer Leitfaden durch die Musik des "Parsifal" nebst einem Vorworte über den Sagenstoff des Wagner'schen Dramas* (Leipzig: Gebrüder Senf, 1882), 17. Much has been written about the problem of naming the leitmotives; I am using here the names that have become most familiar from Wolzogen's study.

[68] In addition, the harmonic structures have their own semantic connotations. On the music of *Parsifal*, see especially Alfred Lorenz, *Der musikalische Aufbau von Richard Wagners "Parsifal"* (Berlin: Max Hesses Verlag, 1933; repr. Tutzing: Verlag Hans Schneider, 1966); Hans-Joachim Bauer, *Wagners "Parsifal": Kriterien der Kompositionstechnik* (Munich: Musikverlag E. Katzbichler, 1977); and more recently William Kinderman's studies "Wagner's *Parsifal*: Musical Form and the Drama of Redemption," *The Journal of Musicology* 4 (1986–87): 431–46; and "Dramatic Recapitulation and Tonal Pairing in Wagner's *Tristan und Isolde* and *Parsifal*," in *The Second Practice of Nineteenth-Century Tonality*, ed. William Kinderman and Harald Krebs (Lincoln and London: U of Nebraska P, 1996), 195–214. Also see the essays by Claus-Steffen Mahnkopf and Bernd Asmus in *Richard Wagner: Konstrukteur der Moderne*, ed. Claus-Steffen Mahnkopf (Stuttgart: Klett-Cotta, 1999).

qualities. The music of *Parsifal* is hard to decipher; it refuses to fully divulge its secrets.

Several musical factors work together to create the aura of the sacred that radiates from the Communion theme — the unison intonation that rises from the mystical darkness of silence; the recollection of Gregorian chant, which sounds here in the expressive tonality of the late nineteenth century; the syncopations that are veiled by the meter; and the instrumentation, which dampens the colors of the woodwinds by the bright sound of the strings. The theme unfolds in an "aura" of upward — and downward — floating A♭ major figurations in many kinds of rhythmical combinations, which makes the music seem to convey a transcendental moment. The melody of the Communion theme dissolves into pure sound. As Theodor W. Adorno wrote, "Es ist, als suchte der *"Parsifal"*-Stil nicht bloß die musikalischen Gedanken darzustellen, sondern deren Aura mitzukomponieren" (It is as if the *"Parsifal"* style sought not merely to convey the musical ideas, but to compose their aura along with them).[69]

The "Heilandsklage"

In the last part of the prelude, following the exposition of the Grail and Faith motives, the Communion theme is transformed. It is rendered in a musical language that has a sensitive, chromatic harmony and a surging sequential presentation reminiscent of passages in *Tristan und Isolde*. Before the curtain opens, Wagner moves towards a more worldly type of dramatic conflict, developing elements from the opening Communion theme. Beginning in measure 77, the musical progression seems to stand still, with a connection to what has sounded before temporarily suspended.[70] The pedal-point on A♭ serves as a bridge between the preceding middle section of the prelude and a new statement of the Communion

---

[69] Adorno, "Zur Partitur des 'Parsifal'," in *Theodor W. Adorno: Musikalische Schriften*, vol. 4 (Frankfurt: Suhrkamp, 1982); reprinted in Attila Csampai and Dietmar Holland, eds., *Richard Wagner: Parsifal: Texte, Materialien, Kommentare*, 192 (Reinbeck bei Hamburg: Rowohlt, 1984). For a discussion of Adorno's approach to Wagner's late style, see Anthony Barone, "Richard Wagner's *Parsifal* and the Theory of Late Style," *Cambridge Opera Journal* 7 (1995), 37–54.

[70] The score of *Parsifal* is cited from the complete works: Richard Wagner, *Sämtliche Werke*, ed. Carl Dahlhaus, vol. 14: *Parsifal*, ed. Egon Voss and Martin Geck (Mainz: Schott, 1972). In subsequent references, the first number refers to the act; the second number refers to the measure. The musical examples follow the piano score by Felix Mottl (Leipzig: Peters, 1914).

theme, now heard above the deep tones of a string tremolo on F, and intoned solely by the woodwinds (1, 79). Through the addition of the sixth, F, to the tonic A♭, the music is darkened toward F minor. The theme is not continued to the end, but ends instead with the Pain motive, which is repeated with a shift of the deepest note to D♭ followed by a rise to F♭, upon which the ensuing G♭ major chord sounds alienating and grating. The process culminates in several stages with new harmonic changes at intervals of a minor third. String *tremoli* and accentuation by the percussion in *pianissimo* underscore the expressive, agonizing character of the music. At last the Communion theme continues with the spear motive (1, 95). Immediately thereafter, the spear motive is developed, in polyphonic sequences, loosened from the context of the Communion theme. In such a process, it is as if the Communion theme is formally "deconstructed" and fragmented into its component parts.

The goal of this development is the motive that Hans von Wolzogen designated as the "*Heilandsklage*" (Savior's lament) in connection with its texted appearance during Parsifal's identification with Amfortas in the second act (ex. 3.2).

With its characteristic turn figure, the *Heilandsklage* becomes the expression of an eloquent lament, an individual expression of a subject rendered in instrumental recitative. In the context of the sparse ornamentation of the *Parsifal* score, this figure is anything but a playful decoration, and represents a poignant means of expression. Here Wagner builds on a long musical tradition. Carl Philipp Emmanuel Bach (1714–88) recommended the use of the musical turn to intensify musical expression, especially in the imitation of speech in recitative passages of a free fantasy, passages that have the character of a lament involving a direct expression of feeling.

In Wagner's programmatic explanation of the *Parsifal* prelude, he wrote about the last part of the prelude as follows: "Da noch einmal aus Schauern der Einsamkeit erbebt die Klage des liebenden Mitleides: das Bangen, der heilige Angstschweiß des Ölberges, das göttliche Schmerzensleiden des Golgatha" (There once more from the shudders of solitude sounds the lament of loving compassion: the fear, the sacred

Example 3.2: Prelude, Act 1, mm. 97–99

agony on the Mount of Olives, the divine suffering of Golgatha; *DEAP*, 46; *SSD* 12:347). The beginning and end of the prelude may be regarded as representing two different aspects of the Christian drama of salvation: the instigation of the Eucharist and thereby the foundation of the Christian religion, and the representation of a compassionate, self-sacrificing redeemer.

This connection is rendered more explicit at the climax of the communion ceremony as the Grail is uncovered. The *Heilandsklage* sounds with the soft musical turn, as a light from above illuminates the blood in the Grail, causing it to glow (1, 1470–78). Here the lament of the Savior develops out of the Communion theme with its mystical aura, serving as an aural symbol of the self-sacrificing Christ and as the musical counterpart of the revelation symbolized by light.

In the Transformation music of the first act we hear the *Heilandsklage* in a very different way. In a complex polyphonic manner that characterizes the labyrinthine path to the Grail Temple, a powerful instrumental scream suddenly breaks through (1, 1123). Once more, several motivic layers are simultaneously stacked up (ex. 3.3).

Example 3.3: Transformation Music, Act 1

A relationship to the earlier motivic complex from the prelude is immediately evident, but its character is fully changed:

1) The theme develops not gradually from the spear motive, but instead is initiated by an emphatic octave leap. A *fortissimo* C♯-minor sonority yields to downward chromatic motion through parallel thirds, which is shrilly orchestrated with woodwinds and horns. The syncopated rhythm opposes the meter and halts the forward motion. Hans von Wolzogen calls this motivic form the "*Wehelaute*" (sounds of pain); in the course of the drama it will gain a particular meaning and in certain dramatic situations takes the place of the *Heilandsklage*.[71] The *Wehelaute* motive does not lead into a subtle musical turn as the *Heilandsklage* does in the prelude. Instead, a quarter note E♯ is heard at the end of its second measure, and then the motive continues with a rising third, which is followed by a downward motion in whole tones, then in half tones, before it ebbs away.
2) Against the background of the syncopations of the *Wehelaute* motive, a motive sounds in the middle register that is strikingly orchestrated with trumpets, percussion, and celli (and in part also the woodwinds). The energetic leap of a fourth and concluding downward triplet motion can be recognized as a variation of the Amfortas motive.
3) A third motivic element sounds a jagged configuration in the violins, which begins with a rapid *fortissimo* rising scale followed by upward leaps of a fifth and tritone (1, 1123).

Following this dramatic outburst a soft string passage marked "ausdrucksvoll" (expressive) intones a thematic variation whose rising turn-figure reminds us of the turn-figure sounded in the prelude (1, 1131–32). The *Wehelaute* form of the *Heilandsklage* is then played twice (beginning on D minor and F minor sonorities; 1, 1134 and 1, 1137) most emphatically, before the musical tension is resolved and the Grail bells ring to announce the arrival at the Grail temple.

As it is articulated here, the *Heilandsklage* harmonically resembles a piece of Baroque music with its sequences of falling fifths. Yet because of its chromatic augmentation with secondary tones, it gains a specifically modern and alienated aural character.[72] The result is a paradoxical combination of the archaic and the modern. Similarly, the motivic structures are archaic in their employment of Baroque topoi of weeping and lament (in the downward motion of thirds in the *Wehelaute*) as well as in the use of the ornamented scale passage or *tirata* and the leaps of a tritone, which recall the topoi of Baroque opera; yet modern in the polyrhythmic nature

---

[71] Wolzogen, *Thematischer Leitfaden*, 35.
[72] See Lorenz, *Der musikalische Aufbau von Richard Wagners "Parsifal,"* 67.

of the motivic layers and the expressive force of the instrumental screams. Wagner's characterization quoted above, "in *Parsifal* everything is abrupt, the Savior on the cross, it is all bloody," evidently refers to the *Heilands-klage* and related ideas, which assume outstanding dramatic significance.

The *Heilandsklage* later appears in the choral passages of the young boys singing from the dome: "Den sündigen Welten, mit tausend Schmerzen, wie einst sein Blut geflossen" (as once His blood was painfully shed for the sinful world). A repetition of the theme occurs at the words "dem Erlösungs-helden sei nun mit freudigem Herzen mein Blut vergossen" (my blood shall now be shed with a joyful heart for the redeeming hero; 1, 1205–9, ex. 3.4).

Example 3.4: Grail Scene, Act 1

Wagner connects the *Heilandsklage* here with text that refers to Christ's self-sacrifice. The theme that Wagner had shaped in the prelude as a ponderous lament and in the Transformation music as a dramatic outburst now sounds in an atmosphere of mysterious sanctity and prophecy. Strangely contrary to the atmosphere of the sacred in classical vocal polyphony is the expressive harmony of the chorus, with its half-diminished seventh at "Blut," a sounding variant of the "Tristan Chord." In its chromaticism, this passage contrasts strongly with the diatonicism of the previous chorus.

The Lament of Amfortas and Parsifal's Enlightenment

As a priest figure who celebrates the Grail ceremony as a cultic repetition of the Last Supper, Amfortas is a representative of Christ and is identified somewhat mystically with him. I maintain that this remains the case despite Amfortas's "fall" and his "original sin," which betray this role. That Christ and Amfortas are inextricably bound together is reflected by the circumstance that Amfortas was wounded with the same weapon and in the same place as Christ. Therefore Amfortas suffers not only physically (from the pain of the wound) but spiritually (from his awareness of his guilt). Complex psychological processes, linking the drama about Christ with the drama of the fallen king, are made explicit for the first time in the second act, in Parsifal's response to Kundry's seduction, which develops the motivic complex of the *Heilandsklage* established in Amfortas's lament.[73] In act 2, we realize that Amfortas's suffering is but one layer of meaning bound up with Christ's suffering as expressed in the *Heilandsklage,* whose deeper significance is now revealed as a divine lament intended for the ears of a redeemer.[74]

Amfortas anticipates the connections and deeper meanings that will be revealed in act 2 when he yearns for redemption: "aus tiefster Seele Heilesbuße zu ihm muß ich gelangen" (from a contrition deep within my soul, I turn toward Him; 1, 1335 ff.): In his torment, Amfortas longs for Christ,

---

[73] For further analytical details of these scenes and the relationships between them, see Katherine Syer's chapter "Unseen Voices: Wagner's Musical-Dramatic Shaping of the Grail Scene of Act 1" in this volume.

[74] While Hans von Wolzogen has seized on this central significance in his choice of labels for the *Heilandsklage* motive, one also encounters "Sündenqualmotiv" (motive of the torment of sin), which focuses more on the motive's role as it appears in the *Amfortasklage.*

for his "Weihegruße" (blessing). Here the motive of the *Heilandsklage* sounds in a fragmented, faltering form broken by rests. The figures used are common in the Baroque tradition of the Doctrine of the Affects — the sighs or "sospiri" designate the affects of hesitation and anxiety. The motive continues with the sixths characteristic of the Grail Realm, which signify the hope for a confrontation and reconciliation with Christ.[75] The god who is here addressed is a forgiving god; the Grail King who is tormented with remorse makes a gesture of pleading.

The parallelism of Amfortas's wound and the wound of Christ is emphasized at his reference to the spear "der dort dem Erlöser die Wunde stach, aus der mit blut'gen Tränen, der Göttliche weint' ob der Menschheit Schmach" (that wounded the side of the Savior, from which the Divine wept bloody tears for the shame of mankind; 1, 1369). The text of this passage recalls, with its blood- and wound mysticism, the eighteenth-century tradition of Pietism. Even the oratorio texts of Johann Sebastian Bach (for example, the tenor aria "Erwäge, wie sein blutgefleckter Rücken in allen Stücken dem Himmel gleich geht" [Consider how His blood-spattered back has risen into heaven] from the *St. John Passion*) are characterized by an almost sensual pleasure in viewing the wounds of Christ. Quite differently, Amfortas's meditation on the physical sufferings of Christ is not accompanied by an assurance of his own redemption; instead he is confronted with the awareness of his own sinfulness. This too is a theme in Protestant theology: the sight of the crucified Christ arouses in the believer a deep feeling of contrition, because the original sin of mankind was the precondition that ultimately caused the suffering of Christ.

The climax and conclusion of Amfortas's great lament is a pressing plea for compassion and forgiveness, directed at Christ as the "all-merciful one": "Du Allerbarmer, ach Erbarmen! Nimm mir mein Erbe, schliesse die Wunde." (O All-Merciful One, have mercy on me! Take this inheritance from me, close the wound; 1, 1393–99). The *Wehelaute* form of the *Heilandsklage* is at the heart of this material, framed by two appearances of the spear motive that recall the prelude. The following "Seufzerfiguren" (sigh figures; 1, 1399) also correspond to a similar passage at the end of the prelude (1, 101). Unlike that earlier passage, these now lead to the prophecy "Durch Mitleid wissend, der reine Tor, harre sein, den ich erkor" (Made wise through compassion, the pure fool, wait for him whom I have chosen) — the crucial response that Christ gives to the despairing pleas of Amfortas.

---

[75] Similarly, Kundry's hope for a re-encounter with Christ will also be accompanied by the Grail motive, as is the musical representation of Parsifal's wanderings in the prelude to the third act.

Parsifal's initial reaction to the *Amfortasklage* is expressed primarily through stage directions that suggest stances and wordless motions: "er [kann] Amfortas sehen. Er folgt dessen Gebaren mit starrer Aufmerksamkeit" (He can see Amfortas. He follows his gestures with a fixed stare).[76] A later direction states: "Parsifal hatte bei dem vorangehenden stärksten Klagerufe des Amfortas eine heftige Bewegung nach dem Herzen gemacht, welches er krampfhaft eine Zeitlang gefaßt hielt" (Parsifal had grasped at his heart during the most powerful cries of lament that Amfortas expressed, and he kept this stance for awhile); finally he stands there "wie erstarrt und regungslos" (transfixed and motionless).[77] When Gurnemanz asks, "Weißt du, was du sahst?" (Do you know what you just saw?) Parsifal does not answer, but he grasps at his heart ("faßt sich krampfhaft am Herzen"), thus repeating a spontaneous gesture of compassion. To accompany this, the orchestra plays an abbreviated version of the *Heilandsklage* — the *Wehelaute* — followed by the "Mitleidsmotiv," which had also accompanied Parsifal's reaction to the death of the swan after Gurnemanz had scolded him (1, 1640–43). Parsifal had learned something then, but his realization remained in a preconscious state of feeling and could not yet be expressed in words.

When Parsifal meets Kundry in the second act, he learns his name and therefore gains an identity and self-consciousness. He attains insight into his guilt in the death of his mother. His regret about forgetting his mother is associated then with his neglect of another responsibility: "Ha! Was alles vergaß ich wohl noch? Wess' war ich je noch eingedenk?" (Ha! What have I forgotten? What am I remembering since then?; 2, 952–54). This refers to the lament of Amfortas and to the spear. The orchestra plays the motive of the *Heilandsklage* in the variation from the prelude to accompany this — the "Klage des liebenden Mitleides" (lament of loving compassion) with its triple exposition of the Spear motive and the Compassion motive. The usual musical turn in which the tension should be resolved is here replaced, significantly enough, by an abbreviated version of the Kundry motive (2, 955) — an indication that in feeling sensual desire for the first time, Parsifal becomes aware of the connection between the suffering of Amfortas and that of the redeemer. Parsifal's mission, of which he has not yet become conscious, consists not merely in the healing of Amfortas, but also in the redemption of the redeemer, the rescue of the relic from guilt-stained hands (2, 1071). Because Wagner felt that God is to be

---

[76] According to the piano score by Felix Mottl, who jotted down these directions during the rehearsals for the premiere. Mottl's directions can also be found in the Dover reprint of the original Peters full score: see pp. 176–77.

[77] Mottl, piano score, 99.

found "im Inneren der Menschenbrust" (deep in the human heart), his use of the *Heilandsklage* here can be understood literally: as the voice of the suffering god coming from within the human heart and the subconscious of the human being, and as a call to Parsifal to become conscious of his mission.

This happens in several stages. From the seduction attempt his erotic urges are awakened, but in response he becomes one with the suffering Amfortas. Thus he sees that the gratification of sexual drives merely reinforces an egotism that cannot possibly be satisfied, and realizes the universality of suffering. According to a stage direction that Wagner's musical assistant Heinrich Porges inserted into his score during a rehearsal for the premiere, Wagner said, "Jetzt sieht Parsifal auf einmal, wie die ganze Welt ein Schlachtopfer ist" (Now Parsifal suddenly sees that the whole world is a place of sacrificial slaughter; *DEAP*, 203). At this point Parsifal comes to the same recognition that had moved Christ to give His life, becoming the "Sühnungsopfer" (expiatory sacrifice) for suffering mankind. "Die Wahrheit zu sehen, nicht mehr den Schein der Dinge, macht den Gott aus" (God consists in seeing truth, not just the appearance of things), Wagner said to Cosima (*CT* 2:376). Parsifal, too, realizes this truth. Thus, he becomes a follower of Christ, and he even becomes, for a Schopenhauerian moment, one with Him.

Wagner's orchestral commentary underscores this "unio mystica" by having the music of the *Heilandsklage* accompany Parsifal's outburst in various different ways. Immediately after Parsifal's words, "Amfortas! Die Wunde! Sie brennt in meinem Herzen" (Amfortas! The wound! It is burning in my heart), we hear the *Heilandsklage,* as he sings "Oh! Klage! Klage! Furchtbare Klage! Aus tiefstem Herzen schreit sie mir auf!" (Oh! Awful lament! It is screaming from the depths of my heart!) This seems to refer to the lament of Amfortas. When we recall Wagner's statement that God resides within the breast of humankind, thus in the heart, where Parsifal hears this lament, we can interpret the music of the *Heilandsklage* that sounds here as referring to the redeemer or Christ figure. The lament of the suffering Amfortas is one with the lament of the suffering god. A similar conclusion can be drawn about the next passage, in which the *Heilandsklage* resounds: "Die Wunde sah ich bluten, nun blutet sie in mir!" (I saw the wound bleed; now it is bleeding in me!) The music that designates pain, along with the motive of the spear, leads directly into the *Wehelaute* motive, which ends abruptly. If Parsifal's cry "O Qual der Liebe" (O torment of love) is underscored by the *Wehelaute* (2, 1037–40), this suggests that the music harbors more than Parsifal himself can express: it is not the torment of sexuality that Amfortas has suffered that is the goal of the psychological process, but rather (as Wagner's stage direction indicates) the recognition of the world as a place of sacrificial slaughter, whereby the experiences of Christ's lament are implied.

In a third stage, the meaning of Parsifal's experience finally becomes clear to him. This recognition happens through the remembrance of the uncovering of the Grail, which Parsifal here re-lives from Amfortas's perspective ("Es starrt der Blick dumpf auf das Heilsgefäß" [He stares transfixed at the sacramental vessel; 2, 1045–47]). The music repeats, albeit in altered ways, the most important stations in Amfortas's monologue, in which the *Heilandsklage* has already played a significant role. The fusion of Parsifal's experience in the Grail Temple with Amfortas's lament and the uncovering of the Grail leads Parsifal to the recognition that Christ, not Amfortas, is the central focus: "Des Heilands Klage da vernehm ich, die Klage um das entweihte Heiligtum" (I hear the lament of the Savior, the lament over the desecrated sanctuary; see ex. 3.5).

Example 3.5: Parsifal's response to Kundry's kiss, Act 2

Parsifal hears words that were not actually spoken in the first act, but hinted at through the music. Through the suffering of Amfortas, Parsifal now experiences a breakthrough to mystic insight. In so doing he explicates a substratum of the drama that concerns the undisclosed redeemer and, by implication, Christ. The music of this passage includes a reordering and reversal of motivic elements from the Communion theme. The expression of the "Gottesklage," the words of the Savior, is accompanied by the repeatedly fragmented and finally integrated Communion theme. The direct speech of Christ is conveyed here and set into relief by quotation marks: "Erlöse, rette mich aus schuldbefleckten Händen!" (Redeem me, save me, from guilt-stained hands!).

Kundry's Encounter with Christ

Less complex but dramatically just as moving is Kundry's experience of Christ. As early as the prelude of the second act, many interpolations of the *Wehelaute* in combination with the motives of Klingsor and Kundry seem to suggest that Christ is also present for the antagonists of the Grail Realm. The "blut'ge Tränen" (bloody tears), with which the Divine wept for the shame of mankind are also meant for Klingsor, who committed a perversion of the negation of the will to life by violently silencinghis sexual urges[78] and for Kundry too. The first sounds she makes in the second act are associated with the *Heilandsklage*: at the very moment she emits a piercing scream, the *Wehelaute* motive sounds (2, 143), before her characteristic motive is heard. Shortly thereafter, a variation on the *Heilandsklage* sounds as attention is drawn to her "Sehnen" (longing; 2, 186–90).[79]

That the *Heilandsklage* emerges here and in other places that concern Kundry's hope for redemption (2, 208, 274, 281, 286) encourages us to contemplate the causal moment of her endless reincarnations before she reveals the actual events to Parsifal: "Ich sah ihn — ihn — und lachte . . . da traf mich sein Blick" (I saw Him — Him — and laughed . . . then His glance rested upon me) (ex. 3.6).

The text only hints at the immense significance of this encounter, but the music expresses a level of feeling suggesting that Kundry's recall

---

[78] The *Heilandsklage* sounds at his words "Furchtbare Not" in 2, 236–37.

[79] For an interpretation of Kundry's psychological conflict, which I will not discuss in detail here, see my essay, "Komponierte Weiblichkeit im *Parsifal*: Kundry," in *Das Weib der Zukunft: Frauengestalten und Frauenstimmen bei Richard Wagner,* ed. Susanne Strasser-Vill (Stuttgart: Metzler, 2000), 153–90.

Example 3.6: Kundry's narrative of her laughter, Act 2

involves understanding that she has gained through time but that she lacked altogether at the original moment. The suffering Christ is signified by the characteristic drum that had already played an important part in the first presentation of the *Heilandsklage*, as well as by the rhythmically slow, formally compressed Communion theme. When she describes Christ's glance falling upon her, a psychologically exceptional moment occurs that is musically "staged." Kundry demonstrates awareness of the compassion-ate nature of Christ's glance, and she soon reveals that she knows her atonement is bound up with a re-encounter with the glance of "loving compassion." On the symbolic level of the music, this re-encounter occurs in the third act. After Kundry is baptized, the chords leading into the "Karfreitagszauber" (Good Friday spell) music sound in the orchestra with additional accents (the *pizzicato* of the violoncellos) joined to the expres-sive turn figure of the *Heilandsklage* (3, 623–24). Kundry's spasmodic laughter is now replaced by her tears. The ensuing Good Friday music expresses a utopia reconciling mankind and nature, mediated through the loving self-sacrifice of the suffering Christ.

"Erlösung dem Erlöser"

The *Heilandsklage* resounds for the last time after Amfortas is healed, now closely tied to the Spear: "Der deine Wunde durfte schließen, ihm seh ich heil'ges Blut entfließen in Sehnsucht nach dem verwandten Quelle, der dort fließt in des Grales Welle" (I see holy blood flowing from the one who should heal your wound, in longing for the kindred fount that is flowing from the Grail; 3, 1069–80). Here we encounter once more a mysticism that recalls the tradition of Pietism. The essence of the suffering of Christ, preserved in the blood, comes alive when reunited with the spear, and fem-inine and masculine principles are united. This moment of revelation again involves a soft glowing of the Grail and a growing light from above. The return of the spear and the resultant reuniting of the relics forms a *restitu-tio in integrum,* with matters coming full circle.[80] The conclusion of this cycle finally resolves the pain and suffering with which the *Heilandsklage* has been so closely connected throughout the drama.

Wagner's last music drama ends with the formula "Höchsten Heiles Wunder: Erlösung dem Erlöser" (Supreme miracle of salvation: Redemp-tion for the Redeemer). Much has been written about the possible mean-ings of these words. In the context of Wagner's understanding of Christianity, one could postulate the following: the music of the *Heilands-klage* shows us the ongoing cyclical suffering of Christ as humankind re-learns compassion, with Christ suffering along with humankind. In this sense, the redemption of humankind is also the redemption of Christ. But this is just one facet of a larger complex of ideas. The intended outcome of Christ's voluntary deed of suffering is fulfilled through imitation. At the onset of the drama, Amfortas and the Grail Knights have failed to follow

---

[80] See: Borchmeyer, "Erlösung und Apokatastasis," 39.

Christ's example of loving compassion. They remain trapped in isolation; they fall prey to sensual seduction and to the egotistical love of self. They react to Klingsor's challenge with inappropriate violence. Therefore, they have undermined Christ's redemptive deed. When Parsifal takes upon himself the conflicts of the guilt-ridden Kundry and Amfortas, thus gaining the ability to redeem them, he restores power to Christ's redemptive deed. Parsifal becomes, as Wagner wrote in a letter to Mathilde Wesendonk, "Erlöser der Welt" (redeemer of the world). More than that, he redeems the Redeemer Himself, and becomes "Erlöser dem Erlöser."

This multi-leveled redemption is what the music expresses as we hear the last words of the drama. "Höchsten Heiles Wunder" employs a variation of the prophecy, "Durch Mitleid wissend der reine Tor" (the pure fool, made wise through compassion), which has now been fulfilled by Parsifal. By contrast, "Erlösung dem Erlöser" involves a variation of the Communion theme and can be interpreted as expressing Christ's redemption. The theme no longer leads into the *Schmerzensfigur;* instead the melody leads upward to a diatonic resolution. In this context, Parsifal and Christ are inextricably bound together — Parsifal is both the pure fool made wise through compassion and the redeemer of the Redeemer. He is an imitation of Christ and he completes Christ's deed of salvation through this imitation. This likeness becomes clear for the first time when Parsifal brings back the regained spear, after long wanderings, "unentweiht" (undesecrated). At this juncture the Communion theme sounds without a trace of suffering and lament for the first time (3, 332 ff.).

The conclusion of *Parsifal* reconciles many conflicts and suggests some sustainability of the present, as "Erlösung dem Erlöser" is repeated in different ways in a long circle of fifths that leads upward — from D major through A, E, B (C♭ major), and further to G♭. In reaching D♭ major, we arrive at the subdominant of A♭ major, with which the prelude to *Parsifal* began. It is as if the rising circle of fifths carries the listener into exalted regions. The orchestral conclusion of *Parsifal* encompasses an expanded plagal cadence (from subdominant to tonic), from D♭ major harmony to the concluding chords of A♭ major. In Wagner's age, the plagal cadence was a topos of sacred music. Many of Wagner's redemptive conclusions to his operas employ this gesture, often involving the minor subdominant.[81] Yet in the midst of this process, Kundry sinks lifeless to the ground as two D♭ major triads enclose a dynamically emphasized A minor triad (3, 1123–25). A window into another world is briefly opened, into the

---

[81] For a recent consideration of Wagner's use of this cadential formula, see Hermann Danuser, "Musical Manifestations of the End in Wagner and Post-Wagnerian *Weltanschauungsmusik,*" *19th-Century Music* 18/1 (1992), 64–82.

"nirvana" that Kundry has longed for. This musical inflection sounded once before, at the end of the Grail liturgy in the first act. Now it closes the cycle of rebirths, and Kundry enters into the eternal presence of the divine as glimpsed in the Grail ceremony. The melody of the Communion theme, now freed from suffering, has the last word in the drama: "Erlösung dem Erlöser."

Is *Parsifal* a Christian music drama? We need to answer "no" to this question if we wish to regard Wagner's last work as reinforcing the dogmas of the church, whether Protestant or Catholic. However, we can answer "yes" if we take the interwoven paths of medieval and modern mysticism seriously as components of the Christian tradition. Wagner's mysticism derives in part from the philosophy of Schopenhauer and in this respect is a mysticism without God. *Parsifal* thus seems to ask whether it is possible to have any kind of a religion in an irreligious age. Like *Der Ring des Nibelungen* and *Die Meistersinger von Nürnberg*, *Parsifal* is an attempt to rescue the ideals of the age of revolution through art.[82] Such ideals have nevertheless undergone substantial change. In his last music drama, Wagner propounds an ethic of nonviolence and advocates a reconciliation of mankind and nature. His attempt at forming a synthesis of Indian and Christian beliefs participates in an interreligious dialogue that is still being carried out today. Wagner was aware of the problematic nature of such a utopian vision. His longing for metaphysical solutions found a home in his music, where a resounding vision of "nirvana" is somewhat tenable. As an expression of this utopia, the cryptic sentence "Erlösung dem Erlöser" can be read as an assertion, or we can understand it as a call to undertake the redemption of the redeemer.

Translated by Mary A. Cicora

---

[82] See Udo Bermbach, *Der Wahn des Gesamtkunstwerks: Richard Wagners politisch-ästhetische Utopie* (Frankfurt am Main: Fischer Taschenbuch Verlag, 1994).

II. The Music:
Evolution, Structure, Aesthetics

4: The Genesis of the Music

William Kinderman

The Earliest Stages in Composition

Introduction

THE EVOLUTION OF THE TEXT of *Parsifal* spanned several decades, from Wagner's early enthusiasm for the subject at Marienbad in 1845 to the completion of the poem in 1877.[1] The genesis of the music, by contrast, has been shrouded in obscurity; it underwent a much shorter but more concentrated genesis.[2] Wagner's sustained labors on the music began in the late summer of 1877, though certain individual sketches date from the preceding year. The main creative work on the music of *Parsifal* was finished by April of 1879. The writing-out of the autograph score dragged on until January of 1882. This last labor did not normally involve substantial new composition. It consisted instead of elaboration of the material from Wagner's earlier drafts. Nevertheless, in March of 1881, Wagner made extensive additions to the Transformation music of act 1, which necessitated the replacement of pages in

---

[1] For discussions of the evolution of the poem, see the introduction and Mary Cicora's chapter in this volume, and Lucy Beckett's study *Richard Wagner: Parsifal* (Cambridge: Cambridge UP, 1981). As noted elsewhere, Wagner's original acquaintance with Wolfram von Eschenbach's *Parzival* probably even preceded his reading of that work at Marienbad in 1845. On the other hand, Wagner continued to make adjustments to the text even after the first printing of the poem in 1877. The differences between the poem of 1877 and the printed text in the score published in 1883 are listed in Richard Wagner, *Sämtliche Werke*, vol. 30: *Dokumente zur Entstehung und ersten Aufführung des Bühnenweihfestspiels "Parsifal,"* ed. Martin Geck and Egon Voss (Mainz: Schott, 1970), 90–134.

[2] The present chapter incorporates material that appeared in different form in German in my article "Die Entstehung der *Parsifal*-Musik," *Archiv für Musikwissenschaft* 52 (1995), 66–97 and 145–65. I am grateful to Dr. Manfred Eger, former Director of the Nationalarchiv der Richard-Wagner-Stiftung, and to the present Director, Dr. Sven Friedrich, who granted me access to the manuscripts in their rich collection.

the score, since the autograph of this part of the work had already been written out.

In tracing the evolution of the music, we shall consider several different types of manuscripts in detail, including the two drafts for the entire work, the so-called "Kompositionsskizze" and "Orchesterskizze." Although these sources were described by Wagner himself and by many subsequent writers as "Skizzen," or "sketches," we shall refer to them as drafts, since they each present a sustained musical continuity, virtually unbroken from the beginning to the end of an act. The first draft, or "composition draft," is written mainly in pencil, and generally contains three staves to accommodate the vocal and choral parts, or only two, when voices are not involved. The second draft, or "orchestral draft," was made immediately after the first; it is written mainly in ink and also primarily on three staves, though more are sometimes employed, and it contains abbreviated specifications of the orchestration. Wagner worked back and forth between these two drafts as the music was composed, one act at a time. Only much later, after both drafts had been completed for the entire work, was the autograph score begun at all.[3]

Our study of the musical genesis of *Parsifal* begins not with these sources, however, but with the considerable number of shorter, individual musical sketches made shortly before, and sometimes during, Wagner's work on the drafts. In comparison with surviving manuscript sources for Wagner's other works, the quantity of these early musical sketches is especially impressive: in the catalogue of Wagner's works, the *Wagner-Werk-Verzeichnis*, more than seventy items are listed, and even this tabulation is not entirely complete.[4]

---

[3] I follow Robert Bailey in employing this nomenclature, which brings the terms used into line with standard parlance in the study of the compositional process of other composers, such as Beethoven. In the pioneering work on Wagner's manuscripts by former Wagner Archive Director Otto Strobel, the terms "Kompositionsskizze" and "Orchesterskizze" were used, and John Deathridge has preferred to retain that terminology. See Deathridge, "The Nomenclature of Wagner's Sketches," *Proceedings of the Royal Musical Association* 51 (1974–75), 75–83.

[4] In the *Verzeichnis der musikalischen Werke Richard Wagners und ihrer Quellen*, by John Deathridge, Martin Geck, and Egon Voss (Mainz: Schott, 1986), 71 items are listed in addition to the composition draft and the orchestral draft, and several other manuscripts are listed that are no longer accessible. The listing of Wagner's sketches and drafts is contained on pp. 540–44 of the catalogue, and a basic chronological outline of the genesis of the music is provided on pp. 550–52. The cataloguing system used in the present chapter conforms to that used by the Wagner Archive and in the *Wagner-Werk-Verzeichnis*. It was devised by former Wagner

Many of these sketches are preserved on fragments of music paper of irregular dimensions. Nearly all are housed in the Wagner Archive at Bayreuth, where they are divided, rather arbitrarily, into four basic parcels or envelopes. Because of the complications attending these sketches, we shall examine them in considerable detail, and shall undertake to reconstruct their original condition, at least in concept, as a prerequisite to our investigation of the compositional process.[5] Such a reconstruction is essential, since few of the sketchleaves were in this fragmentary condition when Wagner wrote down the musical entries, and at least some of the cutting up of documents may have been done by persons other than Wagner.

The Sketch Fragments and Their Reconstruction

In a study of the *Parsifal* sketches, Gillian Tucker drew attention to the interpretative difficulties posed by these fragments, observing in one case, for instance, that "we have no idea what other sketches were on the original manuscript from which they were taken."[6] For many of the fragments, this problem now no longer exists, since it has been possible, working from the original documents, to reconstruct their original relationship, which serves in turn to facilitate the identification and interpretation of the sketch content. The reconstruction of the *Parsifal* sketch fragments is shown in table 4.1. This material supplements the basic tabulation of sources in the *Wagner-Werk-Verzeichnis*, in which a reconstruction of the sources was not attempted. In the *Verzeichnis*, the sketches are rightly described as having been cut from larger leaves.[7] The material in table 4.1 represents a reversal of this process with the scissors, in that the manuscripts are restored, whenever possible, to their original condition. The accuracy of this source reconstruction is assured by the paper type and sketch content as well as by the cut profiles of the fragments, which fit together much like the pieces of a jigsaw puzzle.

Archive Director Otto Strobel, and was based in turn on Wagner's own cataloguing system for his home library at Wahnfried.

[5] The reconstruction of the fragmentary sketches for *Parsifal* required sustained access to the original documents at the Nationalarchiv der Richard-Wagner-Stiftung, Bayreuth. I am especially grateful to archivist Günter Fischer for his invaluable assistance.

[6] "Wagner's Individual Sketches for *Parsifal*," *Proceedings of the Royal Musical Association* 60 (1983–84), 94.

[7] John Deathridge, Martin Geck, and Egon Voss, *Wagner-Werk-Verzeichnis (WWV): Verzeichnis der musikalischen Werke Richard Wagners und ihrer Quellen* (Mainz: Schott, 1986), 541.

Table 4.1. A reconstruction of the fragmentary sketch manuscripts for Wagner's *Parsifal* (MSS are in the Wagner Archive at Bayreuth unless otherwise noted)

Manuscripts	Content	Reconstructed leaf: % complete
Parcel 1, 7 verso " ", 24v " ", 21v	Act 3	80
Parcel 1, 14 recto " ", 18r	Act 2	80
Parcel 1, 17v " ", 16r	Acts 2, 3	40
Parcel 1, 3r " ", 2r MS in Wagner-Gedenkstätte (Hs 120/MM)	Acts 2, 3	40
Parcel 1, 22r " ", 12r	Act 3	40
Parcel 2, 7r " 1, 12r " ", 5r " ", 20v	Act 3	70
Parcel 2, 11r MS in Strauss-Sammlung, Garmisch	Act 1	100
Parcel 2, 6r " 1, 6r " ", 4v " ", 8r " ", 9r	Act 3	100
Parcel 2, 16r " 1, 11r	Act 3	30
Parcel 2, 9v " ", 10r " ", 4r	Act 1	70
Parcel 3, 5r " ", 1r	Act 3	100

Note: In these reconstructions, the individual sketch manuscripts are listed according to their position on the page, proceeding from top to bottom and from left to right.

In some cases, manuscripts from other collections can be shown to have belonged with the fragments now in the Bayreuth Wagner Archive. Leaf 11 from the second parcel, for instance, originally formed the upper portion of a sketchleaf, the remainder of which is now found in the

Richard Strauss-Sammlung at Garmisch.[8] The Garmisch sketch was once also part of the Bayreuth collection, but it was separated from the other manuscripts in 1934, when Winifred Wagner gave it to Strauss, surely in appreciation of his contributions as conductor at the Bayreuth Festival.[9] Leaves 2 and 3 from the first parcel, on the other hand, belong with a manuscript fragment catalogued as Hs 120/MM housed in a separate collection in the Wagner-Gedenkstätte at Bayreuth.[10] Yet another sketch fragment for the prelude to act 3 of *Parsifal* became separated from its companion manuscripts when Eva Chamberlain glued it onto a page in Wagner's diary, the "brown book."[11]

In all, thirty of the fragmentary manuscripts can be joined with companions, forming parts or wholes of eleven leaves. In two instances, the manuscripts so joined are not directly contiguous, because of the way in which the leaves were cut. In these cases, the manuscripts can nevertheless be reconstructed with certainty on the basis of the barlines and other markings that extend from one manuscript to the other. It can be assumed, furthermore, that some portions of the original sketchleaves for *Parsifal* were lost or discarded when the manuscripts were cut into fragments. In any case, the forty-odd sketch fragments belonged originally to fewer than half that number of leaves.

Several different paper types were used for these sketches, but practically all the reconstructed manuscripts consist of half-sheets containing fifteen staves, a format identical to that used by Wagner in his composition draft. The correspondence in musical content between the sketchleaves and composition draft is intimate and extensive. These sources preserve an extraordinarily detailed record of the musical genesis of *Parsifal*, which can be precisely dated at many points from the material in Cosima Wagner's diaries. It seems clear from these correspondences that nearly all of Wagner's numerous surviving musical sketches date from the period of his

---

[8] I am indebted to the late Alice Strauss for sending me a copy of this sketch.

[9] Strauss conducted *Parsifal* at the Bayreuth Festival during 1933 and 1934. This was not the only time a conductor received a *Parsifal* manuscript as a token of appreciation. A sketchleaf for *Parsifal* from parcel 3 was given to conductor Hans Knappertsbusch on March 9, 1953, as indicated by a note on the front of the envelope. See Deathridge, Geck, and Voss, *Wagner-Werk-Verzeichnis*, 543, 544.

[10] This manuscript fragment has been catalogued as Hs 120/MM in the collection of the Richard Wagner Gedenkstätte, which is kept in the building housing the Wagner Archive.

[11] This sketch was published in Joachim Bergfeld, ed., *Richard Wagner: Das braune Buch: Tagebuchaufzeichnungen 1865 bis 1882* (Zurich: Atlantis, 1975), 96, in an inadequate transcription that renders Parsifal's motive in the top stave unrecognizable.

sustained work on the composition and orchestral drafts, between about the fall of 1877 and spring of 1879. There is nothing to suggest in these sources that any substantial work on the music occurred before 1876, about twenty years after Wagner's well-known sketch for "Parzival" made during the composition of *Tristan und Isolde*.[12]

Plates 4.1 and 4.2 show the recto and verso, or sides A and B respectively, of one of the reconstructed sketchleaves, which comprises five fragments drawn from two different parcels of manuscripts. Here, as elsewhere, the cutting involved not an entirely arbitrary mutilation of

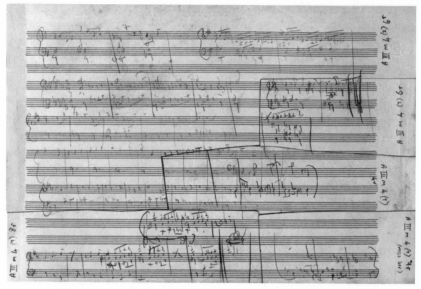

Plate 4.1: Reconstructed worksheet consisting of five manuscript fragments, recto (Side A) Nationalarchiv der Richard-Wagner-Stiftung Bayreuth

---

[12] This sketch appears in the edition of Wagner's letters to Mathilde Wesendonk, edited by Wolfgang Golther, *Richard Wagner an Mathilde Wesendonk: Tagebuchblätter und Briefe 1853–1871* (Berlin: Alexander Duncker Verlag, 1910), facsimile after p. 362, transcription on p. 26. See also Richard Wagner, *Dokumente zur Entstehung und ersten Aufführung des Bühnenweihfestspiels "Parsifal,"* ed. Martin Geck and Egon Voss, vol. 30 of Wagner, *Sämtliche Werke* (Mainz: Schott, 1970), 13. For commentaries on the sketch, see especially Alfred Lorenz, *Der musikalische Aufbau von Richard Wagners "Parsifal"* (Berlin: Max Hesses Verlag, 1933), 12, and Robert Bailey, *The Genesis of "Tristan und Isolde" and a Study of the Sketches and Drafts* (PhD diss., Princeton, 1969), 29–31.

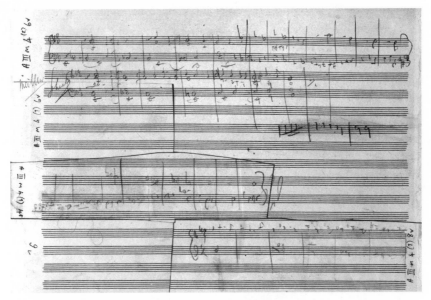

Plate 4.2: Reconstructed worksheet consisting of five manuscript fragments, verso (Side B) Nationalarchiv der Richard-Wagner-Stiftung Bayreuth

the sketchleaf, but an apparent attempt to separate musical entries from their larger context. Inevitably, the attempt was not entirely successful, and through the reconstruction the musical content of some sketches becomes fully comprehensible for the first time since the leaf was dismembered.

The overlapping entries written on the manuscript fragments are characteristic of most of the reconstructed leaves, and indicate that Wagner wrote down most if not all of these sketches before the leaf was cut. Not surprisingly, an affinity in sketch content can also be observed. The sketches on both sides of this reconstructed leaf relate to act 3, and especially to Gurnemanz's narrative of the death of Titurel and the ensuing "Good Friday Spell." No text is in evidence, but the characteristic Öde (wasteland) motive of a falling fifth A–D followed by a falling tritone E–B♭ appears at the top left of side A, on the uppermost system, and in rhythmic diminution further to the right, on the same system. This motive, which is a compressed, dissonant version of the motive of the Temple Bells, is notated at the top left in D minor, which became the tonality associated with Titurel's death; the placement of the motive in this register and key corresponds to the moment in the finished work in Gurnemanz's narrative when he describes how Amfortas refused to again perform the Grail service (at the end of the sentence "Kein Fleh'n, kein Elend seiner Ritter bewog ihm mehr des heil'gen Amt's zu walten"). The other side of the leaf, or side B, contains material for the Good Friday music in the lowest notated system, on MS 8v of Parcel 1, as well as on the top right, written in D Major (this sketch and some of the others appear upside down, and need to be inverted). Another inverted sketch, written on MS 4r of Parcel 1 on the lower half of the leaf, contains an important motivic juxtaposition, with the Prophecy motive followed by the first motive or head of the Communion theme beginning on D♭ and the "Dresden Amen" portion of the Grail motive, such as appears near the end of act 3. The shift in both treble and bass to F♭ four bars from the end of the sketch marks the harmonic inflection corresponding to the A minor chord heard at Kundry's death in the finished work.

Why were this and the other sketchleaves cut into fragments, and by whom? Wagner may not always have been responsible for the cutting, to judge from the inscriptions in other hands found on some of the manuscript fragments. MS 9r, for instance, is inscribed "Parsifal/18ten Dec. 1877," in the hand of Cosima Wagner, who similarly inscribed several other sketch fragments for the work. In some cases, the manuscripts are precisely dated, and it seems likely that the inscriptions were made at the same time that the sketches were cut and removed from their original position on Wagner's sketchleaves.

Another inscribed fragment is entitled "Harmonischer Gang aus Parsifal," and dated "21 Nov. 1877"; the handwriting appears to be that of the pianist Josef Rubinstein, who visited and assisted Wagner around this time.[13] This particular progression was taken into the finished work, in slightly varied form, in Gurnemanz's narrative in act 1 where he describes the founding of the Grail Temple by Titurel. Examination of Cosima Wagner's diary entries for these dates confirms in great detail that Wagner was working on these parts of the score. On November 20 she writes that Wagner played for her Gurnemanz's narrative of the sending of the angel to Titurel, which would indeed have contained the music identified as "Harmonischer Gang aus Parsifal" on the following day.[14] On the twenty-first, Cosima writes that Wagner played for her the "Einsiedelei von Klingsor," the first passage in the work to use the motive in the adjacent sketch on

---

[13] This was determined by the comparison of handwriting samples at the Wagner Archive at Bayreuth. The inscription is attributed to Cosima Wagner in the *Wagner-Werk-Verzeichnis*, 541. Facsimiles of this page and some other reconstructed work sheets are reproduced in my article "Die Entstehung der *Parsifal*-Musik," 66–97.

[14] Cosima Wagner, *Cosima Wagner: Die Tagebücher*, ed. Martin Gregor-Dellin and Dietrich Mack (Munich and Zurich: Piper, 1982) (hereafter *CT*), 1:1087.

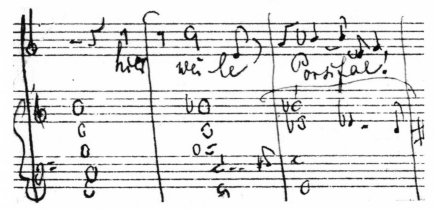

Plate 4.3: Manuscript fragment mounted on brown velvet (AIII m4(2) 5)
Nationalarchiv der Richard-Wagner-Stiftung Bayreuth

9v, while two days later, the twenty-third, we learn that he had finished
Gurnemanz's narrative.[15]

Cosima Wagner's diary entries and the precise dating of these and
other manuscripts have thus preserved an unusually detailed record of the
composition of *Parsifal*. This may not have been her only motivation in
handling Wagner's musical sketches, however. In a number of instances,
pinholes in the manuscripts imply that they were fastened to a larger surface, perhaps for purposes of display on a wall. One of the fragments, furthermore, was elaborately mounted on a piece of dark brown velvet before
being placed on display. This sketch cannot be placed with certainty into
the reconstructed leaves, though it probably belongs with them as a manuscript too fragmentary to permit reconstruction.[16] The manuscript pre-
serves a segment of only three bars, to the text "hier weile Parsifal!" (linger
here Parsifal!), a setting of three of Kundry's first words addressed to
Parsifal at the beginning of the seduction scene in act 2. An enlarged
reproduction of this sketch is shown in plate 4.3.

Holes in the circular mounting of this manuscript fragment show that
it was originally fastened to a wall. Examination of the collection of early
photographs of Wahnfried at Bayreuth indicates, though, that this sketch
was not displayed in the music room on the ground floor. In all available

---

[15] Both entries are found in *CT* 1:1087.

[16] The sketch is catalogued as AIII m4(2) 5. In the cataloguing system, the
number in parenthesis designates the parcel or envelope in which the manuscript is
kept — in this case, the second envelope, or parcel 2.

photographs, the sketch is absent from view; no photographs are available of the private rooms upstairs where it may have been displayed. This sketch could well have had a private significance for the Wagners, which motivated the cutting out and elaborate framing of the manuscript.[17] In this instance, if not in others, the cutting up of Wagner's sketches had no apparent function in the compositional process.

In most of these instances, Wagner himself apparently cut out individual sketches from the work sheets to facilitate the comparison of related passages, or simply to better concentrate his attention on the motives and shorter passages in question. There are occasional references in Cosima Wagner's diary to the "Schnipseln" (small scraps of paper) he used for musical sketches, and on October 21, 1878 she even wrote that his room was "full of such scraps or snippets" (*CT* 2:206). There are also sketches on hard cards of small format, including one entitled by Cosima as "Aller erste Skizze aus: 'durch Mitleid wissend'" (the very first sketch for "knowing through compassion"),[18] and another containing entries associated with the prelude to act 1, which were clearly made during the first few weeks of Wagner's sustained labors on the music, probably around the middle of September 1877. Another sketch on a similar card for Kundry's initial appearance in act 1 was dated by Wagner himself as "11 Feb. 78," and represents a revision of a passage that had already been written out in his drafts many months before. We cannot assume in advance that these individual sketches were necessarily written before his drafts; their chronology and function in the compositional process emerges only after careful assessment of the entire body of available manuscripts and the parallel account contained in Cosima Wagner's diaries.[19]

---

[17] In Cosima's diary from October 20, 1877 (*CT* 1:1078), she writes about the placing of her picture in Wagner's workroom as follows: "Einsetzung meines Bildes, 'in Klingsor's Zauberwerkstatt die Kundry', wie R. sagt." (the placing of my picture, "Kundry into Klingsor's magic workshop," as R. puts it). Wagner "lingered" for countless hours in his upstairs studio during the composition of Parsifal, and that was the most likely location for this sketch.

[18] This sketch is catalogued as AIII m4(2) 1, or MS 1 of parcel 2.

[19] There is of course no guarantee of the accuracy of Cosima Wagner's diaries, but her entries correspond closely with the surviving musical manuscripts, and there is no reason to doubt the basic veracity of her accounts of Wagner's compositional activity. The stern warning issued by Berndt Wessling regarding the use of the diaries to present "pure" Wagner is not at issue here, since our concern is focused specifically on issues of compositional genesis. See Wessling's afterword to his edited volume *Bayreuth im Dritten Reich: Richard Wagners politische Erben: Eine Dokumentation* (Weinheim and Basel: Beltz, 1983), 308.

In some instances, Wagner's individual sketches document his concentration on contrapuntal combinations of motives. On October 22, 1878, he wrote out for Cosima a sketch for the passage in the prelude to act 3, beginning in bar 23, in which the motives of the spear, the prophecy, and Klingsor are combined in the expressive context of Parsifal's tortuous return journey to the realm of the Grail. Cosima recorded that day in her diary that "Er schreibt es und spielt es, ich erkenne das Thema von der Lanze, dazu die unheimliche Figur von Klingsor und Parsifal's Motiv, aber wie gehemmt. Man empfindet und sieht im Geiste, wie er den Speer hoch gerade trägt und wie die Irre ihn umschlängelt." (He writes it and plays it, [and] I recognize the theme of the spear, and with it the uncanny figure of Klingsor and Parsifal's motive, but as if restrained. One senses and sees in one's imagination how Parsifal holds the spear high and how darkness and confusion surround him; CT 2:207). This sketch can be identified as MS 22r of parcel 1, and it can be reconstructed together with MS 12r of parcel 2, a source containing material for the Good Friday music heard later in act 3. The related sketches and parallel entries in Cosima's diary indicate that this nodal passage, with its motivic combination, was devised before the immediately preceding music in the prelude associated with Parsifal's "pfadlose[s] Irren" (pathless wandering). Wagner typically needed to conceive such important aspects of the musical setting in advance, as a prerequisite to his writing out the music in his continuous drafts. The individual sketches show Wagner in the act of concentrating on motivic units and short passages, which were nevertheless devised in close relation to the larger formal and dramatic context. As these sources indicate, his treatment of motives is far more flexible and complex than is usually conveyed in guides based on leitmotives, a popularizing approach that reaches back to the work of Hans von Wolzogen during Wagner's lifetime.[20]

The substantial number of early musical sketches for *Parsifal* has important implications for our understanding of Wagner's compositional process more generally. Although Wagner typically wrote out two full drafts in addition to the autograph score, relatively few individual musical sketches documenting the early stages of the compositional process of other works have survived. That *Parsifal* is the best documented of all of Wagner's works is due in part to Cosima Wagner's concern to preserve a

---

[20] For a recent and thorough treatment of leitmotivic analysis and its history, see Christian Thorau, *Semantisierte Sinnlichkeit: Studien zu Rezeption und Zeichenstruktur der Leitmotivtechnik Richard Wagners* (Stuttgart: Franz Steiner, 2003).

detailed record of her husband's artistic legacy for her son Siegfried and the rest of the family;[21] Wagner's obviously failing health added a sense of urgency to her efforts.

The fact that *Parsifal* was written during a settled period of Wagner's life, and mainly at his home, Wahnfried, meant that there was little danger the musical sketches would be unintentionally lost or discarded. Wagner's process of composition for *Parsifal* was especially slow and painstaking, and he doubtless made more preliminary sketches for it than for some of his earlier compositions. Nevertheless, it seems probable that the surviving sketches for earlier works often represent only a fraction of those Wagner must have made. Wagner himself did not usually attach so much importance to these documents, and it seems probable that even for *Parsifal*, a limited number of individual sketches may have been lost or discarded. The substantial number of missing fragments from Wagner's work sheets supports this conclusion.

The Earliest Sketches

In the 1850s, Wagner contemplated, and eventually rejected, an appearance of the character of "Parzival" as wandering pilgrim in the third act of *Tristan und Isolde*, and one sketch for the music has been preserved. It is in the key of E major, and was ultimately replaced by Tristan's vision of Isolde, in the same key, as Robert Bailey has pointed out.[22] There is good reason to believe that this musical sketch is indeed "Parzival's Refrain" as

---

[21] See Zdenko von Kraft, "Wahnfried and the Festival Theatre," in *The Wagner Companion*, ed. Peter Burbidge and Richard Sutton, 429 (London: Faber & Faber, 1979). Von Kraft cites Wagner's letter to King Ludwig II of 9 February 1879: "In days gone by I would simply discard anything which might have served as a memento of me. Then one morning I called out all over the house, 'I have a son.' All of a sudden the whole world looked different! The happy mother realized immediately that my whole past and future had acquired a completely new meaning. . . . From then on, every relic was preserved: letters, manuscripts, books which I once had used, every line I had ever written, were tracked down and collected; my life was recorded in ever greater detail, pictures of all the places and houses I had lived in were accumulated. My son, for all his tender years, shall on reaching maturity, know exactly *who* his father was."

[22] See Robert Bailey, *The Genesis of "Tristan und Isolde"*, 30–31. Martin Geck and Egon Voss, editors of the *Richard Wagner Sämtliche Werke*, vol. 30, claim in the caption to their transcription of this sketch on p. 30 that the date of the sketch rules out any relation to the composition of *Tristan*. Bailey observes, however, that the manuscript has the appearance of a fair copy, and that the original sketch must have been made earlier, so a relation to *Tristan* is entirely plausible. Wagner enclosed the sketch in a letter to Mathilde Wesendonk in 1858.

contained in the prose sketch for the third act of *Tristan* in a small note-book presumably dating from 1855.[23]

Although the sketch does not belong directly with the later musical sketches and drafts for *Parsifal*, it nevertheless bears some definite similarities to the complex of motives subsequently devised in connection with the Grail. The sketch is reproduced below (ex. 4.1).[24] The pervasive emphasis on the interval of the fourth is particularly noteworthy, in view of the importance of this interval in each of the principal themes and motives associated with the Grail in the finished work. Not only are the opening phrases based on the rising fourths B–E and A–D in the treble in bars 1 and 3, respectively; a variant of the ascending fourth in quarter notes is also heard in the tenor voice in bar 4 and in the treble in bar 6, each time outlining the pitches C♯–F♯, and a further ascent to G♯ takes place in the following bars. The second statement of this ascending fifth is set to "Sehnsucht mein Herze" (longing my heart) in the vocal part, supported by parallel sixths in a lower voice. Such rising motion through a

Example 4.1: Sketch for Parzival's appearance in Act 3 of Tristan und Isolde

---

[23] This notebook is held at the Wagner Archive at Bayreuth and catalogued as BII a 5. The passage in question on pp. 76–77 was transcribed by Hans von Wolzogen in "Richard Wagner. Parzival bei Tristan," *Bayreuther Blätter* 38 (1915): 145–57. Also see *Richard Wagner Sämtliche Werke*, vol. 30, 12. In Wagner's diary account for the year 1855 in his "brown book," he writes "Tristan bestimmter concipirt: 3r Akt Ausgangspunkt der Stimmung für das Ganze. (mit Hineinflechtung des Graalsuchenden Parzival.)" (Tristan conceived with more definition: 3rd act point of departure for the atmosphere of the whole [with a weaving in of Parzival seeking the Grail]; *Bergfeld, Das braune Buch*, 125). Wagner's account in his autobiography, however, places this event in 1854 (*My Life*, trans. Andrew Gray [New York: Da Capo, 1992], 510–11).

[24] *The Genesis of "Tristan und Isolde,"* example 3.

fifth supported by parallel sixths is characteristic of the "Dresden Amen" motive, which Wagner employed prominently in the finished work as the second half of the Grail motive. In the "Parzival" sketch, furthermore, a descent of the fourth B–A–G♯–F♯ guides the basic linear movement of the whole theme, with the first two of these pitches stressed at the beginning of the initial two-bar phrases, while the progression G♯–F♯ appears at the beginning of bars 5 and 6 in the tenor voice, and is repeated in the last two bars in the upper part. Entirely apart from this intervallic stress on the fourth, moreover, the music of the sketch has an expressive atmosphere of measured nobility not unlike parts of the prelude to the first act of *Parsifal*.

Wagner did not begin his sustained composition of the music until August of 1877, but he had been eager to begin work the preceding year, while preoccupied with numerous other projects. His thoughts about the musical setting of *Parsifal* had been stimulated as well through his engagement with Liszt's cantata *The Bells of Strasburg Cathedral*, beginning in 1875.[25] His first documented sketches for *Parsifal* date from early February 1876 and show the influence of his lively interest in the United States of America, an interest stimulated by a highly lucrative commission for a march commemorating the American centennial for the World Exhibition at Philadelphia.

Surprisingly, the music in question, the first music written specifically for *Parsifal*, is for the chorus of Flowermaidens in act 2, who sing "Komm! holder Knabe!" (Come! charming boy!) as they surround Parsifal and flirt with him. The song has a decidedly saccharine flavor, which Wagner may have thought characteristic of America, since he wrote "Amerikanisch sein wollend!" (Wanting to be American!) on his sketchleaf, dated "9 Febr. 76."[26] According to Cosima's diary, Wagner had begun work on the American march on that very day, while wondering whether his request of $5,000 as a fee would be accepted, but he had difficulty devising anything for the "American pomp" (*CT* 1:969). Instead, she reports, he conceived "ein sanftes, wiegendes Thema" (a soft, swaying theme), and it seems certain that this indeed was the music contained in Wagner's sketch, since the description and date match precisely. This sketchleaf for "Komm! holder Knabe!" dated February 9, 1876 is only one of three leaves preserving work on the song preceding the composition draft. Almost a year later, Wagner wrote out a clean draft for the piece, inscribing it with the words "So ist es!" (So it is!), and affixed the

---

[25] For a discussion of this relationship, see the introduction to the present volume.

[26] This sketch is catalogued as MS 19 of parcel 3 (AIII m4(3) 19).

date "26 Jan. 77."[27] Once again his thoughts had turned to *Parsifal*; the day before, he told Cosima that "Ich beginne den Parzival und laß nicht eher von ihm, als er fertig ist." (I'm beginning *Parzival* and shall not stop until it's completed; *CT* 1:1027). This leaf also contains sketches for the transition into the Flowermaidens' scene that were added at a later date in pencil, presumably around April 4 or 5, 1878, when Wagner had reached this part of the work in his composition draft. But more important at this point in our discussion is another, earlier source, a sketchleaf used in late January or, more likely, early February 1876, which contains the very first preserved musical entries intended from the beginning for *Parsifal*.

The *recto* side of this leaf (A III m4(3) 12) contains a contrapuntal sketch in pencil in B♭ major inscribed by Wagner "17 Jan 76 (beim Einschlaf)," (17 Jan[uary] [18]76 [while going to sleep]), an entry identified in Cosima's diary of the same date ("R. schrieb ein Thema, welches ihm abends angekommen, auf und findet, daß das Gegenthema bloß in der Umkehr bestehen könne" (R. writes down a theme that occurs to him in the evening and discovers that the countersubject could only consist of its inversion; *CT* 2:965). This entry does not relate directly to *Parsifal*, but other sketches on both sides of the leaf do. There is a sketch for *Götterdämmerung* occupying three systems of the *recto* side; this is surely the oldest entry on the leaf. Apparently Wagner pressed this older sketchleaf into service on the evening of January 17, and later entered three different sketches for *Parsifal*. These include an early version of the music for Kundry's initial entrance in act 1, at the top of the *recto*, and the earliest sketch for "Komm! holder Knabe!" on the *verso*. The ink draft of the song from February 9, although containing a number of revisions and cancellations, was not Wagner's first attempt to write out the piece, but was based on this rough pencil sketch, which thus represents the very first surviving musical sketch used in *Parsifal* (see ex. 4.2). The sketch could well have been made as late as February 9, when Wagner, unable to conceive anything for the "American pomp," first played this "sanftes wiegendes Thema" (soft, swaying theme) for Cosima.[28] (*CT* 1:969). It shows revisions that were incorporated into the sketchleaf of February 9, as can be seen for example in the bassline of the opening bars, which originally fell on the third beat to E♭. The key of the sketch, significantly, is A♭ major, which became a central tonality in the work as a whole. This was not the only time in Wagner's career that the initial music conceived

---

[27] This sketch is catalogued as MS 18 of parcel 3 (AIII m4(3) 18).

[28] The entire passage is as follows: "Wie ich zu Tisch komme, spielt er ein sanftes wiegendes Thema, für den amerikanischen Pomp fiele ihm nichts ein."

Example 4.2: Wagner's first sketch for Parsifal *("Komm! holder Knabe!") (MS AIII m4(3) 12)*

for an important new work came involuntarily and unbidden, as it were, during his labors on another project.[29]

Wagner's next sketches for *Parsifal* may have been written six months later, on a sleepless night from August 4–5, 1876. Cosima's diary entry for this date was evidently added retrospectively, more than a month later; but if her words "Wenig geschlafen, in Sinnen versunken, Sinnen, Seufzen und Flehen; Aufleben der unerbittlichen Mächte!" from August 4 refer to the night following the large gathering that day at Wahnfried, when Liszt was expected to play but did not, they would correspond to a sketchleaf containing the words "4–5 August: Nachts. Hahnruf" (4–5 August. Night. Crowing of the rooster; A III m(3) 21v).[30] (If this association is not valid, the sketch would date from a year later, in 1877.) On the systems above this inscription, and in the same shade of ink, Wagner made two entries, which are transcribed in example 4.3.

The first of these simply outlines the tonal space from A♭ to C a tenth above, an interval roughly filled out in the important sketch to the right. Here, Wagner enters the head of Parsifal's motive, with a fermata above G, the last note; and then juxtaposes with it an early version of what became

---

[29] See Bailey's discussion of the intersection of Wagner's work on the third act of *Siegfried* with his work on *Tristan* in "The Method of Composition" in *The Wagner Companion*, ed. Peter Burbidge and Richard Sutton, 308–27 *passim* (London: Faber & Faber, 1979).

[30] See *CT* 1:998, and the editorial notes on 1234.

Example 4.3: MS AIII m4(3) 21v

the head of the Communion or Last Supper theme from the very outset of *Parsifal*. The rhythmic subtlety of the Communion theme as we know it is not yet in evidence; the initial A♭ begins on the downbeat, and the following E♭ is not tied over the bar, as in the finished work, but repeated at the beginning of the second bar. The notes at the end of this second bar are unclear; but Wagner obviously intended the line to reach up to B♭ at the beginning of the next measure, just as occurs when this motive is resolved in the third act of the work as we know it. The second statement of the motive is indicated as beginning on E♭ on the bass; and the last note written, G♭, may stand for yet another entry of the subject, while it also clarifies the key of the sketch as A♭ major. The sketch for the "Parsifal" motive also shown in example 4.3 is presumably intended to be read in B♭ major, as in the finished work. Like the entries for the Communion theme, this motive is based on a triadic ascent reaching the sixth degree, an intervallic configuration of special importance in *Parsifal*.

At this time in 1876, Wagner had not yet begun to write out the final version of the text. His third and most polished copy of the Flowermaidens' song "Komm! holder Knabe!," dated January 26, 1877, corresponded closely with his work on the poem for this part of *Parsifal*. Cosima's diary entries from around this time mention his work on the text and particularly his deliberations about the names of the principal characters. On the thirtieth, she writes, "Bei Tische sagte mir R., er sei über das Schwerste im Parzival hinüber" ("At the table he told me that he was past the most difficult part in Parzival"; *CT* 1:1028). At this point, work on the poem was well advanced, to be finished in April. Several months later, in early August, Wagner began his sustained labors on the music.

The "Core of the Whole": The Music for the Grail

Nearly all accounts of the genesis of *Parsifal* have stressed Wagner's story as related in his autobiography that the central idea for the work grew out of his inspiration on Good Friday of 1857. Recent authors are more likely to dismiss this account, since it is not literally true, as Wagner himself noted on April 22, 1879 to Cosima: "eigentlich alles bei den Haaren herbeigezogen wie meine Liebschaften, denn es war kein Karfreitag, nichts, nur eine hübsche Stimmung in der Natur, von welcher ich mir sagte: So müßte es sein am Karfreitag" (In fact it is all as far-fetched as my love affairs, for it was not a Good Friday at all — just a pleasant mood in Nature that made me think, "This is how a Good Friday ought to be"; *CT* 2:335). This story assumes significance only in relationship to Wagner's interest in the basic dramatic potential of *Parsifal*; it could have had little bearing on the music, which was conceived twenty years later, and prominent features of the text also postdate the period in question, as is well known. For the evolution of the music, however, there exists an authentic and vastly more important statement concerning Wagner's central musical-dramatic idea, which is related in Cosima's diary from 11 August 1877:

> "Nehmt hin mein Blut" — R. sagt mir, er habe es aufgeschrieben noch kurz vor meiner Rueckkehr, mit Hut und Rock an, wie er mich eben abholen wollte. Nun habe er den Text umzumodeln gehabt; diese Abendmahl-Scene wuerde die Hauptscene sein, der Kern des Ganzen; bei dem Meistersinger-Preislied habe er auch die Melodie zuerst gehabt, und er habe den Text darauf umgeformt. Gestern sagte er schon, man müsse sich hüten, einer Melodie zuliebe den Text verlängern zu müssen — heute nun ist die Hauptstelle "Nehmet hin mein Blut um unsrer Liebe willen, nehmet hin meinen Leib und gedenket mein' ewiglich" gänzlich da, in ihrer Milde, in ihrem Schmerz, in ihrer Einfalt und Hoheit. " 'Die Schmerzen Amfortas' sind darin enthalten," sagt mir R. — Mich überwältigt der Eindruck, und ich bin unfähig zu irgend einer Beschäftigung. (*CT* 1:1065)

> ["Take my blood" — R.[ichard] tells me he wrote it down just shortly before my return, with his hat and coat on, just as he was about to meet me. Now he had to remodel the text; this Communion scene would be the main scene, the core of the whole. With the *Meistersinger* Prize song he also had the melody first, and had to reshape the text around it. Yesterday he told me that one had to avoid having to extend a melody on account of the text. Today, now the main passage "Take my blood, so be our love betokened, take my body and think of me for ever" is fully there, in its mildness, in its pain, in its simplicity and sublimity. "The sufferings of Amfortas are contained in it," R.[ichard] says to me. — The impression overwhelms me, and I am unable to do anything.]

The "core of the whole," or "Kern des Ganzen," in Wagner's own words, was centered in the Communion theme heard for the first time at the very beginning of the prelude of act 1. As we shall see, this claim is quite literally true: the initial Communion theme assumes crucial importance in the work as a whole, and can be fully understood only in retrospect, in light of the later ramifications and dramatic associations acquired by the musical motives comprising this theme. We begin to be confronted, at this point in our investigation, with major issues of musical structure and significance that can only be properly addressed in a broader analytical context. In particular, the opening Communion theme already foreshadows a central tonal axis of the work, the tonal pairing of A♭ and C, and it also introduces a subtle and complex web of motivic relations of symbolic importance, a matter to which we shall return. Our primary concern here is to trace Wagner's process of composition, which necessarily involved the creation of a network of relationships spanning vast stretches of musical time. For, as the sketches clearly show, Wagner needed to work out the music for the scene where the Grail is revealed before composing the prelude to act 1, consisting as it does of a foreshadowing of the later choral scene. A symphonic prelude for Wagner characteristically anticipates the crux of the drama to follow, and before beginning his composition draft of such a prelude, the related passages had to be thought through, a process that is well documented in the sketches and drafts for *Parsifal*.

As we gradually come to expect in the extraordinarily detailed sources for this work, the leaf containing the entries for the crucial Grail scene, which were written just before Cosima's return home on August 11 (after Wagner had donned his hat and coat and was about to leave) can be precisely identified (AIII m4(3) 14v). The text is different from that employed in the finished work, but the theme has now undergone rhythmic revisions that lend to it a suspended, syncopated character (see ex. 4.4).

In the opening thematic statement, only the closing bars differ much from the work as we know it: Wagner eventually decided to augment the rhythmic values of the last notes, elongating thereby two bars into three. The second thematic statement, restating the Communion theme in C minor, differs more substantially from the finished work, and lacks, for instance, the stress on B in its penultimate bar. Wagner revised the bassline considerably, and closes this statement surprisingly with an A♭, not C, in the bass, quite unlike the harmonized version of this theme in the completed work. These entries were made in pencil and later written over in purple ink. Beneath the sketches for the Communion theme in A♭ and C, Wagner made further sketches for the following choral music of the Grail scene.

Two more drafts for this passage preceded the composition draft. (In this respect, Wagner's composition of the Communion theme parallels that of the Flowermaidens' song, which was also written out three times, first as a rough sketch and then in two increasingly detailed drafts, before the material was entered into the composition draft.) It is revealing that the first of these drafts, on MS AIII m4(3) 15r, appears on a leaf otherwise filled with sketches for the prelude to act 1; this source documents the transition from Wagner's work on the choral Grail scene to his labors on the orchestral prelude. In this draft the Communion theme appears with the text in its final form, beginning "Nehmet hin meinen Leib, nehmet hin mein Blut." The instrumental sketches filling most of the remainder of both sides of this leaf record Wagner's first attempt to conceive the music of the prelude, beginning with the passage in 6/4 meter featuring the so-called "Faith" motive (measure 43), and extending to the beginning of scene 1. Comparison of leaf 15 *recto* and

Example 4.4: MS AIII m4(3) 14v

verso with the first leaf of Wagner's composition draft reveals, in fact, that the work sheet contains the early draft version of the prelude that formed the basis for the composition draft. The transference of this material into the beginning of the composition draft surely began around September 17, for Cosima writes that "Am Montag 17ten begibt sich R. wieder an die Arbeit; er scheint jetzt wirklich zu skizzieren." (On Monday the seventeenth, Richard turns again to his work; he really seems to be able to sketch now; *CT* 1:1071). Several days later, on the twenty-third, she records that "Abends spielt mir R. ein herrliches Thema und sagt mir, er könnte das ganze Vorspiel mir spielen, wenn er dies schon mit Tinte geschrieben." (In the evening Richard played me a marvelous theme and told me that he could play me the entire prelude, if he had written it out in ink; *CT* 1:1072).

Three days later, on September 26, Wagner in fact played the prelude from the orchestral draft for Cosima, and on the following day she quotes him that "Für M[ademois]elle Condrie habe ich einige Akzente auch schon, z.B. das Lachen habe ich schon.'" (For M[ademois]elle Condrie[31] I already have a few features, for example, I already have her laughter.) The theme sheet in question (AIII m4(3) 17) contains this "laughter of Condrie" near the top of the *verso* side, following entries for Parsifal's theme. The text set is "und lachte." It is a revealing sketch (see ex. 4.5a). The setting of Kundry's words from her monologue in act 2 is written immediately above the rapidly falling chromatic motive associated with her, and the pitches assigned to the two syllables of "lach-te" span the register of this powerful falling musical gesture. The sketch thus confirms an association between Kundry's laughter and the instrumental motive, but in the end, Wagner

Example 4.5a: MS AIII m4(3) 17v, system 1

Example 4.5b: Setting of "lachte," Parsifal, Act 2

---

[31] This way of referring to Kundry seems related to an entry in Cosima's diary from October 5, 1877, in which she writes that "Er beschäftigt sich mit der 'laide demoiselle', wie Kundry in Chrêtien de Troyes heißt." (He busies himself with the "ugly spinster," as she is called in Chrêtien de Troyes.)

Example 4.6: MS AIII m4(1) 1v, system 1

removed this motive from the setting of these crucial words in the second act, while intensifying the vocal setting to a nearly two-octave fall, from high B to C♯ above middle C (see ex. 4.5b).

The primary focus of the related material on this leaf is Kundry's initial appearance in act 1, sketches for which occupy much of the *recto* of the work-sheet. But here again, we can observe that Wagner has anticipated the musical setting of a passage of special dramatic weight and intensity — Kundry's scornful laughter at the savior on the cross, the source of her curse — from an early stage in the process of composition. Other sketches made in advance of the composition draft include the earliest surviving entries for Klingsor's music on the sketchleaf fragment AIII m4(1) 1v (the first of these is shown in ex. 4.6).

These entries show that Wagner did not settle immediately on the associated tonality for Klingsor of B minor. Eventually, B minor became the framing tonality of the entire second act, the act set in Klingsor's magic garden. In view of Wagner's early decision to incorporate a tension between A♭ major and C minor into the Communion theme, his choice of the key of C minor for this early sketch is fascinating. Ultimately, of course, it is Klingsor, and his unwilling agent, Kundry, who are associated dramatically with the wound of Amfortas, and Wagner may well have intended at this stage to coordinate the dissonant turn within the Communion theme with the use of C minor as an associated tonality for Klingsor. If so, the notion was soon discarded, as later sources show. Another noteworthy feature of the sketch consists in the simplicity and clarity of its phrasing and harmonic progression, which were later rendered in a far more fluid and dissonant manner by Wagner.[32]

---

[32] As Robert Bailey has observed about the *Tristan* sources, some of Wagner's early sketches are written in two- or four-bar phrases clearly marked off by cadences, in a manner quite unlike the open, extensible motivic characteristics of the finished work. See Bailey, *The Genesis of Tristan und Isolde*, 16–18. Another illustration of this tendency is the sketch for the beginning to the prelude to act 3 of *Parsifal* found on the sketchleaf fragment in parcel 1, MS 17r, which is shaped as a eight-measure unit in two four-measure phrases. Wagner later obscured the square phrase structure of this sketch, while extending the material melodically through use of a series of syncopations.

The Relation of Sketches and Drafts

As we have seen, a considerable amount of preliminary work preceded Wagner's labors on his composition and orchestral drafts for *Parsifal*. In the case of the first act prelude, the material of the opening passages, based on the Communion theme and Grail motive, was first developed on individual work sheets. The main body of the prelude was then drafted on both sides of folio 15 (AIII m4(3)), a source that already contained an entry for the Communion theme with text, as we have seen. This draft contains numerous revisions, but approaches the finished work closely in its general outlines. It lacks a measure in the last section, for instance (bar 99),[33] and also differs in the concluding passage leading into the first scene. Wagner must have completed this part of the draft by the middle of September, to judge from Cosima's diaries. It seems likely that her comment for September 17 ("er scheint jetzt wirklich zu skizzieren" [He really seems to be writing the sketch now]), refers to Wagner's writing out of the composition draft on the basis of the earlier work on folio 15. By the time Wagner began the composition draft, the most essential part of the creative process was already behind him, and he could then indeed have begun to write more quickly, since he was to a considerable extent transcribing and elaborating material that already existed.

Consequently, the composition and orchestral drafts of the prelude generally resemble the completed work very closely, and reveal relatively little about compositional process. Folio 15 is a much more important source in this regard. It is interesting, for example, that in it Wagner completes the cadence to A♭ major at the very end of the prelude by having the head of the Communion theme return in the tonic key, unlike the finished work, where this cadence is avoided by a harmonic shift to F♭ when the head of the Communion theme is played by trombones behind the stage. A related individual sketch is transcribed in example 4.7. It differs crucially from the finished version of this passage, for what it contains is very close to the resolved form of the progression used by Wagner at the final cadence of the entire work. At the end of *Parsifal*, the excerpt begins a fifth lower, in order that it can close on the tonic triad A♭ major. By the time Wagner entered this material into his composition draft, of course, he had decided to change the pitch level of the head of the Communion theme played by the trombones behind stage to F♭, leaving the protracted dominant-seventh chord of A♭ unresolved, and he also restored the original form of the head of the Communion theme,

---

[33] The insertion of two new measures replacing one measure in the draft versions was made in September 1879, when Wagner also made several other revisions to *Parsifal*.

Example 4.7: MS AIII m4(3) 15v, system 4

with a descending semitone in the third bar. Meanwhile, the idea sketched on folio 15v was broken free of its original musical context. It represents, in a sense, Wagner's first sketch for the final cadence of the entire work, though apparently it was intended originally for another passage altogether.

The orchestral preludes of each act required more preliminary labors on Wagner's part than some other portions of the work, and since such substantial work preceded the writing-out of the composition and orchestral drafts, these documents are rather neat and free of revisions. Nothing would be more misleading, of course, than to conclude from this that the preludes did not offer Wagner formidable challenges in composition. The portions of the work based on text generally required less sketching, and precisely for this reason, the pages of the composition draft are sometimes more heavily revised, since they were based on less preliminary work. For instance, at the very beginning of act 1, Wagner made a very substantial change in the composition draft version of the music heard during Gurnemanz's morning prayer with the two boys. Here, Wagner's penchant for extended musical recapitulation was carried too far; he originally intended to restate a lengthy passage from the prelude, beginning at bar 44, where the Faith motive appears *forte* and then *fortissimo* in a sequence leading to a climactic statement in D major in bar 51. Wagner surely soon recognized that the material would be too forceful to use in this quiet dramatic context, and abridged the passage to begin by recalling the more gentle statements of the same motivic material beginning at measure 73 of the prelude. The revised version was written into the orchestral draft of the passage, and subsequently taken into the finished work.

We have already seen that many of the early sketches for *Parsifal* consist of instrumental segments. This is also true of the numerous sketches for the Good Friday music in act 3, where the vocal lines and words are hardly ever notated. Most of the preliminary vocal sketches are for the choral music of the Grail scenes in acts 1 and 3, and for Kundry in act 2. In writing the vocal parts, Wagner made distinctly fewer sketches and revisions than in the more complex orchestral texture. Unlike the composition draft for the orchestral preludes, which prove to be based completely on earlier drafts on loose papers, he was evidently able to write out parts of the vocal sections for the first time in his composition draft. Even here, Wagner often relied on earlier sketches, however, and occasionally heavily revised pages had to be removed altogether from the composition draft and the material was rewritten on new sheets. This brings us to the paper structure and organization of the composition draft, and its relationship to Wagner's individual work sheets and orchestral draft.

The composition draft, unlike the orchestral draft, consists of separate half-sheets of the same paper as Wagner used for the autograph score. Each original sheet contained thirty staves, but these leaves were cut in half, creating oblong pages with fifteen staves each, and all of the bifolia were separated into folia. This provided Wagner the flexibility to replace pages of his draft at will. In order to keep the separate pages in order, Wagner always numbered the folia, and usually each side of the page (fol. 1r = "1/I," fol. 1v = "1/II," etc.). Because of this numbering system, pages that were discarded from the composition draft and later used as work sheets can be easily identified. In the orchestral draft, on the other hand, Wagner employed a different kind of paper in upright format with 21 staves. Since this draft was based on the composition draft, Wagner could expect to make relatively few revisions, and the format of the source did not require the same flexibility as the composition draft. The paper structure of the orchestral draft consists normally of bifolia in gathered sheets, and each side is paginated. Later, as an orientation aid in writing out the autograph score, Wagner would enter page numbers from the autograph into the orchestral draft, and this draft also contains other indications concerning orchestration that were written retrospectively, while he was at work on the autograph.

The inks used by Wagner are also helpful in establishing the chronology of composition and the relationships between these sources. Many early sketches and work in the composition draft were made in ordinary pencil or blue *Tintenstift*,[34] whereas the orchestral draft, autograph, and also many sketches and the later parts of the composition draft, including all of act 3, were made in ink of a very distinctive violet shade. In the composition draft of act 1, Wagner occasionally entered passages in violet ink; these entries were apparently made while Wagner was occupied primarily with the orchestral draft, and turned to the composition draft without changing his writing instrument. Beginning during his work on act 2, Wagner often made even his most fragmentary and preliminary sketches in violet ink.

---

[34] *Tintenstift* is an indelible or copying-ink pencil. It was in wide use in the nineteenth century, but had virtually disappeared by the 1940s. For an article on the *Tintenstift*, see Berharde Woerdehoff, "Bruder des Bleistifts," in *Die Zeit* (45: 10 November 1989), 23.

The fortunate survival of these voluminous sources for *Parsifal*, in conjunction with Cosima's diaries, presents us with an almost unparalleled opportunity to trace the compositional genesis of a major work of art, and gain insights into aspects of the creative process. Our primary interest here is not to describe the documents exhaustively, but rather to offer critical interpretation of the evolution of the music, based on these primary sources. To that end, we shall now turn to a specific section of the score whose genesis can be traced through several stages on the basis of individual sketches, the composition and orchestral drafts, and the autograph score.

The Transformation Music of Act 1

The Original Version of 1877–78

The most surprising single revelation of the manuscript sources for *Parsifal* is probably the radically different form of the Transformation music in its original version. This orchestral transition passage heard during the procession into the Grail Temple posed considerable difficulties for Wagner, to judge from the evidence of the sources. In addition to appearing in numerous sketches and drafts on various leaves, the passage is still very incomplete in the composition draft, while the orchestral draft and autograph score also show signs of extensive revision at this point. It appears, in fact, that this long evolution of the Transformation music was connected in part with the development of a complex of large-scale tonal and thematic relationships spanning the entire work. Practical and non-musical factors also played an important role, however, as we shall see.

From the detailed entries in Cosima's diary, we can judge that Wagner's first sustained work on the Transformation music occupied the last week of December, 1877. The first section of the processional march notated in four flats may have been finished before Christmas, but the modulating sequences that follow required an intensive bout of sketching for five days until December 30. On the twenty-sixth, Cosima writes: "Gestern am Nachmittag, wie ich noch im Saal war, freute sich R. einer großen Terz von fis, ais, zu f, a, welche ihm eben eingefallen. Heute arbeitet er sie aus in dem Marsch der Gralsritter." (Yesterday in the afternoon, when I was still in the room, R. was pleased with the major third of F♯, A♯, to F, A, which just occurred to him. Today he worked this out in the March of the Knights of the Grail; *CT* 1:1100). Such a chromatic descent of a third appears several times in the finished march, and the last time, two bars before the entrance of the trombones behind stage, it is indeed heard at this pitch level, spelled enharmonically as G♭–B♭ to F–A, though the entire progression begins a whole tone higher. This motive, known as the "Wehelaute," has a dramatic association with earthly sin and the painful sacrifice of the redeemer's blood. It assumes special importance in connection with Amfortas, and appears later at the very beginning of Amfortas's great lament where he exclaims "Wehe!" (Woe!), in response to Titurel's request to reveal the Grail. There it is heard precisely at the pitch level that had occurred to Wagner on Christmas Day of 1877. The working-out of this idea, in combination and juxtaposition with other motives, was Wagner's major preoccupation in his sketches for the Transformation music. Every one of Cosima's diary entries during these days mentions his work on the march, which is described humorously by Wagner as a "Bademarsch" (March to the Baths) appropriate for the resort spas of Marienbad or Bad Ems (*CT* 1: 1100). On the afternoon of the twenty-ninth, according to Cosima's report, he was "sehr zufrieden mit einem Kontrapunkt" (very satisfied with the counterpoint; *CT* 1:1101). On the following day, she relates that "R. spielt mir den 'Marsch' vor, der überwältigend herrlich nun erklingt!" (R. played me the "March," which now sounds overwhelmingly wonderful!; *CT* 1:1101).

One of Wagner's first sketches containing the chromatic descending thirds appears in parcel 2, MS 4v, on staves 7–8 of the reconstructed leaf. In this instance, the context of the sketch on the reconstructed leaf helps to confirm its chronology, since other entries from this leaf were dated. To judge from its context, and from Cosima's diary entries, the sketch must have been written down around December 26, approximately a week after the adjoining sketch on MS 9r, which had probably been removed from the leaf when it was dated by Cosima on the eighteenth. Here the third involved is E–G♯ descending to E♭–G, the first appearance of this material in the march. In the sketch, this series of descending thirds is prolonged and incorporated into a phrase six bars long. Wagner subsequently revised the third to fifth bars of the sketch on staves 5–6 immediately above. It was not this revised version of the phrase, however, but the original version, that was taken into Wagner's composition draft for the passage, where it is joined with an overlapping phrase of four bars stressing the processional dotted rhythm from the beginning of the march (see the transcription in ex. 4.8). The resulting nine-bar unit occupies the entire second system on staves 4–6 of this page from Wagner's composition draft. (In this instance, the descending thirds are spelled enharmonically as F♭–A♭ going to E♭–G; a key signature of four flats is initially assumed but not actually notated by Wagner.)

By comparing the third system of Wagner's composition draft (staves 7–9) with the second (staves 4–6), we can see that it consists of an exact transposition of this nine-bar unit up a whole tone, with the descending thirds beginning on G♭–B♭, the same pitch level that had preoccupied Wagner on Christmas day. In the draft, this somewhat mechanical transposition

Example 4.8: Composition Draft, Act 1, fol. 14/ II, system 2

already provides the setting for Gurnemanz's words "Nun achte wohl, und lass' mich seh'n: bist du ein Thor und rein, welch' Wissen dir auch mag beschieden sein," while the following statement of the Grail motive in the full orchestra marks the entrance into the Temple of the Grail. In this draft of the passage, therefore, the sequence employing the chromatic descending thirds already forms part of the transition bringing the purely orchestral passage to a close — it is more than twenty measures shorter than in the work as we know it.

Wagner made one important revision in these plans for the Transformation music when he set out to elaborate this material in his orchestral draft. He first entered the six-bar phrase with the chromatically descending thirds into this second draft, in a version corresponding to staves 7–8 of the reconstructed sketchleaf and staves 4–6 of the page from the composition draft. This sketch then underwent a crucial rhythmic revision: bars 3 and 4 of the earlier phrase were crossed out in the orchestral draft and replaced by a single bar with note values half as long, so that the entire phrase to be transposed occupies one measure less (see ex. 4.9). This revised passage was also entered by Wagner on individual sketchleaves, including one page rejected from an earlier section of the composition draft.

With the incorporation of this rhythmic revision, the passage was evidently finished in its basic compositional substance. According to Cosima's diary, Wagner played the passage for her twice during the following weeks, on January 5 and 15, 1878, each time in conjunction with related musical

Example 4.9: Orchestral Draft, page 26, second last system

excerpts from the passages for Titurel and Amfortas later in the act (*CT* 2:34; 37). More than three years were to pass before Wagner returned, unexpectedly, to work on the Transformation music.

The Expansion of the Transformation Music in 1881

In spite of Wagner's satisfaction with the first act Transformation music at the beginning of 1878, he radically revised and expanded it in March of 1881. The manuscript sources reveal, in fact, that the Transformation music as we know it was the last part of the score composed by Wagner. He did not welcome this return to composition of the Transformation music in 1881, but was compelled to it against his will. On March 3, Cosima wrote that "Er . . . ärgert sich darüber, daß er nun Musik für die Dekorations-maler machen müsse (Wandlungs-D. im ersten Akt)." (He . . . is angry that he has to write music for the stage painter! (the decorative transition in the first act; *CT* 2:704). Evidently, Wagner had just learned that the amount of music supplied for the transition was too short for purposes of the staging. Wagner's irritation about the need for a longer transition was certainly not lessened by the fact that he had finished writing out the auto-graph score for this part of the work only two or three weeks earlier.[35] In subsequent diary entries on March 6 and 12, Cosima reports that Wagner composed additional music three or four minutes in length "mit der Uhr in der Hand" (with a watch in his hand: *CT* 2:706; 709). Nevertheless, he still failed to supply the amount of music needed. More than a year later, as is well known, Engelbert Humperdinck arranged repetitions in the music to extend the music to the necessary length.[36] Wagner's own expansion of the passage in 1881 has not previously received attention, but it is of considerable biographical and analytical interest. In the end, the work was to benefit substantially from Wagner's inconvenience. It is precisely this revised pas-sage whose expressive power is enhanced through its closer structural rela-tionship to the work as a whole. If Wagner failed in his practical objective, he nevertheless succeeded artistically in strengthening this important orchestral transition.

The extent of Wagner's expansion of the Transformation music is made clear from the orchestral draft as well as the autograph, both of

[35] Wagner's progress in writing out the autograph can be followed from the page numbers provided in Cosima's diaries. On March 23, 1881, for instance, after the delay brought by the revision of the Transformation music, she reports that he fin-ished page 80 of the score, whereas eight days later, on March 31, he had finished page 88. See *CT* 2:715, 719.

[36] Humperdinck's extension of the passage is preserved on a manuscript housed in the Bayreuth Wagner Archive and entitled "Ergänzungsstück zu der Partitur."

which contain inserted pages. Plate 4.4 shows a page inserted into the orchestral draft, and added to the pagination as 27(a), while the original page 27 became 27(b). Once this insertion was made in the draft, it was necessary for Wagner to cancel the bars at the top of page 27(b), since these are superseded in the new version. The numbers from 81–85 seen on page 27(a) refer to the corresponding pages of the autograph score, which was written out as an elaboration of this draft.

As a result of Wagner's expansion of the passage, several pages were added to the autograph score, and many pages were subsequently renumbered, to conform to the new pagination.[37] This renumbering begins at page 85 of the autograph, which was originally page 81, as can be seen at the bottom of plate 4.3; the new pages were inserted immediately preceding page 85. Examination of the original manuscript of the autograph shows that pages 85–86 and 87–88 each represented the second leaf of bifolia which originally formed a gathered sheet; the stumps of the two leaves so joined are clearly visible in the manuscript, but are not reproduced in the published facsimile of the score. Two folia, or four pages, were thus removed with scissors before Wagner replaced these leaves with new pages containing his expanded version of the Transformation music.

What did Wagner's revisions consist in? In the first version of the passage from 1877, as we saw in example 4.8, the five-bar unit with the chromatically descending thirds was joined with an overlapping phrase of four bars based on the processional dotted rhythm of the march, and these eight measures were then repeated sequentially a tone higher. Gurnemanz's words to Parsifal beginning "Nun achte wohl" were superimposed on the last several bars of the sequential repetition, on the measures employing the processional dotted rhythm. By contrast, in the work as we know it, Wagner built up the passage into a complex series of interlocking sequences culminating in two appearances of the head of the Communion theme heard from behind stage, first in the trombones, and subsequently by trombones reinforced by trumpets. Following this second statement of the head of the Communion theme, the bells of the Grail Temple are heard, outlining the fourths C–G and A–E derived from the processional march, but with the dotted rhythm removed. In the original version of the passage, the bells of the Grail were not heard at all until after Gurnemanz's words to Parsifal.

---

[37] The autograph score is housed in the Wagner Archive and catalogued as "Partitur" (AIII o). A facsimile of this score was published by the Drei Masken Verlag at Munich in 1925.

*Plate 4.4: Leaf inserted into the Orchestral Draft as p. 27(a) during
the expansion of the Transformation Music in 1881
Nationalarchiv der Richard-Wagner-Stiftung Bayreuth*

The beginning of Wagner's insertion consists of seven bars in a
reduced orchestration of strings alone, placed immediately after the
first appearance of the five-bar phrase from the earlier version employing
the "Wehelaute" motive of chromatically descending thirds associated

Example 4.10: Beginning of insertion, Transformation Music, Act 1

dramatically with "sinful worlds, with a thousand agonies." The third bar of this phrase employs a rhythmic diminution of the descending motive in eighth notes, as we have seen, and the basic descending chromatic line is extended through a tritone at the end of the third bar of the phrase (see ex. 4.10). Wagner's new continuation of 1881 provides a series of imitations of this descending motive, which gradually rise in pitch, and lead to a climactic two-fold restatement of the chromatically descending thirds or "Wehelaute" motive heard in the full orchestra. In this twofold restatement, Wagner curtails the five-bar phrase to three bars, and he intensifies the climax by means of a rising pitch level for each sequence and by means of the orchestration, with the timpani reserved for the last and most climactic statement of the phrase.

Consequently, in the passage as we know it, the narrative outline of the Transformation music unites several contrasting elements into an effective synthesis. The processional march first absorbs (or confronts) the "painful" affect of the chromatically-descending thirds (measure 1123 ff.),[38] before developing this thematic material in the inserted passage (mm.1127ff.). The lowering of tension at the beginning of the inserted passage, due to the soft dynamic level and reduced orchestration, allows Wagner to build gradually to the powerful climax placed just before the entry into the Temple. The more weighty, differentiated character of the Transformation music in its final version also fits more convincingly with the philosophical dictum uttered by Gurnemanz at the outset of the processional march: "Du siehst, mein Sohn, zum Raum wird hier die Zeit." (You see, my son, here time becomes space.) For as so often in Wagner, the temporal unfolding embodied in the music exposes dramatic elements that will be displayed visually on stage, or in "space," at a later point. Regarded in this way, Gurnemanz's comment is but one more of those familiar Wagnerian formulations asserting the priority of music in his artistic synthesis: music seen as the "Schoß des Dramas" (womb of the drama) or inversely, the drama as "ersichtlich gewordene Taten der Musik" (deeds of music become visible).

---

[38] Measure numbers will henceforth be indicated by the abbreviation m.

The climax is enhanced by the ensuing appearances of the head of the Communion theme heard from behind stage, which are joined with the processional material in dotted rhythm into a larger musical unit repeated sequentially, in a manner similar to Wagner's earlier and more primitive sequences using the descending thirds in his composition draft from 1877. The introduction of this new motive is highly appropriate in this dramatic context, since it represents the first segment of the theme sung to the communion text when the Grail is revealed. There is a much broader musical and dramatic significance to this gesture, however, which may only have been evident to Wagner in retrospect, when he was faced with the need to expand the passage in 1881. This brings us to one of the central elements in the tonal structure of the entire work, the tonal pairing of A♭ and C, which is developed and ultimately resolved in the primary musical complex associated with the Grail.

The device of tonal pairing, whereby extended musical passages are based on the tension between two key centers, usually a third apart, assumes special importance in Wagner's works, beginning with *Tristan und Isolde*, but the most far-reaching example is found in the music for the Grail in *Parsifal*.[39] In applying this concept to the music associated with the Grail, including the expanded version of the Transformation music, we shall attempt to respond to Reinhold Brinkmann's proposal "die Quellenforschung voranzutreiben und doch zu versuchen, der Forderung Schönbergs, Musikwissenschaft habe *Forschung in den Tiefen der musikalischen Sprache* zu sein, zu genügen" (to pursue research on sources while also conforming to Schönberg's requirement that musicology be *an investigation into the depths of the musical language*.)[40] What we are addressing here

---

[39] For the concept of "tonal pairing" in Wagner's music I am indebted to Robert Bailey, who has elaborated on the "double tonic complex" in his Norton Critical Score of *Tristan* (*Prelude and Transfiguration from "Tristan und Isolde"* [New York, 1985]). Analyses based on this approach are offered in my articles "Dramatic Recapitulation in Wagner's *Götterdämmerung*," *19th-Century Music* 4 (1980): 101–12; "Das 'Geheimnis der Form' in Wagners 'Tristan und Isolde'," *Archiv für Musikwissenschaft* 40 (1983): 174–88; "Wagner's *Parsifal:* Musical Form and the Drama of Redemption," *The Journal of Musicology* (Fall 1986): 431–46, and (Spring 1987): 315–16; and "Dramatic Recapitulation and Tonal Pairing in Wagner's *Tristan und Isolde* and *Parsifal*," in *The Second Practice of Nineteenth-Century Tonality*, ed. William Kinderman and Harald Krebs, 178–214 (Lincoln and London: U of Nebraska P, 1996).

[40] Reinhold Brinkmann, "Musikforschung und Musikliteratur: Eine Niederschrift von Improvisationen über ein so nicht gegebenes Thema," in *Wagnerliteratur, Wagnerforschung: Bericht über das Wagner-Symposium, München 1983*, ed. Carl Dahlhaus and Egon Voss (Mainz: Schott, 1985), 155.

is essentially the musical ramifications of Wagner's shaping of the Communion theme such that, as he put it to Cosima, " 'Die Schmerzen Amfortas' sind darin enthalten' " (the pain of Amfortas is contained in it). These ramifications are at once structural and symbolic, and cannot be grasped on the basis of a sharp distinction between "pure" orchestral music and music with text. Indeed, as we have seen, Wagner's point of departure in composing the first act was the Grail scene, which preceded his work on the prelude. The device of tonal pairing enabled Wagner to project the symbolic content of the drama not merely on a motivic level but also on the larger structural levels of the musical form. A full discussion of these relations is impossible here, but the following brief summary should suffice to provide a context for evaluating Wagner's expansion of the Transformation music.

The central dramatic tension in *Parsifal* consists in the threat to the Order of the Grail posed by the plight of Amfortas, whose festering wound opens afresh when he reveals the Grail at the Communion Service. This threat to the Grail is removed only in act 3, when Parsifal appears as redeemer, bringing the holy spear he gained during his encounter with Kundry and Klingsor in act 2. In order to embody this dramatic tension in the music, Wagner juxtaposes the sonorities of A♭ major and C minor in the opening Communion theme, whose several motives are each capable of independent development (see ex. 4.11).

The "pain of Amfortas" is reflected in the turn to the C-minor harmony in measure 3, which is emphasized by the crescendo to *forte* and the rhythmic context, with the suspended, syncopated rhythm of the initial ascending line leading to a stressed arrival on a strong beat at the fall of the semitone A♭–G. This motive is often described as the "Schmerzensfigur" or "pain motive," but its dramatic role is far more subtle and differentiated than is indicated by any such label. The harmonic tension created by this striking inflection casts a shadow of ambiguity over the tonic key of A♭ major, which sounds, momentarily, like the flat sixth of C minor. As is later made clear, this tension introduced by the motive in m.3 after the stable beginning in A♭ embodies in germinal form the dramatic relation between the anguished, sinful condition of Amfortas on the one hand and the

Example 4.11: Communion Theme

purity of the Grail on the other. An intensification of this descending semitone relation is evident in the ensuing statements of the Communion theme in C minor, where the semitone C–B is stressed twice, in different registers.

Ab major and C minor are thus used in the tonal structure of the opening of the prelude as keys for the larger thematic statements, each of which is twenty measures long. In turn, this key relation parallels the tonal framework of the entire act, which closes in the major mode of C. In this case, as elsewhere in Wagner's later works, the initial tonal areas of the prelude signal the polar tonalities of the act to follow.[41] In *Parsifal*, this represents one aspect of a general musical foreshadowing in the prelude of the first Grail scene at the end of the act.

The most telling and dramatically significant anticipation of the Grail scene is contained in the last section of the prelude, however. This passage foreshadows the music of Amfortas's great lament, as well as a number of other passages associated with Amfortas. Here the opening Communion theme is greatly expanded from within. Its first three measures are treated sequentially, with the motive from the third bar serving as a pivot for modulations to keys rising in thirds. This tonal framework thereby parallels on the larger structural level the intervallic pattern of rising thirds in the theme itself. Subsequently, the increasingly chromatic texture of the passage culminates in the isolation and development of the descending semitone figure at its original pitch level, Ab–G (see ex. 4.12). Here, the semitone is reinterpreted as an ascending appoggiatura and repeated threefold. Syncopations and diminished and minor harmonies contribute to the expressive intensity of the passage. At the end of Amfortas's tortured narrative in the Grail scene, this poignant appoggiatura and its resolution will be set to the two syllables of "Wunde" (wound).

The chromatic intensity of this passage abates as the music approaches the cadence in Ab, corresponding to m.6 of the original theme, in the closing measures of the prelude (these are also shown in ex. 4.12). Here again, the thematic model of the Communion theme is greatly expanded: the cadential dominant chord is protracted for eight bars, while the serene, rising triadic figure penetrates the highest register in the violins. Yet the expected cadence in Ab is not granted: as the curtain opens, the trombones behind the stage sound the head of the Communion theme on the pitch level of Fb, with much the effect of a deceptive cadence. The diatonic rise through the octave drops chromatically from Fb to Eb, through the same

---

[41] For other examples of this procedure in Wagner, see Robert Bailey, "The Structure of the *Ring* and its Evolution," *19th-Century Music* I (1977): 59.

Example 4.12: End of prelude, Act 1

crucial descending semitone figure that will remain attached to this theme
until Parsifal's return of the holy spear in act 3.

Wagner's subsequent development of the Communion theme in relation to the tonal pairing of A♭ and C is complex, and has been discussed in
some detail elsewhere.[42] Most important in relation to Wagner's expansion
of the Transformation music is the eventual resolution of the tonal pairing

---

[42] More detailed discussion is offered in my chapter "Dramatic Recapitulation and
Tonal Pairing in Wagner's *Tristan* and *Parsifal*," in Kinderman and Krebs, *The Second*

in the closing orchestral passages of act 3, following Parsifal's opening of the Grail Shrine. A motivic resolution of the Communion theme had already occurred earlier in that act, when Parsifal revealed the spear to Gurnemanz. In the closing orchestral passages, this resolved version of the head of the Communion theme is absorbed into a new thematic synthesis encompassing the so-called Faith and Grail motives, so that all of the motives associated with the Grail are combined for the first time into larger formal units. Never before in the work was such integration evident in the music associated with the Grail. In the first act prelude, by contrast, these motives were merely juxtaposed, without being directly connected to one another.

In the closing measures of *Parsifal*, the Grail motive (with its "Dresden Amen" formula) and the head of the Communion theme are overlapped and combined to form the final cadence (see fig. 4.1 and ex. 4.13). In the first two bars of the example, the first half of the Grail motive appears in rhythmically augmented form in the highest register. This rhythmically augmented form of the motive, in a similar register and orchestration, was heard several times in the first Grail scene of act 1, and again in the closing moments of act 2, when Parsifal made the sign of the cross, banishing Klingsor's evil magic. But whereas the tonality of these earlier appearances of the augmented motive was C major, it is now heard in A♭ major, further resolving the tension of the tonal pairing.

The rest of the Grail motive is omitted in the final cadence, since its pitches are duplicated when the Communion theme in its resolved form, heard on the subdominant in the trumpets and trombones, rises stepwise from B♭ through C and D♭ to E♭, the dominant note of the tonic triad

Fig. 4.1: End of Parsifal, *showing overlapping of Grail Motive and Communion Theme*

Practice of Nineteenth-Century Tonality, 195–214; see also Ulrike Kienzle's chapter in the present volume. Studies addressing aspects of the motivic development of the Communion theme in *Parsifal* include Hans Grunsky, "Die Symbolik der Parsifalmusik," in the *Bayreuther Festspiele 1955: Programmheft*, 28–31, 34–40; Uwe Faerber, "Über die musikalische Thematik des 'Parsifal'," *Richard Wagner Blätter* 6 (1982): 17–31; and the more thorough discussion contained in Hans-Joachim Bauer, *Wagners Parsifal: Kriterien der Kompositionstechnik* (Munich: Katzbichler, 1977).

Example 4.13: Conclusion of Act 3

reached in the third-to-last measure. The arrival of this final tonic chord of Ab major thus provides the simultaneous resolution of both motives, standing in place of the dissonant falling semitone that had represented a primary source of musical tension from the very beginning of the work, four hours earlier. In these closing measures, both motives are subsumed into the final subdominant cadence, completing and perfecting the musical form as an audible symbol for the utopia of redemption.

We are now in a position to better appreciate Wagner's incorporation of an important element in the tonal and dramatic structure of the work at a very late stage in composition, when he expanded the Transformation music in 1881. Here, our investigation of the compositional process can serve as a guide for analysis of the music by providing a key to the unique internal context that lies within the work as we know it. For the twofold statement of the head of the Communion theme at the end of the Transformation music shows an especially close connection with two striking musical gestures spanning the entire work: the avoidance of a cadence in A♭ through the shift to the flat sixth degree, F♭, at the end of the first act prelude, and the final cadence at the end of act 3. As we have seen, the long-protracted dominant-seventh chord of A♭ major at the end of the prelude is followed not by the expected tonic triad, but by a shift to the minor sixth degree, as the head of the Communion theme is heard on the pitch level of F♭. The gesture is all the more striking because it is heard from trombones behind the stage. This inflection is closely recalled in the first statement of the motive near the end of the Transformation music, which precisely coincides with it in its pitch level and orchestration, with the trombones again heard from behind the stage. The harmonic context is also parallel, since the shift to F♭ follows a progression through a circle of fifths to the dominant of A♭, and has much the effect of a deceptive cadence (see ex. 4.14; cf. ex. 4.12).

The second statement of the head of the Communion theme on the pitch level of D♭, on the other hand, bears an analogous relationship to the final cadence of act 3 (this is also shown in ex. 4.14; cf. ex. 4.13). In this case, however, there is a crucial difference of one note between the two statements of the motive, which embodies the shift in the tonal pairing from C major, as the framing central key of the first Grail scene, to A♭ major, the key of the conclusion of the whole work. The statement on D♭ at the end of the Transformation music falls to C, opening a gateway to that tonality, as embodied in the fixed pitches of the Temple Bells, whereas the corresponding statement of this motive at the final cadence rises triumphantly to E♭, the dominant note of the tonic triad of A♭. Here again, the orchestration matches exactly, consisting of trombones reinforced by trumpets.

Wagner's insertion of the twofold statement of the head of the Communion theme into the Transformation music thus contributes in far-reaching ways to the rich web of relations in *Parsifal*. Not only does it add to the motivic density of this dramatically important transition and foreshadow the imminent entry into the Temple and ensuing ritual music of the Grail, but it also contributes to the narrative continuity of the whole work through its recall of the trombone passage from the very outset of the act, and its correspondence with the final cadence of the entire work. And whereas the downward resolution of the head of the Communion theme from D♭ to C at the entrance into the Temple in act 1 opens up the "paired" key, C, the gigantic simplicity of Wagner's tonal plan allows the change in a single interval — the replacement of the falling semitone by a rising whole step, the upward resolution of D♭ to E♭ — to confirm the viability of the resolved form of the original tonic, A♭ major, at the conclusion. This is no abstract relation, but a highly

Example 4.14: Conclusion of Transformation Music, Act 1

audible device encapsulating crucial aspects of the drama into a single, concentrated gesture.

In the Transformation music, the close juxtaposition of the two motives we have discussed — the falling chromatic thirds of the "Wehe-laute" with their subsequent rhythmic diminution, and the original head of the Communion theme, with its crucial descending semitone — touches a deeper level of the drama by exposing the underlying substratum of dissonant chromaticism that takes on such a weighty symbolic importance in *Parsifal*. In the first statement of the head of the Communion theme in the Transformation music, the falling semitone F♭–E♭ echoes the same notes heard one measure earlier as part of the thematic material derived from the chromatic descending thirds; these musical ideas are thereby directly linked to one another (see ex. 4.14). Both motives, of course, share a common dramatic association with "pain," as Wagner himself observed, and further analysis could specify their relation to the music of Klingsor and Kundry, some of which was even devised as a chromatic distortion of the stable diatonic music associated with the Grail.[43] We are dealing here with an identification of dramatic relations with musical structure whereby the dissonant elements — including the turn to C minor in the tonal pairing — reflect the threat to the Grail, and all that this may imply. The meaning of the Grail in *Parsifal*, and of the collective transfiguration in act 3, is inherently ambiguous, however, and can be interpreted positively or negatively.[44] Far

---

[43] The so-called "compulsive desire" or "magic" motive heard when Kundry delivers her poisoned kiss to Parsifal in act 2, for instance, replaces the rising triadic configuration from the head of the Communion theme by ascending minor thirds followed by semitones, so that the motive circles around the dissonant tritone. Various writers have commented on the relation between chromaticism and diatonicism in *Parsifal*, and Patrick McCreless has probed more deeply into one aspect of this chromaticism, the F-E dyad heard at Parsifal's anguished cry of enlightenment "Amfortas!" after receiving Kundry's kiss in act 2. See McCreless, "Motive and Magic: A Referential Dyad in *Parsifal*," *Music Analysis* 9 (1990): 227–65.

[44] Negative interpretations have gone so far as to dismiss *Parsifal* as a proto-Nazi tract. See, in this regard, especially Robert W. Gutman, *Richard Wagner: The Man, his Mind, and his Music* (New York: Harcourt, Brace and World, 1968); and the studies of Helmut Zelinsky, some of whose essays treating *Parsifal* appear in *Richard Wagner: Wie antisemitisch darf ein Künstler sein?* ed. Heinz-Klaus Metzger and Rainer Riehn, Musik-Konzepte 5 (Munich: Text + Kritik, 1978); *Richard Wagner: Parsifal*, Musik-Konzepte 25 (Munich: Text + Kritik, 1982); and *Richard Wagner: Parsifal: Texte, Materialien, Kommentare*, ed. Attila Csampai and Dietmar Holland (Reinbek bei Hamburg: Rowohlt, 1984). These studies are less than fully convincing, especially in their treatment of the music, but they raise issues that require more attention. The critical dilemma affecting evaluation of *Parsifal* is lodged above all in the collective yet limited nature of Wagner's treatment of the idea of redemption: inasmuch as the Order of the Grail is viewed as an elite society, it is weakened or even disqualified as a potential model for enlightened social transformation, such as we find in Beethoven's setting of Schiller in the choral finale of the Ninth Symphony, for example. On the other hand, it seems clear that Parsifal's embracing of compassion involves much critique of Amfortas and the Grail community. Some Nazi ideologists responded negatively to this aspect of *Parsifal*, and Alfred Rosenberg stated that "*Parsifal* represents a church-influenced enfeeblement in favor of the value of renunciation." See *Alfred Rosenberg. Selected Writings*, ed. with an introduction by Robert Pois (London: Jonathan Cape, 1970), 139. This quotation comes from Rosenberg's widely-circulated book *Der Mythus des 20. Jahrhunderts* (Munich: Hoheneichen Verlag, 1939; first published 1930), 434. In his recent study, *Opera and Politics: From Monteverdi to Henze* (New Haven and London: Yale UP, 1997), John Bokina finds in *Parsifal* a "utopian vision of Romantic

less ambiguous is Wagner's musical symbolism. In evaluating *Parsifal*, we may do well to recognize this priority of Wagner's music, and consider the possibility that the unfolding of the music as an "unconsummated symbol," in Susanne Langer's formulation, represents the richest dimension of the work.[45] By contrast, the symbolic content of Wagner's text may seem "consummated" and shaped by ideological tendencies that require further interpretation. Our study of the musical genesis of *Parsifal*, and particularly the evolution of the Transformation music, reveals how Wagner sought to equate the development of the music with the development of the entire drama. His late additions to the Transformation music made it a centerpiece of the overall tonal structure, which can be heard in relationship to other passages over vast stretches of musical time by virtue of Wagner's control of the orchestration, tonality, and dramatic context of the recurring thematic material. This was not a premeditated idea, devised in advance of the unique internal context of the work, but, on the contrary, grew out of the work as a final, logical consequence of its internal relations. What Wagner regarded as the "core of the whole" containing "the sufferings of Amfortas" in his early sketching of the Communion Scene and the prelude continued to guide his very last revisions to *Parsifal*. In this instance, revelation of the genesis of the work allows us to recognize not only what Wagner did, but why he did it. We have arrived here at a point where the genesis and structure of the work intersect, providing insight into the nature of the creative process itself.

Anticapitalism" tied to Wagner's pessimism "about the prospects of redemption through political means." (107); a similar interpretation of *Parsifal* as an "anticapitalistic utopia" is advanced by Dieter Borchmeyer in *Das Theater Richard Wagners: Idee — Dichtung — Wirkung* (Stuttgart: Reclam, 1982), 294.

[45] The complex integration of Wagner's music seems to conform to Susanne Langer's requirement of a "process of articulation" whereby "*music as its highest, though clearly a symbolic form, is an unconsummated symbol*" (author's italics). See Langer, *Philosophy in a New Key: A Study in the Symbolism of Reason, Rite, and Art* (1942; New York, 1961), 204.

5: Unseen Voices: Wagner's Musical-Dramatic Shaping of the Grail Scene of Act 1

Katherine R. Syer

O F ALL WAGNER'S OPERAS, *Parsifal* profiles unseen voices and offstage instruments most extensively. Invisible voices — human and instrumental — function as integral elements of the drama in the framing acts. As Wagner planned it, two choruses sing from above the stage at different heights, and Titurel sings from the extreme background of the stage area, out of sight but as if below ground. Six trumpets, six trombones, tenor drum, and bells signal moments of religious ceremony from the wings. This call for sound produced offstage is intended in part to evoke objectively real or phenomenal music making.[1] Locating brass instruments away from their orchestral partners can both signify the realistic nature of their calls and their physical distance from the locale represented onstage. Placing choral forces above the stage design of a temple can allude to the traditional practice of church choirs singing from balconies. The frequent *a capella* nature of the unseen voices in *Parsifal* similarly suggests realistic or non-operatic types of performance, including secular male-voice choral singing.

At the same time, Wagner's use of invisible sources of sound is bound up with a sense that the meaning of the Grail extends beyond the phenomenal level, beyond the visible and immediate realm of experience.[2] This is

---

[1] Carolyn Abbate has opened far-ranging analytical perspectives on phenomenal music (stage music) and noumenal music in her *Unsung Voices: Opera and Musical Narrative in the Nineteenth Century* (Princeton, Princeton UP, 1991).

[2] Much earlier, in 1843, Wagner employed an invisible choir to personify an unnamed divine entity. This chorus sings just once in *Das Liebesmahl der Apostel*, a half-hour oratorio-style work: "Seid getrost! Ich bin euch nah, und mein Geist ist mit euch. Machet euch auf! Redet freudig das Wort, das nie in Ewigkeit vergeht!" (Be of good cheer, for I am near you and my spirit is with you. Rouse yourselves! Joyfully speak the word that will never pass away in eternity.) Singing *a capella,* the unseen chorus is tonally and harmonically distinguished by its diatonic C major music, setting it apart from the work's chorus of youths and the 12 apostles. The work was

particularly the case in the Grail scenes, in which the vertical organization of space is aligned with a range of vocal registers and states of being. Lacking a specific physical identity, the *Knaben* or boys' chorus of sopranos and altos sings as if from the top of the temple dome while the *Jünglinge* — youths' chorus — of altos and tenors sings from halfway up the dome. Anchoring the spectrum of vocal registers, and grounding the communal realm of the visible earth-bound knights (tenors and basses), is the bass Titurel. This framework of unseen voices is inextricably tied to the Grail: the choral conglomerate of voices in the dome functions as ambassador and even spokesperson for the Grail and the undisclosed redeemer with which it is associated, while Titurel, once keeper of the Grail, clings to life through its power. Wagner's nuanced motivic, harmonic, tonal, and instrumentational strategies connect these invisible realms with the world we see onstage. The extended musico-theatrical space reveals itself by this means to be an intricate system of interconnected levels through which we can overcome the barrier of the Grail's ineffability and feel its rejuvenating forces.[3]

The association between invisible voices and the Grail is already intimated in the opera's opening scene.[4] The curtain rises after the prelude has ended, *pianissimo*, with a gently repeating dominant seventh of A♭.[5] Gurnemanz and two squires are seen sleeping at dawn. The first sound of the staged opera is not the tonic resolution of A♭, but a *forte* F♭ played by offstage trombones, supposedly from the direction of the Grail temple (see ex. 5.1). The

---

premiered with massive choral forces in Dresden's Frauenkirche, which is architecturally remarkable for its verticality. The unseen chorus sang from up in the dome, as do the unseen choruses in *Parsifal*. For further details about this work see Werner Breig's "The Musical Works: *Das Liebesmahl der Apostel*," in *Wagner Handbook,* ed. Ulrich Müller and Peter Wapnewski, article trans. Paul Knight and Horst Loeschmann, translation ed. John Deathridge, 420–21 (Cambridge, MA: Harvard UP, 1992).

[3] The most detailed account of motivic relations in *Parsifal* is Hans-Joachim Bauer's *Wagner's 'Parsifal': Kriterien der Kompositionstechnik* (Munich and Salzburg: Katzbichler, 1977). For a study of Wagner's instrumentation, see especially Egon Voss, *Studien zur Instrumentation Richard Wagners* (Regensburg: G. Bosse, 1970). Parts of the analysis presented here are drawn from my "Altered States: Musical and Psychological Processes in Wagner" (PhD diss., University of Victoria, Canada, 1999), 156–88.

[4] We can also regard the purely instrumental prelude as preparing this relationship, featuring as it does Wagner's invisible orchestra. More specifically, and recognizable only in hindsight, the opening material of the prelude prepares the recapitulated version with unseen voices in the Grail scene later in the act.

[5] Tempo and dynamic markings and stage directions (unless noted otherwise) are drawn from Richard Wagner, *Sämtliche Werke,* vol. 14, *Parsifal* (Mainz: B. Schotts Söhne, 1972–73).

Das vorige Zeitmaß: Langsam

Example 5.1: Parsifal, *beginning of Act 1, mm.114–27*

trombones unfold the opening of the so-called *Liebesmahl* or Communion theme (114–16)[6] through a triadic ascent in F♭ major before continued motion through the octave pivots to settle on E♭, strengthened by offstage trumpets. This harmonically and spatially differentiated call to prayer briefly explores the tension between F♭ and E♭ before Gurnemanz awakens and takes E♭ as his point of entry, with the regular orchestra making its first contribution as string pizzicato reinforcement. Gurnemanz wakes the squires, who spring up as the trombones and trumpets sound the Grail theme in A♭ major (mm.119–21). In this important expository segment, the delayed

---

[6] For reference purposes, measure numbers have been provided, hereafter abbreviated as m. and mm.

resolution of the dominant seventh of A♭ exposes a hierarchical ambiguity between A♭ and E♭ that will recur in the harmonic interface between the realm of the Grail and that of the earth-bound knights. As Gurnemanz comments on the call to prayer, woodwinds in the pit orchestra sequence the rising tail gesture of the Grail theme, the "Dresden Amen" figure, emphasizing E♭ major. The faith theme's characteristic plagal progression from A♭ major to E♭ major accompanies the gesture of prayer with offstage trombones and trumpets (measures 124–27). Muted strings echo the theme, extending it sequentially until its close in A♭ major overlaps with another offstage brass statement of the Grail theme. The woodwinds echo this theme in full, with an additional concluding plagal cadence in A♭ major that rises into the highest register as Gurnemanz and the squires slowly stand up.

The trio of brass themes presented in association with the morning prayer is already familiar from the prelude, where they appear in the same order but are sequenced and otherwise varied as the purely instrumental section unfolds. A♭ major is tonally prominent in their initial presentation and at structurally important moments such as the beginning and the close of the prelude's expository section. The developmental section beginning in m.78 concerns itself with various reworkings of the Communion theme, the most differentiated and complex of the three themes. However, the Communion theme is never stated in full after the exposition and the prelude unfolds without any literal recapitulation. Thus the trombone variant that opens the staged part of the opera may initially raise expectations of a recapitulatory gesture, even as the harmonic disjunction and ultimate inconclusiveness signal at least momentary denial. Retrospectively, the trombone gesture can be heard as leaning into E♭ major, which enables Gurnemanz's participation. In the prelude, the second and third brass entries readily offer close interaction between A♭ major and E♭ major, rendering their harmonic relation ambiguous in terms of a single tonic. Through the sequencing of the Faith theme during the actual moment of prayer, A♭ major emerges as the more prominent sonority. Both the closing echoed statement of the tonally-rounded unit of the Grail theme and the added plagal cadence clearly favor A♭ major, which envelopes all in the aftermath of the prayer. Then the stable serenity of the moment changes abruptly when Gurnemanz instructs the youths that it is time to prepare for the King's bath. As at the beginning of this scene, the harmonic disjunction between A♭ major and F♭(E) major signals the shift towards differentiated musical-dramatic space, this time involving new motivic material in a new harmonic space, as the tragic character of Amfortas is introduced.

The drama is refocused on the Grail in the act's second and final scene with its performance of the Grail service. Verbal references to time mark the transition: Gurnemanz, observing that the King's bath is finished and that the sun is reaching its peak, notes that it will soon be time for the Grail meal. Kundry also keenly observes time but will not be taking part in the service. Her "Die Zeit ist da" (The time has come) of mm.1067–68 links up with Klingsor's first line in the second act; this connection causes Kundry to be overcome by sleep and initiates her tormented transition to enslavement in Klingsor's realm. Meanwhile, the transition that Gurnemanz announces and that is enacted directly onstage involves new processional music facilitating the shift in locale to the Grail temple. Interwoven with the "Dresden Amen" cadence, first in E major and then in E♭ major (mm.1076–77 and 1082–83 respectively), the semitone relation that motivated the opening morning prayer is re-employed. The offstage trombones that first presented this semitone relation *in nuce* return here to cap the ensuing *Verwandlungsmusik*, the Transformation music bridging the first and second scenes during the elaborate scene change.

Recalling the beginning of the communion theme starting on F♭ (m. 1140), the offstage trombones distinctively reengage with the notion of a much-delayed recapitulation (see ex. 5.2). Dramatically, this ups the ante: the religious ceremony concerned is not morning prayer in the countryside but midday communion in the Grail temple, and a potential hero is now in the picture. The unseen instruments beckon Gurnemanz and Parsifal as they are drawn ever closer to their acoustical source, the Grail temple. Again, however, the Communion theme does not sound as first heard in the prelude. Only at the beginning of the Grail service will the theme unmistakably return in its initial thematic guise, initiating the much-delayed recapitulation in which, of course, a choral presentation replaces the purely orchestral version heard in the prelude. Towards the end of the *Verwandlungsmusik*, three climactic waves involve sequences of the *Heilandsklage* (Savior's lament; mm.1137–39 shows one such sequence).[7] Out of a fourth climax in F♭(E) major (m. 1140) emerges the Communion theme starting on F♭, effectively displacing the *Heilandsklage*. Sounded by

---

[7] As William Kinderman shows elsewhere in this volume, Wagner expanded the original *Verwandlungsmusik* in March 1881, in reluctant response to requirements of the staging. As originally conceived, the anti-climax following the *fortissimo* D♭ minor sonority at the beginning of m.1123 lasted for five measures and then switched to the processional music, marked *F-dur* (F major) in the sketches. Rising up through the "Dresden Amen" to B♭, the previous climax and diminuendo aftermath was then sequenced a whole tone higher. Again passing into the processional music, Gurnemanz's entry, varied only in its starting pitch, occurred in the first bar featuring its characteristic dotted rhythm. The subsequent music remained the same, as a variant of the previous processional stretch (with voice) that reaches up through the "Dresden Amen" to a C major cadence, the beginning of an expansive diatonic section featuring the off-stage bells. The off-stage trombones, trumpets and bells prior to Gurnemanz's entry were part of the revisions and extensions of the passage. Consistencies between these conceptions of the transformation's ending include: the

*) Originale Anmerkung: *Diese Posaunen, sowie die hierauf noch mit hinzu kommenden Trompeten, sind, je nach Bedürfnis der beabsichtigten Wirkung, nötigenfalls durch die entsprechenden Militärmusik - Instrumente zu verstärken.*

Example 5.2: Act 1 Verwandlungsmusik, *mm.1137–53*

the full complement of six offstage trombones, with an earthshaking off-stage bass drum tremolo, the Communion theme variant is barely audible amidst the terrible tutti *fortissimo.* (See figure 5.1 for an overview from this moment to the end of the act. Off-stage voices and instruments are indicated in italics in the second column.) Becoming more clearly audible

---

juxtaposition of fearful climaxes with more mundane motion-oriented music; the penultimate climax as embedded in music associated with pain and sin; and the final climax as reached through a Grail-like ascent, a gesture which aligns with the end of Gurnemanz's introductory comments and the end of the journey, reached as C major is firmly established with a full statement of the Grail theme.

m.1140	*trumpets* *trombones*	Trumpets sound the head of the communion theme first at m.1440 and again at m.1148, joined by trombones.	F♭+ → E♭+ D♭+ → C+
1150	*bells*	This first sounding of the bells dovetails with the long-held final C of the trumpets and trombones. They ring out for four measures before orchestral accompaniment harmonizes the pair of fourths as C+ and A–. They fade out as Gurnemanz and Parsifal enter the main hall of the Grail castle.	C♭+
1160	*bells*	The Grail theme and the resumption of the bells (m.1162) restore C+.	C+
1168	knights/ *bells*	As before, the bells sound in between but not during vocal passages. After each of the first two vocal phrases they support harmonic motion towards A–. The third and fourth vocal phrases modulate towards flatter keys, E♭+/B♭+, and G♭+/D♭+. An augmented fourth pivot in m.1991 leads further afield through sharp keys, en route back to the final cadence in C+.	C+
1198	*bells*	The Grail theme and bells reenter, anchoring C+ and framing the passage involving the knights, who reach their places at the feast–table.	C+
1203		As Amfortas is carried into the hall, modal inflection of C+ serves as a pivot towards E♭–.	C → E♭–
1204	*youths*	Altos and tenors sing from halfway up the dome, recalling the original act of self-sacrifice and its ongoing redemptive potential. The contrast between E♭ and E is explored, with an overall shift from minor to major.	E♭/E E♭ +

Fig. 5.1: Parsifal, act 1, scene 2: The coordination of unseen sources of sound

1226		A varied statement of the Grail theme bridges the two choruses.	→(A♭+)
1229	*boys*	Sopranos and altos sing *a capella* from the top of the dome, sequencing the faith theme. Their A♭+ cadence overlaps with the re-entry of the orchestra in E♭+.	A♭+→ E♭+
1246 1259	*Titurel* Amfortas/ *Titurel*	*A capella,* Titurel poses three questions to Amfortas. Each emphasizes D♭–, but, in closing, gestures towards E♭+ and is followed by E♭ timpani triplet figures. After the first two questions, the timpani figures are followed by long silences, eerily resounding Titurel's doubts. Amfortas's entry draws in tension between E♭ and F♭(E).	(D♭–)/E♭ E♭/E
1281	Amfortas	The *Amfortasklage,* the only extended solo in this scene, is the most tonally and motivically complex passage. It involves three principal sections and a concluding passage, each featuring a change in psychological state that involves the tonal area of C. The solo technically ends in m.1404, when Amfortas sinks back as if unconscious, but can be understood as extending through the entries of the choruses and Titurel to reach a more palpable level of closure at m.1421. mm.1297–1322 mm.1322–56 mm.1356–92 mm.1393–1404.	 E– E♭+/– E♭–/E– (→ D–)
1405	*boys/* *youths* knights *Titurel*	Altos and tenors from halfway up the dome sing the *Torenspruch* (prophecy), *a capella.* Their consequential phrases "harre sein, den ich erkor!" yield the awaited cadence in D, with the overlapping knights' entrance in m.1410 reinforcing its G+ plagal preparation. The knights' varied form of the Grail theme reroutes the harmonic emphasis towards E♭+, secured at Titurel's softly sung "Enthüllet den Gral!".	→ (E♭+) →D–/+ → E♭+

Fig. 5.1: (Continued)

1422		As Amfortas rises with difficulty, the *Schmerzensfigur* gradually takes shape. Initially drawing attention to A, an augmented fourth above the otherwise bare E♭ timpani pedal, the gesture is reoriented towards A♭ beginning in m.1432.	E♭+ → A♭+
1440	*boys and youths*	Altos and 1st tenors sing the communion theme in its fullest and most basic form, *pianissimo*. After their cadence in m.1445, Amfortas bows devoutly in silent prayer before the chalice; the light in the Hall gradually wanes to a mere dusky glimmer. A luxurious orchestral tutti expands A♭+ before the communion theme is repeated by trumpet, three oboes and the second half of divisi violins at m.1448. A♭+ sounds from the theme's close at m.1453–58 and the stage becomes completely dark as the orchestral texture thins to woodwinds and brass and the rhythmic pulse slackens.	A♭+
1459	*boys* *Titurel*	Sopranos and altos begin the communion theme in C minor. The sequence unfolds unremarkably until the theme's E minor central section is reached within the instrumental section. This climax serves as a pivot away from the theme's regular conclusion into a modulatory section which correlates with changes in the dramatic scenario and lighting but nevertheless returns to E minor. Amfortas, with a transfigured expression, consecrates the bread and wine as modulations incline towards A♭-related keys. Titurel quietly expresses exaltation and cadences in C+ (m.1478) as a striking variant of the communion theme emerges, shorn of its central section and tonally rounded form. As Amfortas sets the Grail down, and its glow fades, the theme's opening triadic gesture reaches over to the sixth, as part of an A– sonority that yields a modulation to a third below, instead of the theme's usual turn to the minor mediant.	C– → C+ →

Fig. 5.1: (Continued)

cont.		Continued step-wise ascent up a fourth to D, harmonized as G+, alludes to the related tail sections of the communion and Grail themes. Semi-tonal swells embrace E♭+ then E♭–, before a similar rhythmically augmented ascent reaches D♭+. Another semi-tonal swell, to A– and back, precedes the final ascent to A♭+, the most direct reference to the Grail theme. Throughout this stretch, natural daylight has gradually been restored. At m.1485, the interlocking fourths of the bell motive sound in the lower strings and timpani, reinforcing A♭+, which gradually settles in middle registers in the woodwinds.	A♭+
1493	*boys* *youths*	Sopranos and a few altos sing of the transformation, through divine love, of body and blood to bread and wine. The melody is a modified and significantly expanded version of the communion theme. Altos and a few high tenors immediately follow in m.1510 with a passage that continues to profile E♭+ through its dominant and is similar in its structure and textual meaning.	E♭+
1528	knights	The knights sing a further modified form of the Communion theme, also in unison and embracing the E♭+ tonic established by the boys' chorus. The theme's characteristic interior turn towards a third related minor sonority is no longer featured, and new upward-striving gestures are introduced. The first group of knights praises the bodily strength yielded by the bread. The second group, in a cadentially overlapping entry, echoes the first group, praising the energy offered by the wine. At m.1528, the first group reenters and the imitative passage is concluded in four-part choral harmony. While vocal parts imply a V–I cadence in E♭+, deceptive instrumental harmonization precludes closure and steers towards a V–I cadence in A♭+ via the ascending "Dresden Amen" figure.	E♭+

Fig. 5.1: (Continued)

1562	knights/ youths/ boys	Knights (basses then tenors), youths, and boys enter successively, every two measures. They complete a double statement of the Grail theme in A♭+, praising faith and love in a continuous registral ascent.	A♭+
1574		The extended instrumental passage momentarily reasserts E♭ as tonic with C+ soon vying for tonal prominence and capping a climax at m.1585. Meanwhile, the squires' attention has turned towards their leader. Amfortas, who has taken no part in the meal, has gradually sunk down from his state of inspired exaltation; he bows his head, and presses his hand to his wound. The squires attend to his freshly opened wound and prepare to depart. The *Heilandsklage* motive recurs at m.1588. This turn towards B♭– leads into the music familiar from the processional, in E♭+, which now serves for the recession. Two further musical allusions to Amfortas's suffering emerge at mm.1597 and 1603, both times emphasizing E♭–. With Amfortas's disappearance at m.1606, the E♭ coloring gives way. The lighting on-stage diminishes. C+ quietly assumes tonal stability, and is the fundamental sonority for the Grail theme that begins in m.1612. At its close, the onstage bells reenter and continue to sound as the other squires and knights depart from the hall.	E♭+→
			C+
	bells		
1634	Gurnemanz	The bells fade to silence as Gurnemanz questions Parsifal. While "Parsifal presses his heart convulsively and slightly shakes his head," a chromatically descending passage in the strings emphasizes E–, before resting on A♭. As a form of criticism, Gurnemanz employs a distorted version of the *Torenspruch* and his music vacillates between D and B♭+ in orientation, but tonal stability is not sustained. He abruptly dismisses Parsifal.	

Fig. 5.1: (Continued)

1653	*alto solo,*	The alto soloist restores the *Torenspruch* in its basic form. The vocal closing in E– is harmonized as C+ as the overlapping entry of the youths' chorus begins the Grail theme, with the boys' chorus entering at m.1659 to sing the theme's concluding ascent. The bells reenter at m.1161, securing the act's closure in C+, and Gurnemanz heads off in the direction of the departed knights.	C+
	youths,		
	boys		
	bells		

Fig. 5.1: (Continued)

as the orchestra recedes, the trombones come to rest on E♭ and the processional music begins. This qualitative shift enabled through the potent F♭/E♭ semitone recalls the simplicity with which the journey began and refocuses attention on the physical goal. The Communion theme begins again at m.1148, this time spanning the semitone relation from D♭ major to C major. With the addition of six offstage trumpets, its entry is recognizable from the onset. Even more than its antecedent, this awesome cry is a striking embodiment of the fearful, infinitely great sublime against which the ensuing plodding and human-scale music seems to exist with humility. The overall effect is a sort of split screen juxtaposing the spiritual and physical planes of the drama. As the music guides the focus back and forth, our aesthetic engagement negotiates multiple planes in this transition.[8]

A new sonic timbre offstage is introduced just after the variant of the Communion theme starting in D♭ major and ending on C. Offstage bells sound briefly in m.1150 before resuming in a more regular way in m.1662, but their descending interlocking fourths have become familiar since Gurnemanz noted the approaching time of the Grail service. Much varied throughout the *Verwandlungsmusik,* the processional gesture now sounds in its most fundamental form: single-rhythm fixed pitches of C, G, A, and E. The realistic nature of the bells, which always sound the same four pitches, fills a delimited harmonic and tonal space that tends to reinforce

---

[8] A similar process occurs near the end of the scene in the reversal of this procession after the communion scene has ended. The communion theme is no longer dramatically relevant but Amfortas's suffering is. The music exemplifying his state is associated with the first three climaxes of the *Verwandlungsmusik* and alternates with the processional music now as recessional music as the squires remove him from the Grail temple.

C major in this scene. As the offstage brass disappear, the bells ring out *a capella* for at least four measures. The orchestra rejoins the texture with strings supplying the dotted rhythm characteristic of the processional gesture's orchestral forms. After Gurnemanz's introductory remarks to Parsifal, the bells resume as the Grail theme cadences in C major. Preparations for the Grail service have begun, and they continue as the three choral groups sing in succession, in ever-higher registers and physical locations.

Initially, the bells are included in the instrumental passages between the knights' phrases, as squires move briskly across the stage. But while the fixed pitches of the bells support the harmonic motion towards A minor, they necessarily drop out at the turn to E♭ major in m.1183. The transformational and regenerative powers of the Grail that are celebrated in the knights' text are vividly suggested by the modulatory nature of the rest of this choral passage. E♭ major serves as the gateway to this more adventurous path, which eventually concludes in C major. The focal pillars of E♭ major and C major call attention to tonal spaces differentiated by instrumentation, harmonic language and textual context and may remind us that the two brass statements of the communion theme in the *Verwandlungsmusik* came to rest on these harmonies. Returning to frame the chorus as a whole, the Grail theme and bells extend the *fortissimo* C-major cadence while the knights arrange themselves at the feast table.

Another harmonic development prevents the bells from ongoing harmonious participation, as C major turns to C minor in m.1203 and the tempo slackens. The E♭-minor sonority reached at the downbeat of m.1204 signals two changes: Amfortas is carried onstage and the lower offstage chorus begins to sing for the first time. In a gesture of mutual cross-referencing, the youths' first phrase "Den sündigen Welten, mit tausend Schmerzen" (For the sinful world, amid a thousand pains) refers obliquely to Amfortas. The orchestra is drastically reduced as the offstage chorus enters and their first vocal phrase dwindles to *piano*. Both of the chorus's first two phrases begin in E♭ minor and invoke the unstable *Heilandsklage* of the *Verwandlungsmusik*. Throughout, the youths' chorus dwells upon the semitone relation of E♭/F♭(E) that has recurred so significantly since the first entry of the offstage trombones. As a localized tonal duality, each of the youths' phrases explores further shifts of meaning through modal fluctuation. Here, as in the knights' chorus, E♭ serves as a springboard for unconventional modulations in conjunction with a text that centers on the notion of transformation. Where the knights refer to the Grail and the Grail service, the youths also mention the source of these symbols: the original act of self-sacrifice that redeemed the sinning world. The theme of transformation is thus connected to an act of substitution, of taking on the burdens of others. The youths' chorus also adopts a more authoritative tone than the dependent knights. The invisible chorus offers redemption to its audience as if it were the Redeemer, shifting from E♭ minor to B major (the dominant of E) in the process of offering the redeeming blood (mm.1213–8).[9] Both E♭ and E are realized in the major mode in the concluding measures of this choral passage (mm.1222–7). Rhetorical impetus underscores the reconciling reinterpretation of the blood of the original sacrifice as the blood of present-moment redemption when the opening E♭ minor of "Den sündigen Welten" is modally altered by the end of the last phrase "er lebt in uns durch seinen Tod" (he lives in us through his death). En route to this synthesizing conclusion, the distantly contrasting key areas are deployed to render sonorous differences between the ideas of sin and sacrifice, suffering and healing, death and life, while broadly evoking the notion of transformation that is central to the Grail service.

The youths' final cadence overlaps with an unusually varied statement of the Grail theme that serves as a bridging passage (see ex. 5.3a). Pit trombones and trumpets absent from the choral passage begin the theme's initial pattern of I–vi–IV (assuming the E♭ tonic of the choral cadence). An ensuing F-minor sonority strengthened by woodwinds leads off a chain of secondary dominants — F minor/B♭[7]/E♭[7] — as a metrical shift and syncopations are introduced in m.1229. At the height of a chromatically-charged dynamic swell in the center of this measure, inner voices featuring first bassoon, trumpet, and trombone descend stepwise from E♭ to D♮ to D♭. At the same time, appoggiaturas occur in the scalar ascent carried by the upper woodwinds as sixths. E♭ moves to F♭ under C, before shifting to F under D♭. Contrary motion in inner voices continues, implying a goal of A♭ as tonic sonority at the point that this orchestral transition breaks off. While the overlapping first entry of the highest unseen chorus does in fact complete this cadence, it does so *a capella*. This extreme shift in instrumentation, following the unstable metrical and harmonic preparatory elements of this cadence, calls attention to the shift from one unseen chorus to the other. In hindsight, once the highest chorus has finished its second phrase, we can hear that Wagner has remarkably distinguished the two unseen choruses. The highest voices are conspicuously more stable and grant A♭, as local tonic, a secure position as they sing by themselves. The two choruses feature distinct thematic material that is metrically differentiated. There is no overlapping of the two choruses or shared

---

[9] Christ's name never appears in the libretto. Although allusions abound, and Wagner referred to Christ in discussing the work, he clearly did not want to limit the identity of the Redeemer to a singular individual in a conventional religious context.

Example 5.3a: Act 1, Grail Scene, mm.1224–30

vocal forces, and disjunctive acoustical surprises surface in the bridging material. This set of conditions will be adjusted in all subsequent performances of the unseen choruses in the act as Wagner develops musical metaphors for the transference and embracing nature of the Grail's redemptive powers.

The earlier transition that took place between the knights' chorus and the first offstage chorus involved a full and powerful instrumental passage, after which the orchestra gradually assumed a less substantial role before dropping out altogether during the second offstage chorus. When the orchestra returns at the vocal cadence at m.1240, it offers a single muted string echo of the faith theme torso sequenced in the preceding boys' chorus (see ex. 5.3b). In this echo, the closing vocal pitches of A♭ and C are not harmonized as A♭ major but as F minor. The favoring of A♭ (as opposed to E♭) as local tonic of the previous transition is soon reversed; the swing towards E♭ major does not immediately negate what has just transpired, but there is the sense of taking a small step backwards. A further suspension of energy occurs with the direction *immer noch langsamer werdend* just as the compound processional/bell motive is fleetingly reintroduced in the horns in m.1242, as all those onstage reach their final positions. With all of the choral forces having completed their preparatory offerings, the gradual de-emphasis on the orchestra reaches an awkward extreme. Onstage motion has drawn to a halt and all are in place waiting for a service to begin. It does not.

A new unseen voice, Titurel's, emerges after prolonged silence. Up until m.1244, there has been no reason to suppose that the Grail service would not continue normally; we might presume that the trio of choruses has sung just as they would before any service. The silent pivot from anticipation to uncertainty registers as something of a surprise for those onstage as well as for us. The same goes for hearing Titurel's voice. As the only member of the Grail community with authority over Amfortas, Titurel speaks on behalf of his original responsibility to the Grail as well as for all those who are awaiting the service. But he also speaks on his own behalf, as Amfortas's father, in an effort to remain alive. Aged and near death, Titurel is the most sensitive to the possibility that the rejuvenating qualities of the Grail might not be offered. These many facets of his voice coexist in his invisibility, as he sings a capella from far behind and perhaps even below the visible stage area, "wie aus einem Grabe" (as if from a tomb). From Gurnemanz we have learned of Titurel's heroic and divinely charged career as leader of the Grail community; this larger-than-life impression benefits from Titurel's invisibility (and may even encourage us to de-emphasize the effects of old age), while Amfortas's relative failures are thrust into visibility onstage. Titurel's morally and religiously authoritative operatic ancestors include the statue of the Commendatore in *Don Giovanni* — whose "back-up" includes an offstage

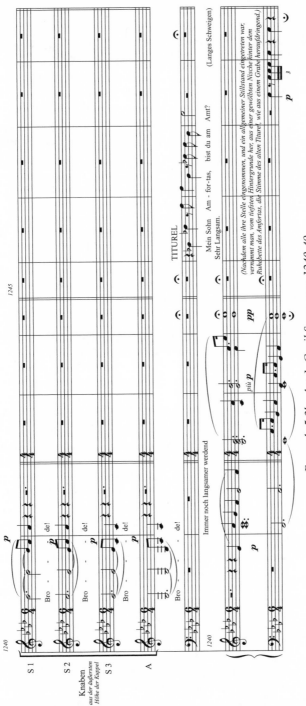

Example 5.3b: Act 1, Grail Scene, mm.1240-49

chorus — as well as the pope, who is never seen but is quoted in Tannhäuser's "Rome Narration."[10]

Titurel poses three questions to Amfortas. Each dwells on D♭ minor but closes with a gesture that moves towards pitches of the triad of E♭ major, followed by E♭ triplet timpani figures. After the first two questions, the timpani figures are followed by long silences. The uncertainty thereby deepens while Titurel's chromaticism moves along a regressive timeline, undoing what for a while seemed inevitable. He seems to reach back to the dissonances of the transition between the two choruses and even further to the semitone relations of the youths' chorus and the beginning of the Communion theme in the *Verwandlungsmusik*. More immediately, Titurel's harmonic otherness also emphasizes his physical distance from the onstage drama. After his third question, his efforts see E♭ harmonically realized as E♭ minor in a momentous orchestral climax with Amfortas finally rising to respond.

The *Amfortasklage* (Amfortas's lament) is exceptional: it is the only extended solo in this scene and presents a highly charged, emotional account of individual experience to which we would not normally be privy. Within the symmetrical construct of the procession, the Grail service, and the recession, the *Amfortasklage* occurs just before the service, threatening to displace it, while occupying roughly one quarter of the entire scene. Although Amfortas initially resists the forward flow of events, the Grail service becomes inevitable by the time he collapses as if unconscious. A turning point between suspense and anticipation occurs in the middle section of Amfortas's solo, with a vision that draws on painful memories of prior services, presented or re-experienced as if in the present. Because Amfortas's experience of the service is substantially different from that of the rest of the knights, his vision serves as an indirect exposition to the public ceremony that follows. His vastly more negative experience is rendered through the motivic, harmonic, and structural distortion of music already heard, including material from the prelude. A large-scale recapitulation from the prelude undergirds the actual ceremony.

Before Amfortas begins his solo proper, he responds to Titurel with vocal anguished outbursts (m.1259–61) of a dminished fifth, from E♭ to A♮, before traversing a D♭-minor sonority that leads into C♭, harmonized as F♭ major. The augmented fourth or diminished fifth has by this point been associated with many expressions embodying pain. As a rising interval, it

---

[10] With Titurel, Wagner bypassed the trope of a predominantly monotone vocal line, which serves an even more important psychological purpose at the beginning of Amfortas's vision, in the central portion of the *Amfortasklage*.

ends Titurel's first question, "Bist du am Amt?" (Are you at your appointed place?) And much earlier, when Amfortas was first introduced in act 1, another rising augmented fourth, F to B, concludes Gurnemanz's announcement of the arrival of their suffering leader: "Behutsam! Hört, der König stöhnt" (Pay attention! Hear, the king groans), while descending versions of the same pitches sound in the lower strings. Paradoxically, Amfortas initially seems quite peaceful when he is subsequently brought onstage; his opening vocal line emphasizes perfect fourths and fifths (mm.259–62). Soon, however, the augmented sonority F/A/C♯ characterizes his accompanimental material (m.264) and underscores his mention of his "Schmerzensnacht" (night of pain) before giving way to a gently unfolding B♭ major at "Morgenpracht" (morning splendor). Amfortas looks forward to further relief from his customary bath, while the augmented sonority returns in targeted fashion as he refers to the pain that his bath will relieve.

If we are tempted to believe that Amfortas is the optimist that he certainly is not, another layer is soon peeled away when a knight announces that Gawain has ventured forth in search of a potent healing balm for the wounded leader. Amfortas's response "Ohn' Urlaub" (Without permission!) unleashes a series of augmented fourths (m.298) as he voices his fear that Gawain could meet a fate similar to his own. This potential fate is projected as a version of Amfortas's own woe, "Oh wehe ihm" (Oh woe to him), with a vocally-traced augmented fourth that forms part of a diminished sonority. Amfortas now seems less assured about positive developments. As he concludes with the profession that he is waiting for the promised redeemer, he intones the *Torenspruch* (prophecy)[11] with its characteristic descending augmented fourth at "Mitleid" (compassion), harmonized as a diminished seventh. But Amfortas does not invest faith in the prophecy of a compassionate redeemer. Within what could unfold as an unremarkable iv–V–i cadence in D minor (mm.331–33), the so-called "Mystic" chord or "Tristan" chord variant is substituted for the dominant sonority as Amfortas names the redeemer "Death," to the vocal augmented fourth E♭–A. This substitution is revealed to us only later, when Gurnemanz accurately quotes the *Torenspruch* (see ex. 5.4, mm.728–35).

Amfortas's tendency to negate or invert meanings is coupled with his strong desire to shed the responsibilities that have been placed upon him by his father. At the scheduled onset of the Grail service, he is quick to propose

---

[11] This is the first hearing of this striking theme, which is selectively presented at crucial moments in the drama. As with Amfortas's personal account of the Grail service in the *Amfortasklage,* we encounter Wagner employing an indirect type of exposition of musico-dramatic material, whereby a rather negative interpretation, involving motivic distortion, is used to anticipate the more characteristic and positive form of the idea and its musical shaping.

Example 5.4: Act 1, Gurnemanz's Narrative, mm.718–35

that he could swap roles with his father: Titurel would perform the service and live, and Amfortas, presumably not partaking of the sacrament, would die.[12] Amfortas turns from E♭ minor towards F♭-related sonorities as he appeals to Titurel, and then closes with a perfect cadence in A♭ (mm.1259–66). By contrast with the previous A♭-major section, when the boys' chorus had praised the harmonizing and healing power of the sacrament, Amfortas's turn towards A♭ minor inverts their message; denying life and the sacrament as the only solution. The negotiation with and negation of the musical language and ideas of preceding passages in this scene continues: the F♭ prominent in Titurel's preceding passage recurs vocally

---

[12] For a discussion of musico-dramatic substitutions in Amfortas's solo in act 3, see David Lewin's "Amfortas's Prayer to Titurel and the Role of D in *Parsifal:* The Tonal Spaces of the Drama and the Enharmonic C♭/B," *19th-Century Music* 7/3 (1984): 336–49.

and instrumentally in m.1260, as part of a D♭-minor harmony en route to F♭ major, and then as a descending vocal augmented fourth, B♭ to F♭, within the diminished sonority that yields to A♭ minor. Sounding in the cadential aftermath, as violas and celli descend through the augmented A♭ triad, F♭ is reclaimed by Titurel as the starting point of his response in m.1267.

Rephrasing his earlier questions as statements and then as stern commands, Titurel reiterates his dependency on the Redeemer's grace. Trombones and bass tuba sound the opening phrase of the Grail theme, *pianissimo*, moving from A♭ major to D♭ major, but the musical idea remains a torso, as does the similar gesture initiated in m.1276, when Titurel commands Amfortas to uncover the Grail. Amfortas's blatant refusal overrides an implied cadence in D major, with his "Nein!" sounding a C atop a diminished sonority that the violins continue in the rapid chromatically descending gesture associated with Kundry. Augmented fourths abound as Amfortas orders the Grail, and his pain, to remain concealed. Amfortas faces paradoxes at every turn. What gives joy to others causes him pain. His wish to isolate his suffering from those who have not sinned motivates his appeals to death, as he has lost faith in the arrival of a redeemer, but suffering would become widespread if he left the Grail community without someone to carry out the Grail service. Rhetorically, he asks, "Was ist die Wunde, ihrer Schmerzen Wuth gegen die Noth, die Höllenpein, zu diesem Amt – verdammt zu sein!" (What is the wound and its raging torment compared to the agony, the hellish pain of being damned to serve this office?) Above all, it is his role in leading the service that troubles him. Amfortas moves awkwardly towards a cadence in F♭ that frames his position of resistance, before launching into his effort to explain himself more fully.

Tension abates somewhat once the *lebhaft* section gets underway (m.1297). A sense of regular structure begins to emerge, while the orchestra assumes a more integrated and uncharacteristically conventional role. Mm.1297–1301 are akin to a ritornello, loosely establishing E, both in the minor mode and within a diminished sonority, together with the syncopated melody and accompaniment by which Amfortas makes his reentry in m.1306. The tonal orientation towards E(F♭) stretches back to Titurel's command to uncover the Grail, and Amfortas attempts once more to launch an explanation of why that responsibility troubles him. What follows is a more objectively-oriented mode of narration, but it proves too difficult to sustain. Several changes occur at m.1309, following Amfortas's identification as the only sinner in his community and preceding mention of his duty to the Grail and his brethren. This gross irony — that a sinner should enable the blessing of non-sinners — is an insurmountable problem. Trombones and bass tuba solemnly underscore the phrase beginning "des höchsten Heiligthums zu pflegen," (to tend this most elevated shrine) *pianissimo*, with a C-major sonority of referential quality. The brass timbres reverberate from his father's command and allude to his filial duty to lead the Grail community. This is the first significant presence of C major since it distinguished the knights' choral passage and its statements of the Grail theme with bell reinforcement. Here, the brass opening leads into a much-distorted and chromatic string version of the Grail theme ascent, with the regular rhythmic pattern arrested. The irony of the situation is further musically manifested as the gesture climaxes in m.1312 at the word "Reine" with a negating chromatic descent like that of m.1281. Momentarily, but unconvincingly, Amfortas reclaims the earlier more stable music-rhythmic patterns to close his phrase with an E^7 sonority that resolves conventionally to A minor. But nothing has really been resolved, and Amfortas seems to lose control again as full orchestral accompaniment underscores emotional and obscure kinds of outbursts. The *Heilandsklage* familiar from Amfortas's first response to Titurel and the first youths' chorus emerges in m.1316. Despite the passage's possible claim towards functional harmony, as a modulation to the subdominant of E minor, Amfortas is unable to logically develop his explanation, and a version of the chromatic descent of m.1312 returns in m.1320. This breakdown of formal/narrative patterns continues as an implied return to E is consumed by the diminished sonority of mm.1320–22.

Another course is pursued as syncopated string chords pulse through the instrumental introduction to Amfortas's next entry. Formally similar to the beginning of the *lebhaft* section at m.1297, the character of the moment is nevertheless quite different (see ex. 5.5). The tempo is relaxed, *langsamer werdend*, and earlier dynamic flux gives way to a restrained *pianissimo*. Although C♯ lingers quietly in the lower strings after the last texted measure (m.1322), the upper strings discard their diminished identity and restore E minor with the second violins shifting from B♭ to B♮ (mm.1322–23), before semitonal alterations in both string groups yield C major in the following measure. In the preceding section, the single deep brass chord that announced C major, atypical in its immediate context and fleeting, had triggered an unusual variant of the Grail theme tail, or "Dresden Amen" figure, distorted by diminished sonorities. In m.1324, C major is again not sustained, but it takes shape more subtly. Flutes and bassoons initiate the head of the Grail theme, in a rhythmically augmented form that moves from C major through an augmented E♭ sonority to a dominant seventh chord built on A♭. This realignment towards E♭/A♭ re-engages with the divine realm of the two offstage choruses and assumes the aura of a prayer as Amfortas professes a desire for divine redemption. His second phrase recaptures the head of the Grail theme, beginning in A♭ minor and reaching D major in m.1332. Neither the augmented sonority of the theme's beginning nor melodic motion through the augmented fourth conveys strain. On the contrary, the relaxed rhythms and non-strident instrumentation both lend a gentle, otherworldly quality to the harmonic palette. D major melts into an augmented D sonority and then E♭ minor. The *Heilandsklage* returns, also sounding unusually relaxed as Amfortas rephrases his humble plea for forgiveness. A syncopated

Example 5.5: Act 1, Amfortasklage, *mm.1322–32*

variant of the Grail theme ends his phrase in G major (m.1339), featuring the
trombones and bass tuba, which have not sounded since the first appearance
of the Grail theme in the solo (m.1309). They continue to sound G major,
underpinned by timpani tremolo, in the rhythmically augmented form of the
Grail theme opening, as Amfortas turns his attention to the impending com-
mencement of the Grail service.

"Die Stunde naht," (The hour approaches) marks a turning point in the
solo (see ex. 5.6). The Communion theme, which has not been heard for
some time, sounds as Amfortas's eyes fix on the Grail (m.1346). He alone, of
those onstage, experiences what he relates, and several clues signal to us that
he experiences an altered state of consciousness during this episode. Unusual,
visionary experiences involving the Grail have already been relayed by Gurnemanz in his extended narrative. The first such scenario involves Titurel in his
battle against the evil forces of Klingsor; the only nearly full statements of the
Communion theme in the first scene occur in this passage.[13] Beginning in
G♭ major (m.581), the theme sounds after Gurnemanz relates how divine

---

[13] The first time the theme sounds in conjunction with a texted vocal line is earlier,
when Gurnemanz defends Kundry from the mockery of the squires. The theme's
opening phrase sounds twice, supporting his interpretation of her as a repentant individual deserving of their tolerance. The first time, the theme begins in D♭ major. The
second time it starts in A minor and dovetails with the *Torenspruch,* as Gurnemanz
recognizes goodness in her deeds. The A minor statement is the only time that the
beginning of the Communion theme sounds in the minor mode in the first scene.

Example 5.6: Act 1, Amfortasklage, mm.1340–50

messengers came to Titurel's aid. As Gurnemanz describes the chalice offered to Titurel as the same one used at the original *Liebesmahl,* the theme unfolds through the *Schmerzensfigur* and returns to its initial key. Instead of cadencing, it dovetails with another statement of the theme beginning in C♭ major. The Communion theme again does not close, but is joined this time with the head of the Grail theme. The explanation of the consecrated nature of the chalice — as *the* chalice that caught the blood of the dying Redeemer on the cross, from the wound inflicted by the spear — profiles expanded treatment of the *Schmerzensfigur* separated from the rest of the communion theme (mm.592–97). Gurnemanz's motivically-dense account of prior events reaches the recent past when he tells of Amfortas's loss of the spear to Klingsor. At this dire point, we learn that Amfortas prayed for a *Rettungszeichen* (a sign of salvation), and that his prayers were answered by the animation of the Grail, including a wondrous vision at the center of which is the Ur-form of the *Torenspruch* and the pronouncement that a redeemer is forthcoming.

The musical presentation of Amfortas's first vision evokes the shimmering of the Grail through ascending A♭-major sonorities (see ex. 5.4) that evolve into the Grail theme's opening in D♭ major. From this point, a full statement of the Grail theme unfolds. The Communion theme melody begins in D♭ major in the oboes and alto oboe, and peaks on its tonic, which is then reinterpreted as the mediant of A major at the mid-point of Gurnemanz's text "durch hell erschauter, Wortezeichen Male" (in the brightest, clearest language). An A-major harmony hovers radiantly for three measures before the *Torenspruch* sounds in full and cadences in D major. This passage, from the Grail's glowing to the divine command to wait for the "reine Thor" (pure fool) unfolds semitonally-related progressions of a fourth: A♭ major→D♭ major/A major→D major.[14]

Amfortas's vision in the Grail scene conveys the severe physical and psychological pain that he has experienced when, after the Grail has been illuminated, its symbolic contents are shared with the community of knights. Amfortas's vision is more than a reenactment of a regular service, for it is accessed through his prayerful plea, thereby recalling in form the first vision narrated by Gurnemanz. Since Amfortas's troubles began, the service has become increasingly valuable in providing sustenance for all waiting for the "reine Thor." The glowing Grail and its contents are tangible symbols of the apparition's message of hope and encouragement to have faith that the prophecy will come true. Precisely because Amfortas's faith has waned, and the Grail service torments him, we see him desperately recalling the moment when he experienced the miraculous prophecy, the realization of which has become most urgent. In his prayer-like plea in his Grail scene vision (mm.1326–32), the focus on A♭ and the internal climax of the Grail theme variant traversing A♭ to D major attempt to reclaim that moment when his prayers were answered by the message that initially gave him hope. The desired response to his prayer — the *Torenspruch* — is substantially delayed by his vision of the illuminated Grail.

As Amfortas imagines that the Grail service is beginning, it is as if another force is controlling time and he becomes an uncomfortable participant in the experiences that he relates. At the mention of time (m.1340), the woodwinds climb to C major through the opening of the Grail theme. String tremolos join the texture as Amfortas "sees" the Grail being illuminated and a fuller sounding of the Grail theme reaches further upwards. When Amfortas envisions the cover falling from the Grail, a luminescent C major turns mysteriously towards the minor, with English horn and clarinet intoning the beginning of the Communion theme. This theme's minor mode version has been heard but rarely; its unfamiliarity works together with the modal shift to create an uncanny feeling as Amfortas slips more deeply into an altered state of consciousness.[15] At the same time, the

---

[14] Patrick McCreless has noted the importance of this passage in focusing attention on the A♭–D relationship, which figures significantly in the relationship of the *Torenspruch* to the opera as a whole. See his "Motive and Magic: A Referential Dyad in *Parsifal*," *Music Analysis* 9/3 (1990): 239.

[15] David Lewin has discussed the difference of these versions in terms of Riemannian functions. He notes that the minor mode version frequently involves *Leittonwechsel* transformations, the most characteristic harmonic feature of the *Schmerzensfigur* as it is first heard. See David Lewin, "Some Notes on Analyzing Wagner: The *Ring* and *Parsifal*," *19th-Century Music* 16/1 (1992): 49–57.

C-minor Communion theme represents the first time in the entire act that we again hear the theme begun on either of the paired tonics heard in the exposition of the prelude.[16] As the C-minor Communion theme unfolds towards the *Schmerzensfigur,* Amfortas's transfixed state is made manifest through his monotone vocal line, with his repeated Fs emphasizing an augmented fourth against the *Schmerzensfigur*'s climax on B. But the treatment of the *Schmerzensfigur* itself is atypical. Instead of tracing an expected E-minor sonority, the melody descends from B to F then rises to A♭, as part of a diminished harmony. At m.1349, the Communion theme has not progressed but instead has lingered on a repetition of the *Schmerzensfigur.* The shortened treatment of the Communion theme and the form of the *Schmerzensfigur* re-orient the listener to the developmental section of the prelude, not its beginning. At "erglüht" (it glows), a propelling dominant-seventh emerges (m.1350) and the *Schmerzensfigur* disappears. When in the next measure Amfortas's vocal line finally line rises from F to G♭, and the dominant seventh of E♭ minor resolves to the tonic, the Communion theme begins again (m.1351), moving in yet unheard directions.

The E♭-minor variant of the Communion theme takes us into a highly subjective realm where we learn of Amfortas's personal response to the Grail service. This response differs completely from that of the knights. We are offered a glimpse of those agonies Amfortas experiences when the Grail service actually takes place — suffering that is impossible to show alongside a communal Grail experience without detracting from the positive experience of the knights. In effect, the individual account of the *Amfortasklage* precludes the need to show two simultaneous levels of experience, for it explains why Amfortas does not himself partake of the sacrament when he eventually leads the service. The vivid opening up of his world of pain is also an opportunity for us to sympathetically identify with Amfortas's choice not to participate in the service. We are exposed to the tremendous guilt that rests on Amfortas through his sharp self-critique, which links several ideas that have already emerged in the harmonic-dramatic space of E♭ minor: Amfortas's sin and suffering, the larger sinning world, and the anguish endured by the Redeemer.

Amfortas's efforts to establish analogies between himself and the Redeemer stem from the bold if misguided role he attempted to play in

---

[16] The ambiguity of this motivic gesture, as one both familiar and yet different, is captured in Heinrich Porges's rehearsal notes from 1882 about how Wagner wanted the theme to be played: "nicht die volle Bedeutung des Themas, also nicht zu langsam" (not the full import of the theme, thus not too slowly). See *Dokumente zur Enstehung und ersten Aufführung des Bühnenweihfestspiels "Parsifal,"* ed. Martin Geck and Egon Voss, vol. 30 of Richard Wagner, *Sämtliche Werke* (Mainz: B. Schotts Söhne, 1970), 185.

confronting Klingsor. He attempted to prove himself resistant to and even stronger than Klingsor's powers, but succumbed to Kundry's seduction like many knights before him. This failing is hardly extraordinary (indeed, quite the contrary), but that is not what makes Amfortas's comparisons with the Redeemer so tragically easy to collapse, despite the ease with which he himself does just that. Amfortas fails in the comparison because his suffering is not really a burden that he bears solely for the greater good of his community; his suffering involves his own sin and misjudgment. While Amfortas's inability to resist Kundry makes him no better or worse than the other knights who had met the same fate, his decision to carry the sacred spear into combat against Klingsor marks a greater failing and original sin in this context. But it is the sin of sexual desire that reminds Amfortas so overwhelmingly of the source of his recurring physical pain; this somewhat narrow perspective drives much of the distortion of musical material in the *Amfortasklage*. This serves an important function locally, as indirect musical exposition for the actual Grail service. But, as it turns out, the larger musico-dramatic purpose of Amfortas's extended solo is held in reserve until that juncture in act 2 when Parsifal takes the place of Amfortas in Kundry's arms.[17]

In the prose drafts of August 28 and 29, 1865, Wagner already had a very clear idea — even a blueprint — of the successive experiences and layers of understanding that Parsifal would undergo at the crux of the drama. What appears as a radical reordering of the material of the *Amfortasklage*, as Parsifal reprocesses what he earlier observed but did not fully comprehend, is actually a fully conceived psychological process that was the precedent for the *Amfortasklage*, not the other way around.[18] The actual musical and formal shaping of the material that would be employed in the *Amfortasklage* was eventually determined by the context of the act 1 Grail service, with much consideration of the possible musical links that

---

[17] Wagner had used a similar strategy in act 1, scene 3 of *Götterdämmerung*. Waltraute's appeals to Brünnhilde fall on deaf ears initially, but her message and its musical presentation are central to the conclusion of the opera, when her message is fully digested and realized.

[18] Given the remarkable detail, including complete lines of text, that Wagner fleshed out at this stage, it is noteworthy that any description of the *Amfortasklage* in act 1 is missing, but that Parsifal's epiphany is completely mapped out as a re-experiencing of what he witnessed in the act 1 Grail scene. The evidence at this stage that the Grail service triggers renewed suffering for Amfortas is highly compressed; Wagner notes merely that Amfortas alone is not positively renewed from the service and that his wound opens afresh. See Joachim Bergfeld, ed., *Richard Wagner: Das braune Buch, Tagebuchaufzeichnungen 1865 bis 1882* (Zurich: Atlantis Verlag, 1975), 61–67.

could be forged between Amfortas's sinful behavior with Kundry and the reenactment of the seduction in act 2. In this respect we can note that musical ideas associated with the Grail service function as a type of musical memory in act 2, while the similarity of Amfortas's so-called *Erbarmen-schrei* (cry for mercy) to the plunging musical gestures associated with Kundry anticipate Parsifal's recognition of Kundry as the agent of Amfortas's sexual sin.[19] Furthermore, we can see how Amfortas's problematic analogies with the undisclosed redeemer will bear fruitful reinterpretation when the potential hero begins to take Amfortas's place and shows himself capable of reversing the mistakes of the fallen leader.

In his act 1 lament, Amfortas prepares the co-mingling of identities of the Grail leader and a supreme redeemer when the Communion theme begins in E♭ minor (m.1351). He describes the reanimation of the Redeemer's redemptive blood in the Grail as that which he painfully feels within his own body and which reawakens the sinful lust of his own blood. Energy gradually gathers in the stream of motivic ideas at the marking *Allmählich etwas belebter* (gradually somewhat more lively) while Amfortas's characteristic augmented triad figures and music associated with Klingsor start to erode the sense of harmonic order. In m.1363, Amfortas's strange experience of strong contrary forces within him so completely overrides his normally physically restricted state that he jumps up.[20] The diminished form of the *Schmerzensfigur* is repeated as Amfortas links his own wound to that of the Redeemer by recounting that it was inflicted by the same spear. The *Heilandsklage*, beginning in E♭ minor and E minor (m.1369 and m.1372 respectively), underscores the description of the Redeemer's wound as the embodiment of the suffering he bore for humanity's shame. While the tempo intensifies, *wieder belebend* (m.1375), the orchestration thins and Amfortas contrasts his role with that of the Redeemer. Amfortas's failings seem to resound in the Communion theme's false starts and endings. Opening in C major, the Grail theme collapses just before its climactic cadence; the theme begins again in C minor. This schism recalls two earlier points in the *Amfortasklage*. The link to the moment at which Amfortas enters an unusual, transfixed state — the beginning proper of his

---

[19] For studies of the relationships between these two extended passages, see David R. Murray's "Major Analytical Approaches to Wagner's Style: A Critique," *Music Review* 39 (1978): 220, and William Kinderman, "Wagner's *Parsifal*: Musical Form and the Drama of Redemption," *Journal of Musicology* 4 (1985–86): 438–42. For the most detailed correlation, see John Daverio "*Tristan, Parsifal, and the 'New' Organicism*," in *Nineteenth-Century Music and the German Romantic Ideology* (New York: Schirmer Books, 1993), particularly 197–207.

[20] This stage direction is noted by Julius Kniese. See *Richard Wagner: Sämtliche Werke*, vol. 30, 185.

"vision" — is highlighted by the stage direction, recorded in Heinrich Porges's notes, that Amfortas was to return to his usual physical position lying down (m.1377) during his reference to his formal office.[21] The Grail theme variant beginning in C minor reaches E major and B major but a repetition of the "Dresden Amen" ends with a negating diminished sonority and the *Erbarmensschrei*/Kundry motive. The first sounding of part of the Grail theme in the solo (m.1309) had been similarly treated. The thematic distortion in both cases reflects how mismatched Amfortas and his office have become.

The closing section of the *Amfortasklage* is an intensified version of the earlier prayer, with Amfortas now desperate for the Redeemer's forgiveness: "Du Allerbarmer! Ach, Erbarmen! Nimm mir mein Erbe, schließe die Wunde, daß heilig ich sterbe, rein Dir gesunde!" (All-merciful one! Have mercy on me! Relieve me of my inheritance, heal my wound, so that I may die holy, pure and healthy for thee!) Tristanesque coloring and diminished sonorities enshroud localized motion from B major→D major→A minor (mm.1394–99) and D minor→G minor→E♭→A^7→D minor→A^7 (mm.1400–1404), while the dynamic level is reduced to *ppp*. Amfortas does not reach his implied goal of D. As "er sinkt wie bewußtlos zurück" (he sinks back as if unconscious), his orchestral accompaniment also passes into silence, save for an A that lingers for two measures on two horns. The melodic contour outlining an augmented fourth and the harmonic nature of Amfortas's final phrase refer obscurely to the *Torenspruch*.[22] Altos and tenors from both of the offstage choruses assume Amfortas's unrealized A^7 sonority as the starting point for a full statement of the *Torenspruch*. Two different sonorities overlap momentarily: a diminished sonority embracing the augmented fourth, and A major. The gesture continues through F major, G minor, and E♭ major sonorities, after which the awaited D cadence is supplied with the consequential command "harre sein, den ich erkor!" (wait for him whom I have chosen!) Initially ambiguous, and inclined towards the minor mode, D is ultimately confirmed in the major mode as the onstage knights affirm the prophecy and reorient the music towards E♭ major.

The main sections and conclusion of the *Amfortasklage* are demarcated by moments involving the greatest degree of change in all of the musical-dramatic parameters, but none of these sections is formally closed and the entire solo utilizes motivic/harmonic material that is reworked

---

[21] *Wagner: Sämtliche Werke*, vol. 30, 185.

[22] As with Amfortas's first reference to the divine prophecy and the *Torenspruch* (mm.320–30), he is incapable of realizing the gesture in a continuous and full form. In the earlier passage, fragmentation of the theme's first phrase occurs when Amfortas breaks off to seek validation from Gurnemanz.

across the opera as a whole.[23] The intent of the narration is to explain why Amfortas resists Titurel's expectations. Crucial insights are not forthcoming immediately or directly, but emerge as Amfortas undergoes a psychological transformation whereby he fully reveals the physical and spiritual suffering that he normally tries to conceal. In the process, conventional formal strategies are bypassed, but a rich harmonic, motivic and rhetorical network is in evidence.

As already discussed, the semitonally related key areas of E and E♭ figure prominently in each of the three main sections, as does the local tonal area of C, which emerges in specific association with the Grail theme to mark shifts in Amfortas's psychological state. In the first section of Amfortas's solo (mm.1297–1322), the presence of C in m.1309 is subtle yet nonetheless seems to lead into a more subjective layer of events that challenge the autonomy of formal strategies already set in motion. This signal gains strength in the second section (mm.1322–56), and occurs similarly at a moment in which we are reminded of Amfortas's responsibilities. Earlier in the scene, C-dominated passages had concerned the knights and their preparations for the Grail ceremony, for which ultimately they require Amfortas to act as leader. With the second symbolic allusion to the key of C, Amfortas passes into a kind of trance, in which he relates a different and vivid reality, which from m.1356 turns most inward and persists until the Grail theme begins in C major at m.1376. The degree of activity and sensitivity that Amfortas displays in this state is suggestive of a sort of intense waking-within-sleeping state. Coming out of this state he is not so much enlightened or refreshed as exhausted — he lies down again, in a state of despair, and dwells on his own physical and spiritual weaknesses. The conclusion of the lament reclaims musical material from before the trance, including intensified features of the plea that had earlier been shaped as a prayer. This material thereby reconnects with processes that earlier inclined towards recreating the visionary experience recounted by Gurnemanz. In a surprising twist, Amfortas undergoes yet another transition, this time into a more conventional state of unconsciousness, and the announcement of the prophecy does indeed follow, sung by both of the

---

[23] In his analysis of the *Amfortasklage*, Alfred Lorenz characteristically overstates the case for balancing symmetries, finding a "vollkommene Bogen" in seven parts. He does not elucidate the dramatic significance of related sections within these symmetrical forms, nor how this material connects to other important passages in the act or opera as a whole. See Lorenz, *Der musikalische Aufbau von Richard Wagners Parsifal* (Berlin: Max Hesses Verlag, 1933), 78–84. For a more probing and satisfying exploration of symmetrical structures in *Parsifal*, see Heiko Jacobs's *Die dramaturgische Konstruktion des Parsifal von Richard Wagner: Von der Architektur der Partitur zur Architektur auf der Bühne* (Frankfurt am Main: Peter Lang, 2002).

unseen choruses. Thus everyone onstage, except Amfortas, fully experiences the miraculous announcement of the prophecy. The completion of this recapitulation comes after the *Torenspruch* theme. Earlier in the act, the squires affirmed Gurnemanz's account with their echo of the first portion of the theme, cadencing in E♭ major. After the *Amfortasklage*, the knights validate the invisible chorus's message and paraphrase it so as to reflect their own needs, firmly urging Amfortas to have faith, and to continue to carry out his office. The Grail theme shifts from C minor to E♭ major, before sounding again in a fully rounded way in E♭ major, as Titurel utters once more the command "Enthüllet den Gral!" (Reveal the Grail!)

An obvious formal prototype for Amfortas's lament is the Dutchman's monologue early on in *Der fliegende Holländer;* the shared harmonic language of their respective prayer-like sections, including augmented sonorities, is thought-provoking. Both solos employ rhetorical gestures that negate conventional types of musical and formal meaning. Both protagonists experience unusual psychological states and collapse at the conclusion, as if unconscious and convinced of their unending suffering, while offstage voices supply a hopeful postlude. As Wagner was completing the final version of the first act of *Parsifal,* he was also working closely with the conductor Anton Seidl on the *Holländer* score, the first act of which they went through together on the evening of October 27, 1877. Cosima recorded the following from their conversation:

> Vom *Holländer* zum *Parsifal,* wie groß der Weg und doch wie gleich das Wesen! — Nach der Musik spricht R. von den Einflüssen des "Kosmos," der äußern Welt, auf Naturen, welche, gut angelegt, vielleicht nicht genug Kraft haben, um dem zu widerstreben, und welche nun ganz besonders schlecht, pervers werden. "Nichts von außen kommt ja wohltätig solchen Naturen entgegen!"

> [From *Holländer* to *Parsifal* — how long the path and yet how similar the character! — Following the music, R. talks about the influence of the "cosmos," the outside world, on characters who, though basically good, do not perhaps possess the strength to resist it, and who then become quite exceptionally bad, indeed perverse. "Nothing from the outside world is of benefit to such characters!"][24]

Wagner indeed seems to return to a familiar character here, since Amfortas, like the Dutchman, meets his fate ignorant of the consequences

---

[24] Cosima Wagner, *Cosima Wagner: Die Tagebücher,* ed. Martin Gregor-Dellin and Dietrich Mack, 2 vols. (Munich and Zurich: Piper, 1982), 1:1079–80; hereafter *CT.* In English: *Cosima Wagner's Diaries,* trans. Geoffrey Skelton (New York and London: Harcourt Brace Jovanovich, 1980), 1:1990.

of his actions. Amfortas also shares with his forerunner a double cycle of suffering: nights of endless pain followed by brief respites seemingly without real solutions. He too has been offered the hope of salvation, but has lost faith with the passing of time and wishes for death by the time we first encounter him. In *Parsifal*, however, faith is maintained on a community level and Amfortas is beholden to that community. After the chorus and Titurel have sung, Amfortas slowly re-engages with the external world and now no longer refuses to carry out the service, which seems to have an independent source of momentum, although he resists active participation. The Dutchman, too, seems not fully connected to the real world after the invisible members of his crew have sung. It is as if he is only going through the motions of his ritual visit ashore, but he has no real faith that he will soon encounter his redeemer.

With Amfortas in this relatively passive and doubtful state, Titurel assumes authority with his command to uncover the Grail (mm.1416–18). The squires duly respond and Amfortas slowly rises, as the *Schmerzensfigur* gradually takes shape in the celli and is then sequenced over an E♭ timpani pedal, with the motive passing through A♭ minor, E minor, and C minor. The long-awaited recapitulation of the opening of the prelude in A♭ major that now begins (m.1440) is enhanced and varied not only through the involvement of singers and text; the next forty-five measures contain the most detailed lighting conception in the entire score, shifting from midday light to a dark twilight and, after the special illumination of the Grail, a return to normal light. Wagner had specific ideas about the vocal effect he wanted to achieve here, according to Cosima's account of June 27, 1880:

> Er spielt darauf für sich das erste Thema von Parsifal und kommt zurück und teilt mit, wie er durch einen Chor die Worte habe aussprechen lassen, um daß es weder weiblich noch männlich erscheine, ganz ungenerell müßte Christus sein, weder Frau noch Mann.

> [He then plays the first theme of *Parsifal* to himself and, returning, says that he gave the words to a chorus so that the effect would be neither masculine nor feminine; Christ must be entirely sexless, neither man nor woman.][25]

Wagner's use of young male voices in the invisible choruses accords with long-standing religious practices. These voices are pre-pubescent and ostensibly pre-sexual, and have obvious blending potential with female voice ranges, thus offering the closest natural, aural form of gender ambiguity. Early in the Grail scene, Wagner uses the youths' chorus, with its particular blend of young male and female voices, to personify the

---

[25] *CT* 2:556 (trans. 2:498–99).

Redeemer, as they offer the Redeemer's blood. The higher boys' chorus sing text as if they were the Grail, offering the Grail's wine. For the divine prophecy at the end of the *Amfortasklage* and the first texted Ab-major version of the Communion theme, Wagner set the respective texts in quotation marks, emphasizing the external source of the words. In both these cases, Wagner combined the two invisible choruses and narrowed their overall range by dropping the lowest and highest voice types.[26]

As the Grail service gets underway, altos and first tenors assume the function of the prelude's bassoons, clarinets, and English horn in singing the melody of the Communion theme. For the first time, the offstage voices sing not in part-harmony but in unison as the singular collective voice of the Redeemer. While they often sing *a capella* elsewhere, they are continuously accompanied by the orchestra here. The orchestra picks up the cadence of this full and tonally-rounded form of the theme and luxuriously expands the Ab-major sonority with predominantly triplet figures in the woodwinds and thirty-second-note arpeggiation in the upper strings reaching into the higher registers. Amfortas prays, and the stage starts to darken. Trumpet, three oboes, and the second half of divisi violins enter at m.1448 to unfold this version of the communion theme melody once more. With Ab major resounding at the theme's close (m.1453–58), the stage becomes completely dark, the texture thins to woodwinds and brass, the rhythmic pulse slackens, and a brief pause ensues.

The sopranos and altos from both offstage choruses now enter smoothly with the communion theme in its second most fundamental

---

[26] Jean-Jacques Nattiez cites the aforementioned diary entry in his analysis of Kundry's death in his larger argument that *Parsifal* is misogynistic. See his *Wagner Androgyne*, trans. Stewart Spencer (Princeton: Princeton UP, 1993), 167–72. Nattiez assumes that Wagner conceived a mixed chorus as the solution to a sexless representation of the Redeemer, and that he was thereby referring to the end of the work. He claims on p. 171 that "this final chorus is the only mixed chorus in the entire work and Kundry dies on a sustained Ab sung by the sopranos." Kundry does not in fact die *while* the sopranos are singing. Their sustained high Ab drops an octave and sounds only for the first quarter note of m.1123, and then the stage directions indicate that "Kundry, with her gaze uplifted to Parsifal, sinks slowly lifeless to the ground." Her death transpires during a purely instrumental passage, coinciding with the semitonal swell from Db major to A minor and back. More important, regarding the idea of a mixed chorus, the invisible youths' chorus halfway up the temple dome is always a mixed chorus unto itself, as is Wagner's combination of the unseen choruses. Concerning the comments made in June of 1880, Wagner was clearly referring to the passage in act 1 beginning at m.1440. These recapitulated, texted versions of the full Communion theme in Ab major and C minor represent the only passage in the entire opera when the original forms of the theme sound with words that are indicated in quotation as possibly emanating from a supreme Redeemer.

form, in C minor (m.1459). Again the cadential close is expanded in a richly serene instrumental passage and the theme is repeated by the orchestra alone. Yet when the inner third-related minor triad is reached in this purely instrumental unfolding, at the *Schmerzensfigur*, the E-minor sonority does not lead back to C minor but modulates out of the theme altogether into the first dynamic climax of the passage, capped by the *Heilandsklage*. This motivic digression reflects the special atmosphere onstage:

> Hier dringt ein blendender Lichtstrahl von oben auf die Krystallschale herab; diese erglüht sodann immer stärker in leuchtender Purpurfarbe, alles sanft bestrahlend. Amfortas, mit verklärter Miene, erhebt den "Gral" hoch und schwenkt ihn sanft nach allen Seiten, worauf er dann Brot und Wein segnet. Alles ist auf den Knieen.

> [A dazzling ray of light falls from above upon the crystal cup, which now glows, ever more deeply, a radiant purple color, shedding a soft light all around. Amfortas, with a transfigured expression, raises the Grail high and waves it slowly to all sides, and then consecrates the bread and wine. All are kneeling.]

As these gestures are realized, the modulatory passage inclines towards A♭-related keys before returning momentarily to E minor at Titurel's entrance. With full orchestration reduced to primarily string accompaniment, Titurel's quiet expression of exaltation effects a V⁷–I cadence in C major, a tonal area that by now correlates to several C-major passages earlier in the scene. These passages tangibly anticipate the ritual of renewal awaited by the knights and Titurel. The subtlety of Titurel's cadence works with an overlapping and different variant of the Communion theme to maintain momentum. The theme's rising opening triadic ascent reaches to the sixth degree (m.1479), a major sixth in keeping with the modal shift to C major. In lieu of the theme's usual profile of the *Schmerzensfigur*, an A-minor sonority begins an ascent of a fourth, characteristic of the "Dresden Amen" figure, reaching G major. Semitonal swells embrace E♭ major then E♭ minor, before another similar motivic ascent reaches D♭ minor, and a semitonal swell to A minor and back.[27] A final ascent comes to rest in A♭ major (m.1485). These musical gestures are coupled to evolving dramatic details of the Grail service: "Amfortas setzt den 'Gral' wieder nieder, welcher nun, während die tiefe Dämmerung wieder entweicht, immer mehr erblaßt: hierauf schließen die Knaben das Gefäß wieder in den Schrein, und bedecken

---

[27] The precedent of these swells, as an expanded treatment of the *Schmerzensfigur*, occurs in Gurnemanz's narrative when he describes the chalice as once having caught the blood of the Redeemer on the cross (mm.592–95). Wagner recapitulates a variant of this progression at the moment of Kundry's death.

diesen, wie zuvor." (Amfortas sets the Grail down again, and the glow slowly fades, as the deep twilight lightens; hereupon the squires enclose the vessel in its shrine, and cover it as before.) By the time A♭ major has been reached, daylight has been restored and the interlocking fourths of the bell motive begin to sound in the lower strings and timpani, while repeated A♭-major sonorities gradually settle in middle registers in the woodwinds.

The animation of the Grail — a mysterious, mystical event — spans a notably integrated and balanced musical stretch that nevertheless allows for new musical and harmonic evolutions. By contrast with some of the distortions of central musical material that are allied with destructive dramatic elements, Wagner here seems to be evoking a powerful reach beyond the diatonic and formally regular musical sphere into the realm of the sublime and wondrous. As we are so often reminded in this work, similar means can be put to very different ends.

With the actual sharing of the sacrament amongst the knights, the focus on the mystical nature of the Grail's content shifts to those processes whereby the beneficial properties of the sacrament are transferred to the earthly realm. For this purpose, Wagner uses the tiered choral effects that he has in place throughout the scene, but in different ways than before. Now, instead of drawing attention to differentiation within and between these choral groups, Wagner employs metaphors of transformation and transference. Cascading downwards in register and vertical location, the boys are followed by the youths and then the knights. The texts of the invisible choruses no longer assume the Redeemer's voice but play a more objective role noting the transformation of blood and body into wine and bread. The boys and youths both sing material derived from the Communion theme, with an initial C-minor orientation (m.1493) that turns to E♭ major (m.1509), suggestive of a closer affiliation with the knights. The knights extend the tonal area of E♭ major and it is clear when they enter (m.1528), that they have absorbed the divine message as they urge each other to gain strength through the sacrament. For the first time, the knights sing as two different groups though they are not strongly differentiated. When they come together in m.1551, the layering effect realizes the strengthening powers that they praise in song. The highly varied treatment of the Communion theme in this extended choral passage attains the quality of an anthem. A culminating and communally embracing coda develops out of the knights' cadence in E♭ major (m.1560), bridged by the Grail theme and a shift to A♭ major.

With the singers divided according to vocal type, four choral entries with their shared texts praising faith and love climb through ever-higher registers (see ex. 5.7). The orchestra participates at both thresholds of this coda, with the Grail theme sounding on trombones as the basses enter (m.1563–65) and the woodwinds supporting the sopranos' extended cadence. This is the only point in the scene where the knights freely occupy

Example 5.7: Act 1, Grail Scene, mm.1563–75

a tonal area that prioritizes A♭ major; it is achieved through the gateway of E♭ major, and the consumption of the sacrament, and thus we are reminded that the Grail service symbolizes cyclical processes of renewal that richly unfold through time and space. Hence Wagner summarizes here the idea of registral ascent strongly interconnected with the progression from visible to unseen sources of sound. Rejuvenated, the knights can now affirm the positive sustaining power of faith and love, which the offstage choruses can echo, having temporarily fulfilled their role. After the sopranos dissolve into the instrumental cadential gesture of the Grail theme heard in the oboes and flutes, the subsequent sequencing of the faith theme beginning in m.1574 recalls the first time we heard the highest invisible chorus; now, without voices, muted strings briefly reach beyond the upper register of the unseen voices.

The sequenced faith theme is a purely instrumental passage during which the knights embrace each other, signaling that the service proper has ended. While the music gradually modulates towards C major, a registral descent mirrors the restoration of normal reality. Since Amfortas has not partaken of the sacrament himself, the transfigured state of exaltation that he had attained when the Grail was brilliantly illuminated has had no substantial impact. His quick reversion to a state of pain emerges as fragments of E♭ minor, featuring the *Heilandsklage* melody, alternate with the knights' recession in C major. This split musical-dramatic plane is resolved in favor of C major once Amfortas is carried off the stage. With the fading of the bells the sense of time marching on abates, and Gurnemanz takes stock of the situation.

Parsifal's inability to express in words his reaction to what he has seen is severely misunderstood by Gurnemanz to mean that the young fool is not a candidate for the redeemer; quirky modifications of the *Torenspruch* mock the boy as it were in frustration. There is more than a little irony in the situation as it follows on the heels of the celebration of faith. However, the Grail service primarily concerns faith in the cycles felt from one midday Grail service to the next. The larger and more pressing cycle of faith whereby a new redeemer figure will emerge involves a different level of belief. We have already seen the terrible challenge posed by this expectation with regard to Amfortas. Here, the uncharacteristic weakening of Gurnemanz's faith induces a partial recall of the prophecy that was heard at the end of the *Amfortasklage*. Prepared by an F♯ viola tremolo, an unseen alto soloist restores the basic form of the *Torenspruch* and its text (mm.1653–57), harmonically transposed so as to lead into C major. The soloist's vocal close in E minor overlaps with a re-entry of the youths' chorus, who initiate the Grail theme in C major and are joined in m.1659 by the boys' chorus. This concluding ascent recapitulates in a more removed tonal sphere the unseen choral conclusion to the sweeping series of rising choral passages beginning at m.1563. The bells re-emerge at m.1661 as the act closes with a thrice-repeated C-major sonority. With this final repetition of the messages of hope and faith, unseen human voices are not heard again until the end of the opera.[28]

Unbeknownst to Gurnemanz, he and his fellow knights have failed to grasp the deeper meanings of the *Amfortasklage,* and thus the voice of Amfortas is also a sort of "invisible" voice in this complex scene. Furthermore, Gurnemanz cannot imagine that Parsifal is capable of the level of compassion that will enable him to fruitfully re-hear and re-experience core material of the *Amfortasklage.* In the closing measures of the act, the distorted version of the *Torenspruch* followed by the restatement in its original form thus serves as a reminder to Gurnemanz that his faith in a redeemer should remain strong, while also signaling that the *Torenspruch* is already in the process of being realized.

---

[28] An exception might be Kundry's initial call "Par-si-fal" in act 2, since Parsifal and the audience should not initially see Kundry through the Flowermaidens. This ploy in part concerns Kundry's disturbing means of seduction, in which she attempts to bring to life a distant (both in time and space) past, with herself playing the role of Parsifal's mother.

6: "Die Zeit ist da": Rotational Form and Hexatonic Magic in Act 2, Scene 1 of *Parsifal*

Warren Darcy

IN ACT 2, SCENE 1 OF *Parsifal,* the evil sorcerer Klingsor lures Parsifal to his magic castle and conjures up the seductress Kundry to be the agent of the boy's undoing. Although the dramatic power of this scene is indisputable, its musical structure has stubbornly resisted traditional methods of formal and tonal analysis. Patrick McCreless claims that one harmonic stretch "comes close to breaking the bonds of tonal logic";[1] while Alfred Lorenz opines that "Die Formen in dieser Szene sind durchweg sehr undeutlich, zackig und unsymmetrisch, ein Abbild von Klingsors unfruchtbarem, häßlichem Wesen" (the forms in this scene are all unclear, jagged, and asymmetrical, an image of Klingsor's sterile, ugly nature).[2]

This study proposes that the scene may profitably be viewed through two new analytical lenses: the theory of rotational form developed by James Hepokoski and the present author,[3] and the theory of hexatonic

---

[1] Patrick McCreless, "Motive and Magic: A Referential Dyad in *Parsifal,*" *Music Analysis* 9/3 (1990): 243.

[2] Alfred Lorenz, *Das Geheimnis der Form bei Richard Wagner,* vol. 4: *Der musikalische Aufbau von Richard Wagners Parsifal* (Berlin: Max Hesses Verlag, 1933; repr. Tutzing: Verlag Hans Schneider, 1966), 98. Lorenz's analysis of this scene is contained in pages 98–110.

[3] See James Hepokoski, *Sibelius: Symphony No. 5* (Cambridge: Cambridge UP, 1993), 23–26; "The Essence of Sibelius: Creation Myths and Rotational Cycles in *Luonnotar*" in *The Sibelius Companion,* ed. Glenda Dawn Goss, 121–46 (Westport, CT: Greenwood Press, 1996); and "Rotations, Sketches, and [Sibelius's] Sixth Symphony" in *Sibelius Studies,* ed. Timothy L. Jackson and Veijo Murtomaki, 322–51 (Cambridge: Cambridge UP, 2001). See also Warren Darcy, "The Metaphysics of Annihilation: Wagner, Schopenhauer, and the Ending of the *Ring,*" *Music Theory Spectrum* 16/1 (1994): 1–40; "Bruckner's Sonata Deformations" in *Bruckner Studies,* ed. Timothy L. Jackson and Paul Hawkshaw, 256–77 (Cambridge: Cambridge UP, 1997); and "Rotational Form, Teleological Genesis,

systems elaborated by Richard Cohn.[4] In the analytical framework advanced here, these two musical processes (one formal, the other harmonic) are seen as intimately connected and closely coordinated with the dramatic and poetic content.

Rotational form is a cyclical, repetitive process that begins by unfolding a series of differentiated motives or themes as a referential statement or "first rotation"; subsequent rotations recycle and rework all or most of the referential statement, normally retaining the sequential ordering of the selected musical ideas. In addition, it sometimes happens that a brief motivic gesture or hint planted in an early rotation grows larger in later rotations and is ultimately unfurled as the *telos,* or final structural goal, in the last rotation. Thus the successive rotations become a sort of generative matrix within which this *telos* is engendered, processed, nurtured, and brought to full presence.

An interpretation of act 2, scene 1 of *Parsifal* in terms of rotational form leads to results rather different from those of the analysis of Lorenz, who relied upon the sometimes slippery concept of the "poetic-musical period."[5] Lorenz was at pains to find terminal points for his designated periods based upon the return of the original key and related thematic material, and his insistence on formal segmentation often works at cross-purposes with the all-embracing continuities of Wagner's music and drama. For Lorenz, act 2, scene 1 comprises seven periods of highly variable length. The first and longest of these extends from measure 1 to 131, beginning with the prelude in B minor dominated by Klingsor's theme and ending with the return of that theme in the same key at the point when Klingsor recites Kundry's previous incarnations as Gundryggia, Herodias, "und was noch?" (and what else?). In the alternative view proposed here, this return to Klingsor's theme in B minor in m.108 beginning with the text "Dein Meister ruft dich" (Your master calls you) is regarded as the beginning of a

---

and Fantasy-Projection in the Slow Movement of Mahler's Sixth Symphony," *19th-Century Music* 25/1 (2001): 49–74. The ways in which rotational form intersects with the sonata paradigm, as well as a grounding of the term itself in philosophy, literary theory, and the natural sciences, may be found in Hepokoski and Darcy, *Elements of Sonata Theory: Norms, Types, and Deformations in the Late Eighteenth-Century Sonata* (New York and Oxford: Oxford UP, forthcoming).

[4] See Richard Cohn, "Maximally Smooth Cycles, Hexatonic Systems, and the Analysis of Late-Romantic Triadic Progressions," *Music Analysis* 15/1 (1996): 9–40; and "As Wonderful as Star Clusters: Instruments for Gazing at Tonality in Schubert," *19th-Century Music* 22/3 (1999): 213–32.

[5] For a discussion of the limitations of Lorenz's approach, see especially Anthony Newcomb, "The Birth of Music out of the Spirit of Drama," *19th-Century Music* 5 (1981), 38–66.

second large formal rotation. The third rotation also begins with this theme in the related tonality of F# minor at m.239, near the beginning of Klingsor's tortured monologue in response to Kundry's biting comment "Bist du keusch?" (Are you chaste?). The fourth rotation, on the other hand, initially dispenses with this material, although Klingsor's active role at m.321 is reflected by his blowing of a horn to summon his knights, whereas the very end of this rotation, just preceding the change of scene to the magic garden, brings yet another return of the music of Klingsor's theme in B minor.

Thus *Parsifal* II/1 unfolds in four broad rotations (fig. 6.1). Each rotation comprises two sections: an agitated passage dominated by Klingsor (section A), and a recitative-like series of exchanges between Klingsor and Kundry (section B). In its simplest form the rotational structure unfolds as shown in fig. 6.1a.

However, the internal structure of section B is variable (fig. 6.1b). In its complete form, which is revealed only in rotation 2, section B comprises three subsections: x, y, and z. The commonality between the two z subsections lies in the treatment of Kundry's resistance to Klingsor, with her reluctance to serve him continuing at her despairing questions "Muß ich? Muß?" (Must I? Must?) in mm.310–11. Only Subsection y appears in each of the four rotations as a sort of refrain, bringing forth each time the Prophecy or *Torenspruch* motive.[6]

On a somewhat more detailed level, the scene unfolds as shown in figure 6.2. The measure numbers in column 1 refer to the beginnings of sections, which may precede the subsections indicated in the chart.

a.	AB AB AB AB				
b.	Rotation 1:	A		y	
	Rotation 2:	A	x	y	z
	Rotation 3:	A		y	z
	Rotation 4:	A		y	

Fig. 6.1: Rotational form of Parsifal *II/1 (simplified)*

---

[6] Leitmotive labels are placed in italics, to differentiate the musical motive (the signifier) from the person, object, or concept to which it refers (the signified). The labels employed in this chapter are those used by Alfred Lorenz, who took over and modified the names proposed by Hans von Wolzogen, and also added a few labels of his own devising. See Hans von Wolzogen, *Thematischer Leitfaden durch die Musik zu Richard Wagners Parsifal* (Leipzig: Feodor Reinboth, n.d.). The *Torenspruch* is the harmonized melody first sung in act 1, scene 1 to the words "Durch Mitleid wissend, / der reine Tor." Wolzogen (*Thematischer Leitfaden*, 22) actually dubbed it "*Der Verheissungsspruch (Thorenmotiv),*" but Lorenz simplified this to "*Torenspruch,*" modernizing the spelling of "Thor" ("fool").

Measure	Rotation	Section	Subsection	Dramatic Content
1	R_1	A_1	Prelude (orch.)	Battle of wills: Klingsor vs. Kundry
61		B_1	y [Torenspruch, *Parsifal*]	Klingsor sees Parsifal approach his magic realm
85		Retrans.		Klingsor prepares to summon Kundry
108	R_2	A_2	Aria	Klingsor summons Kundry
132		B_2	x	Kundry awakens
180			y [Torenspruch]	Kundry's refusal
214			z	Kundry mocks Klingsor
239	R_3	A_3	Aria	Klingsor's rage at being mocked
268		B_3	y [Torenspruch]	Kundry's reluctance
299			z [*Parsifal*]	Klingsor sights Parsifal
321	R_4	A_4	Telos! [*Parsifal*]	Parsifal storms the castle
387		B_4	y [Torenspruch]	Kundry goes to work

Fig. 6.2: Rotational structure of Parsifal *II/1 (moderately detailed)*

Just as Klingsor's goal is to lure Parsifal to his castle, so the musical goal of this scene is to bring forth the diatonic *Parsifal* motive. The thematic seed of this theme is planted in Rotation 1, Subsection y; the motive resurfaces in an expanded form in Rotation 3, Subsection z; and is fully unfurled in Rotation 4, Section A_4, as Klingsor describes how Parsifal storms the castle and appears on the ramparts.

The music associated with Klingsor and Kundry is complex and highly chromatic. It often employs distinctive sets of six, eight, or nine pitches and can thus be regarded as hexatonic/octatonic/enneatonic, remaining for the most part harmonically non-functional, whereas the Parsifal music is diatonic and firmly anchored in functional harmony. A process of teleological genesis operative in this scene involves not merely a thematic growth, but a transformation of harmonic language: the "magical" hexatonic matrix ultimately gives birth to the "heroic" diatonic *Parsifal* motive.

In terms of their contrasting effect and dramatic meanings, these different manifestations of the tonal language invite close analytical study. The music of the Klingsor/Kundry sphere tends to be not only highly chromatic but also "geometric," since it relies upon equal division of the octave. Such an idiom is rich in dissonance and instability, and stands in a polar relation to the "natural" diatonic music that Wagner employs to represent the vigorous young hero Parsifal. The traditional tonal system relies on the hierarchical position of the triad, whose defining interval of a perfect fifth spans seven of the twelve semitones making up the octave. Equal division of the octave, as in the "magic" tonality of Klingsor/Kundry, aspects of which are effectively mapped in Cohn's hexatonic system, results in dissonant configurations in which the perfect fifth is avoided. The bisection of the octave into two intervals each containing six semitones produces the tritone, the most dissonant relation of all, which was known in the middle ages as the "diabolus in musica." The division of the octave into four equal units, on the other hand, yields a series of minor thirds, which can make up a diminished-seventh chord. The trisection of the octave into three major thirds provides the material for the augmented triad, and it is this configuration that is particularly relevant to the music of the Klingsor/Kundry sphere in *Parsifal*.

As Arnold Whittall has pointed out, act 2 of *Parsifal* is the only act in all Wagner's music dramas to begin and end in the same key.[7] It progresses by ascending major thirds from B minor (Klingsor's key) through E♭ major (Parsifal's key) and G major (the key of Kundry's attempted seduction) to conclude in B minor, as Parsifal defeats Klingsor and destroys his magic realm (fig. 6.3).[8] The presence of these tonal relations based on major thirds as well as of important thematic material based on similar third relations, such as the *Klingsor* theme, encourages us to apply the aforementioned theory of hexatonic systems to this music. The act thus moves counterclockwise through Cohn's Western Hexatonic System (fig. 6.4).[9] The first two tonic triads (B minor and E♭ major) are hexatonic poles,[10]

---

[7] Arnold Whittall, "The Music," in Lucy Beckett, *Richard Wagner: Parsifal* (Cambridge: Cambridge UP, 1981), 76. Unfortunately, Whittall's further remarks about the tonal relationships in act 2 are not very enlightening.

[8] E♭ major is the key of the scherzo-like opening section of the Flowermaiden scene, whose ensuing trio-like song "Komm! Holder Knabe!" (Come! Dear boy!) is cast in A♭, a key in subdominant relation to E♭. Kundry's seduction lullaby is set in G major. The poisoned kiss triggers a highly modulatory finale, which concludes resoundingly in B minor.

[9] Figure 6.4 is reproduced from Cohn, "Maximally Smooth Cycles," 17. The geographic labels match the placement of each system on the page, and possess no further significance.

[10] Two triads are hexatonic poles if together they comprise a complete hexatonic pitch-class collection (i.e., set-class 6–20, whose prime form is [0, 1, 4, 5, 8, 9]).

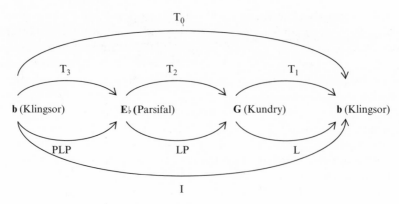

Western Hexatonic Collection: {B D D♯ F♯ G B♭}

[T = hexatonic transposition; P = parallel; L = Leittonwechsel; I = identity]

Fig. 6.3: Tonal structure of Parsifal act 2 — hexatonic and neo-Riemannian interpretations

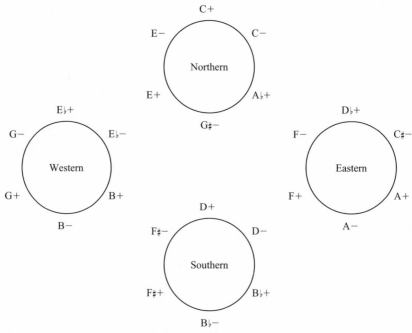

[+ designates a major triad; − designates a minor triad]

Fig. 6.4: Cohn's four hexatonic systems

and the succession of all four tonic triads displays a systematic semitonal displacement of three, two, and one pitch-classes. Figure 6.3 analyzes this semitonal displacement in two ways: as hexatonic transformations using Cohn's transposition labels (T_1, T_2, etc.) and as contextual neo-Riemannian transformations using Brian Hyer's labels (P, L, etc.).[11]

The *Klingsor* theme that opens act 2 is harmonized by a hexatonic progression that reverses the ascending thirds of figure 6.3, but employs all minor triads: B minor, G minor, E♭ minor, and B minor (fig. 6.5).

It thus traverses the Western Hexatonic System in a clockwise direction, generating modally-matched harmonies through a consistent

---

One pole will be a major triad, the other a minor triad a major third lower (e.g., E major and C minor).

[11] Hexatonic transposition refers to the number of semitonal pitch-class displacements between two triads that lie within a hexatonic system. For example, a C-major and a C-minor triad are related by T_1 because one pitch-class is semitonally displaced when moving from the first to the second (E is displaced by E♭). A C-minor and an A♭-minor triad are related by T_2 because two pitch-classes are displaced when moving from the first to the second (first G is displaced by A♭, then C is displaced by C♭). A C-major and an A♭-minor triad (hexatonic poles) are related by T_3 because of the three pitch-classes displaced; note that $T_1 + T_2 = T_3$. Two transpositions of T_3 would result in T_0 (the original triad) because this is a closed system with a modulus of 6, and 6 = 0 mod 6. Enharmonic equivalence is assumed. See Cohn, "Maximally Smooth Cycles," for a more detailed explanation. Building on writings of David Lewin, Brian Hyer uses the symbols P, L, and R to describe certain triadic transformations. The P (parallel), L (Leittonwechsel), and R (relative) operations are defined in terms of contextual inversions around an invariant dyad, which might be a perfect fifth, a major third, or a minor third. For example, the P operation inverts a C-major triad around its perfect-fifth axis to produce a C-minor triad, or vice versa; the L operation inverts a C-major triad around its minor-third axis to produce an E-minor triad, or a C-minor triad around its minor-third axis to produce an A♭-major triad; and the R operation inverts a C-major triad around its major-third axis to produce an A-minor triad, or a C-minor triad around its major-third axis to produce an E♭-major triad. These three simple transformations may be combined in various ways to form compound transformations; for example, LP applied to a C-major triad generates an E-major triad, while PLP applied to a C-major triad generates an A♭-minor triad. Some (but not all) of these operations are equivalent to hexatonic transpositions, as shown in fig. 6.3. See Bryan Hyer, "Tonal Intuitions in *Tristan und Isolde*" (PhD diss., Yale University, 1989); and "Reimag(in)ing Riemann," *Journal of Music Theory* 39/1 (1995): 101–38. For an overview of the development of what is variously referred to as neo-Riemannian theory and transformational theory, see Richard Cohn, "Introduction to Neo-Riemannian Theory: A Survey and a Historical Perspective," *Journal of Music Theory* 42/2 (1998): 167–80.

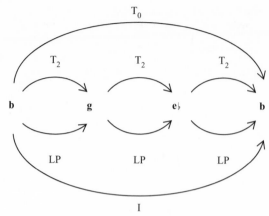

Western Hexatonic Collection: {B D D♯ F♯ G B♭}

[T = hexatonic transposition; L = Leittonwechsel; P = parallel; I = identity]

Fig. 6.5: Tonal structure of Klingsor theme — hexatonic and neo-Riemannian interpretations

semitonal displacement of two pitch classes, or by a threefold application of the LP transformation. It also generates the Western Hexatonic Collection, a specific pitch-class representation of the third-order all-combinatorial hexachord.[12]

Example 6.1a reproduces the *Klingsor* theme as it first appears in act 1. As example 6.1b shows, the melodic line adds three pitches (an augmented triad) to the Western hexatonic collection, to produce a nine-note or enneatonic collection.[13]

Like its hexatonic counterpart, this enneatonic scale (Messiaen's Third Mode of Limited Transposition) is symmetrical, alternating a whole step with two half-steps. It may be understood as combining three of the possible four augmented triads, or in this case, as adding a third augmented triad to the two that make up the hexatonic collection.

Notice that in example 6.1a not all these triads are sounded in root position: the G-minor and E♭-minor triads enter in first inversion, while the final B-minor triad is sounded in $\frac{6}{4}$ position. The theme is prepared by

---

[12] Set-class 6–20 combines with all four forms of itself (prime, inversion, retrograde, and retrograde-inversion) at three different transposition levels to produce a twelve-note aggregate.

[13] The non-enneatonic eighth-note E♮ at the end of the third measure of the theme clearly functions as a "chromatic" passing tone.

a. Initial Appearance in *Parsifal* I/1 during Gunemanz's Narrative

b. Hexatonic Harmonization and Enneatonic Scale

Example 6.1: Klingsor *Theme*

a half cadence in B minor, and the final B-minor $\frac{6}{4}$ chord resolves as a cadential $\frac{6}{4}$ to an F♯ dominant. However, although the theme is framed by these functional signifiers, its interior structure is best understood in non-functional, transformational terms.

The Western Hexatonic Collection may be viewed as three overlapping major-minor tetrachords, on B, E♭, and G. Each of these tetrachords can generate one of the three octatonic collections by combining with its transposition at the tritone (fig. 6.6).

Figure 6.7 displays these three collections as modal scales beginning with either a half step or a whole step on B, E♭, and G. Obviously the three other hexatonic systems will generate octatonic modes with different fundamentals.

$$\{B\ D\ D\sharp\ F\sharp\ G\ B\flat\} = \{B\ D\ D\sharp\ F\sharp\} + \{E\flat\ G\flat\ G\ B\flat\} + \{G\ B\flat\ B\ D\}$$

$$\{B\ D\ D\sharp\ F\sharp\} + \{F\ A\flat\ A\ C\} \quad \rightarrow \quad \{B\ C\ D\ D\sharp\ E\sharp\ F\sharp\ G\sharp\ A\}$$

$$\{E\flat\ G\flat\ G\ B\flat\} + \{A\ C\ C\sharp\ E\} \quad \rightarrow \quad \{E\flat\ F\flat\ G\flat\ G\ A\ B\flat\ C\ D\flat\}$$

$$\{G\ B\flat\ B\ D\} + \{C\sharp\ E\ E\sharp\ G\sharp\} \quad \rightarrow \quad \{G\ A\flat\ B\flat\ B\ C\sharp\ D\ E\ F\}$$

Fig. 6.6: Generation of the Three Octatonic Collections from the Major-Minor Tetrachords of the Western Hexatonic Collection

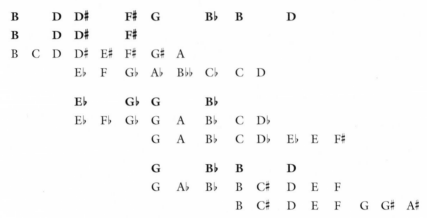

Fig. 6.7: Octatonic Modes from the Western Hexatonic Collection

{B D F Ab}

{C# E G Bb}

Example 6.2: The Kundry motive and its octatonic transpositions
(act 2 Prelude, mm.30ff.)

Octatonicism characterizes the music associated with Kundry, the unwilling agent of Klingsor's scheme. Example 6.2 shows how successive transpositions of Kundry's leitmotiv generate an octatonic collection.

In m.30 of the act 2 prelude, the *Kundry* motive arpeggiates a descending C♯ diminished seventh chord, but its third, E, is delayed by a drawn-out appoggiatura F♮ that creates a half-diminished sonority. Transposing this motive by interval class 3 holds the C♯ diminished seventh invariant, while the appoggiaturas unfold a diminished seventh on B. This combination of two diminished-seventh chords yields an octatonic mode on G, one of those related to the western hexatonic collection; alternatively, the scale could be viewed as generated by ic3 transpositions of the initial half-diminished-seventh chord. The mode is written with G as fundamental due to the emphasis placed upon this pitch class by the bassline (not shown in ex. 6.2).

We see therefore that the western hexatonic collection can generate both an enneatonic and an octatonic collection. Wagner associates hexatonicism with magic in general, its enneatonic aspect with Klingsor, and its octatonic aspect with Kundry, reserving functional diatonicism for the innocent hero Parsifal.

Figure 6.8 displays the interior structure of rotation 1 in some detail. The stormy orchestral prelude (section A_1) suggests a battle of wills between Klingsor and Kundry; its first subrotation presents the *Klingsor* theme followed by an exegesis on the *Zaubermotiv*, while its second subrotation (m.25) features a threefold cycling through this material, enriched with the *Wehelaute* and *Kundry* motives. Section B_1 (m.61) comprises a brief recitative-like passage for Klingsor; here the *Zaubermotiv* frames a contrapuntal combination of the *Torenspruch*, which will recur as a refrain, and the *Parsifal* motive, which will ultimately flower into the thematic *telos* of the scene. An orchestral retransition based upon the *Zaubermotiv* (m.85) accompanies the sorcerer as he readies his magical apparatus in preparation for the conjuring of Kundry.

Measure	Section	Subsection	Interior Structure		Motives
1	A_1	Prelude	Intro.		
5			SR_1		*Klingsor*
11					*Zauber* (bar: 3+5+6)
25			SR_2	sr_1	*Klingsor/Wehelaute*
30					*Zauber/Kundry* (bar: 2+2+6)
40				sr_2	*Klingsor/Wehelaute*
42					*Zauber/Kundry* (bar: 2+2+4)
50				sr_3	*Wehelaute*
55					*Kundry*
61	B_1	y		a	*Zauber* (bar: 3+3+4)
71				b	*Torenspruch/Parsifal*
75				a'	*Zauber* (ro: 5 + 5)
85	Retrans.				*Zauber* (bar: [4+] 4+4+11)

[SR = Subrotation; sr = lower-level subrotation; ro = rotational]

Fig. 6.8: Parsifal *II/1, rotation 1 (moderately detailed)*

Meas.   5   6   7   8   9   10   11

| Hexatonic | Octatonic | Octatonic |

Example 6.3: Harmonic structure of Act 2 Prelude, mm.5–11
(harmonization of Klingsor *theme)*

Example 6.3 displays the harmonic situation at the onset of the prelude. In m.9, the hexatonic harmonization of the *Klingsor* theme dissolves into octatonicism, as the expected B-minor triad is replaced by a diminished-seventh chord. This joins with the half-diminished seventh in m.10 to create an octatonic collection. This half-diminished seventh (Lorenz's "mystic chord") resolves to an Eb-minor triad, which combines with the half-diminished seventh in m.11 to produce a different octatonic collection.[14] All this time, the *Klingsor* melody pursues its enneatonic course.

Example 6.4a shows the derivation of the *Zaubermotiv* from the final measures of the *Klingsor* theme. In m.11 (ex. 6.4b), an eighth-note variant of this enneatonic fragment is harmonized by a half-diminished-seventh chord on A resolving to an Ab-major triad; as shown beneath the lower staff of example 6.4b, this harmonization generates an enneatonic collection different from that implied by the melody. The pattern is transposed a whole step higher in m.12, producing two new enneatonic collections, one melodic, the other harmonic.

In all, mm.11–12 generate incomplete forms of the four possible enneatonic collections. However, these same chords combine across the barlines to form octatonic collections; this process is speeded up in the second half of m.13. We see, therefore, that upon its initial appearance in act 2 the *Zaubermotiv* mediates between enneatonicism and octatonicism.

This mediation continues in Subrotation 2 (m.25), which opens by restoring the hexatonic harmonization of the *Klingsor* theme. The final two bars of the *Klingsor* theme (Eb minor followed by B minor) are now combined with the *Wehelaute,* a descending chromatic hexachord harmonized in parallel major thirds (ex. 6.5).

In m.30, the dotted-rhythm form of the enneatonic *Zaubermotiv* appears on G, combined with the octatonic *Kundry* motive; the latter falls in

---

[14] When octatonic or enneatonic pitch-class collections are incomplete, the absent pitches are enclosed within parentheses.

a. Generation of *Zauber* motive from second half of *Klingsor* theme

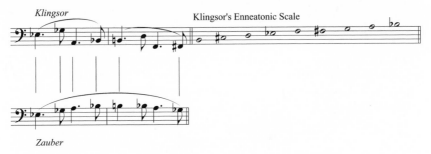

b. Harmonization of *Zauber* motive: Act II Prelude, mm. 11-13

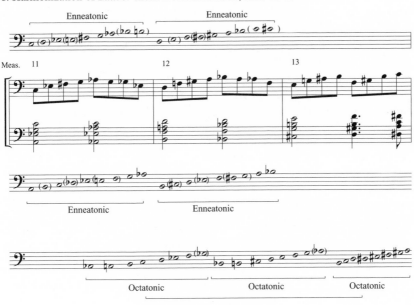

Example 6.4: Zauber *motive*

Example 6.5: Act 2 Prelude, mm.28–31

m.31 to an enneatonic E♭, suggesting that Kundry is beginning to fall under the sorcerer's influence. G and E♭, the outer limits of the *Zaubermotiv,* are of course nodal points in the Western Hexatonic System.

Example 6.6 displays the three-tiered harmonic structure of mm.28–50 of the prelude.

The *Klingsor* theme (bottom staff) progresses hexatonically from E♭ minor to B minor through four applications of the T_2 transposition, which combine sequentially to form two applications of T_4. The *Wehelaute* (top staff) begins on B♭, the fifth of the underlying E♭-minor triad, and descends a fourth to F, which is picked up in m.30 by the *Kundry* motive (middle staff); this ascends octatonically through a minor-third cycle to D (m.38). D is then picked up as the fifth of the G-minor triad by the *Wehelaute* (m.40), which descends a fourth to A; the *Kundry* motive picks this up in m.42 and ascends octatonically to F♯. F♯ (m.50) functions as the fifth of a *fortissimo* B-minor triad; this climactic chord, the harmonic goal of the prelude, has thus been approached in three ways, through ascending and descending major thirds and ascending minor thirds. It appears in $^6_4$ position, so that at a background level the prelude may be understood as unfolding the perfect fifth of the B-minor triad (ex. 6.7). At the foreground and middleground levels, however, this unfolding does not involve a single functional progression.

Example 6.6: Act 2 Prelude, mm.28–50 (harmonic structure)

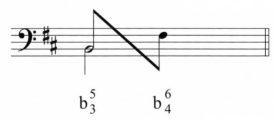

Example 6.7: Background structure of Parsifal *Act 2 Prelude*

Example 6.8 reproduces the piano/vocal score of section B$_1$. During this brief recitative, sequential statements of the *Zaubermotiv* (mm.61 and 75) frame a contrapuntal combination of the *Torenspruch* and *Parsifal* motives (m.71).

Example 6.8: Rotation 1, section B$_1$ (piano/vocal score)

a.

b.

"Mystic Chord"

Example 6.9: Section B₁: some octatonic and enneatonic elements

This central moment, during which Wagner plants the thematic seed that will ultimately flower into the *telos* of the scene, is ushered in by Klingsor's words "die Zeit ist da" (the time has come). These were the final words uttered by Kundry in act 1, as she felt herself succumbing to a trance-like sleep. William Kinderman has suggested that these two utterances are contemporaneous, that Kundry disappears from the realm of the Grail at the same moment Klingsor announces that the time has come for her to reenter the abode of evil.[15]

During this passage, the interpenetration of hexatonic, octatonic, and enneatonic elements continues. As shown in example 6.9a, the diminished-seventh chords that trigger the first two statements of the *Zaubermotiv* (mm.61 and 64) unite to form the descending octatonic scale that undergirds mm.70–82. Example 6.9b analyzes the second appearance of the *Zaubermotiv* (m.64) as an interpenetration of octatonic and enneatonic collections.

The first and last pitches of the new three-note prefix derive from an octatonic and enneatonic collection respectively, while the second pitch is common to both. The truncated *Zaubermotiv* is also common to both collections, while its "mystic chord" harmonization is octatonic. The *Torenspruch* (mm.71–74) perhaps retains some functional residue from its previous appearances in act 1, but its harmonic changes can also be analyzed transformationally.[16] In addition, the progression in m.82 from an E major

---

[15] William Kinderman, private communication.

[16] For example, the progression from the E-major root position triad in m.71 to the C-major first inversion triad of m.72 could be analyzed as the PL transformation (or as a T_2 hexatonic transposition, moving two notches clockwise around the Northern Hexatonic System). The progression from the D-minor root position triad of m.73 to the Bb-major first inversion triad of m.74 could be analyzed as the L transformation (or as a T_1 hexatonic transposition, moving one notch clockwise

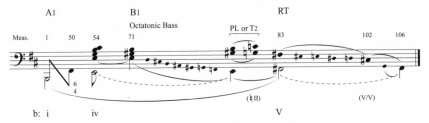

Ex. 6.10: Tonal structure of Rotation 1

to a C major triad is a PL transform (or T_2 transposition), although when the resultant C_3^5 chord resolves to an F♯ pedal (not shown), it creates the impression of a Neapolitan half cadence that points to and signifies a B-minor tonic.[17]

Example 6.10 offers a tonal interpretation of Rotation 1 as a whole. The B-minor $^6_4$ chord from the climax of the prelude leads to an E-minor triad with added major sixth, momentarily suggesting a pre-dominant supertonic $^6_5$ chord. Although the octatonic bassline of Section B_1 supports hexatonic and octatonic harmonies,[18] its final PL transform again suggests a functional harmony, here a Neapolitan leading to a dominant. This dominant is prolonged during the retransition by a chromatic bassline that generates octatonic collections.

We see, therefore, that although 95% of this music is harmonically non-functional, Wagner does place functional signifiers at crucial structural points. This means that despite the Schenkerian appearance of example 6.10, the structural levels are not recursive: the background level may suggest a functional progression (I–iv–V in B minor), but the lower-level prolongational spans are non-functional and transformative.

Figure 6.9 displays the formal structure of rotation 2. Section A_2 (m.108) is a short but powerful aria for Klingsor, during which he summons Kundry. In terms of motives, tonality, and tempo, this section harks back to the orchestral prelude, suggesting that we have begun a second large sweep through the musical material of the scene.

---

around the Southern Hexatonic System); the C♮ in m.73 can be interpreted not as a true chordal seventh, but as a suspension of the C from m.72 that resolves (via a chromatic passing tone) to the B♭ of m.74.

[17] For an explanation of how a dominant triad plus added seventh, or a subdominant triad plus added sixth, can point to and signify a withheld tonic triad, see Hyer, "Tonal Intuitions," 21–98.

[18] For example, the A♯-minor triad of m.77 combines with the E-major triad of m.78 to form an incomplete version of the octatonic scale that undergirds mm.70–82 (omitting G and D). It would be difficult to produce a meaningful functional interpretation of these tritone-related triads.

Meas.	Section	Subsection	Interior Structure	Motives
108	A₂	Aria	a	*Klingsor*
113			b	*Zauber* (ro: 4 + 4)
121			a'	*Klingsor*
132	B₂	x	Orch.	*Wehelaute/ Zauber*
143			Klingsor	*Wehelaute, Kundry* (bar: 6+9+7)
165			Kundry	*Leiden, Zauber* (arch: 3+6+6)
180		y	Both	Recit., *Kundry*
186				*Wehelaute, Kundry*
194			Klingsor	*Leiden, Speer, Klingsor* (bar: 3+2+7)
206				*Torenspruch, Leiden* (bar: 2+2+4)
			(+ Ku.)	("Ich will nicht!")
214		z	Both	*Leiden, Lachen* (bar: 3+3+7)
227			Klingsor	*Lachen, Wehelaute* (bar: 3+3+7)

[ro = rotational; Ku. = Kundry]

Fig. 6.9: Parsifal *II/1, rotation 2 (moderately detailed)*

The bi-rotational structure of the prelude is here replaced by the aria's aba' ternary form, during which two statements of the *Klingsor* theme (mm.108 and 121) frame a sequential treatment of the *Zaubermotiv* (m.113). Kundry's theme and its related octatonicism are conspicuous by their absence; in contrast to the battle of wills depicted by the prelude, Klingsor is now firmly in control.

Example 6.11 offers a harmonic reduction of Klingsor's aria.

The outer sections move clockwise through the Western Hexatonic System, their T_2 or LP transforms generating minor triads on B, G, E♭, and B. During section a', however, the E♭ and B triads are sustained for four times their normal value, and the latter, respelled as C♭, appears in its parallel major. The music then "backs up" counterclockwise to the forceful E♭-minor triad that punctuates Kundry's materialization (m.132).

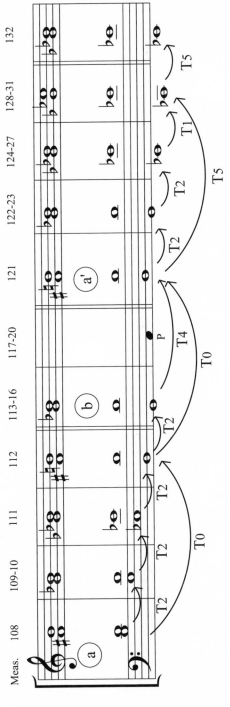

Example 6.11: Rotation 2, section A₂ (Klingsor's aria): Harmonic reduction

As mentioned earlier, Section B$_2$ comprises three subsections: x, y, and z (fig. 6.9). During Subsection x (m.132), Kundry awakens and gradually regains her power of speech. The passage beginning at m.165, during which, "hoarsely and brokenly," she sings her first words ("Tiefe Nacht … Wahnsinn,") is built upon the same descending octatonic bassline (from e to E) that undergirded Section B$_1$ of Rotation 1. During Subsection y (m.180), Klingsor mocks Kundry's service to the knights of the Grail, whom she has been seducing one by one; his subsequent reference to Parsifal, the "pure fool" who will afford Kundry her greatest challenge, is accompanied by the second appearance of the *Torenspruch* (m.206), which first surfaced (at the same pitch level) in Subsection y of Rotation 1. Kundry's refusal to seduce Parsifal ("Ich will nicht!") triggers Subsection z (m.214), during which the sorcerer attempts to assert his mastery over the woman. Klingsor's boast that he himself is impervious to Kundry's charms is countered by her mocking reference to his self-mutilation. Klingsor flies into a rage, and launches into the aria that opens Rotation 3.

Space limitations forbid a detailed tonal analysis of this second rotation. Suffice it to say that six-, eight-, and nine-note pitch collections predominate, and that harmonic progressions are largely transformational rather than functional in nature. The E♭ minor that initiated Subsection x (m.132) returns at the opening of Subsection y (m.180), and yields to an F♯ dominant at the opening of Subsection z (m.214), which ultimately cadences in F♯ minor (m.239). As a result, the rotation as a whole could be viewed as a background arpeggiation from B through D♯ (or E♭) to F♯, an unfolding of the B-major tonic triad. At the surface level, however, functional signifiers are invoked but rarely; and even this background arpeggiation could be analyzed in transformational terms, as suggested in figure 6.10.[19]

Figure 6.11 displays the formal structure of Rotation 3. Like its predecessor, this rotation begins with an aria for Klingsor, Section A$_3$. Beginning in F♯, the dominant minor of Klingsor's associative key, this brief but effective set piece (m.239) allows the villain an opportunity to pour out all his rage and frustration. It culminates in a C-major statement of the *Gral* theme (m.261), a motive not heard since the end of act 1; however, the theme's cadence is undercut by an F♯ dominant (m.264) that restores the sense of a B-minor tonic.

---

[19] In neo-Riemannian theory, the D (dominant) operation transforms a triad into a modally-matched triad a perfect fifth *lower*, not a perfect fifth higher. Thus D applied to a B-minor triad transforms it into an E minor triad. In order to transform a B-minor triad into an F♯-minor triad, we must apply the dominant inverse (D^{-1}) or S (subdominant) operation. However, D, S, and their inverses are actually redundant, inasmuch as the same results can be obtained through the application of compound transformations (e.g., in ex. 6.10, D^{-1} = PLRP).

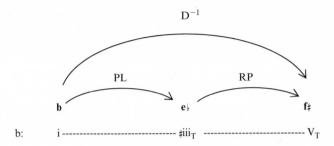

[P = parallel; L = Leittonwechsel; R = relative; D^{-1} = dominant inverse; T = tonicized]

Fig. 6.10: Neo-Riemannian and functional interpretations of background arpeggiation

Meas.	Section	Subsection	Interior Structure		Motives
239	A_3	Aria	Orch.		*Klingsor*
241			Pt. 1		*Klingsor, Lachen*
253			Pt. 2		*Klingsor, Amfortas, Gral*
268	B_3	y	SR1	Kl.	*Amfortas,* Chords
274				Ku.	*Leiden, Schwachtriolen, Wehelaute*
290			SR2	Kl.	*Torenspruch*
296				Ku.	Tremolo ("Ich will nicht!")
299		z	SR1	Kl.	***Parsifal***
305				Ku.	*Schwachtriolen, Kundry*
312			SR2	Kl.	Tremolo ("Ha! Er ist schön, der Knabe!")
316				Ku.	*Kundry*

[SR = subrotation; Kl. = Klingsor; Ku. = Kundry]

Fig. 6.11: Parsifal II/1, Rotation 3 (moderately detailed)

All three rotations have thus begun with an agitated set-piece based upon the *Klingsor* theme and its hexatonic harmonization, the first two focused upon B minor, the third upon F# minor.

Section B_3 eliminates Subsection x and retains only Subsections y and z from the previous rotation. Each subsection comprises two subrotations, in each of which a statement by Klingsor elicits an anguished response from Kundry. In Subsection y (m.268), Klingsor reminds Kundry that the man who can resist her charms will release her from her curse; to the accompaniment of the *Torenspruch* refrain (m.290), he urges her to try her luck with Parsifal, who draws near. Kundry refuses a second time ("Ich will nicht!").

Subsection z (m.299) opens with the *Parsifal* motive (ex. 6.12), not heard since Rotation 1. It appears over a B♭-major $^6_4$ chord, suggesting the functional dominant of the hero's associative key; however, its progression to a G-minor triad can still be viewed transformationally, as the R operation.[20] Nevertheless, a subsequent dominant seventh on E♭ (m.314) that underscores Klingsor's taunt "Ha! Er ist schön, der Knabe!" ultimately resolves to A♭ minor (m.321) to launch Rotation 4; the resultant pattern of falling fifths (B♭–E♭–A♭) suggests that, although functional harmony has not yet taken hold, it has certainly appeared on the horizon. Parsifal, the embodiment of functional diatonicism, is climbing the castle walls.[21]

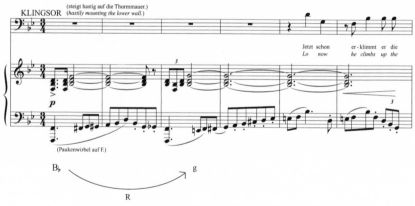

Example 6.12: Parsifal *motive (act 2 scene 1, mm.299–304)*

---

[20] In more traditional terms, it could of course be viewed as a diatonic 5–6 shift.

[21] Lorenz (107) slavishly followed the key signature in assigning m.321 a tonal center of D♭ minor, but the harmonic context (especially the dominant ninth chord

Figure 6.12 displays the formal structure of the final rotation. Like its two predecessors, this opens with an agitated solo for Klingsor (section A_4), during which he describes Parsifal's assault on the fortress.

This solo (m.321) is shaped as a bar form whose first two formal units, or *Stollen,* are based upon the *Knabentatenmotiv,* a theme previously associated with Parsifal's youthful energy.[22] Example 6.13 interprets this

Meas.	Section	Subsection	Interior Structure		Motives
321	A_4	Solo	Stollen 1		*Knabentaten* (bar: 2+2+4+4)
333			Stollen 2		*Knabentaten* (bar: 2+2+7+5)
349			Abgesang	a	*Parsifal*
357				b	*Torenspruch* (bar: 4+4+4)
369				a'	*Parsifal* (Telos!)
387	B_4	y	Pt. 1		*Schwachtriolen*
394					*Herzeleide, Klingsor*
403			Pt. 2		*Torenspruch*
418					*Klingsor*

Fig. 6.12: Parsifal *II/1, rotation 4 (moderately detailed)*

Example 6.13: Relationship between Zauber *and* Knabentaten *motives*

---

on E♭ and the sustained pedal on A♭) surely suggests A♭ minor. By analogy, he assigned m.333 a tonal center of D minor, this time *despite* the key signature; here a dominant ninth on E and a pedal on A suggest A minor.

[22] Each Stollen is internally structured as a bar with repeated (and varied) Abgesang.

motive as a reshaping of the *Zaubermotiv* that featured prominently in sections A_1 and A_2.

Toward the end of *Stollen* 2, as Klingsor relishes the sight of his vassals being hacked to pieces, Kundry breaks into demonic laughter, surely one of the most chilling moments in Wagnerian opera. The more extended succeeding formal section, or *Abgesang* (m.349), is an aba' ternary form whose outer sections bring forth the complete diatonic *Parsifal* motive as the thematic *telos* of the entire scene; its two appearances (mm.349 and 369) frame a sequential development of the *Torenspruch* (m.357).

Section B_4 (m.387) is limited to subsection y, during which Klingsor notices that Kundry has disappeared; unable to resist the sorcerer's description of Parsifal's physical beauty, she is already preparing to seduce the lad. After a final statement of the *Torenspruch* refrain (m.405), the music dissolves back into Klingsor's B-minor hexatonic matrix (m.418).

Example 6.14 shows how functional diatonicism evolves during section A_4. The bassline rises from A♭ (*Stollen* 1: m.321) through A♮ (*Stollen* 2: m.333) to the B♭ that underpins the *Abgesang* (m.349). This B♭ supports a cadential $^6_4$ chord that resolves to a dominant $^5_3$ of E♭ (m.356) during the initial statement of the *Parsifal* motive; as a result, the previous A♭ may be retrospectively interpreted as subdominant.

The sequential development of the *Torenspruch* (m.357), an urgent intensification or *Steigerung*, projects a more elaborate resolution of the cadential $^6_4$, and the resultant B♭ dominant this time resolves to a root position E♭-major triad (m.369). Overall, therefore, Section A_4 may be understood in Schenkerian terms as an auxiliary cadence, IV–V–I, in the key of

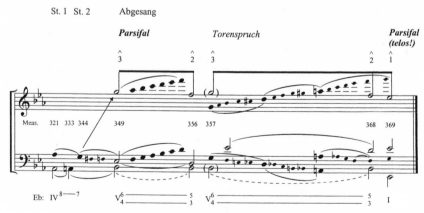

Example 6.14: Rotation 4, section A_4 (Parsifal storms the castle): voice-leading graph

Eb major. The *fortissimo* authentic cadence at m.369 coincides with the final complete statement of the *Parsifal* motive, the goal or *telos* of the scene. This peak moment marks the culmination and simultaneous resolution of the formal, thematic, and harmonic trajectories set in motion by the initial rotation — trajectories that Wagner has brilliantly synchronized with the dramatic progression of the scene.

Example 6.15 shows how functional diatonicism dissolves back into transformational harmony. The *Parsifal* motive moves through IV to V of Eb, but is denied cadential closure; instead the music slips into G major (m.385) as Klingsor notices that Kundry is absent. G major, of course, lies on the Western Hexatonic System, and is the key in which Kundry will attempt to seduce Parsifal in scene 3. Here, however, it is sounded in $^6_3$ position, with B in the bass. Each of the two parts of section B_4 features a descending bass arpeggiation through the B triad, first major, then minor; however, the individual harmonies supported by these arpeggiations relate transformationally rather than functionally.[23]

Finally, figure 6.13 offers an interpretation of the background tonal structure of the entire scene. The symmetrical arpeggiation from B through Eb to F# and back again was noted by Lorenz (109), who seemed unsure what to do with it. Figure 6.13 suggests a transformational reading that stresses the motion from B minor (Klingsor's key) to and from its hexatonic counterpole, Eb major (Parsifal's key).

Although exceptions exist, most practitioners of transformational theory limit their analytical applications to brief, carefully chosen musical snippets.[24] By contrast, I have attempted to demonstrate how neo-Riemannian theory, especially its hexatonic subset, may profitably be applied to an entire operatic scene. I have also tried to show how hexatonicism can interact with octatonicism and enneatonicism, and how these symmetrical patterns can ultimately give way to functional diatonicism. Finally, I have suggested how these tonal processes may be coordinated with the dramatic teleology of the scene, and how they are shaped by its rotational macro-structure. Viewing act 2, scene 1 of *Parsifal* through the twin lenses of rotational form and hexatonic theory can open up this otherwise refractory music to a more intense, more rewarding reflection than that offered by traditional methodologies. After a decade

---

[23] This twofold arpeggiation suggests a double-rotational structure for section B_4.

[24] As an example, see David Clampitt, "Alternative Interpretations of Some Measures from *Parsifal*," *Journal of Music Theory* 42/2 (1998): 321–34. Clampitt's densely argued exegesis focuses on only three measures of music (the *Gral* motive).

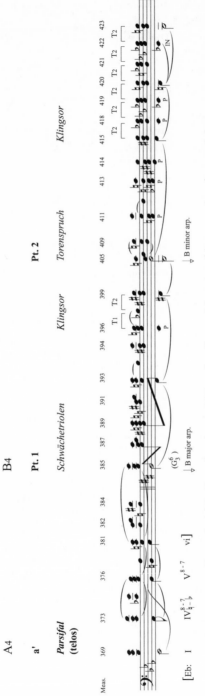

Example 6.15: Rotation 4, mm.369–end: collapse of functional harmony into hexatonicism

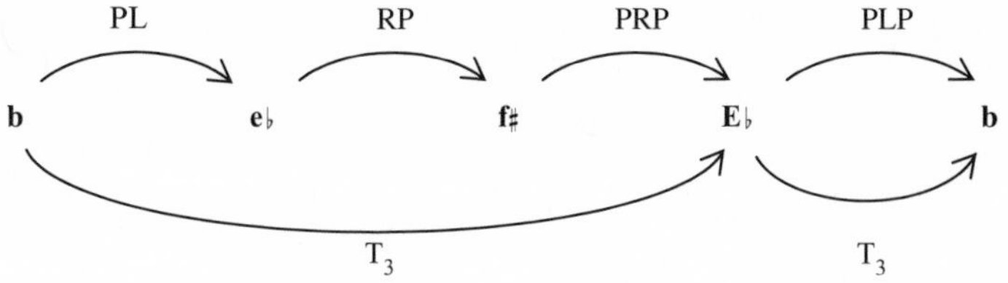

[P = parallel; L = Leittonwechsel; R = relative; T = hexatonic transposition]

Fig. 6.13: Parsifal *II/1 tonal background: Neo-Riemannian and hexatonic interpretations*

during which the sophisticated musical analysis of Wagnerian opera has declined into an almost moribund state, surely the time has come for such a new analytical approach. Or, as that old magician Klingsor would put it, "die Zeit ist da."

III. Reception and Interpretation

7: *Die Weihe des Hauses* (The Consecration of the House):[1] Houston Stewart Chamberlain and the Early Reception of *Parsifal*

Roger Allen

Wer mit richtigem Sinne und Blicke den Hergang alles dessen, was während jener beiden Monate in den Räumen dieses Bühnenfestspielhauses sich zutrug, dem Charakter der hierin sich geltend machenden produktiven wie rezeptiven Tätigkeit gemäß zu erfassen vermochte, konnte dies nicht anders als mit der Wirkung einer Weihe bezeichnen, welche, ohne irgend eine Weisung, frei über alles sich ergoß.

[Whoever had the mind and eye to seize the character of all that passed within the walls of that house during those two months, both the productive and the receptive, could not describe it otherwise than as governed by a consecration that shed itself on everything without the smallest prompting.][2]

THE PREMIÈRE OF *Parsifal* on 26 July 1882 was a cultural event of considerable magnitude and of immense significance to Wagner and his ever-widening circle of devotees. Since the first performance of *Der Ring des Nibelungen* in 1876, the aging composer had achieved what amounted to little less than iconic status amongst musicians, literati, and the bourgeois intelligentsia of Europe and America, and it was an eclectic audience that was assembled in the small Franconian town of Bayreuth to pay him homage. Franz Liszt and Anton Bruckner were prominent amongst the gathering of composers; the redoubtable Eduard Hanslick led the critical

---

[1] The title is suggested by Beethoven's overture *Die Weihe des Hauses* (op. 124).

[2] Richard Wagner, "Das Bühnenweihfestspiel in Bayreuth 1882," vol. 10 of *Sämtliche Schriften und Dichtungen* (Leipzig: Breitkopf & Härtel/C. F. W. Siegel (R. Linnemann)), 297; In English: *Religion and Art,* trans. W. Ashton Ellis (Lincoln and London: U of Nebraska P, 1994), 303. Reprinted from the original English translation of vol. 6 (*Religion and Art*) of *Richard Wagner's Prose Works* (London: Kegan Paul, Trench, Trübner, 1897).

vanguard, and executive musicians such as Felix Weingartner, subsequently
to become internationally prominent in the concert hall and opera house,
were among the throng on Bayreuth's green hill. Many others made the
journey to Upper Franconia in order to experience Wagner's new work at
first hand in the remarkable theater he himself had designed: among them
was a young Englishman who later assumed a leading role in the dissemination of Wagner's ideas and the publicizing of Bayreuth: Houston
Stewart Chamberlain.[3]

Chamberlain is today remembered primarily as a racial theorizer and
precursor of Nazi ideologues. Viewed from a post-1945 perspective he is a
disturbing figure. Many of his ideas, when considered with the benefit of
hindsight, seem repellent; his historiography appears unsystematic and
underpinned by a particularly pernicious form of racist ideology. Yet to dismiss or, worse still, ignore him as an intellectual charlatan who was nothing
more than a corrosive precursor of Nazi ideologues is to run the risk of over-
looking a significant historical resource. As the critic Lucy Beckett writes, "It
is necessary to forget Chamberlain's later career as a vitriolic anti-Semite and
Nazi ideologue to give his early writing the credit it deserves."[4] While the
consequences of Chamberlain's later career were too extreme for us simply
to "forget," Beckett is right in reminding us that we should be aware of the
dubious benefits of hindsight when reading his earlier work. As she writes
elsewhere, "His accounts of the operas are largely unaffected by his opinions, are based on very thorough knowledge of the scores and sketches and
are — within the limits of uncritical admiration — sensible and perceptive."[5]

Chamberlain was born at Southsea on the south coast of England on
September 9, 1855. His father was an admiral in the Royal Navy and his
mother a lady of aristocratic Scottish descent; he was therefore a true scion
of the upper middle class so much in the ascendant in mid-Victorian
Britain. Within a year of his birth, his mother died and he spent his early
years living in Versailles as the ward of his paternal grandmother and speaking French as his first language. Following the death of his grandmother, he
returned to England and attended Cheltenham College, where he developed a strong distaste for the militaristic rigors of Victorian boarding school
life. By 1870, his indifferent health had deteriorated to the point where it

---

[3] The literature on the 1882 Bayreuth Festival is extensive. For present purposes
see Frederic Spotts, *Bayreuth: A History of the Wagner Festival* (New Haven and
London: Yale UP, 1994), 78–89; and Robert Hartford, ed., *Bayreuth: The Early
Years* (London: Victor Gollancz Ltd, 1980).

[4] Lucy Beckett, *Richard Wagner: Parsifal*, Cambridge Opera Handbook
(Cambridge: Cambridge UP, 1981), 109.

[5] Lucy Beckett, "Houston Stewart Chamberlain," in *The New Grove Dictionary
of Music and Musicians*, ed. Stanley Sadie (1980), 4:113.

became necessary for him to leave Cheltenham, and he subsequently traveled widely on the continent in the company of a maiden aunt in search of a more propitious climate. Thus began the peripatetic wanderings that were to take him to some of the major intellectual centers of Europe. An important influence at this time was that of Otto Kuntze, a young German theology student hired as Chamberlain's tutor and an ardent nationalist who fired his impressionable pupil with enthusiasm for the cultural heritage of Germany. He widened his knowledge of art in the winter of 1878–79 in Florence, immersing himself in art treasures and avidly reading the works of the notable German historian of the Italian Renaissance, Jakob Burckhardt, before his developing interest in botany and the physiology of plants prompted him to study for a degree in natural sciences in Geneva.

Chamberlain had little in the way of formal musical education save introductory lessons in piano, cello, and music theory. Nevertheless, he showed a considerable degree of musical response: in his autobiography, *Lebenswege meines Denkens* (Paths of My Thought, 1919), he relates that it was through the magic of Beethoven's art that he was first introduced to the innermost shrine of music, before a note of Richard Wagner's had even reached his ears.[6] He first heard Wagner's name while taking a boat trip on Lake Lucerne during the summer of 1870, when the guide happened to mention the famous occupant of the Villa Triebschen. This prompted him to read the texts of the *Ring* operas, and he became so enthusiastic that he attempted to attend the premier of the cycle at Bayreuth in 1876. He could not afford the cost of a ticket, and wrote to Wagner personally, asking for subsidized or free admission to one of the cycles. In response to his plea, he received a reply not from Wagner himself but from the festival administration informing him that tickets were still available for the second and third cycles, but failing to include the requested free tickets. Chamberlain first encountered the *Ring* cycle in performance in 1878 in Munich, after which he sent an unsolicited essay to Hans von Wolzogen, editor of the *Bayreuther Blätter*, in which he was critical, not of Wagner and his works, but of the journal itself, for attaching extraneous philosophical and social ideas to Wagner's art.

Chamberlain did not consider that Wagnerian music dramas had any didactic purpose: they were autonomous aesthetic works in their own right. This is the first sign of the intellectual distance that Chamberlain tried to

---

[6] Houston Stewart Chamberlain, *Lebenswege meines Denkens* (Munich: F. Bruckmann, 1919), 161. A shortened version of this autobiography was published as *Mein Weg nach Bayreuth* (Munich: F. Bruckmann, 1919). This contains material exclusively concerned with Bayreuth and includes an introductory chapter, "Houston Stewart Chamberlain und der Bayreuther Kulturkreis," by Paul Bülow.

maintain between himself and the orthodox view of Wagner that Cosima
Wagner and her circle at Wahnfried had fostered, no matter how devoted he
was to the Wagnerian cause.[7] Wolzogen did not publish the essay, although
he did refer to it in a subsequent issue in support of his thesis that only a
German, and certainly not a pretentious young Englishman, could possibly
understand the deeper subtleties of Wagner's art. In the mid 1880s Chamberlain spent a period in Paris, in which he contributed regularly to the
short-lived but influential journal, *Revue wagnérienne*.[8] By 1889 he finally
settled in Vienna, remaining there for the next twenty years. When in
December 1908 he married Wagner's younger daughter, Eva, and moved
to Bayreuth, he became an indispensable member of the fractious and
quarrelsome inner circle around the aging and increasingly infirm Cosima.
Here he spent the remaining nineteen years of his life, acting as Cosima's
spokesman and establishing himself as a major influence on the workings of
Wahnfried and the Festival. His last years were dominated by a paralyzing
illness that eventually left him bedridden and resulted in his early death on
January 9, 1927 — three years before that of the woman whose cause he
had served with such loyalty and devotion. At his funeral service he was
lionized as one who had devoted his life to the cause of Wagner and greater
Germany; among the mourners were members of the Wagner family,
Prince August Wilhelm Hohenzollern, representatives of the Pan-German
league, and a rising young nationalist politician: Adolf Hitler.

As with so many of his contemporaries, Chamberlain's initial attraction
to the Wagner movement was idealistic: as the historian Geoffrey Field
observes

> For him, as for so many contemporaries, the Wagner movement heralded
> cultural rebirth: he was deeply attracted by its anti-capitalist leanings and
> its critique of the spiritual emptiness and fragmented nature of modern
> society . . . Chamberlain's initial enthusiasm had little to do with nation-
> alist or political feeling. It was the aesthetic utopianism of Bayreuth that
> fascinated him [with] its stress on the inward condition of the individual
> and on self-realization through art.[9]

---

[7] Chamberlain first met Cosima Wagner, whom he subsequently addressed as
"Meisterin," on June 12, 1888, at the house of a mutual friend in Dresden. The
extensive correspondence that developed between the two, and which lasted until
his move to Bayreuth in 1908, is one of the main sources we have for the study of
Chamberlain and his role in the developing phenomenon of Wagnerism; see
Cosima Wagner and Houston Stewart Chamberlain im Briefwechsel 1888–1908, ed.
Paul Pretzsch (Leipzig: Philipp Reclam Jun., 1934).

[8] The *Revue wagnérienne* was published from 1885–88.

[9] See Geoffrey G. Field, *Evangelist of Race: The Germanic Vision of Houston Stewart
Chamberlain* (New York: Columbia UP, 1981), 54–55. This compelling, thoroughly

In the summer of 1882 Chamberlain's ambition to visit Bayreuth was finally realized when he attended several of the first series of *Parsifal* performances. The heady atmosphere of this second Bayreuth Festival is vividly captured in his memoir:

> Am nächsten Morgen — ich hatte lange geschlafen — wurde ich durch das wiederholte eindringliche Pfeifen einer Melodie aus Klingsors Zaubergarten geweckt; und obwohl ich mir nicht schmeicheln konnte, dieser Frühgruß gelte mir — kannte ich doch in Bayreuth keine einzige Seele —, er wirkte doch magisch auf mich, indem er mir bestätigte, daß es kein Traum war und ich wirklich im lange ersehnten Bayreuth erwachte; und so sprang ich schnell aus dem Bette und lief ans Fenster, wo ich einen energischen, Lebensfreude ausströmenden Mann erblickte, der von der Straße aus zu meinem Nachbarnfenster hinaufschaute, an dem im selben Augenblick zwischen den Vorhängen zwei Mädchenköpfe hervorlugten, deren Inhaberinnen offenbar, wie ich, bis jetzt geschlafen hatten, wofür der Mann sie unter vielem Gescherze auszankte. Mein freundlicher Hauswirt, der, sobald er meine Schritte hörte, herbeieilte, um sich meinen Wünschen zu erkundigen, gab dem Fremdling mit dem Behagen eines Wissenden die Erläuterung: "Das ist Felix Mottl von der musikalischen Assistenz, und die beiden Damen sind Soloblumenmädchen." Diese kleine Episode erwähne ich nur als tonangebend für den ganzen Tag.

> [The next morning — I had slept for a long time — I was awakened by the repeated insistent whistling of a melody from Klingsor's magic garden; and although I could not flatter myself that this early greeting was for me — for as yet I knew not a single soul in Bayreuth — its effect on me was magical for it confirmed that it was no dream and that I awoke in the long desired Bayreuth. I sprang quickly out of bed and ran to the window, where I saw an energetic man, full of zest for life, who looked up from the street toward the adjacent window. At the same moment the heads of two girls, who like me had obviously until now been asleep, peeped out from between the curtains and were light-heartedly reprimanded. My friendly landlord who as soon as he heard my steps rushed over to see what was the matter, explained with the pleasure of one "in the know": "that is Felix Mottl, one of the musical assistants, and the two girls are solo Flowermaidens." I mention this small episode as it set the tone for the entire day.][10]

---

researched work is the standard study of Chamberlain and is indispensable to the understanding of his role in Wagner reception. This chapter also draws heavily for biographical material on the excellent anthology edited by David Large and William Weber, *Wagnerism in European Culture and Politics* (Ithaca and London: Cornell UP, 1984), 113–25.

[10] Chamberlain, *Lebenswege meines Denkens*, 235. All translations are my own.

On the eve of the first performance, a gathering of all concerned with the enterprise took place in the restaurant adjacent to the Festspielhaus. Chamberlain somehow contrived to be present and left a vivid description of the event — the only time he encountered Wagner in person — in his memoir of the occasion:

> Endlich kam der langersehnte Augenblick: schnellen Schrittes, eine Dame am Arme, betrat Er den Saal, durchschritt die Reihe der sich verneigen- den Gäste und erreichte in wenigen Sekunden die mittleren Sitze an der Wandseite — mir also genau gegenüber. Ich glaube, mein Herz hat während dieser Sekunden nicht geschlagen, und ich erinnere mich, mich krampfhaft am Geländer festgehalten zu haben. Kein Mensch, der es nicht erlebt hat, kann sich den Eindruck dieser Erscheinung vorstellen: die stramme Haltung des Oberkörpers — an die Jugendbildnisse Goethe's erinnernd — das zurückgeworfene Haupt, das verklärte Antlitz, das unbezwinglich stolze, sichere Schreiten. [. . .] Als Muncker ausge- sprochen hatte, sprang Wagner von seinem Stuhle auf, gebot durch zwei resolute Schläge auf sein Glas Schweigen [. . .]. Diese Rede sprach Wagner mit so feierlicher Würde, mit so heiligem Ernste, daß selbst zwei Franzosen in meiner Nähe, die kein Wort verstanden, tief ergriffen waren, so weihevoll wirkten Ton und Gebärde.[11]

> [Finally, the long-awaited moment arrived: with rapid steps and a lady on his arm. He entered the room, strode through the rows of bowing guests and in a few seconds reached the center seats on the side wall — exactly opposite me. I believe that during these seconds my heart ceased to beat and I recall desperately grasping the banisters [for support]. No man who has not experienced it can imagine the impression made by this appari- tion: the erect posture of the upper part of the body — reminiscent of the portraits of Goethe as a young man — the head thrown back, the trans- figured countenance [and] the unconquerably proud walk. [. . .] When Muncker had finished speaking, Wagner jumped up from his seat and with two resolute taps on his glass demanded silence [. . .]. He spoke with such solemn dignity and seriousness that two Frenchmen near me, who understood not one word, were deeply moved — so profound was the effect of speech and gesture.]

Chamberlain then describes how Wagner spoke of his attempts since the first Festival of 1876 to establish his ideal and correct the many misunder- standings of his intentions. Finally, he relates how the composer concluded his remarks:

> "Jetzt," bei diesem Worte "jetzt" brach ihm die Stimme und er schwieg; ich weiß nicht, waren es Sekunden, waren es Minuten; in dem großen Raume und unter den Hunderten von Menschen herrschte ein Schweigen,

---

[11] Chamberlain, *Lebenswege meines Denkens*, 237–38.

daß man eine Fliege hätte summen hören; endlich wiederholte der Meister das Wort "jetzt," aber diesmal im Flüsterton, und dann noch ein drittes Mal, indem er, unmächtig der Stimme, leise flüsterte: "Jetzt habe ich zu schweigen gelernt."[12]

["Now" — with this word "now" his voice faltered and he became silent — I do not know whether it was for seconds or minutes — and silence so intense that one could have heard the buzzing of a fly prevailed amongst the hundreds of people in the great room. At last the Master repeated the word "now," but this time in a whisper, and then again a third time when he softly whispered, "Now I have learnt to be silent."]

The quasi-religiosity of Bayreuth so vividly captured in the description of this pre-performance gathering gained an enthusiastic convert in the young idealistic Englishman. Here he found presented on the stage the dramatic and musical realization of the aesthetic utopianism that initially drew him to Wagner and his works. This utopianism was to inform his early writings on Wagner and his interpretation of *Parsifal*.[13]

One of the first literary fruits of Chamberlain's enthusiasm for Wagner was his collaboration with a young French writer he had met on his return to Bayreuth for the 1883 Festival: Edouard Dujardin (1861–1949). The two Wagner enthusiasts became the prime movers behind the *Revue wagnérienne*, which played a crucial role in the dissemination of Wagner's ideas in France. Following the ill-fated staging of *Tannhäuser* at the Paris Opéra in 1861, Wagner performances in France had been limited. A small group of poets and intellectuals had kindled a limited interest in Wagner in the 1860s, but Dujardin, Chamberlain, and their associates hoped that the new journal would stimulate a broader substratum of support.[14] In his role as Paris representative of the Wagner Association, Chamberlain also hoped to interest French adherents of Wagner in the work of Bayreuth.[15] As it turned out, the journal saw only thirty-six issues, published between 1885 and 1888. Chamberlain contributed reviews of performances in Central Europe, notes on issues associated with Wagner in Germany, and a number of perceptive assessments of the dramas themselves. His essay on *Parsifal*

---

[12] Chamberlain, *Lebenswege meines Denkens*, 238.

[13] A vivid account of the 1882 Bayreuth Festival and the première of *Parsifal* is to be found in Ernest Newman's classic, *The Life of Richard Wagner*, 4 vols. (New York: Alfred A. Knopf, 1933–46), 4, 684–96.

[14] For an introduction to the reception of Wagner's ideas in France, together with associated extracts from the *Revue wagnérienne*, see Bojan Bujić, ed., *Music in European Thought 1851–1912* (Cambridge: Cambridge UP, 1988), 222–59.

[15] For a more detailed account of Chamberlain's involvement with the *Revue wagnérienne*, see Field, *Evangelist of Race*, 64–69.

in the August 1886 issue attempts to refute the idea that *Parsifal* is the creation of exhausted old age by arguing that a long period of time was needed to produce the finished work. At the same time it bolstered the organicist idea that *Tristan und Isolde, Der Ring des Nibelungen,* and *Parsifal* formed a complete whole in Wagner's mind. Binding this idea was Chamberlain's emphasis on the symbolic nature of the works, a perspective that informed his understanding of the religious features in *Parsifal.*

> It is unnecessary . . . to state that *Parsifal* is not the glorification of a religious dogma. There is no more Christianity in *Parsifal* than there is paganism in the *Ring* or in *Tristan.* These three works, as we have seen, are contemporary; Wagner worked on them simultaneously; they are connected to each other by many imaginative links, and form for us — as they formed in the thought of the Master — a whole. Wagner always recognized the bonds that unite Art and Religion; he never overstepped the frontiers that separate them . . . In 1880 he said: "If someone asked me, 'Do you want to create a religion?' I would answer that that is impossible; my ideas on this subject come to me only as a creative artist" . . . [16]

This organicist, almost anti-religious interpretation of *Parsifal* is in striking contrast to the more literal interpretations that flourished in the high period of Wagnerism in Britain and the United States before the First World War. In New York a "*Parsifal* Entertainment" extravaganza was organized to introduce Americans to Wagner's last work and amongst the introductory lectures was one billed as "*Parsifal,* the Finding of Christ through Art."[17] In Britain a little known Scotsman, David Irvine, published "Parsifal" *and Wagner's Christianity,* a long and convoluted study that places the work and its composer at the center of any true understanding of Christianity.[18]

The short-lived *Revue wagnérienne* brought Chamberlain's name to the fore in Wagnerian circles. In Dresden, on June 12, 1888, he first met Cosima Wagner. The extensive correspondence that developed between the two, and which continued until his move to Bayreuth in 1908, reveals the extent to which the older woman became increasingly reliant on the opinions and judgment of the younger man; it is one of the main sources we have for the study of Chamberlain and his role in the growing

---

[16] *Revue wagnérienne* 2 (1886–87): 225–26. Quoted in Lucy Beckett, *Richard Wagner: Parsifal,* 109–10.

[17] March 31, 1890. See Joseph Horowitz, *Wagner Nights* (Berkeley: U of California P, 1994), 181–98.

[18] David Irvine, *"Parsifal" and Wagner's Christianity* (London: H. Grevel and Co., 1899). For a detailed study of Irvine see Gulliver Ralston, "David Irvine: The Case of a British Wagnerian," in *Wagner* 24/1 (2003): 23–43.

phenomenon of Wagnerism.[19] His articles for the *Revue* also served as a preliminary exercise for his first full-length study of Wagner: *Das Drama Richard Wagners*, published in 1892.[20] His authorial purpose in this short work is described on the title page of the English edition as "an attempt to inspire a better appreciation of Wagner as dramatic poet," and he begins his introduction with an unequivocal statement of intent. "The first and most essential point to be realized is that Wagner from the very beginning was first and foremost a dramatic poet; the second is that his dramatic gift is manifested from the outset in a special and individual creative impulse in which words and music played an equal part" (*DDRW 7*; 1).

Chamberlain considers that Wagner's creative processes were marked by a shift around the year 1848:

> Bis 1848 suchte Wagner die Lösung, wo sie auf den ersten Blick zu liegen schien, nämlich in einem "Wie?" "Wie können Wort und Ton zu einem höchsten, erschöpfenden dramatischen Ausdruck zusammenwirken?" — Daß sie es können, bezweifelte er nicht. [. . .] Nicht so darf man fragen: "wie können Wort und Ton zu einem höchsten, erschöpfenden Ausdruck zusammenwirken?," sondern: "was für ein Gegenstand ist es, der eines so erhabenen Ausdruckes bedarf? Und der ihn folglich für seine künstlerisch vollendete Darstellung erheischt?" [. . .] Denn aus diesem "Was?" entsprang die neue und vollkommenste dramatische Kunst[. . .]

> [Up to 1848 Wagner looked for the solution where at first glance it would seem to be found, namely in a "how" i.e., "How can word and tone work together towards the realization of a supreme and exhaustive dramatic expression?" That they were able to do so he did not doubt. [Later, he decided that] the question to be put must not be: "How can word and tone together work towards the realization of a supreme and exhaustive dramatic expression?" but: "What subject calls for such a lofty expression, and consequently requires it, for its artistically complete representation?" . . . from this "what" emanated the new and most perfect dramatic art . . . (*DDRW* 12–14; 11–14)[21]]

---

[19] Paul Pretzsch, ed., *Cosima Wagner und Houston Stewart Chamberlain im Briefwechsel 1888–1908* (Leipzig: Philipp Reclam jun. Verlag, 1934). See also Joachim Köhler, *Wagners Hitler: Der Prophet und sein Vollstrecker* (Karl Blessing Verlag, 1997); In English: *Wagner's Hitler: The Prophet and his Disciple*, trans. Ronald Taylor (Cambridge: Polity Press, 2000), 115–32. This highly tendentious, not to say lurid, account of the relationship between Chamberlain and Cosima is unconvincing.

[20] Houston Stewart Chamberlain, *Das Drama Richard Wagners* (Leipzig: Breitkopf & Härtel, 1892); *The Wagnerian Drama* (London: John Lane The Bodley Head, 1923). Translator not named. Hereafter referred to as *DDRW*, with German edition page numbers followed by English edition page numbers.

[21] See also Wagner's letter to Theodor Uhlig, February 15, 1852.

254 ◆ ROGER ALLEN

This notion is central to Chamberlain's evolving concept of Wagner's mature works as Wort-Tondramen (word-tone-dramas), which he considered "in [their] balance of tone and word a perfect means of communication between the subjective, unconscious realm and the objective world."[22] He develops the concept of the word-tone-drama more fully in the second chapter of *Das Drama Richard Wagners*, which he entitles "Die Lehre vom Wort-Tondrama" (The Teaching of the Word-Tone-Drama). This exegesis draws heavily on ideas and aesthetic metaphors from *Parsifal*, and is superscripted with the enigmatic final words of the opera, "Erlösung dem Erlöser" (Redemption to the Redeemer). Quoting Wagner, Chamberlain's interpretation of the fundamental message of the word-tone-drama is that man is both interior and exterior:

> Wo es den unmittelbarsten und doch sichersten Ausdruck des Höchsten, Wahrsten, dem Menschen überhaupt Ausdrückbaren gilt, da muß auch der ganze vollkommene Mensch beisammen sein, und dies ist der mit dem Leibes- und Herzensmenschen in innigster, durchdringendster Liebe vereinigte Verstandesmensch, — keiner aber für sich allein.

> [Wherever it is a case of finding the most direct and, at the same time, surest expression of what mankind can find to say that is highest and truest, there the entirely complete man must come into action and that is the intellectual man, blended with the bodily and the emotional man in closest and all transfusing love — but no one of these by himself. (*DDRW* 22; 23–24; quoting *Das Kunstwerk der Zukunft*, GS III, 66, 2nd edition onwards)]

It is the blending of the intellectual, as represented by the poetic text, with the emotional power of music that creates the perfect drama.

> wenn . . . der dramatische Dichter sich an Phantasie und Auge, der Musiker sich an das Ohr richtet, beide vereint dem "ganzen, vollkommenen Menschen" Genüge tun müssen; wobei wohl zu bemerken ist, daß der Dichter nicht durch den Verstand auf die Phantasie wirkt, sondern auch als Seher dem Auge die greifbare Gestalt auf der Bühne und die bestimmende Gebärde, sowie auch die szenische Umgebung gibt. In diesem Sinne können wir nunmehr die Behauptung aufstellen: das vollkommene Drama verlange die Zusammenwirkung von Dichter und Musiker.

> [When the dramatic poet appeals to the imagination and the eye, and the musician to the ear, the two combined must satisfy the requirements of the "entire, complete"; whereby we must not fail to note that the poet acts on the imagination not only through the intellect, but, as seer, also provides the tangible figure on the stage for the eye, as well as the defining

---

[22] Field, *Evangelist of Race*, 68.

gesture and the scenic surroundings. In this sense we can therefore affirm that the perfect drama requires the co-operation of Poet and Musician. (*DDRW* 23; 25)]

Chamberlain's exegesis of the synthesis of poetry and music draws heavily on Wagner's own as defined in his essay *Beethoven* (1870): the other world of music, the world of the inner man, mediates between the inner and outer man — the world of poetry.[23] This synthesis renders conventional opera an absurdity: "eine absolute Musik, die sich also nur an den Gefühlsmenschen wendet, aufgepfropft auf ein Gedicht welches sich schon erschöpfend an den Verstandesmenschen richtet, und welches, mit Ausnahme einer Anzahl lyrischer Momente, in gar keiner Beziehung zu der unsichtbaren Welt der Musik steht" (absolute music, which accordingly only appeals to the "emotional man," engrafted on a poem which is already exhaustive in its appeal to the "intellectual man" and which, with the exception of a number of lyrical episodes, stands in no relation whatever to the invisible world of music; *DDRW* 26; 29). Echoing Nietzsche's *Birth of Tragedy,* Chamberlain argues that the poem must be "born out of the spirit of music" in order that the longing of music for form (Gestalt) may be satisfied: the designation of the poetic material is determined by music, by the inner man, for the expressive powers of music reveal the inner substance of all phenomena. The artwork, therefore, evolves from the inner man. It is the longing of the inner man for form (compare Homunculus in Goethe's *Faust* Part II, act 2), the longing of the inner man to connect with the exterior man, that is the *fons et origo* of the word-tone-drama: ". . . wie soll dieser nie endenden Sehnsucht der Musik nach sichtbarer Gestaltung, nach greifbaren Wesen, die sie umarmen und zu ihren Regionen reinen Gefühlslebens mit hinaufziehen kann, entsprochen werden?" (how shall this never-ending longing of music for a visible form, for a tangible shape, which it may embrace and draw up with it to its own spheres of pure emotional life, be satisfied?; *DDRW* 26; 29). Chamberlain's concept of the word-tone-drama here comes close to paraphrasing the composer's own words to the effect that the essence of Wagnerian music drama is "ersichtlich gewordene Thaten der Musik" (deeds of music made visible). It is the internal action as realized in the music that constitutes the substance of the drama; the poem is the exterior surface.[24]

---

[23] Richard Wagner, *Beethoven* (Leipzig: Verlag von E. W. Fritzsch, 1870); trans. W. Ashton Ellis in Richard Wagner, *Actors and Singers,* 59–126 (Lincoln and London: U of Nebraska P, 1995). New translation with critical commentary by Brian Hitch and Roger Allen forthcoming.

[24] Richard Wagner, "Über die Benennung 'Musikdrama'," *Gesammelte Schriften und Dichtungen,* 9:306, 2nd edition and later.

Chamberlain's explanation of the essence of the word-tone-drama is rooted in the romantic aesthetic of Schopenhauer and Wagner's interpretation of Schopenhauer. He caps his discussion by saying that music is the redeeming art and that Wagner has therefore redeemed the redeeming art from the fetters of so called absolute music: "Und man kann seine Tat nicht treffender und nicht erschöpfender kennzeichnen als mit den Schluß-worten des *Parsifal:* 'O höchsten Heiles Wunder — Erlösung dem Erlöser'! Ja, die Erlösung der Musik! Die Erlösung des 'inneren Menschen'! — das war die große Tat Wagners; die Erlösung der Musik in dem Drama und durch das Drama." (This achievement cannot be more fittingly and exhaustively characterized than by the closing words of "Parsifal": "Oh, miracle of sublimest salvation — Redemption for the Redeemer"! Yes, the redemption of music! the redemption of the "inner man"! — that was Wagner's great achievement, the redemption of music in and through the drama; *DDRW* 34; 45).

Such was Chamberlain's evaluation of Wagnerian music drama in 1892, and such is the set of intellectual assumptions that informs his reception of *Parsifal*. For him, Wagner's final opera is the epitome of his concept of the word-tone-drama. The dramatic content is in essence simple in the extreme and easily summarized: act 1 — pity aroused; act 2 — pity leads to knowledge; act 3 — knowledge of pity calls forth the redeemer. The dramatic action takes place within Parsifal himself as he moves in each act from a passive to an active state that is the dramatic symbol of the invisible musical process. "Auch hier, wiederum, findet die Verbindung des eigentlichen Dramas und des umgebenden Bildes zu einer organischen Einheit vermittelst der Wundermacht der Musik statt." (Here again, the blending of the real drama with the surrounding picture into an organic whole is brought out by the miraculous power of music; *DDRW* 135; 214).[25] Parsifal represents the victory of the "inner" over the "exterior" man and the "inner" man can only be expressed through music.

In Chamberlain's view, the religious element in *Parsifal* is primarily symbolic and an extension of the dual concept of the inner and outer man:

> Wagner hatte ursprünglich an Buddha gedacht; daß er die christliche Symbolik wählte, erkläre ich mir daraus: erstens, daß er das Gemeinte in dieser erschöpfender als in irgend einer anderen darstellen konnte; zweitens [. . .] aus der Erwägung, daß ein Allbekanntes weniger Auseinandersetzungen vor dem Verstande nötig macht und folglich für die unmittelbare, künstlerische Aufnahme vorzuziehen ist.

> [Originally Wagner had thought of Buddha. The fact that he chose Christian symbolism appears to me accountable for the following reasons: first,

---

[25] Translation emended by the author.

that he could more exhaustively express his intention in this than any other symbolism; secondly [. . .] what is generally known requires less demonstration for the understanding and is consequently more compatible with immediate artistic reception. (*DDRW* 139; 220–21)]

The religious symbolism is an allegory of the inner dramatic process, aesthetically represented by the striving of music for form; in no sense does it represent a specific dogma or doctrine; hence Chamberlain's assertion that "there is no more Christianity in *Parsifal* than paganism in the *Ring* or *Tristan*." In *Parsifal*, music, as it strives to attain perceptible forms, expresses the innermost essence of the drama simultaneously with the representation on stage. The action is born out of the spirit of music engendered by the inner man, and to emphasize his point still further Chamberlain this time quotes directly from Wagner: "Nun ist das wesentlich Unterscheidende des Dramas, namentlich aber des Wagnerschen, daß es sich an den ganzen Menschen wendet, und daß in ihm 'die Taten der Musik sichtbar werden'" (Now that which essentially differentiates the drama, especially Wagnerian drama, is the fact that it makes the approach to the entire man, and that it is the "achievements of music made visible"; *DDRW* 139; 220).

The fact that Chamberlain draws so heavily on *Parsifal* in his definition of the word-tone-drama suggests that it held a special place for him within his defined organic grouping of *Der Ring des Nibelungen, Tristan und Isolde*, and *Parsifal*. Indeed, as Mary Cicora points out, *Parsifal*, with its regular performances at the Bayreuth Festival, was the work with which the emerging Bayreuth Circle identified and defined itself.[26] Chamberlain's concept of the word-tone-drama and the realization of the idea in *Parsifal* were formulated less than a decade after the opera's première, during the period when to experience the work in performance necessitated attendance at the Bayreuth Festival. In giving prominence to the musical processes as the origin of the drama (which he carefully differentiates from the more specific text and stage action) he is following both Schopenhauer's conception of music as the primary art and Wagner's rationalization of his compositional processes in the essay *Beethoven*. In *Das Drama Richard Wagners*, as in his earlier articles for the *Revue wagnérienne*, Chamberlain shows an in-depth knowledge that could only have been acquired from extensive study of the score and the associated prose writings. This short book, for all its many lapses into uncritical admiration, represents the best of Chamberlain's writings on Wagner. His concept of the word-tone-drama is an attempt to engage with the aesthetic issues raised

[26] Mary Cicora, *Parsifal Reception in the Bayreuther Blätter* (New York: Peter Lang, 1987), 5.

by Wagnerian music drama without being conditioned by the necessity of contributing to the construction of the Wagner myth so carefully orchestrated by Cosima and her associates.

His attempts at intellectual distance notwithstanding, Chamberlain became ever more closely associated with Wahnfried and the Bayreuth Circle: his articles in the *Revue wagnérienne* had already proved his potential value as a publicist and promulgator of Wagner's ideas to the world outside the immediate influence of Bayreuth.[27] When Cosima was seeking a reliable and articulate author to write an approachable biography of the composer that would interest the general reader, her choice fell on Chamberlain. Cosima covertly arranged for the Munich publishing house of Bruckmann, which subsequently published all of Chamberlain's works, to commission the book. John Deathridge has described Chamberlain's historical methodology as "trying to stress Wagner's artistic mission by fusing his art into a quasi-mystical unity."[28] To a certain extent this is true of *Das Drama Richard Wagners,* but in *Richard Wagner* the author states his intention to provide "nicht eine chronistische Aufzählung aller Vorkommnisse der aufeinanderfolgenden Lebensjahre, sondern eine möglichst einheitliche Skizze des Lebens sowie namentlich des gesamten Denkens und Schaffens dieses großen Mannes zu geben. [. . .] Hier hat mich vom ersten bis zum letzten Wort das eine Bestreben geleitet, Wagner 'von innen' zu erblicken, ihn und die Welt so darzustellen wie *er* beide sah" (not a chronological enumeration of all the events of his [Wagner's] life in proper order, but rather a sketch of the entire thought and work of the great man . . . I have been led, from first to last, by the wish to view Wagner *from within,* to represent him and the world as *he* saw them both).[29] Chamberlain's new book was widely distributed, lavishly illustrated, and luxuriously bound in a manner that would grace the bookshelves of any respectable bourgeois household. In its iconography it often lapses into a form of bloated hyperbole that has resulted in its subsequent dismissal as mere sycophantic hagiography written to please the watching eye of Haus Wahnfried.

---

[27] For an account of the activities of the Bayreuth circle, see Winfried Schüler, *Der Bayreuther Kreis von seiner Entstehung bis zum Ausgang der wilhelminischen Ära* (Münster: Aschendorff, 1971).

[28] John Deathridge, "A Brief History of Wagner Research," in *The Wagner Handbook,* edited by Ulrich Müller and Peter Wapnewski, 210 (Cambridge: Harvard UP, 1992).

[29] Houston Stewart Chamberlain, *Richard Wagner* (Munich: F. Bruckmann 1895; 3rd ed., 1904) vii; trans. G. Ainslie Hight (London: J. M. Dent; Philadelphia: J. B. Lippincott Company, 1900), v. Hereafter referred to as *RW,* with German and English page numbers following. Quotation is from the 1904 edition.

The sweeping condemnation that Chamberlain's work so often receives risks consigning to the dustbin of history a significant cultural text that was an important vehicle for the dissemination of Wagner's ideas in the decades immediately following his death. It is certainly true that his extensive explanation in the second chapter of what he describes as the Wagnerian doctrine of regeneration marks a stage in the process through which late Wagnerian thought as defined in the prose writings flowed into a repellent Germanic ideology. The doctrine of regeneration was a complex agglomeration of quasi-scientific principles that evolved through a synthesis of ideas gleaned from Wagner's *Das Judenthum in der Musik* (1850) through to the so-called regeneration writings of Wagner's last years and underpinned by Chamberlain's thesis that, for the first time, in *Das Judenthum in der Musik*, Wagner "dem zunehmenden Einfluß der Juden in der deutschen Kunst warnend entgegentrat" (raised his warning voice against the increasing influence of the Jews on German art; *RW* 226; 175) and continued to do so until the end of his life. However, there is no attempt to use the content of the music dramas themselves to support a particular ideological position, and Chamberlain's detailed descriptions display a thorough knowledge of the texts and scores. In the course of the biographical material, he specifically detaches the works from the circumstances of Wagner's life:

> Bemerkenswert ist dagegen . . . das eigentlich schöpferische Schaffen des Künstlers in einem nur sehr lockeren, ja meist in gar keinem Zusammenhang mit den äußeren Ereignissen seines Lebens steht. In den jämmerlichen Pariser und Wiener Jahren entsteht die Dichtung zu den *Meistersingern* und die Komposition der heitersten Szenen aus dem ersten Akt; die furchtbare Welttragik der *Götterdämmerung* dagegen während des friedlichen Idylls in Triebschen! Darum bin ich weit entfernt, *Parsifal*, das letzte grosse Werk des Meisters, mit diesen Eindrücken und Erlebnissen der letzten Lebensjahre in irgend einen genetischen Zusammenhang bringen zu wollen.

> [It is remarkable how . . . one peculiarity of all real works of artistic genius becomes intelligible; namely that the real creative work of the artist has only a very loose connection, or generally no connection at all, with the external events of his life. The gay poem of *Die Meistersinger* and the music of the most lively scenes of the first act were composed during the miserable years at Paris and Vienna; the terrible world tragedy of *Götterdämmerung* on the other hand was composed during the peaceful idyll of Triebschen. For this reason I am very far from wishing to bring *Parsifal*, the last great work of the master, in any way into genetic connection with these impressions and experiences from the last years of his life. (*RW* 125; 102)][30]

---

[30] Translation emended by the editors.

Chamberlain's evaluation of *Parsifal* in *Richard Wagner* is consistent with that in *Das Drama Richard Wagners*. In a Schopenhauerian sense, Parsifal's life is controlled by the impulse of his will, and the object of the tragedy is to awaken sympathy in his heart within the harmonically sounding space of the word-tone-drama. Chamberlain sees Parsifal as the embodiment of the romantic idea of genius — the intensification of vision that penetrates the single given fact to the eternity beyond: the action of *Parsifal* is entirely "internal," becoming a drama of pure thought that has at its center the concept of the Grail (*RW* 441; 328). Chamberlain also makes claims for a common origin of the early sketches for *Parsifal* and those for the Buddhist drama *Die Sieger*, both dating from 1854, and calls attention to the Buddhist content in the music drama. The drama consists of the gradual development of a simple youth who blindly follows his own will and through purification of the will emerges as a strong hero. The music is the source of the whole process.

> Wagner wußte das von allem Anfang an; nie hat seine musikalische Gestaltung der Wortsprache und des scenischen Bildes entraten zu können gewähnt; nur im Drama kann die Musik Gestalt werden, nur im Drama kann sie aus dem Reich der Willkür in das Reich der Notwendigkeit treten; dieses höchste menschliche Kunstwerk: das Drama, war darum auch stets sein Ziel. Gerade weil er ein so großer Musiker war, mußte er das Drama wollen.[. . .] Mit ungestümer Macht sollte uns die Musik hinreißen, wie Parsifal von seinem Willen fortgerissen wird, und uns dem Dichter gefügig machen.

> [Wagner knew that from the very first; he never tried to separate the music from the language and the scenic picture; only in the drama can music attain form, only in the drama can it pass from the domain of caprice to that of necessity; this highest human art-work, the drama, was therefore always the object for which he strove. *Because* he was a great musician, he could not help desiring the drama.[. . .] As Parsifal is carried along by his will, so too are we carried away by the impetuous force of music, and made to bend to the will of the poet. (*RW* 448; 333; translation emended by author)]

It is entirely consistent with this view that to Chamberlain *Parsifal* is not a specifically religious, and still less a sacred, work: it is not intended to teach morality or religion. Rather it is "die künstlerische Darstellung eines großen, und im edelsten, stolzesten Sinne des Wortes religiösen Charakters . . . in *Parsifal* — wie in *Tannhäuser* — genießt der Autor des Vorteils, der den griechischen Dichtern so sehr zu statten kam, daß er sich nämlich an allgemein bekannte, in uns noch lebendigem mythischreligiöse Vorstellungen wendet" (artistic representation of a great *religious* character, using the word in its noblest, loftiest sense . . . In *Parsifal* — as in *Tannhäuser* — the author enjoys one advantage in common with the Greek poets, namely that he addresses mythical and religious perceptions possessed by all, and still living within us; *RW* 443; 330).

After *Richard Wagner,* Chamberlain produced no further full-length studies of the composer, although he continued to contribute regular articles to the *Bayreuther Blätter* and other journals.[31] Amongst the series of articles written for the *Blätter* were the *Parsifal-Märchen:* three tales written in the style of the Brothers Grimm that show the serious-minded author in quite a different light. "Parsifal's Christbescherung, ein Weihnachtsmärchen" (1892); "Parsifal's Gebet, ein Ostermärchen" (1893) and "Parsifal's Tod, ein Pfingstmärchen" (1894) create imaginary events in the life of Parsifal during the period of his wanderings (between acts 2 and 3 in the opera) and after his return to Montsalvat. These engaging offshoots of Chamberlain's writings on Wagner were dedicated to Manfred Graf Gravina, grandson of Cosima and Hans von Bülow, and subsequently published in a single volume.[32]

The content and style of his Wagner biography broadly, though not entirely, support the notion that Chamberlain was an uncritical, idolatrous Wagnerite intent on mystifying the composer and promoting his image as a suitable icon for the cultivated and increasingly conservative middle classes. Yet in 1898, when invited to address the prestigious Philosophical Society of the University of Vienna on the subject of Wagner's philosophy, Chamberlain adopted a more critical position.[33] He drew attention not to the unity but to the inconsistencies in Wagner's thought and depicted the composer as a brilliant but essentially unsystematic dilettante. This lecture is significant: not least for the way in which it anticipates by thirty-five years the central thesis of Thomas Mann's "Leiden und Größe Richard Wagners."[34] But it is most noteworthy for the manner in which Chamberlain was prepared to modify and to some extent recast his interpretation of Wagnerian philosophy when addressing a critically astute academic audience. He was by no means Cosima Wagner's poodle: he was

---

[31] For a full list of Chamberlain's writings see the bibliography in Field, *Evangelist of Race,* 519–29.

[32] Houston Stewart Chamberlain, *Parsifal-Märchen* (Munich: F. Bruckmann, 1900).

[33] See Field, *Evangelist of Race,* 341–42. The lecture, "Richard Wagners Philosophie" was given on December 16, 1898 and published in the *Münchener Allgemeine Zeitung,* Feb. 25–28, 1899.

[34] Thomas Mann, "Leiden und Grösse Richard Wagners," in *Wagner und unsere Zeit,* ed. Erika Mann, 63–121 (Frankfurt am Main: S. Fischer, 1983); in English: *Thomas Mann: Pro and Contra Wagner,* trans. Allan Blunden (London: Faber, 1985), 91–148.

not prepared to compromise his intellectual independence by bowing to the demands of Wahnfried orthodoxy when by so doing he might impugn his academic integrity. The lecture was published in the *Münchener Allgemeine Zeitung* from February 25 to 28, 1899, and through this public distancing of himself from Wahnfried, Chamberlain gained greater credibility amongst those who regarded Cosima's growing dogmatism with suspicion. When the "Meisterin" read the text, she retorted tartly that Chamberlain was in error regarding the facts, but she stopped short of ostracizing him from her circle: his perceived intellectual respectability and growing reputation as a writer made him much too valuable to her cause.

By making extensive use of evolutionary models in his biography of Wagner, Chamberlain brought the developing phenomenon of Wagnerism into the mainstream of pan-German ideology, increasingly dominated as it was by a sociology based on the theories of Charles Darwin: *Richard Wagner* marks the point at which the converging streams flow into one another. It was in his next major work, the hugely influential and widely-read *Die Grundlagen des neunzehnten Jahrhunderts* (The Foundations of the Nineteenth Century) that Chamberlain placed himself and the doctrines of Bayreuth orthodoxy in the centre of the cultural platform already constructed by such *völkisch* writers as Paul Lagarde and Julius Langbehn.[35] He created a literary crucible in which the ideas of Wagner's later years were perceived as sharing the same assumptions as a particularly tendentious form of late nineteenth-century Germanic ideology rooted in racial and cultural idealism.

The work was suggested to Chamberlain by his publisher in a letter of February 6, 1896 as a literary homage to the cultural achievements of the waning nineteenth century. Chamberlain, uncertain as to his personal suitability for so momentous an undertaking, sought the advice of Cosima Wagner. Cosima strongly encouraged him, as she envisaged a work that would be a view of history in accordance with Wagnerian ideals; indeed, the initial tripartite plan of the book was to have identified Wagner and his work as no less than the culminating point of the entire span of human history.[36] In the event, only the first part, the two-volume *Grundlagen,* was ever published, and, much to Cosima's annoyance, it contained scant

---

[35] Houston Stewart Chamberlain, *Die Grundlagen des neunzehnten Jahrhunderts* (Munich: F. Bruckmann, 1899; 4th ed., 1903); in English: *The Foundations of the Nineteenth Century,* trans. John Lees (London: John Lane The Bodley Head; New York: John Lane Company, 1911).

[36] The exchange of correspondence between Cosima Wagner and Chamberlain is to be found in Pretzsch, *Cosima Wagner und Houston Stewart Chamberlain im Briefwechsel,* 441–54.

reference to Wagner. In the first volume, Chamberlain surveys the entire sweep of European history up to the year 1200 in terms of a dialectical struggle between conflicting racial groups; his historiography casts the Teutons (Germanen) as the true progenitors of European culture, while the Jews in particular were depicted as a disruptive, degenerate influence. The anthropology is tortuous in the extreme: the intellectual acrobatics to which the author resorts when advancing his thesis that Christ, whose birth he called the most important date in the history of mankind, was not and could not have been of Jewish origin, illustrate how in this work Chamberlain's intellectual integrity was increasingly compromised by his ideological purpose. The second volume follows on from the first by charting the rise of modern European culture in terms of Teutonic superiority. In Chamberlain's distorted view, all achievements in science, political economy, industry, and art were a result of Teutonic influence: thus the achievements of the nineteenth century rested on secure Teutonic foundations.

Chamberlain's *Grundlagen* was widely disseminated amongst the educated bourgeoisie of the Wilhelmine empire, and amongst its most enthusiastic readers was Kaiser Wilhelm II, who initiated a prolific correspondence with the author. Critical reaction, however, was mixed: many reviewers pointed to the unsystematic nature of Chamberlain's historiography; Friedrich Hertz, in the *Sozialistische Monatshefte,* warned that Chamberlain's enthusiasm led many people to embrace his ideas without being concerned about his reasoning.[37]

The initial reaction from Wahnfried to the publication of the *Grundlagen* was favorable. However, when some months later Cosima began to reflect in depth upon the contents in consultation with her son-in-law Henry Thode, she changed her mind, declaring that the intellectual debt to Wagner was inadequately acknowledged: she was displeased that the composer's name was so little in evidence. Henry Thode, husband of Daniela von Bülow, was an art historian whose best-known work, *Franz von Assisi,* drew on the work of Jacob Burckhardt; in it the author appropriated the visual arts for ideological purposes by interpreting the art of the Italian Renaissance along *völkisch* lines. This doughty defender of Bayreuth orthodoxy took up the cudgels on Cosima's behalf; in March 1900 he published a lengthy review in the *Literarisches Centralblatt für Deutschland* that accused Chamberlain of plagiarizing the central thesis of the book from Wagner's late essays and Count Gobineau's *Essai sur l'inégalité des races humaines.* Chamberlain, always hyper-sensitive to press criticism, and especially so when his antagonist was a trusted confidant of Cosima, answered the charges leveled against him by publishing a new preface to

---

[37] Quoted in Field, *Evangelist of Race,* 228.

the third edition of the *Foundations* (1901). This long and detailed apologia, here made available to the English reader for the first time, is important in helping us to understand the extent to which Wagnerian thought was, or was not, responsible for underpinning Chamberlain's ideas. It therefore merits extensive quotation:

> Ein Mitarbeiter des *Literarischen Centralblattes* hat mich des mehr oder minder bewußten Plagiats an Richard Wagner bezichtigt. Wären Wagners Schriften bekannter als sie sind, ich könnte schweigen; der Vorwurf würde sich von selber richten. So aber drucken selbst wohlwollende Rezensenten die betreffende Behauptung nach; Wagners *Religion und Kunst* haben sie — leider — nie gelesen, und da die verwandtschaftlichen Beziehungen des betreffenden Gelehrten seine Vertrautheit mit den Schriften des Bayreuther Meisters gewährleisten, nehmen sie ohne weiteres an, meine *Grundlagen* seien in der Hauptsache ein Breittreten von Wagners hundert Seiten auf den Umfang von tausend Seiten, im besten Falle — um mit dem Rezensenten zu reden — ein Sammeln von "Belegen für die Wahrheit dieser (von Wagner) gegebenen Fundamentalsätze." In Wirklichkeit ist die Behauptung ebenso irrig als injuriös, und indem sie mir das Meine raubt, raubt sie auch dem großen Wort- und Tondichter das Seine, dasjenige, meine ich, was er mir in der That gegeben hat und wofür ich ihm mit jedem Atemzuge meines Lebens danke.
>
> Wohl darf ich mich in einem gewissen Sinne einen "Jünger" Wagners nennen, doch müßte das Wort genau definiert werden, ehe ich es als berechtigt anerkennen könnte. Descartes sagt: die großen Geister reden Unsinn, sobald ihre Jünger in ihrem Namen sprechen. Das habe ich an Wagners angeblichen Jüngern oft genug erfahren, und ich geize nicht danach, ihnen beigezählt zu werden. Als ich ein Werk über Wagner zu schreiben hatte, habe ich mir strengste Selbstbeherrschung zum Gesetz gemacht: erstens, damit Wagner möglichst rein zu Worte komme, zweitens, weil ich empfinden mußte, daß uns nicht bloß ein Höhenabstand, sondern fast die ganze geistige Anlage und damit zugleich viele "Fundamentalsätze" der Überzeugung von einander schieden. Meine Ehrfurcht vor Richard Wagner ist viel zu groß, als daß ich es jemals wagen könnte, "seine Ideen auszuführen" (wie das *Centralblatt* sich ausdrückt), das heißt also, gleichsam in seinem Namen zu sprechen. Ich möchte den Mann sehen, der sich dessen unterfinge; ein zweiter Richard Wagner thäte es gewiß nicht.

[A collaborator on the *Literarisches Centralblatt* [*für Deutschland*] has accused me of more or less consciously plagiarizing Richard Wagner. If Wagner's writings were better known than they are, I could keep silent. The reproach would right itself. As it is, even well-meaning reviewers repeat this claim; they have unfortunately never read Wagner's *Religion und Kunst*, and since the relationship of the scholar concerned with Wagner's family guarantees his familiarity with the writings of the Bayreuth master, they simply assume that my *Grundlagen* essentially extends Wagner's 100 pages to 1000 pages; at best — in the words of the reviewer — a collection of "evidence for the truth of these fundamental assertions of Wagner." In reality the claim is as erroneous as it is injurious, and while it robs me of what is mine, it also robs the great poet and composer of what is his, I mean that which he has actually given me and for which I thank him with every breath of my being.

I may well call myself in a certain sense a disciple of Wagner's, but the word would need precise definition before I could consider it justified. Descartes said, "great men talk nonsense as soon as their disciples speak in their name." I have often enough experienced this with Wagner's alleged disciples, and I have no ambition to be numbered amongst them. When I had to write a work about Wagner I made it a rule to observe the strictest self control: first so that Wagner should express himself, as far as possible, in his own words and second because I felt that we were separated not only by a difference in level but by our entire intellectual aptitude and at the same time many fundamental convictions. My awe of Richard Wagner is much too strong for me ever to dare to expand his ideas (as the *Centralblatt* has it): that is to say, to speak in his name. I would like to see the man who would undertake that; a second Richard Wagner would certainly not do so.][38]

Chamberlain then vigorously defends his standard of scholarship, assuring his readers that every factual assertion in the *Grundlagen* has been verified and the appropriate source acknowledged. He goes on to describe Wagner as essentially a philosophical and scientific dilettante whose ideas represent an unsystematic mixture of a number of disparate strands of thought.

Mein gelehrter Rezensent muß unter dem Einfluß einer starken Hypnose gestanden haben, als er Richard Wagner Ideen als Eigentum vindicierte, die Wagner einfach aus dem gemeinsamen Kulturgut der europäischen Menschheit schöpfte. Welch ein andrer Geist weht uns aus Wagner's Worten entgegen: "Was einmal öffentlich gesagt ist, gehört der Allgemeinheit an und nicht mehr ist es Eigentum Desjenigen, der es gesagt hat. In diesem Sinne würde ich mir jedes Plagiat verzeihen, weil ich es nicht dafür halten könnte."[39] Und in der That, Wagner hat die Ideen, welche ihm hier zugeschrieben werden, meistens *en bloc* von weltbekannten Autoren übernommen. Sein Geist ist in wissenschaftlicher Beziehung eigentümlich unkritisch, fast möchte ich sagen kindlich naiv. Wer ihm

---

[38] Chamberlain, *Die Grundlagen des neunzehnten Jahrhunderts* (Munich: Bruckmann, 1899). Abbreviated prefatory material newly translated by Brian Hitch and Roger Allen from the 4th edition (1903). The preface to the third edition (1901), from which these excerpts are taken, is to be found between pages xii and xxvi. The assistance of Stewart Spencer is also gratefully acknowledged. A translation of the full text is available on application to the present author.

[39] Here Chamberlain is quoting from a letter Wagner wrote to Theodor Uhlig dated "Anfang Februar 1851" (the beginning of February 1851).

Vertrauen einflößt, dem glaubt er alles, von dem nimmt er alles ungeprüft an. Jedenfalls hängt dies mit dem Wesen des absoluten Künstlers zusammen. Wagner's Weltanschauung — als Bestandteil seiner unvergleichlichen Persönlichkeit — ist und bleibt ein unschätzbares Gut; doch wer wissenschaftliche Belehrung bei ihm holt, ist übel beraten, und wer ein Buch von der Art des vorliegenden auf eine derartige Grundlage aufbauen wollte, wäre — nach meinem Dafürhalten — ein Thor.

[My learned critic must have been under the influence of a strong hypnosis when he vindicated Wagner's ideas as something simply drawn from the common European culture. What a different spirit inspires Wagner's words: "what has once been said publicly belongs to all and is no longer the property of him who said it. In this sense I would forgive every plagiarism because I could not consider it as such." Indeed, Wagner mostly borrowed the ideas ascribed to him here "en bloc" from world-famous authors. In scientific matters his mind is peculiarly uncritical, one might almost say childlike and naïve. Wagner believes everything and accepts everything without examination from anyone inspiring him with confidence. This goes with the nature of the absolute artist. Wagner's *Weltanschauung* — an integral part of his incomparable personality — is and remains an inestimable blessing; yet anyone taking scientific instruction from him is badly advised, and anyone seeking to base a book such as the present one on such a foundation of that kind would, in my judgment, be a fool.]

The thrust of Chamberlain's criticism is twofold: first, he asks to what extent Wagner drew his ideas from the prevailing intellectual assumptions of his time; second, he shows how his own twin concepts of the ruin of the Christian religion and the admixture of racial types — the theses which constitute the framework of the *Foundations* — differ substantially from those of Wagner. In Chamberlain's view, the question of race is not central to Wagner's thinking: where the composer does touch upon the question in the essay "Heldentum und Christentum" it is only to offer a résumé of Gobineau's ideas.

> *Die Grundlagen des neunzehnten Jahrhunderts* sind eine Ausführung der besonders in *Religion und Kunst* von Richard Wagner ausgesprochenen Ideen . . . Ob nun wirklich mit diesem ziemlich mageren Inventarium der Inhalt meines Buches erschöpft ist, das kann ich billig dem Urteil des Lesers überlassen; ich glaube, er wird finden, daß ich nicht bloß stofflich, sondern auch gedanklich etwas mehr biete, und daß eine hochgradige Einseitigkeit dazu gehört, um in einem derartigen Werk nur gerade diejenigen Punkte zu bemerken, die eine mögliche Beziehung zu Richard Wagner gestatten. Was mir obliegt zu zeigen, ist, erstens, daß die genannten "Thesen" nicht Wagner's Eigentum sind, zweitens, daß meine eigene Auffassung in zwei von den drei "Fundamentalsätzen" wesentlich von der seinen abweicht. [. . .]
>
> Meine Auffassung des Begriffes und der Thatsache "Rasse" ist die zweite meiner "Thesen," die angeblich in den Schriften Richard Wagner's

ihren "Quell" hat. Da Wagners Schriften zwölf Bände umfassen und also nicht leicht zu überblicken sind, bitte ich den Leser zu einem vortrefflichen Nachschlagewerk zu greifen, das er gewiß auf jeder Bibliothek finden wird; es heißt: *Wagner-Lexikon, Hauptbgriffe der Kunst- und Weltanschauung Richard Wagner's in wörtlichen Anführungen aus seinen Schriften zusammengestellt;* die Verfasser sind Karl Friedrich Glasenapp, der vortreffliche Wagnerbiograph, und Heinrich von Stein, der begabteste Jünger des Bayreuther Meisters; daß diese beiden Männer, die genauesten Kenner von Wagners Schriften, nichts übersehen haben, was bei Wagner einem "Fundamentalsatz" gleichkommt, ist sicher. Nun schlage der Leser unter diesen Hauptbegriffen den Begriff "Rasse" nach. Es steht ihm eine Überraschung bevor: das Wort ist überhaupt gar nicht genannt! In der That, Wagner hat sich während seines ganzen Lebens niemals mit der Rassenfrage beschäftigt, und so hat er darüber weder Gedanken, noch Ideen, und noch weniger Fundamentalsätze aufgestellt. In seinen allerletzten Lebensjahren hat er aber zufällig auf Reisen den Grafen Gobineau persönlich kennen gelernt; diese Bekanntschaft führte zur Lektüre von Gobineaus *Versuch über die Ungleichheit der Menschenrassen;* und jetzt nahm Wagner — wie das bei ihm üblich war — mit größter Begeisterung und ohne jegliche Kritik die ihm völlig neuen Ideen Gobineaus als nachgewiesene, offenkundige, restlose Wahrheit auf. Und wenige Monate vor seinem Tode schrieb er einen kleinen Aufsatz von zehn Seiten, betitelt *Heldentum und Christentum,* stilistisch eines der schönsten Gebilde seiner Feder, in welchem er, von Gobineau ausgehend und mit Herbeiziehung tiefmystischer Gedanken über die reinigende Wirkung der Religion auf die Rasse, die Bedingungen untersucht, unter denen — trotz Gobineau's düsteren Prophezeiungen — doch noch "eine wahrhaftige ästhetische Kunstblüte" zu erwarten sei. Dies ist die einzige Schrift, in welcher Wagner das Rassenthema berührt hat. Ihr sind die Worte entnommen, die mein Rezensent citiert, und Wagner selber giebt sie für nichts anderes aus, als für eine kürzeste Zusammenfassung von Gobineau's Theorie. Und doch glaubt der betreffende Rezensent, angesichts meiner Kapitel über das Völkerchaos, über die Juden und über die Germanen behaupten zu dürfen: "Chamberlain verdankt die Erkenntnis dieses Problems Richard Wagner." Das ist kühn! [. . .]

Was nun meine Darstellung der Rasse anbetrifft, wird jeder Leser — namentlich jeder, der über naturwissenschaftliche Kenntnisse verfügt — einsehen, daß sie ganz und gar in dem naturwissenschaftlichen Gedankenkreise lebt und webt. Es giebt nur wenige Stellen, wo ich mich mit Gobineau und seiner Welt auch nur berühre. Was ich hier weiß und was ich theoretisierend denke, is alles wissenschaftliches Erbteil aus einem Jahrhundert heißer Arbeit — von Blumenbach bis Ujfalvi —, und mein Meister ist in erster Reihe — wie an Ort und Stelle hervorgehoben — Charles Darwin. Nicht etwa, daß ich diesen großen Namen für meine Auffassung des Wesens und der Bedeutung der Menschenrassen beanspruchen könnte; er aber war es, der mich zwischen "Rasse" und "Art" zu unterscheiden lehrte, und zwar zu einer Zeit, wo ich noch nicht wußte, daß Wagner überhaupt eine Schrift verfaßt hatte. [. . .]

Wer diese Seiten gelesen hat, begreift, warum ich mein Buch hier in Schutz nahm, warum ich versuchen mußte, einer bedauerlichen, irreführenden Konfusion bei Zeiten den Riegel vorzuschieben. Zugleich ging es an meine persönliche Ehre. Denn der Rezensent schreibt: "Die Erkenntnis jener Probleme verdankt Chamberlain Richard Wagner." [. . .] Ich werde somit der absichtlichen Verschweigung meiner Quellen beschuldigt, und einige "doch" und "vielleicht," die dann folgen, vermögen nicht die verletzende Insinuation aufzuheben. Auch hiergegen mußte es mir im Interesse meiner Leser erlaubt sein, mich zu wehren. Und doch, weder die Rücksicht auf mein Buch, noch die auf meinen literarischen Ruf hätte mich zu reden vermocht, wenn nicht jene unüberlegt geschriebene und sorglos nachgedruckte Beurteilung etwas berührt hätte, was ich als ein Heiligstes im Herzen trage, nämlich mein Verhältnis zu Richard Wagner.

"Ist das Genie vorbeigeschritten, so ist es, als habe sich das Wesen der Dinge umgewandelt, denn sein Charakter ergießt sich über alles, was es berührt"; diese Worte Diderots habe ich auf S. 896 dieser *Grundlagen* angeführt; sie sprechen meine eigene Erfahrung aus, eine bestimmende Erfahrung meines Lebens. Ich würde nicht leben wollen und gewiß könnte ich nicht schaffen, wenn nicht jener unvergleichliche Mann, alles um sich verklärend, über die Welt geschritten ware. Seine Kunst ist die höchste und vollendetste, welche die Menschheit besitzt; mehr als jede andere ist sie das, was Goethe forderte: "eine lebendig augenblickliche Offenbarung des Unerforschlichen": wer sich jemals wahrhaft erfahren, glaubt. Für mein Empfinden aber steht die Persönlichkeit Wagners so hoch wie seine Kunst. So vollendet ist sie natürlich nicht, denn er war ganz Mensch: doch bewährt dieser Mensch im ganzen Verlaufe seines Lebens eine so erhabene Gesinnung, er ist so restlos hingegeben an ein ideales Ziel, er ist so hinreißend selbstvergessen, er ist von dem Edlen in der Menschennatur so verwegen überzeugt, es besteht in ihm eine so vollkommene Harmonie zwischen Wollen und Können — der Gendanke kein Phantom, sondern fähig, sich augenblicklich in die That umzusetzen, — daß ihm gegenüber Ehrfurcht, Liebe und Bewunderung in gleichem Maße gefordert werden; mir ist aus der Weltgeschichte kaum ein Mann bekannt, bei dem das in ähnlicher Weise zutreffe. Ein solcher Mann wirkt auf Andere wie eine Naturkraft: er weckt Leben, er schenkt Selbstvertrauen, er regt das auf, was in Seelentiefen unbewußt schlummerte. Wie Diderot sagte: es ist, als habe er das Wesen der Dinge umgewandelt, — darunter auch das Wesen des eigenen Selbst.

Ich sagte oben, ich könne mich nicht unbedingt zu den "Jüngern" Richard Wagners rechnen, und in der That, meinen geistigen Anlagen ist es angemessener, ein Jünger Goethes und Kants und Cuviers zu sein; ich sagte auch, daß ich in manchen Beziehungen Wagners Führerschaft wenig traue, das ich vielmehr ihr kritisch ablehnend gegenüber stehen müsse; doch das sind Erkenntnisse, die mein Verhältnis eines dankbar und liebevoll Empfangenden in keiner Weise berühren. *Le génie laisse loin de lui l'esprit qui le critique avec raison*, fährt Diderot an derselben Stelle fort. Auch wo er von irrtümlichen Voraussetzungen ausgeht, schafft

Wagner Bewundernswertes und Beherzigenswertes, wie z.B. in der obengenannten Schrift *Heldentum und Christentum,* und ich glaube, die leichtfertige Art, in der ein solcher Künstlergeist mit Thatsachen verfährt, wird ihm durch die Gewißheit eingegeben, daß er doch zu einer höheren Wahrheit durchdringt, gleichviel von welchen Voraussetzungen er ausgeht; darum nimmt er die ersten besten an, die er leicht assimilieren kann. Wagner schwört heute bei Feuerbach und morgen bei Schopenhauer, er ist heute Republikaner und morgen Gottesgnadentumverfechter, heute rührt die Entartung der Menschheit von der Nahrung her, morgen von der Rassenvermischung — und doch ist er der selbe, und was er der Menschheit zu sagen hat: über das Wesen der Kunst, über eine künstlerische Kultur, über das Verhältnis zwischen Kunst und Religion u.s.w. bleibt unverändert, gleichviel aus welchen Materialien er den Unterbau gezimmert hat. Künstlerische Intuitionen sind wie die ägyptischen Pyramiden; sie werden von der Spitze nach abwärts zu gebaut; was darunter liegt, ist bloß staubiges Gerüst. Eine "Thatsache" giebt es bei Wagner, in die ich unbedingt vertraue: er selber.

Jener Rezensent rührt nun nicht nur an meiner litterarischen Ehre, sondern er bringt mich in den Verdacht der Undankbarkeit. Mit Recht wird Untreue, wenn auch nicht als das schwerste, so doch als das schwärzeste Verbrechen betrachtet. Für sie giebt es keine Sühne; nur der Wahnsinn kann sie entschuldigen. Seit Jahren streiten die Gelehrten darüber, in welchem Augenblick Nietzsche thatsächlich in Wahnsinn verfiel; und doch liegt es klar vor aller Augen: in dem Augenblick, als er von Wagner abfiel.

[*The Foundations of the Nineteenth Century* expounds the ideas that Wagner propounded especially in *Religion und Kunst.* . . Whether the content of my book is exhausted by this rather meager inventory I properly leave to the judgement of the reader; I believe he will find that both in my material and my thinking I am offering more and that it would be extremely one-sided in a work of this kind only to notice points with a possible connection to Richard Wagner. It is incumbent on me to show, firstly, that the theses outlined above are not Wagner's own creation, and, secondly, that my own views differ substantially from his.

My interpretation of the concept and fact of "race" is the second of my theses allegedly having their origin in Wagner's writings. Since they comprise twelve volumes and are not easy to take in as a whole I ask the reader to reach for an excellent work of reference he will certainly find in every library: *Wagner Lexicon: The Main Ideas in R. Wagner's View of Art and of the World, Compiled from Quotations from His Writings.* The authors are K. F. Glasenapp, Wagner's excellent biographer, and H. von Stein, the most gifted disciple of the Bayreuth Master; it is certain that both these men, with their detailed knowledge of Wagner's writings, have overlooked nothing tantamount to one of Wagner's fundamental clauses. Now the reader may care to look up "race" among these "main ideas." A surprise awaits him: the word is simply not there. In fact, Wagner never in his whole life concerned himself with racial questions; he never devised thoughts or ideas and still less fundamental clauses on this matter. But at the very end of his life he chanced while on a journey to meet Count Gobineau; this acquaintance encouraged him to read Gobineau's *Essai sur l'inégalité des races humaines* (Essay on the Inequality of the Races); as usual with him, Wagner now, with the greatest enthusiasm and without criticizing them in any way, took up Gobineau's ideas, which were completely new to him.[40] He accepted them as the proven, immanent and complete truth. A few months before his death he wrote a short essay of ten pages entitled "Heldentum und Christentum," stylistically one of the most beautiful creations of his pen. Starting with Gobineau and adducing deeply mystical thoughts about the purifying effect of Religion on race, this examines the conditions in which — in spite of Gobineau's dark prophecies — "a true aesthetic cultural blossoming might yet be expected." This is the only place where Wagner touched upon the theme of race.[41] This is the source of the words that my reviewer quotes, and that Wagner himself offers as nothing more than a very brief résumé of Gobineau's theory. Yet on the strength of my chapters on the "Chaos of the Peoples" on Jews and on the Teutons this critic dares to assert: "Chamberlain owes his knowledge of the problem to Richard Wagner." That is bold of him.

As far as my concept of race is concerned, all readers — especially those with scientific knowledge — will understand that it lives and breathes entirely in a scientific context. There are only a few places where I even come into contact with Gobineau and his world. What I know about this and what I think theoretically is the scientific legacy of a century of intensive work — from Blumenbach to Ujfalvi — and my master

---

[40] See L. J. Rather, *Reading Wagner* (Baton Rouge: Louisiana State UP, 1990), 17. Rather makes more specific Wagner's engagement with Gobineau's subject matter by noting that Wagner possessed both the French original and the German translation of Gobineau's work in his library at Wahnfried and that the work "lauds the accomplishments of the Ancient Hebrews in Palestine as the model of what can be accomplished by strictly maintained racial purity." Rather also points out that the work of Gobineau is "now much condemned but seldom intelligently read" — a criticism which could equally well apply to current reception of Chamberlain's writings. See also pp. 275–89 and 304–15, in which the author considers the fundamental differences between Wagner's concept of race and the subsequent Nazi ideology of racial supremacy and purity.

[41] It is important in this context to distinguish between the terms "Geschlecht" and "Rasse." Wagner uses Geschlecht frequently, e.g., "Ich weiss ein wildes Geschlecht," (*Die Walküre* act 1 vs p.32); "Du zeugtest ein edles Geschlecht" (*Die Walküre*, act 3, 281). Chamberlain is correct when he cites "Heldentum und Christentum" as the only reference Wagner makes to "Rasse" when the twin concepts of "Rasse" as race and "Geschlecht" with strong overtones of family lineage occur in close proximity. (R. Wagner, *Gesammelte Schriften* 10:284; *Religion and Art*, 284). Chamberlain refers to "die Rassenfrage" in *Richard Wagner* in connection with the doctrine of regeneration (*RW* 161; 12).

in the first instance — as I have emphasized in the text: Charles Darwin. It is not as if I could make use of this great name for my view of the nature and significance of human races; but it was he who taught me to distinguish between race and species; and this was at a time when I did not know that Wagner had written anything about it.

Those who have read these pages understand why I have defended my book, why I had to try to put a timely end to this regrettable, misleading confusion. At the same time, my personal honour was involved. For the critic writes, "Chamberlain owes the understanding of those problems to R. Wagner" . . . In this way, I am accused of intentionally concealing my sources and some "yets" and "perhapses" which then follow do not manage to remove the wounding insinuation. Against this, too, I had in the interest of my readers to be permitted to defend myself. Neither consideration for my book nor for my literary reputation could have persuaded me to speak out had not this judgment, written without reflection and carelessly copied, concerned something which I hold as most sacred in my heart, namely my relationship to Richard Wagner.

"If genius passes by, it is as if the nature of things is transformed for its character is poured out over all that it touches"; I have quoted these words of Diderot's on p. 896 of the *Foundations;* they express a defining experience in my life. I would not want to live and certainly I could not create if that incomparable man, transfiguring all around him, had not passed through the world. His art is the highest and most complete which mankind possesses; more than any other it is the art which Goethe demanded, "a living and momentary revelation of the unfathomable." Who has ever truly experienced this believes. I feel that Wagner's personality stands as high as his art. It was naturally not as perfect, for he was totally human, yet this man attests in the entire course of his life to such a lofty purpose, he is so totally devoted to an ideal goal, he is so captivatingly self-effacing, he is so audaciously convinced by what is noble in human nature, he has such perfect harmony between will and ability — thought being no phantom but capable of immediate realisation — that he commands awe, love and admiration in equal measure. In the history of the world I scarcely know anybody of whom that is similarly true. Such a man has the effect on other people of a natural force. He awakens life, bestows self-confidence and excites what slumbered unconscious in the depths of the soul. As Diderot said, it is as if he had transformed the nature of things — including the nature of one's self.

I said above, I don't regard myself unconditionally as one of Wagner's "disciples," and in fact, given my own intellectual disposition, it would be more appropriate to describe me as being a disciple of Goethe, Kant and Cuvier; I said too that in many respects I have little confidence in Wagner's leadership and that I have critically to reject it; but this is a recognition in no way affecting my relationship to him as a grateful and affectionate beneficiary. Diderot continues in the same passage that genius leaves far behind the spirit who criticizes him from the standpoint of reason. Even when he starts from erroneous premises, Wagner's works deserve admiration and attention, as for example in the above-mentioned essay "Heldentum und Christentum," and I believe that the slapdash way in which an artistic spirit of this kind deals with facts is prompted by a certainty that he is attaining a higher truth regardless of his initial premises; therefore he accepts whatever ideas he can assimilate. Today Wagner swears by Feuerbach and tomorrow by Schopenhauer; today he is a republican and tomorrow an advocate of the Divine Right of Kings; today the degeneration of humanity derives from food, tomorrow from racial mixing — and yet he remains the same, and what he has to say to mankind about the nature of art, about artistic culture and about the relationship between art and religion remains unaltered, regardless of what material he used for the infrastructure. Artistic intuitions are like Egyptian pyramids; they are built from the top downwards; what lies underneath is merely a dusty framework. There is one fact with Wagner in which I believe unconditionally: himself. That critic is not only impugning my literary honour but opening me to the suspicion of ingratitude. Infidelity is rightly considered, if not as the most grievous, then surely as the blackest of crimes. There is no atonement for it; only madness can excuse it. Scholars have for years disputed when Nietzsche actually went mad; and yet it is crystal clear: at the moment he separated from Wagner.]

Such was Chamberlain's attempt in the preface to the third edition of *Die Grundlagen des neunzehnten Jahrhunderts* to establish his intellectual independence from the ideas of Richard Wagner. His position is essentially defensive in that he is distinguishing and differentiating himself from the artistically driven, naïvely idealistic Wagner, partly to define his territory as intellectually different (indeed, superior) and scientifically more rigorous. The notion of Wagner the philosophical and scientific dilettante is a subtext running just below the surface of this entire preface. In *Das Drama Richard Wagners* he had carefully divided Wagner's creative life into two distinct periods more or less bisected by the year 1848. In the same way the publication of *Foundations* in 1899 may be seen as the decisive point at which Chamberlain's thinking turned from an extreme form of romantic idealism towards the racially-inspired historiography which nourished his later worldview. His concept of the word-tone-drama, of which *Parsifal* was the epitome, belongs entirely to the pre-*Foundations* period. The relationship between the music and the drama — the drama as deeds of music made visible — is founded in the Schopenhauerian view of music as Wagner defined it in his essay *Beethoven* (1870): music is itself the fundamental process of the drama; the drama is music seeking form. Tinged with hyperbole though it may be, Chamberlain's reception of the music dramas in general and *Parsifal* in particular belongs to the pre-*Foundations* phase of *Das Drama Richard Wagners* and the biography *Richard Wagner.*

In spite of a mixed critical reception, the success of the *Foundations* consolidated Chamberlain's position as one of the prime movers and shakers of German culture during the final fifteen years or so of the Wilhelmine Reich. The work itself is an example of the way in which late nineteenth-century idealism hardened into the form of racial and cultural ideology that proved so potent a tool in the hands of the forces of extreme nationalism. At no point, however, does Chamberlain directly use either Wagner's music dramas or his prose writings to buttress his historiography. His biographer Geoffrey Field, in his otherwise scrupulous and balanced account, is carried away by his theme and tendentiously describes *Parsifal* as a "racial odyssey."[42] There is no direct evidence to support the view that Chamberlain saw *Parsifal* as anything more than a spiritual fable; nowhere in his writings does he make the work out to be the myth of racial regeneration constructed by later writers and critics.[43] The "evangelist of race" found no racism in *Parsifal,* nor did he draw on its content to support his racial historiography.[44]

As we have seen, Chamberlain does not call on Wagner to support his theories through either his works or his writings. Yet the situation is shot through with difficulties, for by making an extensive study of the Wagnerian concept of regeneration in his biography of the composer and through his ready use of organic models he inevitably creates an uneasy synthesis between this aspect of late Wagnerian thought and his own later writings. In addition, the immediate effect of the well-publicized controversy with Henry Thode was to bind the regeneration writings of Wagner's last years in the minds of Chamberlain's ever-widening and largely uncritical readership inextricably with the racially motivated agenda of the *Foundations.* Whether intentionally or not, it was Chamberlain who was to forge the links of the ideological chain that connected the growing phenomenon of Wagnerism to the wider movement of nationalist and *völkisch* thought. In the minds of a broad social and intellectual cross-section of the German public, Bayreuth and racist thinking became ideologically synonymous.

Parsifal, the work of Wagner's last years, was not one of the direct links in that chain. To Chamberlain and the ideologues of the Bayreuth

---

[42] Field, *Evangelist of Race,* 88.

[43] See for example Robert Gutman, *Richard Wagner* (London: Secker and Warburg, 1968).

[44] Thus Gutman's view that "Wagner was preparing in *Parsifal* that concept of Aryan Christianity that his future son-in-law Houston Stewart Chamberlain was in turn to bequeath to Alfred Rosenberg and the Nazi movement" (336) is largely unsustainable. As has been seen, there is nothing of a racial nature in Chamberlain's writings on *Parsifal* and he found it necessary to defend himself from accusations that his racial views as formulated in *Die Grundlagen* involved unacknowledged dependence on Wagner. See also Hartmut Zelinsky, *Richard Wagner: Ein deutsches Thema: Eine Dokumentation zur Wirkungsgeschichte Richard Wagners 1876–1976* (Frankfurt am Main: Zweitausendeins, 1976); also Mike Ashman, "A Very Human Epic," in *Parsifal: Richard Wagner,* Opera Guide 34 (London: ENO and Royal Opera, 1986), 10.

Circle, it remained Wagner's *Bühnenweihfestspiel*. In his writings on the opera, Chamberlain fostered the process through which the Bayreuth stage was "consecrated." Echoing Wagner, he regarded *Parsifal* as the artwork that "saved the spirit of religion by recognizing the figurative value of the mythic symbols which the former [religion] would have us believe in their literal sense and revealing their deep and hidden truth through an ideal presentation." The Festspielhaus thus became a temple dedicated to the religion of art.[45] By this means, however, Chamberlain nourished the inexorable process through which Wagner's works were increasingly politicized and Bayreuth became a center of the forces of extreme conservatism. In attempting to keep Wagner and his works apart from ideology, he succeeded only in appropriating him for his ideological purpose.[46]

By the time the copyright expired on January 1, 1914, performances of *Parsifal* had taken on some of the characteristics of a sacred religious rite: Wagner's original production of 1882 had been frozen by Cosima and then by Siegfried Wagner into a ritual of preservation aided and enhanced by the magisterial musical presentation of Karl Muck.[47] The theater on the hill had come to resemble a temple dedicated to the religion of art; the process of consecration was all but complete. To some, the atmosphere of these pre-First World War Festivals could be suffocating in the extreme, as Igor Stravinsky felt when recalling in 1936 his visit to the Festival in 1912:

> What I find revolting in the whole affair is the underlying conception — the principle of putting a work of art on the same level as the sacred and symbolic ritual which constitutes a religious service. And, indeed, is not all this comedy of Bayreuth, with its ridiculous formalities, simply an unconscious aping of a religious rite. [48]

---

[45] Wagner, GS X, 213. *Religion and Art*, trans. W. Ashton Ellis (Lincoln and London: U of Nebraska P, 1994), 213.

[46] For further critical perspectives on these complex issues, see Laurence Dreyfus, "Hermann Levi's Shame and *Parsifal's* Guilt: A Critique of Essentialism in Biography and Criticism," *Cambridge Opera Journal* 6/2 (1994): 125–45.

[47] Karl Muck (1859–1940) directed *Parsifal* at every festival from 1901 to 1930. Extensive extracts from *Parsifal* under his direction, including the Grail scenes from act 1 and an almost complete act 3, were recorded by Columbia in 1927 and 1928 respectively. The Grail scenes were captured in the Festspielhaus itself and, within the limits of the recording technology of the time, give some idea of the magnificence of the Bayreuth Orchestra and Chorus during the era of Siegfried Wagner. Muck's conducting is quite extraordinary in its intensity and overarching sense of line. This is especially evident in the act 1 Transformation music (Naxos 8.110049–50).

[48] Stravinsky writing in 1936. Quoted in Robert Hartford, *Bayreuth: The Early Years*, 252.

The period from the early months of 1914 to the years immediately following the First World War thus presented an anomalous and strikingly divergent situation. On the one hand, *Parsifal* was released to the world beyond Bayreuth in 1914, a process Wagner (and Cosima) had sought to control. The stage consecration festival play was no longer the exclusive preserve of the Festspielhaus; productions, usually closely modeled on Bayreuth, abounded as opera houses throughout the world rushed to bring it before audiences eager to experience Wagner's final work. Ironically, later that same year the arrogant Wilhelmine worldview fostered by Chamberlain helped ignite a conflagration that brought to an abrupt, tragic end the long and mainly peaceful nineteenth century that had nourished the creation of *Parsifal*. Chamberlain's wartime utterances became ever more strident: the quality and critical perception of his pre-1900 writings gave way to the myopic extremism of "politische Ideale" and the tendentious rant of the "Kriegsaufsätze."[49] The idea of a strong leader as savior of Germany came ever more to the fore: in *Politische Ideale* he wrote: "Ein eiserner Besen muß in Deutschland auskehren: wer den Mut hat, ihn zu führen, wird alle Kräfte des Volkes hinter sich finden" (An iron broom must sweep Germany clean: whoever has the courage to wield it will find all the strength of the *Volk* behind him).[50]

On the other hand, in the uncertain political context of post-war Germany the sanctuary of Bayreuth in the Franconian forest was to become, in the period leading up to the reopening of the Festival in 1924, increasingly inward looking — a meeting place for a wide variety of disaffected conservative and *Völkisch* factions. This concentration of hardening ideological attitudes in itself became a limiting factor, one that was soon to have some highly destructive implications and far-reaching consequences in the form of Chamberlain's enthusiastic endorsement of Hitler following the rising young politician's visit to Bayreuth in 1923. On September 30, Hitler was invited as a guest to Haus Wahnfried and in the course of his visit met the aging and increasingly frail Chamberlain. A week later, in an enthusiastic letter to Hitler, Chamberlain wholeheartedly endorsed Hitler as the future savior of Germany. The letter concludes "Das Deutschland in der Stunde seiner höchsten Not sich einen Hitler gebiert, das bezeugt sein Lebendigsein; desgleichen die Wirkungen, die von ihm ausgehen; denn diese zwei Dinge — die Persönlichkeit und ihre Wirkung — gehören zusammen (That Germany in its hour of greatest need has given birth to a Hitler is proof of vitality; your actions offer further evidence, for a man's

---

[49] Chamberlain, *Politische Ideale* (Munich: F. Bruckmann, 1915); *Kriegsaufsätze* (Munich: F. Bruckmann, 1914).

[50] Chamberlain, *Politische Ideale*, 101. My translation.

personality and actions belong together).[51] These words came, "as a bene-diction from the Bayreuth Meister himself,"[52] and, as Barry Millington writes, helped to secure Chamberlain's place in history as "one of the most influential ideologues of the pre-Nazi era, who played a crucial role in link-ing the destinies of Bayreuth to the Third Reich."[53]

For reasons that are not entirely clear, *Parsifal* was relatively neglected during the Nazi period. It was the perceived nationalism of *Lohengrin* and *Die Meistersinger* rather than the use of religious symbolism in *Parsifal* that provided the propagandists with powerful ideological tools. Richard Wag-ner's *Bühnenweihfestspiel*, released by the expiry of copyright from the limiting confines of Bayreuth but in no sense de-mystified, had by this time taken its place securely within the Wagnerian canon represented on the international stage.

---

[51] Houston Stewart Chamberlain, *Briefe 1882–1924 und Briefwechsel mit Kaiser Wilhelm II.* Ed. Paul Pretzsch, 2 vols. (Munich: Bruckmann, 1928), vol. 2, 124–26. For the full English text of Chamberlain's letter to Hitler and a description of the future dictator's visit to Haus Wahnfried, see Field, *Evangelist of Race,* 434–37.

[52] Field, *Evangelist of Race,* 438. See also Joachim Fest, *Hitler* (New York: Vintage, 1975), 181.

[53] Barry Millington, "Houston Stewart Chamberlain," in *The New Grove Dictio-nary of Music and Musicians,* 2nd ed., ed. Stanley Sadie and John Tyrrell (2001), 5:434. See also Erik Levi, *Music in the Third Reich* (London: Macmillan Press 1994), 5–6. Levi writes, "The degree to which Hitler was already taken seriously by the Wagner circle was already manifested in the Spring 1924 edition of the *Bayreuther Blätter* which opened with a quotation from one of his speeches."

8: *Parsifal* on Stage

Katherine R. Syer

1882–1903: From Bayreuth to America

PARALLELS EXIST BETWEEN the production history of *Parsifal* and the first years of Wagner's title character: both lost their fathers in infancy, had an extremely protected childhood, and left home only to encounter war and political strife. At the same time, the opera and the hero-in-the-making share a sort of resilience and strength that has allowed each to endure and persevere amid hardship and resistance. Wagner could not have foreseen how his last operatic child would have fared through the twentieth century, emerging in the twenty-first as an artwork that continues to demand serious attention — and provoke controversy. *Parsifal* has proven to be a particularly rich object of interpretation in its over 120-year existence. From the beginning, however, Wagner handled his *Bühnenweihfestspiel* somewhat differently than all his other stage works.

Efforts to restrict performances of *Parsifal* to Bayreuth began before the opera was completed. Wagner had reluctantly included *Parsifal* in the arrangement that was to compensate for debts incurred by the 1876 *Ring* by forfeiting royalties for performances of his works at the Munich Court Opera. Highly frustrated with his circumstances, Wagner even thought of moving to Minnesota and granting performance rights to the Americans.[1] But as he recognized the singular significance that *Parsifal* could play in the future of his family, Wagner began to regard what he likely knew would be his final opera as a special opportunity. He then made the case that the particular nature of the work could only be fully respected at the Bayreuth Festspielhaus. Months before the 1882 premiere he convinced Ludwig II to exclude *Parsifal* from the debt repayment arrangement. After the

---

[1] See the entry of 1 February, 1880 in Cosima Wagner, *Cosima Wagner: Die Tagebücher,* vol. 2, ed. Martin Gregor-Dellin and Dietrich Mack (Munich and Zurich: Piper, 1982; in English: *Cosimas Wagner's Diaries,* trans. Geoffrey Skelton, 2 vols. (New York and London: Harcourt Brace Jovanovich, 1980; hereafter *CT*), 2:486–87 (trans. 2:435).

premiere, Wagner also sought the consent of the impresario and conductor Angelo Neumann, when he rescinded a verbal offer to grant him performing rights to take *Parsifal* on tour.

After Wagner's death, eight private performances were given for Ludwig in Munich during 1884 and 1885. In the last exchange of letters between the composer and the king, Wagner responded to Ludwig's appeal for private performances with the intention to put on special performances for him right after the end of the Bayreuth season in the summer of 1883. These extra performances would not take place in Munich but in Bayreuth, where Wagner's optimal cast could be involved, and where he could personally oversee complex aspects of the production such as the transformation scenery, which required modification after 1882 and was particularly constructed for the Bayreuth stage.[2] Wagner died a little over a month after he expressed these thoughts, and before he had the chance to produce *Parsifal* a second time.

After Ludwig's death in 1886, Count Christoph Krafft von Crailsheim of the Bavarian government attempted to include *Parsifal* in the Munich Opera's special royalty arrangement. But by 1887, the flexing of authority from Munich came to a temporary end; Bayreuth's hold on *Parsifal* remained secure and the Wagner family was declared owner of all of the composer's works. The Berne Convention for the protection of Literary and Artistic Works that had been set into motion in 1886, with ten signatory countries including much of Europe in 1887, granted copyright protection for thirty years following the death of the artist. Performances of *Parsifal* at Bayreuth thus continued to attract a devoted international audience, as they had at the premiere, while those eager to hear the music elsewhere had mainly to be content with excerpts, which readily found their way onto concert programs. More ambitious and complete concert renderings could be heard in London (1884), New York (1886), and Amsterdam (1894).

In some ways these very production restrictions stimulated interest in *Parsifal* during this initial phase, but this is just part of a more complex picture of the years before the First World War in which Wagnerism, or Wagnerianism, was at its height. Particularly in France, Italy, Russia, the United Kingdom, and the United States — countries where Wagnerism gained momentum during the composer's lifetime — the dissemination and translation of the composer's voluminous writings contributed to the widespread discussion and absorption of Wagner's theoretical ideas. This

---

[2] The relevant letters are included in *Wagner: A Documentary Study*, ed. Herbert Barth, Dietrich Mack, and Egon Voss, trans. P. R. J. Ford and Mary Whittall (London: Thames and Hudson Ltd., 1975), 244–45.

extramusical phenomenon coincided with an eagerness to experience Wagner's works, and had the further effect of influencing people's views about the meaning and significance of the operas themselves.[3] However, the intense enthusiasm that had accumulated around *Parsifal* as it first reached some of the world's prominent stages in early 1914 was soon overwhelmed by international events. A world in flux awkwardly confronted cultural works and political realities, struggling to understand if and when culture, national identity, and politics could be considered separately. From today's vantage point, we know that Germany's political profile and its role in both world wars have indelibly influenced perceptions of Wagner and his operas. Since the mid-twentieth century, when revisionist approaches to opera production gained substantial ground, the complicated interactions of reception history and production history have become hard to imagine away, even if one would wish to do so. In any case, when we consider the production history of *Parsifal* prior to the First World War, we encounter not only a work, but also a world, that seems artificially protected from the darker developments of the twentieth century.

Core German audiences ready and willing to hear Wagner in the latter half of the nineteenth century existed in large numbers in many American cities in the East and Midwest. Conductors such as Theodore Thomas (1835–1905), Leopold Damrosch (1832–85), and Anton Seidl (1850–98) were eager to build a cultural bridge across the Atlantic, often presenting new works not long after audiences in Germany had heard them. Leopold Damrosch had copyists work feverishly to beat Thomas by six days in presenting Brahms's First Symphony in 1877, the same year the work was first published. The prelude to *Parsifal* became part of Damrosch's repertoire almost immediately after the opera's 1882 premiere. It was Damrosch who initiated in 1884 the first German-language opera season at the Metropolitan, including French and Italian repertoire sung in German. Damrosch died before the end of this inaugural season, but Seidl took over as conductor and presented all of the mature Wagner operas, save *Parsifal,* in the course of the next seven years. While the Metropolitan's executive director Edmond C. Stanton was strongly tempted to present Wagner's last opera in this period, he was counseled otherwise by colleagues such as the soprano Lilli Lehmann.

---

[3] See Erwin Koppen, "Wagnerism as Concept and Phenomenon," in *Wagner Handbook,* ed. Ulrich Müller and Peter Wapnewski, translation ed. John Deathridge, 343–53 (Cambridge and London: Harvard UP, 1992), and David C. Large, "Posthumous Reputation and Influence," in *The Wagner Compendium,* ed. Barry Millington, 384–89 (London: Thames and Hudson, 1992).

Seidl of course had an intimate relationship to *Parsifal*, as he had lived in the Wagner household on and off during a six-year period that included the composition of the opera. He worked as Wagner's assistant, and as choral director for the eminent conductor Hans Richter (1843–1916). Long before Seidl had the opportunity to conduct *Parsifal* at Bayreuth in 1897, he had led the first American approximation of a staged performance, which was sponsored and organized by the Seidl Society. "The Parsifal Entertainment," as it was known, took place at the Brooklyn Academy of Music (then in Brooklyn Heights) on March 31, 1890. Henry Hoyt of the Metropolitan Opera designed the expensive white and silver cathedral scene within the auditorium. Patron boxes were decorated in green, red, and white, streamers adorned the ceiling, and fan palms and other foliage surrounded the eighty-four-piece orchestra on the stage. The moderately abridged performance lasted from five to half past six in the evening, and then from eight until ten, following a catered dinner break.[4] A flurry of ancillary events, lectures and publications surrounded this performance, foreshadowing the near frenzy that would emerge a little over a dozen years later, when New York would experience *Parsifal* fully staged at the Metropolitan Opera.

As the nineteenth century drew to a close, Wagner had been produced on many stages of the major cities in the eastern United States and through to Chicago in the Midwest. Tours originating in New York were a main source; Leopold Damrosch's son Walter toured with three Wagner operas in 1885, the same year he became conducting assistant to Seidl after his father's death. In 1886 he presented over three hours of *Parsifal* in a concert at the Metropolitan Opera, even before *Siegfried* and *Götterdämmerung* had their New York premieres. From 1894–99, as the Metropolitan Opera turned more towards the Italian and French repertoires, Walter Damrosch led a touring company that specialized in German opera. His ambitious five-month tour of 1894, which extended as far west as Kansas City, presented only Wagner operas. In the later 1890s, tours featuring German operas, led by Damrosch and the Metropolitan's Maurice Grau, evinced substantial interest in Wagner. Grau found that students at Harvard were so keen that he could actually charge them fifty cents for the privilege of participating in the productions as supernumeraries.[5]

When Maurice Grau did not mount an 1897–98 season at the Metropolitan, the touring Damrosch-Ellis Opera Company rented the house for a five-week engagement that featured much Wagner. Meanwhile, the

---

[4] Joseph Horowitz, *Wagner Nights: An American History* (Berkeley and Los Angeles: U of California P, 1994), 181–82.

[5] Horowitz, *Wagner Nights*, 241.

impresario Henry W. Savage set up shop in a recently erected theater at 42nd Street and Eighth Avenue and presented over two hundred performances of two dozen works in a six-month period. *Lohengrin* proved an early and overwhelming financial success for the company. Savage specialized in producing opera translated into English. His Castle Square Company earned a reputation for its excellent choir, vividly dramatic renderings, and — unusual at the time — gorgeous new work-specific sets and costumes (with the orchestra less often praised). Returning to the Metropolitan in 1898, Grau launched an ambitious season with Franz Schalk (1863–1931) as conductor, following Seidl's death. He opened with *Tannhäuser* and later presented New York's first unabridged *Ring*. In 1900, Grau and Savage combined forces to produce a season of opera in English at the Metropolitan, including *Tannhäuser* and *Lohengrin*. Grau's flexibility and his ability to gauge the tastes of his audience contributed to his success as an opera impresario — few before him had actually been able to make a regular profit, and his efforts helped extend interest in Wagner's operas into the twentieth century.

1903–14: Interest in *Parsifal* Grows

When the Austrian Heinrich Conried took over the Metropolitan from Maurice Grau in 1903, New York encountered a whole new breed of businessman. Up until this point, the Metropolitan was primarily the physical auditorium whose space was leased to a range of impresarios and companies. The Conried Metropolitan Opera Company, incorporated in 1903, gradually evolved into the continuous, resident production company we associate with the Met today. Conried was quick to recognize the publicity and interest that would be aroused if he produced *Parsifal* in his first season.[6] He took every opportunity to make the production a very special affair. The sets were ordered from Hermann Burghart's workshop in Vienna. With support from the Director of the Munich Hofoper, Ernst von Possart, Conried brought Carl Lautenschläger from Munich to renovate the stage of the Metropolitan Opera House, then between 39th and 40th on Broadway. Particular attention was paid to the execution of the

---

[6] The musical performance was made possible when the publishing firm Schott released a pocketsize version of the full score of *Parsifal* in 1902, with Siegfried Wagner's authorization. Previously, Schott had tightly controlled distribution of the full score, but several copies of the smaller score were sent to the United States for sale. From one such score the orchestral parts were copied for the New York premiere.

opera's two transformation scenes.[7] Counterweights were added to fly machinery, and a new floor with traps was installed. Decorative enhancements were also made to the auditorium and Grand Tier foyer.

By contracting several musicians who had worked for Grau, Conried gained instant access to the Bayreuth experience with Alois Burgstaller (Parsifal) and Anton van Rooy (Amfortas), both of whom had sung in the 1882 premiere. Further connections included Milka Ternina (Kundry) and Robert Blass (Gurnemanz), who had performed their roles more recently in Bayreuth. Central to the whole undertaking was Anton Fuchs, the creator of the role of Klingsor. Fuchs essentially oversaw the stage direction and other production matters, a role he would repeat elsewhere. Cosima's efforts to stop the production were denied by the United States Circuit Court on November 24, 1903, exactly one month before opening night, Christmas Eve, which was also the eve of Cosima's birthday. The timing of the premiere fueled vigorous debates amongst the clergy, who discussed the suitability of the subject matter on the commercial stage. For her part, Cosima attempted to extract revenge by blacklisting these singers. The production's conductor, Alfred Hertz, never worked in Germany again.

While Conried attempted to replicate the Bayreuth production on his stage — charges of his theft or "rape" of the Grail were much bandied about — it is also surely true that he wished his production to be superior. With the price of the orchestra seats doubled to ten dollars, and with twelve sold-out performances, the well-nurtured Wagnerian audience from within and outside New York quickly filled the seats. A chartered train from Chicago, "The *Parsifal* Limited," brought many midwestern Wagnerians to the performances. The reviews reported a tremendously impressive success. Able to compare the Met performances with those at Bayreuth, long-time *New York Tribune* critic Henry Krehbiel favored the stage effects in New York, particularly for the Flowermaiden scene, while Bayreuth came out ahead in his view in terms of musical preparation and lighting.[8]

All of the hype and accomplishment left a huge market untapped, but not for long. In the fall of 1904, The Henry Savage Grand Opera Company took to the road with an English version of *Parsifal,* slightly trimmed

---

[7] Many stages around the world were not equipped to meet the mechanical challenges of the transformation scenery; in 1914 some theaters chose to renovate for precisely the same reasons as the Met, while others avoided staging the scene at all, performing the transformation music with drawn curtain. As the trend to imitate some of the original production features waned, the choice of a closed curtain could also be made for non-technical reasons, as with Wieland Wagner's 1951 Bayreuth production.

[8] Horowitz, *Wagner Nights,* 265.

according to the suggestions of *New York Evening Post* critic Henry T. Finck.[9] Stage director Joseph C. Engel was brought from Berlin to prepare Savage's troupe, with principal roles doubly and triply cast to execute the grueling schedule of eight performances per week. After initial rehearsals, the company opened a two-week trial run at Boston's Tremont Theater in October. There, as elsewhere, Savage strove to emulate the unique performance space of the Bayreuth Festspielhaus by forgoing several rows of seats to accommodate an enlarged orchestra (seventy players) in a partially sunken pit. He also imitated the Bayreuth tradition of having a brass quintet play opera themes to the audience in the foyer a few minutes before curtain time. Returning to Manhattan for one week before heading out on the road, Savage's *Parsifal* played to New York audiences just three weeks before the opening of Conried's season, featuring its *Parsifal* revival. By the end of Savage's tour, Conried was touring with the Metropolitan *Parsifal* and occasionally played the same cities; sometimes Savage's show was preferred.[10] It is striking to think that between October 1903 and May 1904, Savage was responsible for more than 200 performances of *Parsifal* in the United States and another eight in Canada. The original Bayreuth production of *Parsifal* was performed a total of 205 times in the entire period from the 1882 premiere until 1933.

Performers and touring companies freely navigated the border between Canada and the eastern United States during these years, distinctly benefiting the Canadian side, which had not really attempted to produce the ambitious Wagnerian repertoire.[11] Leopold Damrosch conducted the prelude to *Parsifal* in Toronto less than four months after the 1882 Bayreuth premiere. Anton Seidl, who took members of the Metropolitan Opera Company on tour when the 1892–93 season was cancelled after a fire, conducted orchestral music from *Parsifal* in his 1893 Toronto concert, as did Theodore Thomas in 1895. In Toronto in April 1904, Walter Damrosch led an evening of substantial excerpts from *Parsifal* with

---

[9] Horowitz notes on p. 266 of *Wagner Nights* that a Yiddish version was also performed on the Lower East Side.

[10] Jim McPherson, "The Savage Innocents, Part 2: On the Road with *Parsifal, Butterfly,* the *Widow,* and the *Girl,*" in *The Opera Quarterly* 19/1 (Winter 2003), see particularly 35–41.

[11] Notably, the first complete Canadian-produced *Ring* will be presented by the Canadian Opera Company in Toronto in the fall of 2006, in their new 2,000-seat opera house scheduled to open earlier that year. The production features a different director for each of the four music dramas, a similar strategy to that of the Stuttgart *Ring* of 2002, although in this case the designs are being carried out by one designer, Michael Levine.

soloists and the New York Symphony Orchestra. The Henry W. Savage Company's contributions to Wagnerian musical life in Canada included touring performances of *Lohengrin, Tannhäuser,* and *Die Walküre* in the years 1904 and 1905. The most anticipated of their productions was clearly *Parsifal,* which was given four performances at Toronto's Princess Theater in April 1905 before moving to Montreal for four more performances. While Canada, as a British "possession," observed the Berne Copyright Convention, these Canadian-staged performances of *Parsifal* seem to have caused little concern, let alone furor, such as had been stirred up by the Metropolitan Opera.[12] Likely few were interested in the copyright matter after the huge New York debate had been silenced, and it could also be that the Canadian performances were hardly perceptible to international eyes, given the US-dominated schedule. *Parsifal* has not been produced in Canada since that time.

Conried contributed mightily to this early twentieth-century peak in North American *Parsifal* reception with twenty-seven performances of *Parsifal* during 1904–5, including tour performances. The Metropolitan scheduled only four performances the following season and two the season after that. The initial hubbub had subsided. After all, *Parsifal* was never exactly destined to be daily operatic fare. The typical pattern, which emerged at the Met after the First World War and lasted until mid-century, was of annual or near annual performances, inevitably around Easter. Similar patterns emerged during the same period at many German and other European opera houses.[13]

Like the United States, Holland was not initially bound to the Berne Copyright Convention. The Dutch Wagner Society had begun presenting concerts consisting mainly of Wagner's music since 1884, gradually tackling more involved scenes and vocal numbers before staging complete operas, the first of which was *Siegfried* in 1893. The Society did not attempt to authenticate their 1905 Amsterdam production of *Parsifal* by hiring Cosima's singers, although singers well known to Bayreuth, such as Burgstaller, Marie Wittich, and Ernst van Dyck, sang in the society's productions before and after 1905. Ernst van Dyck, who sang the title role of *Parsifal* in Bayreuth for nine seasons between 1888 and 1912, sang only other Wagner roles for the Dutch Wagner Society. The Dutch

---

[12] Carl Morey, "The Music of Wagner in Toronto before 1914," *Canadian University Music Review* 18/2 (1998): 25–37.

[13] This pattern at the Metropolitan changed in the era overseen by Sir Rudolf Bing, from 1950–72: *Parsifal* was not performed during nine of those seasons. After the Second World War, Indiana University's School of Music became the first university to produce *Parsifal,* and they embraced a tradition of producing *Parsifal* annually, which continued for the next twenty years.

bass-baritone Van Rooy's first performance for them was as the Wanderer in *Siegfried,* in 1898, the year after he made his Bayreuth debut as Wotan. Van Rooy suffered Cosima's wrath for singing Amfortas (a role he had not sung in Bayreuth) in the 1903 New York *Parsifal.* He continued performing with the Dutch Wagner Society until 1912 in his signature roles of Wotan, Hans Sachs, and Kurwenal, but never Amfortas.[14] Amongst the solid but perhaps not stellar cast for the 1905 Dutch *Parsifal,* Félia Litvinne (Kundry) stands out as a noteworthy Wagnerian singer of the period. Resident forces included director Emil Valdek, and the Concertgebouw Orchestra under the baton of Henri Viotta performing at the Stadsschouwburg in Amsterdam. The Society went to some lengths to have a Grail made by the firm of Schwab and Plettung, the artisans who had made the original costumes and props. Burghart created the scenery based on the designs already developed for New York, a practice he would later repeat. The production was revived in 1906, 1908, and 1912, before copyright protection elsewhere expired.

The New York and Amsterdam cases present early examples of stylistic deviations from the Bayreuth model. Burghart's realization of the Grail temple for Conried was more richly ornamented and detailed than the Bayreuth original. His rendering of the magic garden was more realistically tropical — it was still opulent but in a different way from Wagner's oversized flowers.[15] On the one hand such differences reflect a wish to out-do Bayreuth, but on the other hand we also glimpse the workings-out of a trend towards increased historical realism in stage design that Wagner himself did not embrace. Cosima occasionally moved in this direction as she introduced *Tristan und Isolde* (1886), *Tannhäuser* (1891), and *Lohengrin* (1894) to the Bayreuth stage. Where Wagner would prefer the general suggestion of the Middle Ages, for example, Cosima would sometimes pursue the path of well-researched historical verisimilitude. Her unwillingness to alter the 1882 production of *Parsifal* for many years leaves us with more faithful evidence of Wagner's stage practices than can be found in other productions mounted in Bayreuth in the 1880s and 1890s.[16]

---

[14] *50 Jaar Wagnervereeniging,* Gedenkboek der Wagnervereeniging, ed. Margaret Kropholler (Amsterdam: van Munsters drukkerijen, 1934).

[15] Gustav Gamper's designs for the April 1913 Zurich production were restrained and generally less exotic than Wagner's, although there is the outline of an Arabian temple in the distance.

[16] For insightful surveys of Wagner's own ideas about production and design, and subsequent approaches to his works in general, see Mike Ashman "Producing Wagner" and Patrick Carnegy "Designing Wagner: Deeds of Music Made Visible?" in *Wagner in Performance,* ed. Barry Millington and Stewart

Wagner had good reason to be pleased with the premiere production of *Parsifal*. The preparations for *Parsifal* went much more smoothly than those for the first production of the complete *Ring* in 1876 and the performances attained a higher level of quality. Certainly it was less formidable a task preparing one new opera than four at once. Accounts from the rehearsals and blocking sketches exist; Anton Schittenhelm documented such details to assist his colleague Theodor Reichmann, the first Amfortas.[17] Carryovers from the *Ring* production included Wagner's use of the brothers Gotthold and Max Brückner of Coburg to realize the set designs, and his employment of Karl Brandt as stage manager. Unfortunately, Brandt died in 1881, but his son Franz proved admirably equal to the task, however complicated at times. With regard to the theater itself, Wagner continued the practice of darkening the auditorium, a strategy that he had first tried only with the opening performance of *Das Rheingold* in the Festspielhaus. His initial intention was to have dim lighting, but the gas lighting proved difficult to regulate, so darkness was preferred — the results were deemed desirable in any case. One change that Wagner made in 1882 was the addition of a sound damper extending down over the sunken orchestra pit from the front of the stage. The pit already featured a curved hood on the audience side. The addition of this damper enhanced already special characteristics of the orchestral cavity, namely the blending of sound and a tempering of the brass instruments that enabled them to maximize their expressive potential without overwhelming the orchestra or singers. These acoustical properties particularly enhance musical and aesthetic features of the score of *Parsifal*. Both in the composition of the score and in the development of the production, *Parsifal* was fully integrated with the special acoustics of the Bayreuth Festspielhaus.

Spencer, 29–47 and 48–74 respectively (New Haven and London, Yale UP, 1992). Georg Oswald Bauer devotes a chapter to selected productions of Parsifal from the premiere to the early 1980s. See his *Richard Wagner: Die Bühnenwerke von der Uraufführung bis heute* (Frankfurt am Main: Propyläen, 1982), 253–79. Also see Derrick Everett, Monsalvat Index [on-line], http://home.c2i.net/monsalvat/inx-common.htm. The chapter entitled "Stage History" in the Cambridge Opera Handbook volume considers a small number of productions in detail, mainly the original production and that of Wieland Wagner. See Lucy Beckett, ed., *Richard Wagner: Parsifal* (Cambridge: Cambridge UP, 1981), 87–102.

[17] Schittenhelm's notes and stage diagrams are included in Richard Wagner, *Dokumente zur Entstehung und ersten Aufführung des Bühnenweihfestspiels Parsifal*, ed. Martin Geck and Egon Voss, vol. 30 of *Sämtliche Werke* (Mainz: B. Schotts Söhne, 1970), 139–64, along with the rehearsal observations by Heinrich Porges and Julius Kniese, 165–229.

*Illustration 8.1: Bayreuth, original grail temple set, 1897
(reproduced by permission of the Bildarchiv, Bayreuther Festspiele)*

It is well known that Wagner, when conceptualizing the set designs, was inspired by the Siena Cathedral for the Grail temple scenes, and by the gardens at the Palazzo Ruffolo in Ravello for Klingsor's magic garden (see ill. 8.1). In fact, it was when the painter Paul von Joukovsky accompanied him to Ravello in 1880 and sketched the gardens that Wagner, deeply impressed, immediately asked him to design the scenery and costumes for the new opera. This choice pointed to new directions in visual design, as did Wagner's use of the painter Josef Hoffmann for designs for the *Ring*, and perhaps more provocatively the unsuccessful courting of Arnold Böcklin as designer. However, when Joukowsky set to work on the designs for the magic garden in the first months of 1881, Cosima repeatedly reported Wagner's dissatisfaction in her diary.[18] Ultimately, Gotthold Brückner painted the sets according to Wagner's directions, producing a red-hued fantasy realm in the style of Hans Makart, with crazily shaped flowers so oversized that it appeared that the Flowermaidens had emerged from them. This decorative style was not typical of the Brückner brothers, nor

---

[18] See for instance the entries of February 22, March 8, and March 11 in *CT* 2:699, 707, and 708–9 [trans. 2:630, 637, and 639].

was the more impressionistic style of Joukowsky. No matter; Wagner and Cosima adored the opulent and colorful results.[19]

After a decade and a half, Cosima conceded that the magic garden sets were showing too much wear; the 1901 production reflects Max Brückner's suggestions for something fresher — more tropical and more naturalistically green. The Bayreuth reins clearly passed down a generation to Siegfried after Cosima had a series of severe hearts attacks in December 1906. Siegfried shared the conducting of *Parsifal* with Karl Muck in 1909 and two years later he called for some adjustments to the again badly deteriorated sets and costumes of the second act. Siegfried was an amiable and gentle man, but not the man to challenge the stage designs or ideology he had inherited. He certainly recognized that the world of opera production had been evolving without Bayreuth's participation, but limited his intervention to select spheres. He showed great interest in directing, particularly in the handling of crowd scenes, and in electrical developments that affected lighting and color. His first new production, in 1908, was a *Lohengrin* that introduced for the first time on the Bayreuth stage partially three-dimensional sets instead of painted flats, as well as a cyclorama, or circular horizon, comprising a curved backcloth that enabled a greater sense of depth and illusion. Siegfried's modifications of *Parsifal* showed more restraint. His half-sister Daniela clothed Kundry and the Flowermaidens anew. More striking perhaps were the new backdrops for the magic garden that he created with Max Brückner.

Only rediscovered in 1999, Brückner's models for the 1911 production draw attention to Siegfried's interest in color and lighting in ways that no photographs of the period can, while also revealing a transformation that artfully and symbolically relates to the many other scenic transformations in the work. Shifting away from the large palm leaves and generally realistic representation of foliage, Siegfried chose unreal plant structures for his generally impressionistic design. Two interrelated sets were designed for the scene involving the Flowermaidens and the seduction scene with Kundry respectively. Each set comprised four painted drops that together gave the sense of a dense canopy or even cavern of vegetation. The key difference was that the first set was painted in yellow, gold, and ochre and the second in blue and violet. The set change was aided by coordinated

---

[19] While such production decisions may not immediately seem progressive, Geerd Hellberg-Kupfer stresses Wagner's overall shift in *Parsifal* away from aesthetic realism and towards a rich yet elemental style that could be associated with later developments in production. See his *Richard Wagner als Regisseur: Untersuchungen über das Verhältnis von Werk und Regie* (Berlin: Selbstverlag der Gesellschaft für Theatergeschichte, 1942), 84–88.

lighting that shifted from yellow to blue to violet, effecting a very intimate scene by the time of Kundry's narration of Herzeleide's fate. By the end of the scene, the lighting had shifted to a grim blue-green violet. This set design and lighting plan, enthusiastically received in 1911 and 1912, continued to be used when the festival reopened after the First World War in 1924.

For the *Verwandlungen,* or transformation scenes, in act 1 and act 3, Wagner also aimed for a sense of illusion. Despite mechanical challenges, the effect of a coordinated system of painted scrolls seems to have been quite successful.[20] Brandt had previously used such a system in Darmstadt, and Wagner himself could have seen similar scenic effects in the boulevard theaters when he was in Paris. For *Parsifal,* three scrolls and a fixed rear flat were employed. Each of the twelve-meter high movable scrolls had a unique pattern of cut-outs that interacted with the other scrolls for an overall effect of continual change — the front scroll was the longest and most rapidly moved. Located at regular intervals along the length of the stage, these scrolls were initially hand-wound to shift from left to right, with electric motors employed later on. The intention was to reverse the procedure in act 3. Things did not run technically smoothly enough for this to be undertaken in the premiere season, but in subsequent festivals both transformation scenes were enacted. With regard to Brandt's initial miscalculation, whereby the scenery would move rather quickly, Wagner's retrospective account is telling:

> In diesem Interesse hatte die Vorüberführung einer wandelnden Szene durchaus nicht als, wenn auch noch so künstlerisch ausgeführter, dekorativ-malerischer Effekt zu wirken, sondern, unter der Einwirkung der die Ver-wandelung begleitenden Musik, sollten wir, wie in träumerischer Entrückung, eben nur unmerklich die *pfadlosen* Wege zur Gralsburg geleitet werden, womit zugleich die sagenhafte Unauffindbarkeit derselben für Unberufene in das Gebiet der dramatischen Vorstellung gezogen war.[21]

---

[20] The following summary of the transformation scenery draws from Evan Baker's essay "Wagner and the Ideal Theatrical Space," in *Opera in Context: Essays in Historical Staging from the Late Renaissance to the Time of Puccini,* ed. Mark A. Radice, 241–78 (Portland: Amadeus Press, 1998). For more details see also Carl-Friedrich Baumann, *Bühnentechnik im Festspielhaus Bayreuth* (Munich: Prestel, 1980), 154–63, and Detta and Michael Petzet, *Die Richard Wagner Bühne König Ludwigs II* (Munich: Prestel, 1970), 265–86.
[21] Richard Wagner, "Rückblick Richard Wagners auf die Erstaufführung des *Parsifal,*" *Bayreuther Blätter* 5 (1882): 327.

[In this regard I had never meant the passing of a changing scene to act as a decorative visual effect, however artistically carried out; but, with the help of the accompanying music, we were to be led quite imperceptibly, as if in a dream-like state, along the "pathless" trails to the Gralsburg, whose legendary inaccessibility to the non-elect was thus brought within the bounds of dramatic portrayal.]

The phrase "with the help of accompanying music" seems an understatement, for the music potently enables the feeling of moving in an extraordinary manner through time and space. Rehearsals in the first part of June 1882 did not bode well, with uncertainty about the length of time the mechanical process would take in performance giving Wagner a few headaches in finalizing the Transformation Music in act 1; as we know it, it includes an extension that Wagner composed in March 1881.[22] But the Transformation Music was adjusted more than once in an effort to coordinate with the stage machinery. As rehearsals remained problematic, Engelbert Humperdinck arranged repetitions in the music that were eventually removed when the machinery functioned more smoothly, beginning in 1883. At the 1882 performances more music was indeed needed, and the entire Transformation Music with Wagner's extension had to be repeated in full.[23]

The ambitious visual effects of the *Verwandlungen* in *Parsifal* presented the audience with a set of ever-changing scenery that periodically revealed full use of the stage, yielding a considerable sense of depth. Features such as entrances, rocks, and gateways were seen, together with Parsifal and Gurnemanz coming in and out of view, while in actuality the two characters barely moved. Parsifal tells the truth when he states "Ich schreite kaum, doch wähn' ich mich schon weit" (Scarcely have I moved, yet it seems to me that I am already far). Clearly Wagner wished us to agree with Parsifal, to brush aside normal reality and surrender to the total musical-scenic effect of having strangely traveled to a distant realm. The arrival at the Grail temple was achieved by lowering scenic drops while the stage depth was partitioned by the scrolls.

The temple setting itself was effectively designed, revealing Wagner's interest in special lighting effects. The technology needed to undertake a more sophisticated approach to non-realistic visual representation was not in place in the Festspielhaus until several years after Wagner's death. However, the limited use of electric light in 1882 included a focus on Kundry when she first appears to Parsifal in act 2, as well as the illumination of the

---

[22] As William Kinderman notes in chapter 4 of this volume.

[23] One of the solutions to this problem was to reduce the length of the longer front scroll.

Grail. Joukowsky's designs for the temple featured an open-ended cupola that extended upward beyond the audience's view, facilitating such lighting opportunities from above. At the same time, the design coordinates with Wagner's deliberate blurring of the distinction between the real and the ungraspable, the seen and the invisible. From beyond the visible temple sound the invisible voices that sing ostensibly from the dome's height; their special aura is derived from the fact that they are not physically grounded and that their text speaks of otherworldly experience. On the ground level, Joukowsky's designs realized ideas that Cosima had suggested: the intricate maze of hallways and arches extending beyond the central temple area. The path into the temple was not really clear at all. Thus in several respects the temple design could be perceived as both realistic and versatile, capable of bearing ambiguous metaphors that would enhance the set's longevity as more symbolic modes of theatrical representation came to be explored, quite aside from any pious intent to preserve the Master's work.

As a widow, Cosima spent much of her time and energy trying to protect the Wagnerian legacy crowned by *Parsifal*. Before the controversy over the 1903 New York *Parsifal*, Cosima's main artistic and financial fears had come from nearby. As the place where Wagner's career had been saved and the completion of his later works ensured, Munich claimed a longstanding Wagner tradition of its own. Ernst von Possart at the Munich Court Opera emerged as a particular threat to Cosima with his desire to launch his own Wagner Festival in 1894. Within a few years the ironies multiplied, as Possart put into action the building of a new theater based on Gottfried Semper's original designs for Wagner's desired opera house in Munich. Cosima was relieved when the Bavarian Prince Regent persuaded Possart not to name the new house the "Munich Richard Wagner Festspielhaus," but the "Prinzregententheater." Possart was also directed to defer to Bayreuth on choice of repertoire and performers in any given season.[24] It was difficult for Cosima to completely oppose Possart, since she was reliant on Munich for singers and production staff. Yet his threat to produce *Parsifal* encouraged her to seek greater control at precisely the time when the Reichstag was reviewing copyright laws and considering extending the period of protection from thirty to fifty years. This so-called "Lex Parsifal" initiative was, however, not achieved, despite public outcries that would grow louder in 1903.

---

[24] Frederic Spotts, *Bayreuth: A History of the Wagner Festival* (New Haven and London: Yale UP, 1994), 119–20. The Prinzregententheater mounted Munich's public premiere of *Parsifal* on May 22, 1914, directed by Anton Fuchs and conducted by Bruno Walter, as well as the city's next two productions of 1924 and 1957.

The voices in support of Bayreuth's not surrendering *Parsifal* peaked as 1913 approached. Cities set up their own committees to protect *Parsifal*. Richard Strauss, Humperdinck, Charpentier, Puccini, and Toscanini joined eighteen thousand others in signing a petition for the Reichstag.[25] As an act of protest, and a bizarre prelude to the Bayreuth dark years of 1914–24, no festival was mounted in 1913. The festival had operated roughly two out of every three years for pragmatic reasons. 1913 was a year of Wagnerian celebrations, with memorials erected around the world to mark the one hundredth anniversary of the birth of a composer who was undoubtedly one of the most performed opera composers of all time. As head of the Festival, Siegfried commented ironically "Ja, wir singen das Lied an die Freude, weil Deutschland uns den *Parsifal* stiehlt" (Sure, we're singing a song of joy because Germany is stealing *Parsifal* away from us).[26]

1914–18: Excitement, Confusion and Despair

Enthusiasm but not vindictiveness fueled interest in *Parsifal* as 1914 approached. Production activity got underway outside Bayreuth with a private charity performance in Monte Carlo in February 1913, and there was a performance in April in Zurich, where the copyright had already expired. Italian versions were produced in Buenos Aires and Rio de Janeiro in June and September respectively. The actual dawning of 1914 was dramatically claimed by Barcelona's Gran Teatro del Liceu, with a performance conducted by Franz Beidler, Isolde von Bülow's husband, that started at 10:25 P.M. on December 31 and lasted until five the next morning! Madrid opened their production the next evening. Intra-national competition also took place in Italy, with Bologna's January 1 performance edging out their chief rival, La Scala, by only a week. Acts 1 and 3 had been performed in concert in 1902 at La Scala, where they secured Alois Fuchs as stage director for their first stage production. By beginning especially early, at three o'clock in the afternoon, Bologna also edged out the January 1 premiere in Rome, where *Parsifal* was heard in Italian, just as in Bologna and Milan.[27] Eugenio Giovanetti, music critic of the Bolognese paper *Il resto del Carlino*, is quoted as saying that the Milanese production was "catholic and Latin," whereas the one in Bologna was "Christian and

---

[25] Frederic Spotts, *Bayreuth,* 133.

[26] Quoted in Brigitte Hamann, *Winifred Wagner oder Hitlers Bayreuth* (Munich and Zurich: Piper Verlag, 2002), 20.

[27] Many premiere productions outside Germany were sung in local languages.

universal." However, he commented of both productions, which he jointly named the "Italian *Parsifal*," that they were "the most enchanting *Parsifal* of this world." [28]

At this high-water mark of international Wagnerism, Italy, like many nations, claimed a special relationship with Wagner's works, and particularly with the newly-released *Parsifal*.[29] A broad public enthusiasm was marked in Bologna and in Rome, where a long series of performances took place in 1914 at the Teatro Costanzi. The religious dimension of the work was clearly connected to its powerful impact on the larger public. After the last performance, critic S. A. Luciani wrote:

> *Parsifal* is genuine *musica sacra*, the only such music that has appeared in Europe since Palestrina and Bach . . . Its religiosity is not however a sign of decadence, as Friedrich Nietzsche believed. Wagner's nature is mystical and sensual at the same time, as it manifests itself in the marvelous, tragic and eternal struggle between spirit and flesh . . . Thus our epoch, which is both sensual and spiritual, shows a bent toward devoutness, and *Parsifal* satisfies this instinctive and unconscious desire in all of us . . . With this [work] Wagner's dream has come to fulfillment: the public in the broadest sense of the word, the people, receive the drama in a spirit of religious devotion, as in a ritual.[30]

Others quick to produce *Parsifal* included opera houses in Berlin, Bremen, Breslau, Kiel, Prague, Frankfurt, Mainz, St. Petersburg, Freiburg, and Brussels, in addition to the Paris Opéra, all in just the first week of January. Dozens of productions opened across Europe in the first three months of 1914. Multiple productions could even be seen in the same city at this time, such as those at the Hofoper and the Volksoper in Vienna.

Generally speaking, the unusual circumstances protecting the work for so long seem to have promoted an intention of fidelity to Bayreuth's model, or more correctly, perhaps, of striving towards an ideal of that model. By 1914, parts of the original Bayreuth sets of 1882 were over thirty years old, yet they were virtually unchanged, particularly the transformation scenery and the Grail temple settings of the first and third

---

[28] Marion S. Miller, "Wagnerism in Italy," in *Wagnerism in European Culture and Politics,* ed. David C. Large and William Weber, 178 (Ithaca and London: Cornell UP, 1984).

[29] In Italy, 1914 was often spoken about in the arts as the *"Parsifal* year," after 1913 had been celebrated as a "Verdi year" honoring the centenary of the composer's birth. Of course, Wagner was also born in 1813.

[30] "Dopo l'ultima del *Parsifal*," in *Harmonia,* Rome, A. II, No. 3, 22–23 (22 March 1914), cited in Ute Jung, *Die Rezeption der Kunst Richard Wagners in Italien,* 52 (Regensburg: Gustav Bosse Verlag, 1974).

acts. As the world stood poised to produce *Parsifal,* an examination of Bayreuth's privileged production would have revealed a hybrid of a few isolated impulses in modern directions with much that remained true to the work's origins in the 1880s, technologically and aesthetically.

Opera companies announcing their new 1914 productions of *Parsifal* often stressed the extraordinary expense and attention to detail, and some tangible relationship to Bayreuth, through sets, performers, or production personnel. Typical was Covent Garden's promise to be "faithful" to Bayreuth, with the intention to "spare no pains nor expense in order to render the presentation of the work worthy of the best tradition of the Royal Opera."[31] Legitimizing this claim was the creation of new scenery — not *de rigeur* for new productions at that time — and new costumes supervised by the Arthurian authority Mr. Comyns Carr, who had been sent to study the *mise en scène* at Bayreuth. The production's stage manager, Willi Werk, also had a work history with Bayreuth, while the Bayreuth chorus master, Professor Hugo Rüdel, helped prepare the chorus. Bells were specially cast while the Grail "and other relics from the famous private performances given for King Ludwig of Bavaria, were lent to Covent Garden."[32] Like many opera houses, Covent Garden also imitated the early start time and long intermissions of Bayreuth, stretching the first interval to one and half hours to accommodate a special dinner. The late afternoon start times prompted much social debate concerning proper attire, such as whether one ought to wear formal evening clothes, or jewels, given the work's obvious religious content. Like those in the United States and some other countries, Londoners would not have been altogether unprepared for this premiere. Some of the local audience might have heard the previous year's abridged performance without voices but accompanied by a series of "living tableaux," conducted by Sir Henry Wood at the Coliseum. Others would have already experienced *Parsifal* in Bayreuth.

In reality, the notion of fidelity to a Bayreuth model, or to what Bayreuth was perceived to represent, was somewhat flexible. Unique production features such as the transformation scenes certainly invited more imitation than experimentation at first. And certain props like the Grail were virtually copied, while the Bayreuth firm of Steingräber und Söhne received many orders for the special "Glockenklavier" (bell-piano) with four broad keys that it originally built for Wagner in 1881.[33] In the areas of

---

[31] Quoted in Harold Rosenthal, *Two Centuries of Opera at Covent Garden* (London: Putnam and Company, 1958), 379–80.

[32] Rosenthal, *Two Centuries of Opera at Covent Garden,* 380.

[33] This original instrument, played by Udo Schmidt, can be heard on the Decca *Parsifal* recording made in Vienna in March 1972, conducted by Sir Georg

stage and costume designs, however, it is hardly surprising that 1914 designs might deviate from the 1882 model in at least subtle ways, acknowledging changing aesthetics in production styles and the visual arts.

Radical rethinking of nineteenth-century production practices turns up in the ideas of the Swiss theater theorist Adolphe Appia and the British stage designer Edward Gordon Craig, whose work proved foundational for subsequent developments in non-historical approaches to production. Their experiments with abstract, geometric, three-dimensional props, and their use of highly nuanced lighting and stylized gestures broke new ground on every front. Appia's design strategies were coordinated with an intense focus on the psychological development of characters. The real core of Appia's influence lay in his theories and sketches as presented in his two early publications *La mise en scène du drame wagnérien* (1895) and *Die Musik und die Inscenierung* (1899). In 1912, Appia published his sketches for *Parsifal* in the journal *Türmer*. Shaped by his serious engagement with Wagner's music dramas and by his dissatisfaction with the traditional staging practices he encountered at Bayreuth in the 1880s, Appia's writings offer many prescriptions for new ways to produce Wagner's works. Cosima Wagner rejected his suggestions outright, but traces of Appia's ideas began to appear in Wagner productions in the first years of the twentieth century. In practice, Appia's non-Wagner productions and collaborations in the realm of Eurythmics with Jacques Dalcroze were more impressive and influential than his productions of Wagnerian works themselves. His opportunities to produce Wagner came rather late — *Tristan und Isolde* at La Scala in 1923, and the first two operas of a never-completed *Ring* in Basel in 1924–25 — when his ideas had already much evolved.

One of Appia's design ideas for *Parsifal* that continues to echo in productions is his linking of the forest trees to the columns of the Grail temple in act 1. Through a process of abstraction, one is literally transformed into the other. Ludwig Sievert explored this solution for the 1914 production in Freiburg, where the stage was not otherwise equipped to handle the transformation scenes. Sievert's long-standing association with the Frankfurt Opera, where he also designed a production of *Parsifal*, later yielded an even more rigorously modern *Ring* (1925), a production that must have paralleled avant-garde developments at the Kroll Oper in Berlin. Sievert, like Appia and Craig, made a break from historicism in the

Solti, and in the 1982 film *Wagner* directed by Tony Palmer. Beginning in 1911, Steingräber und Söhne offered three versions of this special instrument and filled orders for many opera houses, including those in Stuttgart, Warsaw, Hildesheim, and Hanover (this instrument is currently in the Niedersächsisches Theatermuseum Hannover). The firm built a new variant of the instrument for Wieland Wagner's 1951 production.

theater, embracing technologies that also invited more moderate approaches to design — quasi-representational approaches that could be vividly symbolic.

The famous 1927 Kroll Oper production of *Der fliegende Holländer,* which made no positive impression on Siegfried Wagner and was criticized as "Bolshevik," was the work of designer Ewald Dühlberg and director Jürgen Fehling. Dühlberg had sketched costumes for the 1914 Hamburg production of *Parsifal* with Flowermaidens who seemed to dance right out of a Tahiti-inspired Gauguin painting. They were rejected as too bold at the time. The sweeter, muted *Jugendstil* palate was more popular and surfaces in design sketches by Remigius Geyling and in those by Heinrich Lefler for Frankfurt am Main and the Vienna Volksoper. The most noteworthy artist to have an impact on stage design at this time was Alfred Roller, who designed *Tristan und Isolde* for Gustav Mahler at the Vienna Hofoper in 1903. This collaboration remains a breakthrough in Wagnerian production history because of its revisionist shift away from historical realism towards a more symbolic interpretation, including revolutionary designs and lighting. Roller prepared the 1914 *Parsifal* premiere at the Vienna Hofoper with Franz Schalk conducting and Wilhelm von Wymetal as director. Immensely popular, the production was repeated twenty-seven times that year.

Excitement over *Parsifal* continued at a more relaxed pace as political tensions waxed. The 1914 Bayreuth Festival got underway on July 25, but Austria attacked Serbia three days later, halfway through the *Ring,* and Germany declared war on Russia four days after that. Despite obvious unease and the dispersion of the international audience, Karl Muck insisted that the August 1 performance of *Parsifal* go on. It turned out to be the last Wagner performance on the Festspielhaus stage until 1924. While Bayreuth remained silent, much of the world rethought German culture in the context of political change. During this same period (1914 to 1924) the German language was not heard at all at Covent Garden. Not performed during the war in London, *Parsifal* was presented in an English version by the Thomas Beecham Opera Company during their lease of the Covent Garden Theater in 1919–20. La Scala, after performing *Parsifal* twenty-seven times in the first part of 1914, did not return to the work again until 1922.[34] Oddly, Stockholm's Royal Opera first produced *Parsifal* in 1917. This was one of the few new productions of the work to appear during the war, together with one in Copenhagen in 1915. Stockholm subsequently performed it every season until 1939–40, resuming

---

[34] The performance of *Parsifal* for two seasons in Milan during the Second World War, in 1940 and 1944, reflects the shifting political positions in that country.

annual performances the following season for another twenty years before another brief hiatus.

In North America, the "early" presentation of *Parsifal* in 1903 did not preclude attention to the landmark year 1914. Chicago's first resident opera company, the Chicago Grand Opera Company, founded in 1910, produced *Parsifal* in the 1913–14 season. It was an affluent time, with thirty different operas produced in the first six weeks of the season. In Chicago, in contrast to New York, German opera had not been favored up to this time. It was actually emphasized in the 1915–16 season as so many of the French and Italian singers usually employed by the conductor Cleofonte Campanini were unavailable. *Parsifal* was revived in that season, which also included *Tristan und Isolde, Tannhäuser,* and the first complete *Ring* seen in Chicago in over twenty-five years.[35] By the following season, however, the trend quickly reversed itself; political tensions discouraged even German audiences from attending. The stronger leaning towards Italian opera in Chicago would last for many years. When performed in 1922, *Parsifal* was not popular at all; it would not return to the Chicago stage until 1931, when it proved to be a complete sellout. In 1914 San Francisco saw its first *Parsifal*, at the Tivoli, thanks to the the Chicago Grand Opera Company's western tour. The San Francisco Opera eventually set down roots in 1923 and in 1935 gained a favorite Wagnerian performer in Kirsten Flagstad, who would sing the company's first Kundry when they finally produced *Parsifal* themselves in 1950.

Many opera companies that first mounted *Parsifal* in 1914 revived their initial productions through the inter-bellum period, which did not see many new productions. Some houses had abandoned German repertoire during the war, and the speed with which it was reclaimed depended conjointly on pre-war levels of interest and post-war sentiments. In New York, the strong Wagner tradition prevailed with little interruption. The American declaration of war was actually heard by the Metropolitan Opera audience on April 6, 1917 — Good Friday — partway through a performance of *Parsifal*. German repertoire was cut at this point, but Wagner returned to the Metropolitan stage in 1920 with *Tristan,* albeit sung in English. *Parsifal* also returned in 1920, like *Tristan,* sung in English, in a new production designed by Joseph Urban.

Together with his brother-in-law Heinrich Lefler, Urban co-founded the Hagenbund in Vienna, an exhibiting society similar to the Secession. Urban emigrated to the United States in 1912 to work for Henry Russell's Boston Grand Opera, where he was set, costume, and lighting designer, as

---

[35] See Ronald L. Davis, *Opera in Chicago* (New York: Appleton Century, 1966), 105–12.

well as stage director. Before the company disbanded two years later, Urban was responsible for productions of *Tristan und Isolde, Die Meistersinger,* and *Parsifal* that were included in a tour to Paris. The four Parisian performances of *Parsifal* in June of 1914, conducted by Felix Weingartner, were the first German renditions of the work in the French capital. Urban subsequently worked with Florenz Ziegfield, and his association with Broadway earned him fame as well as a small fortune. Engaged for a *Tristan und Isolde* that was performed in 1916 in Cleveland and Detroit by the short-lived Tri-Cities Opera, Urban then became one of the principal designers at the Metropolitan Opera in 1917. His new *Parsifal* of 1920 was produced six times in the premiere run — only in the 1939–40 season would the annual number of performances reach this figure again. Urban's work was controversial and revolutionary, as he put into practice in America some of the ideas that had recently taken root in Vienna. His approach to stage design was decorative but stylized and intertwined with his use of colored light, while the *Gesamtkunstwerk* concept guided his shaping of productions as integrated artworks. Compared with the original 1903 Metropolitan production of *Parsifal,* Urban's colors, which owed much to the influence of the Secessionists, yielded a much brighter and livelier stage. More radical was his handling of the scene changes, given the earlier efforts to duplicate the original stage machinery of 1882. For each scene change, Urban used curtains decorated with two classically-inspired figures bearing the sacred spear and Grail respectively. Over time such experiments would seem less daring. Urban's scenic productions for the Metropolitan were generally long-lived; his *Parsifal* remained in use well after his death in 1933, revived in each season but one until 1955.

In Russia, the popularity of Wagner's works before the First World War rivaled that of major east-coast American cities. Especially in St. Petersburg, with the German-born Empress Alexandra's encouragement, interest in Wagner's works grew steadily in the first decade of the twentieth century. The Mariinsky Theater regularly produced four, five, then six Wagner works per year (out of a season featuring between twenty-three and thirty operas).[36] So dominating was the number of Wagner operas in the 1913–14 season in St. Petersburg that "nationalists requested justification of the repertory selected and called for a Russian Bayreuth, a showcase for Russian composers."[37] *Parsifal* was already part of this picture; Count Aleksandr Sheremetiev had arranged a performance in

---

[36] See Rosamund Bartlett, *Wagner and Russia* (Cambridge: Cambridge UP, 1995), Appendix 3, 304–6.

[37] Bernice Glatzer Rosenthal, "Wagner and Wagnerian Ideas in Russia," in Large and Weber, eds., *Wagnerism in European Culture and Politics,* 198.

1906 that was split across three separate concerts to avoid the copyright restrictions.[38] Not surprisingly, Russia joined the widespread rush to bring *Parsifal* to the stage as soon as the copyright expired (December 19, 1913, according to the Julian calendar). Its opening postponed by two days to accommodate a sick singer, the first semi-professional production took place on December 21 on the small stage of the Ermitazh theater in a private performance for the Imperial family and select government officials. Sheremetiev's concert society repeated the production twice more for Military Academy students before relocating it within St. Petersburg to the Theater of Musical Drama.[39]

In Moscow, *Parsifal* was scheduled for the 1914–15 season at the Bolshoi and former Zimin Theaters but shared the fate of all German repertoire in Russia in being banned from performance during the war. After the war and the Russian Revolution, interest in Wagner remained strong enough that *Parsifal* returned to the stage of the Theater of Musical Drama, only days after the signing of the peace treaty. Meanwhile the modernist director Fyodor Komissarzhevsky unveiled new approaches to staging Wagner in the Soviet age, beginning with a striking cubo-futurist *Lohengrin* (1918) designed by Ivan Fedotov at the Zimin Theater. Komissarzhevsky then began rehearsing a new production of *Parsifal* but emigrated before those plans were realized. He abandoned the work at a time when many were coming to regard it as an uneasy ideological fit, seen from the Soviet perspective. From this point, *Parsifal* remained unperformed until the post-Soviet age, when Russia would finally experience its first fully professional staged production of *Parsifal*.

1918–1945: Revival, Change, and Nazism

The years after the First World War were difficult for the Wagner family. The end of 1913 had marked the end of income from performance royalties from all of Wagner's operas, not just *Parsifal*. Then the family had to bear losses from the shortened 1914 season. On the personal side, the summer of 1914 also witnessed the end of a complicated lawsuit, the outcome of which was that Isolde von Bülow's claim to be the daughter of Richard Wagner was legally refuted.[40] After the war, a seemingly successful

---

[38] Bartlett, *Wagner and Russia*, 88.

[39] Bartlett, *Wagner and Russia*, 112–13.

[40] Hereditary rights were denied to the son of Isolde and Franz Beidler, also named Franz, and this placed great pressure on Siegfried to produce a son of his own as the heir to the Wagner legacy. See Brigitte Hamann, *Winifred Wagner oder Hitlers Bayreuth*, 20–21.

fund drive — Siegfried raised five million marks — was devastated by infla-
tion. Only in 1924 could hopes of revitalizing the festival be realized. At
this point, the Wagner family configuration had changed in key ways that
would determine the artistic future of the festival. In 1915, Siegfried had
married the British orphan adopted by Karl and Henriette Klindworth,
Winifred Wagner. Their four children — Verena, Friedelind, Wolfgang,
and Wieland — were born soon after. After years of concern about
Siegfried's lack of family options as he progressed through middle age, not
to mention his promiscuous bisexual lifestyle, the future of the Wagner
family had been secured. The other pivotal event in this period would play
out most critically after Siegfried's death in 1930; Winifred Wagner's
encounter with Hitler in 1923, a man to whom she and her children were
magnetically drawn.[41]

The 1924 and 1925 Bayreuth seasons featured the same program as
the pre-war seasons of 1911 and 1912: two complete *Ring* cycles, five
performances of *Parsifal,* and seven of *Die Meistersinger.* Working with
Kurt Söhnlein, the new stage assistant and successor to Max Brückner,
Siegfried entertained the idea of a completely new production of *Parsifal*
but ultimately decided only to change the sets of the second act, including
creating a new tower for Klingsor, new Flowermaiden costumes, and petal-
bedecked gauzes for the magic garden.[42] The exterior acts, particularly the
Grail temple scenes, remained frozen in time. Any changes, proposed or
actual, always provoked controversy, with plenty of supporters voicing the
need to preserve Wagner's production indefinitely. With the passing of
both Cosima and Siegfried in 1930, a large body of supporters mobilized
themselves to protect *Parsifal* from the ills of modern opera staging and
design. Although a Wagner by marriage and British by birth, young
Winifred Wagner was now responsible for the festival. In 1931 she put
together a solid artistic team featuring Heinz Tietjen, who had held the
position of director of all the Prussian state theaters since 1927.[43] Tietjen
brought with him experience as both conductor and stage director, and he
facilitated bringing Emil Preetorius, the designer, and Wilhelm Furtwängler to Bayreuth. Karl Muck, who had conducted *Parsifal* at Bayreuth each
festival since 1901, took Siegfried's death as the opportunity to end his
relationship with the festival.

Winifred's era owed its very existence to the support of Adolf Hitler.
She certainly needed his financial backing, and since Hitler's association

---

[41] Spotts, *Bayreuth,* 137–38.
[42] Spotts, *Bayreuth,* 150.
[43] Tietjen and the designer Preetorius maintained active creative lives outside
Bayreuth, particularly in Berlin.

with the festival drove away some of the regular audience to some extent, she came to need his audience too. The 1933 season was full of controversy, when Toscanini refused to conduct and then joined forces with Bruno Walter in Salzburg. According to Frederic Spotts, "Hitler responded by requesting artists, such as Furtwängler and Strauss, to withdraw from Salzburg — they compliantly obeyed — and levied an exit tax at the German border so large as to make it impossible for the German public to attend."[44] By 1940, the beginning of the so-called "War Festivals," Bayreuth was completely transformed into a party tool. The audience was composed of "guests" of the Führer rather than of freely paying individuals. Obviously this targeted support of an artistic enterprise during wartime reflects Hitler's special love of Wagnerian opera, but it also reflects his prioritization and protection of the arts in certain confined spheres. Much to the consternation of the head of the Reich Chamber of Culture, Joseph Goebbels, Hitler sympathized with artists and granted many of them special financial arrangements and release from service. Some were even forgiven for criminal behavior. Only in the second half of 1944 were theaters officially closed, when Goebbels finally convinced Hitler that given the state of the war those resources of manpower and money could no longer be devoted to the arts. All along Hitler adamantly maintained that the performing arts were a key to maintaining morale through challenging times.[45]

While some of Hitler's preferences influenced matters at Bayreuth, it would be wrong to view artistic life during this period as a direct reflection of party ideology. The Festival was the only relatively autonomous artistic institution in the Third Reich. Winifred did not answer to Goebbels and she was rightfully wary of other powerful Nazi figures who either envied her position or had little interest in Wagner's music. Paradoxically, she was able to practice in full some of Hitler's idiosyncratic deference to artists that so baffled some party members. Several artists with Jewish background or connections were celebrated for their artistry, as were some homosexuals, such as Max Lorenz, who sang the role of Parsifal in 1933 and 1937. Furthermore, Tietjen and Preetorius walked a delicate tightrope with Winifred as their safety net; they were not party favorites and their wish to modernize productions at Bayreuth had to be managed with subtlety. Winifred deftly circumvented Hitler's occasional suggestions for involving Benno von Arent, the Reich's Theatrical Designer.

---

[44] Frederic Spotts, *Hitler and the Power of Aesthetics* (Woodstock and New York: The Overlook Press, 2002), 258.

[45] Spotts elaborates on the special role that some artists had in Hitler's society. See his *Hitler and the Power of Aesthetics*, 76–94.

In 1933, the Tietjen/Preetorius team launched a complete new *Ring* as well as a new *Die Meistersinger*. By 1939 they had presented new productions of all of the mature Wagner works except *Tannhäuser*. Before this era ended in 1944, two works had been presented, each in two new productions: *Die Meistersinger* and *Parsifal*. Both *Parsifals* were directed by Tietjen but involved other designers. Alfred Roller worked on the 1934 production, but his approach was not well enough received to be long-lived. Thus Wieland Wagner was given the opportunity to prepare new designs for 1937. The strong resistance to these fresh approaches, even before they were conceived, points to the complicated position that *Parsifal* was coming to occupy in Bayreuth during the Third Reich. Winifred's sisters-in-law Daniela von Bülow and Eva Wagner issued the call to return to the 1882 production, bypassing changes introduced by their brother Siegfried. Meanwhile, ultimate authority over such matters rested with Winifred Wagner and Adolf Hitler; both sought change, although perhaps for different reasons.

The exact nature of Roller's invitation is unknown.[46] Hitler had been wildly enthusiastic about Roller's designs ever since he had seen the Vienna production of *Tristan* in 1906, when he still maintained aspirations of working in opera design himself. But Roller was already well-known to Bayreuth before Hitler entered the fold. Siegfried Wagner admired Roller's work and had met him personally when the designer traveled to Bayreuth to experience *Parsifal* in 1911. In Roller's style Siegfried may have seen a style less radical than expressionistic trends of the time, thus one that accorded with his own conservatism and his deference to his mother Cosima's aversion to change. In any case, the path seemed to have been paved for Roller to be a possible designer of a new *Parsifal* production after the passing of Siegfried and Cosima. Hitler was clearly delighted by this prospect, and his financial support enabled the venture. On July 12, 1934, just a couple of weeks before the new production opened, members of the international press were invited for a special viewing of the original manuscript score of *Parsifal*, and, quite unusually, were allowed to observe a stage rehearsal of act 2. The intent of this gathering was to connect the opera's emphasis on peace with the policies of the Reich

---

[46] It is often asserted that Roller's involvement was a command invitation by Hitler. A more nuanced interpretation of the situation is found in Georg Oswald Bauer's "Prüfstein 'Parsifal'," published together with English and French translations in the *Bayreuther Festspiele Programmheft 1998*, 50–77. The discussion here is drawn mainly from Bauer's consideration of the matter. Bauer's appraisal takes into account Roller's sketches for Klingsor's tower and magic garden and the transformation scenes; these sketches were not publicly known prior to 1997.

and Bayreuth's mission. This message was delivered just twelve days after "Die Nacht der langen Messer" (The Night of the Long Knives), the wave of murders intended to eliminate obstacles to Hitler's growing power.[47]

Roller surely did not regard *Parsifal* as a piece of propaganda. His first sketches for the Bayreuth production date from 1932, before Hitler was in power. By this point Roller was approaching seventy and his main concern was that he not appear to have become conservative in his later years. To eyes now accustomed to more substantial rethinkings, the Bayreuth production seems in essence a repetition of Roller's 1914 Vienna production (although the designer would not have voiced that opinion). His work does show a shift towards a simpler type of grandeur in the nature scenes of the framing acts, which differ most from the Vienna designs. Beginning in 1913, Roller, like some other artists, substituted snow-capped Alpine mountains for Wagner's requested "northern slopes of the Pyrenees." His approach to nature was generally abstract — influenced by Appia — and driven by a keen theatrical and dramaturgical sense that focused on the contrast between symbolically interior, personal spaces and the exterior. The most striking design remained unaltered from Vienna: Roller's cavernous tower for Klingsor, which used large expanses of simple, massive stone walls, as did Roller's designs for *Elektra* (1909). In *Parsifal,* the curved walls of the stone tower opened fully upward, with a lookout partway up from which Klingsor spied the approaching hero. It might not be too far-fetched to sense a relationship between the upward-reaching temple of the Grail knights and Klingsor's counterpart, his temple of destruction where he vicariously seeks revenge upon the knights.

Audiences were keenly interested in how Roller would handle the perennially challenging magic garden scene. But here, and at other crucial junctures in the drama including the transformation scenes, Roller's sets were plagued by production problems. Everything was constructed too rapidly and many lighting plans and projected scene changes were not successful in performance. Roller himself did not consider the production finished; he had hoped to achieve this in its second season. With Roller's death in June of 1935, Preetorius took over the production's revival in 1936 and attempted to follow through on some of Roller's plans with the young Wieland Wagner as assistant. The temple scenes remained problematic. Roller's design included eight plastic columns that extended seemingly infinitely upwards. The set-building firm of Müller Godesberg built the columns too short, necessitating the addition

---

[47] Bauer, "Prüfstein 'Parsifal'," 66.

of soffits that compromised Roller's vision. In 1936, Preetorius added capitals and an arch that suggested the architectural form of a cupola. The final assessment in 1936 led to a decision to discontinue the production and to embark on an entirely new production designed by Wieland Wagner.

The gap between the ultra-conservative call for a return to Wagner's original production and the desire to experience a more modern *Parsifal* proved too big to bridge. Wieland's 1937 efforts to restore some sense of realism were considered insufficient, and betrayed by his introduction of modern technology such as film projections during the transformation scenes. Richard Wagner himself had experimented with the possibility of using magic lantern projections in the 1876 *Ring*. However, film had come to be associated with subsequent expressionist developments. Franz Ludwig Hörth's work with the designer Emil Pirchan on the Berlin *Ring* of 1928–29 employed film in the mixed-media style of Erwin Piscator. Wieland's production was revived in 1938 and 1939, before the seemingly unsolvable problems surrounding the production of *Parsifal* in Bayreuth took another new turn.

Parsifal was not produced in Bayreuth during the "War Festivals," from 1940 until 1944. Only the *Ring* and *Der fliegende Holländer* were produced in 1940, 1941, and 1942.[48] In 1943 and 1944 only *Die Meistersinger* was performed. Since 1882, only one Festival season had not featured Wagner's last work. This was in 1896, when Cosima concentrated all her energies on producing four cycles of the first post-1876 performances of the *Ring*. The issues surrounding the disappearance of *Parsifal* from Bayreuth and from many other stages in Germany after the start of the war are complex. It has often been suggested that a ban on the work took effect throughout Germany after the outbreak of war, although details of how the ban was implemented have not been brought to light. Any de-emphasis of the work could be explained in part by its prominent themes of pacifism and compassion.[49] But any prohibitive directive must surely

---

[48] The only Festival performance that Hitler himself attended during the war was one of *Götterdämmerung* in 1940.

[49] Robert R. Gibson, while mistakenly accepting the idea of a de facto ban, richly explores the many possible tensions between *Parsifal* and Nazi ideology. See his "Problematic Propaganda: 'Parsifal' as Forbidden Opera," in *Wagner* 20/2 (1999): 78–87. Recent authors who refer to some sort of Nazi ban on *Parsifal* but who are somewhat misleading about its effectiveness include Nike Wagner, Wagner production history specialist Georg Oswald Bauer, and Frederic Spotts, in his book *Bayreuth: A History of the Bayreuth Festival*. Spotts offers clarification of this complex issue in his later book *Hitler and the Power of Aesthetics*.

have been quasi-official if anything, as there were more variations to the rule than any rule proper.

Cultural authority in Germany was in some ways not consistently centralized. Despite Goebbels' role as head of the Reich Chamber of Culture, his authority did not extend to Bayreuth, where *Parsifal* indeed was not being performed in this period. Furthermore, Göring controlled a number of important Prussian opera houses, Baldur von Schirach was Gauleiter, or party mayor, of Vienna, while Hitler himself managed the "Great German Art" exhibitions and main opera in Munich. Other centers such as Hamburg and Dresden were more locally controlled.[50] Von Schirach's liberal approach and celebration of culture made Vienna attractive to many artists, while making him somewhat unpopular with Hitler, for whom Munich and Berlin were more worthy as cultural centerpieces. *Parsifal* was not performed in Munich during the war, but it was in von Schirach's Vienna. In Hamburg, *Parsifal* was performed annually from the 1929/30 season until that of 1942/43, on average three times per season; in 1936, a new production directed by Oscar Fritz Schuh and designed by Emil Preetorius ran for seven performances. In Frankfurt, which fell within Goebbel's sphere, *Parsifal* had been performed annually in the period between the wars, invariably around Easter time. *Parsifal* suddenly disappeared from the Frankfurt program in 1940, only to resurface in 1941, 1942, and 1943.[51] In Dresden, *Parsifal* was performed every season from 1914 to 1944 inclusive, with the number of annual performances fixed at four from 1933 to 1944.

Hitler envisioned producing *Parsifal* after the war and coming to terms with what seems to have been for him the work's most disquieting element: its religious symbolism.[52] Apparently, Wolfgang Wagner had a discussion with Hitler on November 4, 1940 about which Wolfgang wrote a letter to Wieland telling him that Hitler's projected solution to the religious aspects of the temple scenes was to take a more mystical, indefinable,

---

[50] Spotts, *Hitler and the Power of Aesthetics*, 76–77.

[51] *Parsifal* was also performed at the Nationaltheater in Mannheim on April 15, 1940.

[52] This anti-religious stance is developed into a full-blown revisionist interpretation of *Parsifal* in Hermann Rauschning's *Gespräche mit Hitler* (Zurich: Europa Verlag A.G., 1940). According to Rauschning, Hitler rejected Hans von Wolzogen's interpretation of *Parsifal*, as well as Schopenhauerian ideas and the theme of compassion, and even suggested that Amfortas should be left to die. See *Gespräche mit Hitler*, 216–17. The Swiss historian Wolfgang Hänel has largely discredited this source, calling it inauthentic anti-Nazi propaganda.

and indeterminate approach.[53] As Spotts remarks, Hitler told Goebbels in November 1941:

> He would see to it either that religion was banished from *Parsifal* or that *Parsifal* was banished from the stage. He recalled that the Vienna opera archive held sketches of Roller's 1914 production and he commended these as models for producers. Not waiting for the final victory, Goebbels passed on the word to his ministerial officials with instructions to have photographs of the Roller sketches circulated to every opera house. Managers were informed that any future staging of the work was to follow the Roller model and "was no longer to be done in the Byzantine-sacred style that was common up to then."[54]

Provocative is the claim made by Wieland Wagner's daughter Nike that Hitler would have had the text of *Parsifal* modified by Alfred Rosenberg.[55] In his book *Der Mythus des 20. Jahrhunderts,* originally published in 1930, Rosenberg offers an enthusiastic assessment of Wagner and his artworks with a nearly complete dismissal of *Parsifal.*[56] Rosenberg and Hitler surely agreed that the religious elements of the work were disagreeable, but Hitler could also be dismissive of Rosenberg's reactionary ideology. Rosenberg had a voice as a cultural spokesperson, as editor of the *Völkischer Beobachter,* but Hitler accorded him titles and awards without real power. What a collaboration such as this might have produced is difficult to imagine.

1945–1973: The Post-War Era

While *Parsifal* was performed within and outside Germany during the Second World War, many European opera houses simply were not in full operation throughout. Some houses stopped production altogether, while

---

[53] Hitler's suggestion is conveyed in a letter written by Wolfgang to his brother Wieland, quoted in Bauer's "Prüfstein 'Parsifal,'" 66. One could speculate that modernistic and relatively secular productions, such as had evolved in Frankfurt, may account for some performance continuity in Germany through the early 1940s. However, modernism being deemed positive in the Nazi era is a paradoxical issue. Hitler was never keen on Goebbels's modernist leanings.

[54] Spotts, *Hitler and the Power of Aesthetics,* 236.

[55] Nike Wagner, *Wagner Theater* (Frankfurt am Main and Leipzig: Insel Verlag, 1998), 225; in English *The Wagners: The Dramas of a Musical Dynasty,* trans. Ewald Osers and Michael Downes (Princeton: Princeton UP, 1998), 139.

[56] Alfred Rosenberg, *Der Mythus des 20. Jahrhunderts: Eine Wertung der seelisch-geistigen Gestaltenkämpfe unserer Zeit* (Munich: Hoheneichen-Verlag, 1939), 434.

others offered pared-down seasons, as resources were redirected towards war efforts. Some houses were bombed. Germany was unusual in maintaining operatic life for so long. However, the tables turned by the end of the war, when some of Germany's most notable opera houses were badly bombed. They would take many years to rebuild, as resources permitted. The Berlin Staatsoper was rebuilt by 1955. The Munich Nationaltheater was only reopened in 1963; because of this, the first post-war production of *Parsifal* in Munich took place in 1957 in the Wagner-influenced Prinzregententheater, where the Bayerische Staatsoper resumed operatic activity in 1945. In Dresden, the Semperoper was not functional again until 1985; Theo Adam directed a new *Parsifal* there in 1988. Opera companies could be highly creative in their use of interim alternative performance spaces, but preferred repertoire that made modest technical demands and was easily adapted to generic sets and costumes. As houses were reconstructed, *Parsifal* became particularly attractive, as a way of showing off new production capabilities. Reconstruction offered opportunities to upgrade and rethink stage machinery and other production-related elements, regardless of whether the public areas of the house were rendered in modern ways or were more or less restored to their pre-war appearance.[57] *Parsifal* was sometimes chosen to inaugurate the openings of rebuilt or new opera houses, recalling Wagner's designation *Bühnenweih-festspiel*. The opera house in Chemnitz, for example, reopened with *Parsifal* in 1992, after substantial refurbishing. And in 2003, in Seattle, *Parsifal* became the last of the ten mature Wagner operas to be presented in a new production under general director Speight Jenkins, in celebration of the completely rebuilt opera house Marion Oliver McCaw Hall. Such choices are noteworthy but bear little of the controversy surrounding the first post-war re-opening of an opera house with *Parsifal*.

After Winifred Wagner forfeited the right to control the Bayreuth Festival, her de-Nazification trial proceedings concluded without imposing strong punishment. Bayreuth was severely bombed in the last days of the war. The context for restarting the Festival was not strong and resources were scarce. The Festspielhaus itself had not been bombed, but the costume warehouse had suffered from looting. Wolfgang and Wieland Wagner raised enough capital by 1949 that they could plan to reopen the Festival in 1951. Initially they programmed *Parsifal* and *Die Meistersinger*,

---

[57] In Vienna, for example, the stage machinery dated mostly from 1869 and had presented challenges for quite some time; Alfred Roller's 1914 production of *Parsifal* had not been easy to mount. Reconstruction in the mid-twentieth century involved massive technological changes and a thorough reconceptualization of the stage.

but with growing support they added a new production of the *Ring,* which turned out to be the biggest drawing-card in terms of ticket sales. Restoring *Parsifal* to the program was a priority and it was selected for opening night. Because of the strongly mixed reception of the work amongst Nazis, and its absence from the Bayreuth stage during the war, it was *the* Wagner opera with which to reopen the festival, setting the agenda of returning to some Bayreuth traditions, but not all. Concerning this decision, Nike Wagner adds: "Daß ein antisemitisches Programm in der christlichen Verpackung mitgeliefert sein könnte, auf diese Idee kam man nicht, trotz der Kenntnis des Antisemitismus der Entstehungszeit des *Parsifal,* trotz der Kenntnis jenes verquasten deutschmissionarischen Schrifttums der alten wie der neueren »Bayreuther Blätter«, die das Werk umrahmten" (The idea that there might be an anti-Semitic program inside the Christian packaging did not occur to anyone, in spite of the well-known anti-Semitic ideas voiced by Wagner and others at the time of the piece's composition, and the fervidly Aryan accounts of the work regularly presented in the *Bayreuther Blätter*).[58] As will be discussed later, interpretations of *Parsifal* as deeply anti-Semitic did not become widespread until several years later. Inaugurating the 1951 Festival with a new production of *Parsifal* represented above all an overturning of the recent past.

Wieland Wagner, always favored as the artistic heir of Bayreuth, had enjoyed privileged status during the war. He had pursued his interest in painting in Munich, where he had also studied the musical intricacies of his grandfather's works with Kurt Overhoff. Then as chief operatic producer in Altenburg he had prepared several Wagner productions with Overhoff that can be seen as stepping stones to his post-war style. As he pursued his artistic development, Wieland did not always trust the support of his mother Winifred, or Preetorius, but he was clearly intrigued by Hitler's plans to transform the Bayreuth Festspielhaus into a more impressive structure after the war, and the plans for a "Peace Festival" celebrating Germany's victory. Things of course turned out quite differently and Wieland was forced to reevaluate many aspects of his life in what he called his "schöpferischen schwarze Jahre," (creative black years), the years he

---

[58] Nike Wagner, *Wagner Theater,* 225–26; *The Wagners,* 139. The rampant anti-Semitism of the so-called "Bayreuth circle" is well known, but specific readings of anti-Semitism in *Parsifal* are rather sporadic in the years before the Second World War. Mary Cicora points to two such articles in the *Bayreuther Blätter:* Anton Seidl's "R. Wagner's *Parsifal* und Schopenhauer's 'Nirwâna' " of 1888 and a 1915 article by Erich Schwebsch (who acknowledges a debt to Houston Stewart Chamberlain) entitled "Klingsor und die heilige Lanze." See her *"Parsifal" Reception in the "Bayreuther Blätter,"* (New York: Peter Lang, 1987), 93 n.5.

lived with his family in Winifred's summer house on Lake Constance, reconstructing his life and engaging with many sources and influences that had not yet been part of his rather sheltered world. [59] He studied the writings of Freud and Jung, and a wide variety of avant-garde artists and philosophers whose work was suppressed in the world in which he had grown up. Wieland also continued his in-depth study of Wagner's operas with Overhoff, focusing on the psychological dimensions of the music and drama. At the same time, he was much stimulated by Greek drama and mythology as he re-explored Wagner's own writings on the topic. In many respects, Wieland's reflections during this period respond indirectly to Thomas Mann's famous 1933 essay "Leiden und Größe Richard Wagners" (Sorrows and Grandeur of Richard Wagner).[60] For Mann, the psychological dimension of the operas was complemented by their mythic aspects, but he felt that these facets were not generally regarded as complementary in his own age or in Wagner's. Wieland would bridge this perceived divide in his own work as director and designer.

Wieland stunned audiences of the 1951 *Parsifal* with his non-literal approach to the score's directions for settings and gesture. Those hoping for a return to something resembling the original production found Wieland's abstract minimalism sacrilegious, while others discovered a new and deeper spirituality in the stage presentation. With prominent champions such as Ernest Newman and Carl Dahlhaus, the movement to gain historical distance from the original stage directions gained momentum.[61] Modern staging and design strategies, especially those of Appia and Craig, came together in what must have seemed like a quantum leap, with a rigorous logic that focused on the opera's mythological and psychological dimensions. Wieland's own father, Siegfried, had experimented with colored light and use of the cyclorama, yet with a strong allegiance to older aesthetics. With the assistance of lighting designer Paul Eberhardt, Wieland made these elements the focus of his conception of scenic design, which eschewed all but the most essential props.[62] Projections might hint

---

[59] Walter Panovsky, *Wieland Wagner* (Bremen: Carl Schümann Verlag, 1964), 9–15.

[60] Thomas Mann, "Leiden und Größe Richard Wagners," in *Wagner und unsere Zeit,* ed. Erika Mann, 63–121 (Frankfurt am Main: S. Fischer, 1983); in English: *Thomas Mann: Pro and Contra Wagner,* trans. Allan Blunden, 91–148 (London: Faber, 1985).

[61] Unusual for its time, Dahlhaus's book *Richard Wagners Musikdramen* (Velber: Friedrich, 1971) offers a critical discussion of historical production styles amidst musicological analysis.

[62] While part of a fully integrated aesthetic, the spartan Bayreuth stage of the 1950s also reflected the lean budget of those years.

Illustration 8.2: Bayreuth, Wieland Wagner's 1951 production, beginning of act 2,
Janis Martin shown as Kundry, Gerd Nienstedt as Klingsor, 1973
(reproduced by permission of the Bildarchiv, Bayreuther Festspiele)

at forests or a spider's web, images which gained in complexity, texture, and symbolic allusion over the years (see ill. 8.2).

Much use was made of the realm of twilight, that mysterious transitional zone in which our awareness and perceptions are gradually awoken and things come in and out of focus.[63] A Greek-inspired raised *Scheibe*, or circular dramatic acting space, could be strikingly used in the careful placement of props and performers; the generally uncluttered surface lent to the proximity or distance between performers and objects a special potency. Gestures too were minimal and highly purposeful. With such a selective and tightly controlled visual sphere, much space was left open for the music and text, which Wieland, like his grandfather, believed demanded interpretive sensitivity and precision.

At the time of his death in 1966, Wieland was reevaluating his approach to *Parsifal* with renewed intensity, stimulated by his work with

---

[63] Many critics complained of a pervasive darkness.

Pierre Boulez.[64] His production, bound to change even further, was thus frozen in time and remained in the repertory until 1973, ironically recapitulating the cult-like fame and fate of the original 1882 production. Hans-Peter Lehmann, who became Wieland Wagner's assistant in Bayreuth in 1960, also took on the responsibility of mounting the production in Brussels, Zurich, Hanover, and Posen between 1960 and 1973.[65] Some still feel this production to be definitive. It was undoubtedly influential on many levels. As the initial brouhaha of 1951 dissipated, Wieland's *Parsifal* came to be regarded as generally apolitical in tone, an attractive feature for an operatic world that remained uncertain as to what should be done about the whole association of Hitler and Wagner. Of course Wieland's psychological focus and his favored production means were not entirely driven by a desire to be apolitical; *Parsifal* invited this manner of interpretation, as other directors were discovering on their own. East Germany's first production of *Parsifal*, directed by Wolf Völker and designed by Lothar Schenk von Trapp in Berlin in 1950, aimed for a monumental realization of classical simplicity that would free up the work's deeper, symbolic levels of meaning.[66] In the first production mounted by the San Francisco Opera, on October 27, 1950, Paul Hager set much of the action between a scrim and the cyclorama, suggesting that much of what took place was in a half-waking, half-sleeping state.[67] A series of images by Wolfram Skalicki was projected onto the cyclorama including, in the premiere run, a spinning cathedral in the first act Transformation music. The projections served as "a sort of visual commentary on characters' mood and thinking" while "in the filmy middle world there were frozen, subtly lighted knights suggesting Gothic statuary set free from cathedral niches."[68]

Some opera houses revived pre-war productions in the early 1950s before heading in Wielandesque directions. In 1955, Joseph Urban's long-standing designs for the Metropolitan production yielded to

---

[64] Boulez conducted *Parsifal* from 1966–68 and again in 1970, when his interpretation was recorded. Boulez returned to the work and Bayreuth for the new production directed by Christoph Schlingensief in 2004.

[65] Lehmann later began a long association with the Hanover Opera, where he chose to direct *Parsifal* (1981) for his first production as Intendant.

[66] Völker had previously directed *Parsifal* in Düsseldorf and would go on to direct it in West Berlin at the Theater des Westens (1955) and in Cologne (1958).

[67] Hager directed another new production in Stuttgart (1959), while Skalicki designed the Innsbruck premiere of *Parsifal* (1978).

[68] Arthur Bloomfield, *The San Francisco Opera: 1922–1978* (Sausalito, CA: Comstock Editions, 1978), 213–14.

a neo-Bayreuth approach in the production directed by Herbert Graf, with projections by Leo Kerz.[69] Other quasi-imitative productions include Graf's at Covent Garden in 1959, with designs by Paul Walter, as well as the Frank de Quell production designed by Peter Bissegger at the Teatro di San Carlo in Naples in 1967, and Ernst Poettgen's 1969 Buenos Aires production designed by Roberto Oswald. Graf directed a third *Parsifal* within a decade (Geneva, 1964). For that production Max Röthlisberger based his designs quite literally on Appia's sketches of 1912, and Wieland's production again seemed to hover in the background.

Two conductors who also directed productions of *Parsifal* in the 1960s avoided echoing Wieland's work, at the same time eschewing a traditional 19th-century path. Herbert von Karajan conducted and directed the 1961 Vienna production with designs by Heinrich Wendel. Karajan split the casting of Kundry between Elisabeth Höngen (acts 1 and 3) and Christa Ludwig (act 2), thus realizing the fractured nature of Kundry's existence in a tangible way, while also essentially undoing Wagner's creation of a single complex character from multiple figures in his sources.[70] Karajan did not repeat this approach in his 1980 Salzburg Easter Festival production. In 1965, conductor Lovro von Matačić directed the first production of *Parsifal* in Turin in nearly forty years. Tina Sestini Pallini's designs evoked a sort of magic realism, a blend of the quotidian and the fantastic, but did not impress critics as contributing to a persuasive interpretation. The production was revived the following year at Florence's Teatro Communale, with the chorus singing in Italian and the soloists singing in German.

Wieland's rather secularized interpretation of *Parsifal* contributed to a trend that gained momentum in the 1960s. One may recall that allusions to organized religion had complicated enthusiasm for *Parsifal* amongst some Nazi party members, but it is difficult to regard Wieland's secular approach as an appeal in that direction. The many paradoxes of the intertwined reception and production histories of *Parsifal* in the 1930s and 1940s render meaningless such a straightforward link. Furthermore,

---

[69] Nathaniel Merrill took over the direction of the 1961 revival of this production. Merrill was responsible with designer Robert O'Hearn for the Metropolitan's next new production of *Parsifal* (1970), which was much less dependent on the so-called "New Bayreuth" style of Wieland Wagner.

[70] An inverse strategy was used in the 1972 Bayreuth *Tannhäuser*, directed by Götz Friedrich, in which Gwyneth Jones sang both Venus and Elisabeth. Although cast separately for the production premiere in 1996, Harry Kupfer's *Tannhäuser* also featured Venus and Elizabeth as the same singer, Angela Denoke, for revivals in Berlin and Madrid in 2002.

religiosity in *Parsifal* posed a problem in contrasting ideological camps. In the entire period of the GDR, *Parsifal* received the fewest new productions of all of Wagner's works — only six. The first new *Parsifal* — that directed by Völker — opened April 7, 1950, in East Berlin, somewhat remarkably since the Berlin Staatsoper on Unter den Linden had been heavily bombed in 1945, after having already been damaged in 1941 and rebuilt. During the second reconstruction, operatic activity shifted to the Admiral's Palace, where *Parsifal* was performed from 1950–54. Apparently because of fears of anti-fascist reactions against Wagner, none of his other operas were performed in East Berlin from 1950 until 1955, when the general popularity of *Die Meistersinger* prevailed for the reopening of the Staatsoper.[71] Ultimately, Wagner was thoroughly reintegrated into the repertory in East Germany: *Der fliegende Holländer* received eighty-five new productions, *Tannhäuser* sixty-one, *Die Meistersinger* forty, and *Lohengrin* thirty-two.[72] The ongoing unease toward *Parsifal* in the GDR remained the anomaly.

Willy Bodenstein directed a new production of *Parsifal* in 1956 at the Landestheater in Dessau, which was responsible for more new Wagner productions than any other theater in the GDR (leading the Berlin Staatsoper, Dresden, and Leipzig).[73] The Dessau Theater was substantially renovated and re-opened in 1938 by Goebbels and Hitler, who considered the theater a German jewel. The post-war attention to Wagner in Dessau marked a movement to erase all fascist associations and to reclaim Wagner as a true revolutionary and socialist; this intention was driven by a conservative return to quasi-original staging practices. In 1953, Bodenstein launched the first Richard-Wagner-Westwochen, a kind of proletariat-style Bayreuth of the North that continued until 1958. That same year Wagner's relevance to socialist cultural aims was hotly discussed in the pages of the journal *Theater der Zeit*. This debate "represented an important cathartic moment in GDR

---

[71] For more detailed consideration of this scenario and Wagner in the GDR period, see Sigrid and Hermann Neef, *Deutsche Oper im 20. Jahrhundert: DDR, 1949–1989* (Berlin and New York: Peter Lang, 1992). *Die Meistersinger, Fidelio*, and *Der Freischütz* were all popular choices within Germany for signaling the post-war renewal of operatic life, and the reconstruction of damaged opera houses.

[72] These statistics are drawn from Peter Kupfer's study of Wagner productions in the GDR; see http://www.northfieldfineart.com/peter/gdrprod.html. It should be noted that the popularity of *Der fliegende Holländer*, was, as it is today, in part driven by its relatively more modest production requirements.

[73] Recently, Dessau has entered a phase of marked de-emphasis on Wagner, particularly since Johannes Felsenstein (son of Walther Felsenstein) became Intendant in 1992.

denazification and in the uncritical reception of the German cultural heritage."[74] In contrast to Bodenstein's production style, a powerfully critical mode of interpreting Wagner on the stage would later emerge to address issues raised in this debate.

Wieland Wagner was by no means the only radical and controversial opera director in the early post-war years. In this active phase of cultural renewal, directors such as Peter Brook,[75] Giorgio Strehler, Jonathan Miller, and Walter Felsenstein brought a new and sometimes provocative vitality to opera interpretation. Drawing forth principles then more at home in the world of spoken theater, this wave of directors paid close attention to textual analysis, gesture, and all aspects of design as interactive interpretive media. But Wagner was not high on their list of opera composers to tackle. Thus, for some time, Wieland stood apart in the realm of Wagner production in his integrated revisionist approach to dramatic interpretation and to the visual dimensions of opera production. The primary alternatives — reactionary reliance on old traditions or undistinguished hybrids of Wieland's and more conservative styles — gradually gave way to a spectrum of design-weighted experiments that put *Parsifal* into different contexts and viewed the work from different perspectives through historical and contemporary visual references. In 1970, Thomas Richter-Forgách designed a surreal, space-age *Parsifal* for director Ulrich Melchinger in Kassel. Dietrich Haugk directed the 1973 production at Munich's Nationaltheater, with sets by Günther Schneider-Siemssen that were inspired by the post-Second World War Viennese arts movement known as fantastic realism. Klingsor's magic realm was depicted as an underwater grotto with elaborate imagery of a giant mermaid and a menacing octopus, reminiscent of Hieronymus Bosch, against a backdrop recalling Pieter Breughel the Elder's painting of the tower of Babel. In Hamburg, in 1976, director August Everding turned to one of the founding members of the school of fantastic realism, Ernst Fuchs. The artist's personal style very much characterized the production through an intense use of color, extraordinary visionary power, and a deep attachment to the sacred. Schneider-Siemssen had not put his own

---

[74] Joy Calico Haslam, "The Politics of Opera in the German Democratic Republic, 1945–1961" (PhD diss., Duke University, 1999), 306.

[75] Susanne Vill has drawn attention to the ways in which Wagner's blending of art and religion resonate with twentieth-century theatrical practices such as those of Peter Brook. See her "Kunstreligion und Lebenskunst: zur Aktualität von Richard Wagners Bühnenweihfestspiel," in *"Und jedermann erwartet sich ein Fest": Fest, Theater, Festspiele; Gesammelte Vorträge des Salzburger Symposions 1995,* ed. Peter Csobádi, et al., 137–49 (Anif/Salzburg: Verlag Müller-Speiser, 1996).

original work as a visual artist onstage, but, in accordance with his ideas about the stage as cosmic space, he was attracted to the style developed by Fuchs and other fantastic realist artists. For two later productions of *Parsifal,* with long-time collaborators Herbert von Karajan (1980, Salzburg, Grosses Festspielhaus) and Otto Schenk (1991, The Metropolitan), Schneider-Siemssen created substantially different designs that reflected changes in directorial objectives.

In January of 1973, Filippo Sanjust directed and designed a production in Frankfurt that presented an aestheticized world of the Grail. Nature was rendered through very simple but pleasing means, and Klingsor's garden was a soft green-hued Elysium. Klingsor was seated in a throne like Amfortas, a potent reminder of the drama's many binary oppositions that are inextricably linked. Kundry did not appear in the closing scene, having already been fully redeemed.[76] The overall beauty of this production had the effect of putting the entire drama at a bit of a remove, but certain symbolic features or stage directions drew attention to the illusory surface, and suggested layers of meaning beneath that surface. In April of the same year, in Paris, Rolf Liebermann directed a new production of *Parsifal* with Jürgen Rose's strikingly beautiful Jugendstil designs, including a sumptuous Flowermaiden scene. In the last act, the Grail temple columns were withdrawn, suggesting that Parsifal's leadership marked a break from the Grail community's earlier traditions. These two productions appeared just months before the final revival of Wieland Wagner's *Parsifal,* which had been performed each Bayreuth season since the 1951 reopening, when the festival first became an annual event. As this era drew to a close, and watered-down imitations of Wieland's style lost their appeal, there was no clear indication how the path of *Parsifal*'s production history would unfold, at Bayreuth or anywhere else. It was not simply the case that stylistic norms were falling by the wayside as post-modernism took root. Rather, in hindsight we can see that the directors like Sanjust and Liebermann in 1973 were beginning to raise probing questions in their productions, through staging and design strategies. In each case the final scene of the opera was reinterpreted, introducing questions, if not exactly spelling out the answers. Why did Kundry not appear in the final scene?[77] Where

---

[76] Sanjust carried this idea through to his 1975 West Berlin production, which was more sparing in the use of scenery and had the aura of a dream play with beautiful ever-changing light patterns.

[77] In the Teatro Colón production developed in Buenos Aires (and later revived at the Teatro Municipal de Santiago, in 1999, and at Washington Opera in 2000), director/designer Roberto Oswald also chose to not have Kundry present in the final scene.

did she go and what was her fate after being baptized? What kind of leader will Parsifal be? Is there a new and better alternative for the Grail community? The next phase of *Parsifal*'s production history would largely be shaped by such questions.

Since 1973: The Critical Spotlight Sharpens and Refocuses

In the 1970s, Wagner and Bayreuth were very much in the spotlight. Ownership and control of the Festival, the theater itself, the complex of Wagner family homes in Bayreuth, and the Wagner archives were legally reconfigured in 1973, with the establishment of the Richard-Wagner-Stiftung. The net result of this agreement was that Wolfgang Wagner retained control of the Festival and in some ways even increased his autonomy. Wolfgang, the other two surviving children of Siegfried and Winifred Wagner, Friedelind and Verena, and the children of Wieland all received considerable sums of money for various family holdings, as well as voting rights in the Stiftung. This was a particularly tense time for the Wagner family as family-related documents gradually became accessible and open to public scrutiny. The publication of Cosima's voluminous diaries proved to be a watershed of information about Richard Wagner's personal and artistic life. All in all, a wealth of new material reinvigorated research into the lives of the Wagner family and Wagner's artworks. The availability of new materials added impetus to an intense period of critical reevaluation surrounding the observation of three centenaries between 1976 and 1983: the centenary of the premiere of the complete *Ring,* that of the premiere of *Parsifal,* and that of Wagner's death. During this phase, *Parsifal* would be recast in a particularly harsh light that would spread itself through the popular press, the scholarly world, and the operatic stage.

Artistically, Wolfgang had begun carving out new directions for the Festival by engaging outside directors. August Everding's *Der fliegende Holländer* of 1969 was followed by Götz Friedrich's *Tannhäuser* in 1972. Friedrich was a particularly provocative hire; working closely with Walter Felsenstein in East Berlin he had developed a politically focused and intense dramatic style that exposed difficult issues. Felsenstein himself never directed Wagner, and only once allowed him to be produced at the Komische Oper during his long leadership there. But the exception — Joachim Herz's 1962 production of *Der fliegende Holländer* — was a harbinger of the wave of revisionist Wagner productions that would be undertaken by directors heavily influenced by Felsenstein, including Friedrich and Harry Kupfer. The 1972 *Tannhäuser* was Friedrich's first Wagner production altogether. His interpretation centered on the relationship between the protagonist/artist figure and the society around him that proves highly intolerant of artistic freedom and individuality. The Wartburg society was thus represented as particularly cruel and militaristic, while Tannhäuser was isolated more than usual, right through to the end. Jürgen Rose's designs helped to make it clear that this was an allusion to the Nazi regime. After more than two decades of skirting awkward issues about the relationships between Wagner's art and Hitler's politics — and between Wagner's politics and Hitler's art — Bayreuth had reached the point of confronting its past on its own stage. On the one hand, Friedrich's interpretation called attention to the many artists who could not or would not perform on the very same stage during the 1930s and through the war. On the other, there is the suggestion that Tannhäuser, with whom Wagner identified, represented the composer's independence from the regime that appropriated him. But a critique of socialist realism was surely also at play; Friedrich emigrated to the West soon after and took up a position in Hamburg.

One would not expect such a complex and critical type of staged interpretation from Wolfgang Wagner in his first production of *Parsifal*. After Wieland's death, Wolfgang's tendency had been to become more traditional, and he moved increasingly away from the "New Bayreuth" style. As artistic director of the Festival he did not discourage Friedrich's manner of engaging with Wagner's works. Instead he hired him again, to stage *Lohengrin* in 1979, and then again for the centenary production of *Parsifal* in 1982. And of course, in between these productions came the highly controversial 1976 Bayreuth *Ring*, directed by Patrice Chéreau and designed by Richard Peduzzi. Amidst all of these provocative and challenging productions, each of which involved non-traditional designs, Wolfgang's 1975 *Parsifal* seemed to belong to a different world altogether. It opened with a representation of nature that had not been seen in Bayreuth stagings of *Parsifal* since the 1930s. The critics ran lukewarm, but Wolfgang had taken some significant steps in a critical direction. In his program notes, he raised questions about the basic viability of the Grail community. If the ideals or traditions of the Grail community were not respectable from the onset, then Parsifal's assuming leadership of the community as a purely restorative gesture would also be open to criticism. In his production, Wolfgang chose not to present the characters as symbols or archetypes, but on a more human plane. He thereby opened up awkward perspectives on the complex character of Kundry, in particular the treatment of her death. In the first year of the production, he directed Amfortas to stroke Kundry's hair and to recognize her sympathetically with a glance before she expired. By 1981, when the production was recorded for commercial video distribution, Wolfgang altered his staging so that all of the principal characters remained standing on stage as the curtain closed. Kundry, a Wandering Jew character and the only female principal in the work, did not die and the implication was that she was not excluded from the future of the Grail community. In these brief closing moments Wolfgang had touched on two of the hottest issues concerning *Parsifal:* anti-Semitism and misogyny.

Before the war began, Hitler's love of Wagnerian opera and his affiliation with Bayreuth had already begun to taint the way Wagner's operas were regarded. With the war underway, skepticism towards Wagner and questions about the significance of his operas for Hitler increased. Publications like Peter Viereck's *Metapolitics: from the Romantics to Hitler* of 1941 argued that German Romanticism, with its idealistic thrust, was the foundation of Nazism.[78] Leon Stein's *The Racial Thinking of Richard Wagner* appeared in 1950, followed by Theodor Adorno's *Versuch über Wagner* (Essay on Wagner) in 1952, and widely-read studies by Robert Gutman and Hartmut Zelinsky appeared in 1968 and 1976, respectively.[79] A growing number of such authors focused on Wagner's operas as manifestations of anti-Semitism, beliefs in racial purity and German supremacy, and misogyny. Before the war *Parsifal* had not been so specifically perceived as an embodiment of Wagner's unacceptable prejudices and an essential step in the pathway to Nazism. Sometimes, as has already been mentioned, it was regarded as just the opposite. Nevertheless, this body of criticism spawned public debates that helped to push the burden of history, particularly within Germany, onto the stage as a forum for intense self-criticism and possible catharsis. *Parsifal* would now have to withstand and respond to strong post-war perspectives on ideology as shaped through stage direction and design.

Götz Friedrich directed his first *Parsifal* in Stuttgart in 1976. His design partner was the material artist Gunther Uecker, well-known for his work with natural woods and nails. Uecker's sets were severe and deliberately lacked warmth, implying that the traditions of the Grail realm were uncomfortable, overly rigid, and hollow. While the degree of abstraction in the designs was reminiscent of Wieland's style, Friedrich unleashed considerable energy and development of character in his direction of the performers. Particularly striking was Klingsor's release of the Flowermaidens from

---

[78] Viereck's book *Metapolitics: From the Romantics to Hitler* (New York: A. A. Knopf, 1941) was published in a revised and expanded form as *Metapolitics: The Roots of the Nazi Mind* (New York: Capricorn, 1961 and 1965) and most recently as *Metapolitics: From Wagner and the German Romantics to Hitler* (New Brunswick, NJ: Transaction, 2004). The evolving title reflects the increased tension concerning Wagner and Nazism in public debates of recent decades.

[79] Subsequent authors who have pursued this vein include Paul Lawrence Rose, Barry Millington, and Marc Weiner.

Illustration 8.3: Bayreuth, Götz Friedrich's production (1982),
Simon Estes shown as Amfortas, Leonie Rysanek as Kundry, Hans Sotin as
Gurnemanz, 1983 (reproduced by permission of the Bildarchiv, Bayreuther Festspiele)

a torture chamber so that they could perform their roles as seductresses. Kundry remained alive in the opera's closing scene, suggesting that her membership in the Grail community would be part of its renewal.

In 1982, Friedrich directed the centenary *Parsifal* at Bayreuth working with another designer, Andreas Reinhardt. The production's unit set was an enclosed structure that could have been a catacomb, with the perspective of the viewer skewed so that it seemed that the architectural structure was lying on its side, or the viewer was looking up through the inside towards the ceiling. In either case, the stage floor involved a side of this structure that featured a series of Romanesque windows, like all the other sides (see ill. 8.3). The primary acting area for the main characters was thus deliberately perilous, offering limited paths along which to move and many opportunities to fall. Amfortas's mobility was further challenged by the large crucifix sometimes borne on his back, symbolizing the Christian dimension of his burden while rendering visible how difficult it was for him to carry out his role. Klingsor's power and control were manifested in the form of a nuclear disaster that had destroyed nature in the framing acts, while his platform in the second act was a sort of scientific superstation. Throughout, the interiority of the unit set emphasized a lack of connection with the natural world. In the final scene, however, all this changed.

Friedrich did indeed direct Kundry to die in this production, while the chorus was still singing its closing phrases, hence earlier in the score than Wagner indicated. At the moment when Wagner indicated that Kundry should sink and slowly expire, the back wall of the set opened out, allowing the Flowermaidens to join the knights onstage in a flood of natural, external light.

Director Uwe Wand (Leipzig, 1982) interpreted Kundry's redemption as her opportunity to unite with Amfortas, following Parsifal's death onstage. Joachim Herz, like Friedrich, also incorporated additional women in the final scene in his 1986 production for the English National Opera. By drawing women down from the unseen choruses above the stage, Herz tied into an idea that Wagner entertained during the rehearsals in 1882.[80] Bill Bryden (Covent Garden, 1988) included women and children as part of an onstage audience watching the presentation of the *Parsifal* legend within a bombed-out cathedral.

Friedrich's use of a modern metaphor for the spear and its misuse as a destructive weapon was attractive to other directors in the 1970s, 1980s and 1990s. Rolf Liebermann, with designer Petrika Ionesco, depicted Klingsor's control of atomic power in their Geneva production earlier in 1982. Such a choice has overarching implications for design that are at odds with Wagner's methodology, although they can make a powerful impression that resonates with twentieth and twenty-first century concerns about global well-being and destruction. Wagner's strategy in the first act of *Parsifal*, for example, is to unfold a series of scenarios in which we only gradually learn how dire things have become for the Grail community and its leader. The music of the prelude of course lets us know that all is not well, but Wagner does not initially utilize the natural setting to anticipate our deepening perception of this reality. His primary means of progressive disclosure include Gurnemanz's narration of previous events, and shifts in the behavior of characters that are musically shaped to reveal underlying fears and a lack of faith that things will improve. By the act 1 Transformation scene, we realize that the surface appearance of things has in fact been an illusion, before we are presented with more intricate cycles of illusion and revelation in the following Grail scene and act. In the third act these cycles are modified so that the scenic depiction is more transparent and

---

[80] On July 7, 1882, Wagner abandoned the possibility of including at least the boys from the unseen choruses participating in the communion service, citing (surely humorously) the fact that some of the boys were not themselves confirmed. See *CT* 2:976 [trans. 2:886]. Other earlier ideas that could have affected the final scene include Wagner's plan to momentarily revive Titurel, included in the 1865 prose draft and the 1877 printed version of the poem.

integrated with reconstructive processes. The coordination of emerging signs of spring with Parsifal's return on Good Friday is thus developed musically as a positive and multi-faceted anticipation of the opera's closing scene. What is not preserved so much in setings that foreground devastation from the onset is the concentrated and localized impact that Klingsor's use of the weapon initially has on Amfortas, and the gradual ways in which this comes to impact the Grail community as a whole. Our step-by-step increased awareness of the situation actually parallels the intensification of the problems within the Grail community. With nature immediately and brutally altered from the onset, many of these processes are de-emphasized, if not foregone. No doubt this partially serves today's audiences as an urgent prescription against naïveté concerning the destructive potential of abused power.

As early as 1970, the Melchinger/Richter-Forgách production in Kassel had obtained similar results from their use of space technology as a metaphor for the religious relic and its use as a weapon. The natural world never thrived onstage nor was it involved in any symbolic regeneration. The same was true of Friedrich's 1976 Stuttgart production in which neon lighting during the Good Friday music hinted at an artificial type of nature. The greater the potential destructive threat posed by modern weapons, the more difficult it is to invest hope in a return to a more natural and idyllic state. Friedrich's 1982 Bayreuth production made a more hopeful plea, suggesting that we hold the key to a brighter future in a greater compassion for humanity on a broad scale. In his 1982 production, Liebermann's images of destruction included a decrepit Grail temple that hinted at a tensional relationship between religion and science. In the final scene Parsifal broke the spear after he had returned it to the Grail temple, which then became a cathedral radiantly illuminated by stained glass panels. Later, in 1991, Claude Naville made allusions to the Gulf War in the Finnish premiere of *Parsifal*, in Tampere — here oil was depicted as the instrument of power. A film projection of a bird drowning in oil unfolded during the Good Friday music.[81] Such productions share attention to global concerns and misuses of power that have wide-ranging impact, while highlighting mankind's lack of respect for nature as well as humanity. They vary, however, in their interpretations of what the future of the Grail might entail, from bleak despair to glimmers of hope.

Götz Friedrich directed *Parsifal* four times in his career. After Bayreuth he worked with the designer Peter Sykora (Stockholm, 1995)

---

[81] The image of a dead swan that seems to be covered in oil and is pierced by a red-tipped arrow is part of a sequence that unfolds during the prelude in Hans-Jürgen Syberberg's film *Parsifal*.

and took a slightly different approach to the rendering of Klingsor. No longer a military figure armed with nuclear power, Klingsor appeared as more of a Chinese magician skilled in the art of illusion, but a little pathetic and certainly less threatening. At the close of the opera, Friedrich directed Parsifal to extend the Grail towards Kundry. Reaching up towards the Grail she expired, as did Amfortas simultaneously. All of the stage lights then gradually dimmed until the only thing that could be seen onstage during the music's last few seconds was the glowing Grail, shedding a soft light throughout the auditorium. No Flowermaidens were redeemed at this point. Yet for Friedrich, this staging was another essentially positive rendering of the end of Wagner's opera. Friedrich claimed that his understanding of the work had remained fundamentally the same but that working with new designers across time enabled him to explore different ways of realizing what he saw unequivocally as a culminating message of universal redemption and freedom. Friedrich believed that Wagner's original stage directions, while not clearly translating this positive message to a modern audience, are intended to do so. Kundry's death, he maintained, cannot easily be understood as a Buddhist kind of redemption when this form of redemption is exclusive to her case of suffering. Amfortas too has begged for a release from the cycles of suffering. It is for this reason and not as a form of punishment that Friedrich tied Amfortas's fate to Kundry's. Friedrich initially envisioned a different way to close the opera, but the idea was too technically demanding for the Stockholm stage, as it also was for his Deutsche Oper production in Berlin in 1998. Friedrich would liked to have had Parsifal turn his gaze from Kundry out towards the audience, while still holding the glowing Grail, and to be raised over the first few rows of the audience via a hydraulic lift while the lights dimmed.[82]

Harry Kupfer expressed a change in attitude towards *Parsifal* between his two Staatsoper productions: one in 1977, which was the first production in East Berlin since 1954, and the second in 1991. Around the time of the first of these he was engaged to direct a new production of *Die Meistersinger* in Copenhagen, but insurmountable budget challenges led to the Berlin production of *Parsifal* being offered to that house, where Wagner's last opera had not been seen since 1915. Kupfer's first *Parsifal* proved to be a head-on engagement with Nazi exclusivity. Peter Sykora's sets for the Grail temple adopted the monumental style of Nazi designer Arno Breker for a pair of stage-high statues of idealized youth warriors as cherubim facing an equally oversized image of a crucified Christ. In act 2

---

[82] These ideas were conveyed to the author in personal interviews with Friedrich conducted in May of 1996.

Klingsor was surrounded by fragments of a crumbling giant statue of Christ. Like Friedrich, Kupfer openly criticized the religious dimension of the Grail community en route to an appeal for greater humanism, but he carried the idea further. His rendering of the message of redemption was not so all-encompassing or optimistic, or at least it involved more of an element of individual choice. The production closed with Parsifal redeeming Amfortas and then leaving the Grail temple, taking the spear and Grail with him, followed by Gurnemanz and Kundry.

In 1992, Kupfer had the rare opportunity to replace his own Berlin production with a new one. The situation had changed with the fall of the wall and there was considerable concern about the fate of three opera houses in a reunited city. As head of the Komische Oper, Kupfer had limited possibilities for presenting Wagner operas in his own house and so he joined Daniel Barenboim in a project to produce the major Wagner operas at the Deutsche Staatsoper. *Parsifal* was the first installment of this project. Working this time with the designer Hans Schavernoch, Kupfer offered a biting, but politically less specific, critique of the Grail community using very different means than in 1977. This modernistic Grail is literally locked into a realm devoid of nature, encompassed by cold, high-tech surfaces. The knights seem hopelessly dependent. After the spear is returned to the Grail temple, Amfortas expires in Kundry's stead and Parsifal momentarily seems overcome by doubt at the prospect of his new role, but is gently assured by Gurnemanz and Kundry. With the knights oblivious of the trio and almost drunk at the sight of the glowing Grail and spear, the curtain draws to a close behind Parsifal, Gurnemanz, and Kundry. They alone remain visible onstage, looking out at the audience, self-assured and invitingly hopeful.

This 1992 production offered a unique interpretation of the Flowermaiden scene. The questing Parsifal encounters a wavy red grid supporting several television monitors (see ill. 8.4). The black screens come to life with images of beautiful women who occasionally reveal their bosoms and buttocks as they attempt to seduce the young man. Attracted but perplexed, Parsifal approaches the screens and attempts to get close to the women that he sees, only to find them two-dimensional and inaccessible. The whole presentation makes quite an effect, with Parsifal not only confronting female sexuality for the first time, but also discovering, like a child, how illusory the images that he sees on the screens actually are, no matter how real they look. We are reminded in a flash of the dehumanizing and desensitizing effects of commonplace modern technology. This double discovery is not of course present in Wagner's conception, which uses the initial temptation of the Flowermaidens as a sort of warm-up for Kundry's more masterful seduction. Kupfer's premature unmasking of the initial illusion is effective in its own right in that Parsifal's hopes are inflated when he sees a truly three-dimensional woman in the form of Kundry.

Illustration 8.4: Staatsoper Unter den Linden, Berlin, Harry Kupfer's production (1992), Poul Elming shown as Parsifal (photo: Monika Rittershaus)

Distrust in Wagner's treatment of illusion peaked with two Brechtian interpretations of *Parsifal* that first appeared in 1982: the feature film directed by Hans-Jürgen Syberberg and the Frankfurt stage production directed by Ruth Berghaus. Syberberg's *Hitler* film trilogy of the 1970s and the spin-off *Confessions of Winifred Wagner* (1975) form the backdrop to his *Parsifal* film. That Syberberg would adopt a hyper-skeptical stance towards Wagner's last opera was a foregone conclusion, but the film remains an interesting compilation of images and associations bound up with one hundred years of Wagner and *Parsifal* reception history. A staged performance of the opera it is not. The film features a complete soundtrack of the opera, but the performance could not be reenacted as a live performance on a real stage; the whole presentation is intimately bound up with the medium of film. Some of the roles are performed by the actual singers, while the soundtrack's conductor, Armin Jordan, acted the role of Amfortas. What appears as bad lip-synching is one of several gestures intended to focus on disjunctive layers of the performance, a sort of anti-*Gesamtkunstwerk*. The emphasis on decadence and kitsch runs high, with the result that the creative void behind the illusion of "high art" is simultaneously exposed. Syberberg's handling of the Flowermaiden scene is a case in point.

As the encounter between Klingsor and Kundry draws to a close, the evil magician raises the sleeve of his coat. The drape of fabric is transformed into a projection screen bearing one of Joukovsky's original designs for the Flowermaiden scene, and we enter that realm through the eye of the camera. The painted design proves to be the backdrop for dancing puppet Flowermaidens before the focus shifts to Parsifal. Attired like a dandy, and semi-aloof, he wanders through a craggy maze that we know from earlier scenes to be the crevices of a gigantic version of Wagner's death mask, the basic set for the opera/film. Leaning against the walls are the real Flowermaidens, but they give few if any signs of being alive, let alone seductive. Some of them have exposed breasts, but their skin is covered with a pale paste, while others are completely wrapped in cloth. Scarcely are glances exchanged between Parsifal and the Flowermaidens; all parties seem to be in a trance, and for a time, while the Flowermaidens are singing their appeals, Parsifal is nowhere to be seen. Naïveté and emotion are absent in this decadent reading. As Parsifal moves on, the set charts a sort of decline: wooden beams support the walls and ceilings around him, almost as if he is moving deeper into a mine shaft, while a Flowermaiden appears in bondage on the side. Puppets and props resurface from earlier in the film, and images of Wagner's complete death mask and elements from Hieronymus Bosch's *Earthly Delights* tryptich appear as projections in the background. When Parsifal finally reaches another seemingly interior realm, with painted backdrops alluding to the exterior, he is again dressed as a simpleton. Kundry sits atop a primitive throne modeled after the one today on display in Aachen as Charlemagne's throne. The Flowermaidens are seen one last time as Kundry looks into a crystal ball to bid them farewell.

Syberberg has paid some care in the construction of the film, employing elements like the puppets and Kundry's crystal ball as cross-referencing punctuation. Rich, too, is his interweaving of the worlds of theater and film. No images are carelessly selected, although the endless allusions may escape those less familiar with the opera and Wagner's life. Others may be overwhelmed or may tire of the distractions such that their individual meaning is diminished. Historical references to a stream of militaristic missions, some religious and some not, are impossible to miss. We are reminded of the very brutal realities enacted in the name of higher ideals, from the Christian Crusades to the Nazi regime. This is given extra stress in a hyper self-conscious presentation, and possibly serves as a locus of real meaning amongst the many layers of illusion in this film.

More ambiguous was Ruth Berghaus's centenary production of *Parsifal* in Frankfurt, designed by Axel Manthey. Collaborating with the dramaturg Klaus Zehelein, a onetime student of Adorno, Berghaus did not attempt to point in any single direction to causes or solutions, but aimed to illuminate any and all flaws in the Grail community until nothing meaningful remained. At the conclusion, Kundry lay on the ground before Titurel's coffin, but it was not certain if she was dead. Parsifal, much aged by his years of wandering, wore the paper crown and royal mantle previously worn by Amfortas, but they were several sizes too large. The role was too big for him, but likely also for anyone else; the role becomes a utopian impossibility. Director Cesare Lievi took this premise one step further in his 1991 production at La Scala. From the beginning the knights seemed beyond help, struck by disease and wearing what looked like gas helmets. At the end of the opera the walls of the set broke open, with the knights, Parsifal, and Kundry wandering off in different directions. Jaroslav Chundela's 1992 production in Essen left Kundry in an exalted state with the knights while Parsifal abdicated his position and strode off into the distance. A particularly unusual variant of this abandonment idea took place at the end of Peter Mussbach's 1989 Brussels production: the knights wandered offstage leaving Parsifal staring curiously at a rough drawing of the Grail that Amfortas transfixed with the spear before he expired.

Amidst so much variation in the treatment of the close of *Parsifal*, it is rare to find a production that shows Kundry's death as indicated in Wagner's original stage directions. She is typically shown as sharing her fate with others in some way. One production that is regarded as more faithful than most to Wagner's original stage directions is that of the Metropolitan (1991), directed by Otto Schenk and designed by Günther Schneider-Siemssen. This *Parsifal* belongs to a series of their Wagner productions that employ modern technology but do not take an oppositional stance to the composer's production conception. They are not, as is often misconceived, literal renderings of Wagner's stage directions. In their *Parsifal*, Gurnemanz plays a more active and supportive role in the Grail ceremonies than originally prescribed. And there is none of the gentle ecstasy in Kundry's death that Wagner intended; Kundry drops in an instant to the ground. In several regards, Otto Schenk's stage directions actually smooth out some of the non-traditional (for Wagner's time) dimensions of the original staging, particularly those that involve characters in altered states of consciousness. Director and designer Jean-Pierre Ponnelle also offered a relatively straightforward narrative in the spirit of a fairytale in Cologne in 1983. His production presented a medieval epic full of vivid onstage drama, with lively knights and an unquestioned hero.[83] While popular with audiences, such an approach can seem somewhat naïve in the context of so many other productions confronting "difficult" issues.

Wolfgang Wagner's second production of *Parsifal* can also be considered a straightforward interpretation, much like his first production, but with some different ideas in the area of design. The exterior natural

---

[83] Three years later, Ponnelle undertook a completely different production strategy, presenting *Parsifal* "in the round" in Toulouse.

settings of acts 1 and 3 were modernistic — serene but lifeless — and those for the Grail temple were geometrically primitive. The same graduated columns of the Grail temple framed Klingsor's appearance in act 2. This production was retired in 2001, after which *Parsifal* was not presented in Bayreuth for two consecutive seasons.[84] Christoph Schlingensief directed the new production in 2004, making many allusions to German South-West Africa (Namibia), with much of the cast in blackface. The chorus was wildly eclectic, featuring what appeared to be Osama bin Laden, Ghandi, Napoleon, Patton, and the like. Extensive use of digital projections contributed to an overabundance of references and fragmented narrative.

Many of the challenging issues that were thrust onto the stage in the later 1970s and early 1980s continue to resurface in new guises. Peter Konwitschny's 1995 *Parsifal* in Munich (his Wagner directing debut) considered the idea of misogyny with renewed intensity. For Konwitschny (son of the late conductor Franz Konwitschny), the exclusion of women from the Grail community is the central cause of its downfall. This idea formed the foundation of the staged interpretation, applied with a keen dramaturgical sense of logic from beginning to end. The remnant and reminder of the missing feminine element turns out to be the Grail itself. The sets by Johannes Leiacker are simple but leave room for impressive developments. The opening scene is set in a clinically bare white room with a tree lying on its side. Kundry makes her entrance riding on a wooden horse, using this tree as a ramp. During the transformation scene, the tree is lifted up to its full height and the entire floor rises to reveal a subterranean level with the knights gathered around the roots of the tree (see ill. 8.5). Rendering tangible the physical pain the wounded leader endures in leading the Grail service, Amfortas struggles up to ground level to open two Magritte-like secret doors on the side of the tree.[85] We later recognize that Amfortas is dressed like Klingsor. Inside the tree, a small chamber reveals a medieval tableau: two children bearing bread and wine, together with Kundry as a Madonna/whore image. When Kundry steps out of the tree and walks about, the knights are drawn to her

---

[84] Since the Second World War, *Parsifal* has been produced at Bayreuth annually except during the years between productions: 1974, 1986, 2002, and 2003. Considered together, Wolfgang Wagner's two stagings of *Parsifal* at Bayreuth were seen a total of 104 times, from 1975 to 1981 and 1989 to 2001. Wieland's production was mounted a total of 101 times between 1951 and 1973.

[85] René Magritte (1898–1967), Belgian surrealist painter, whose paintings display startling or amusing juxtapositions of the ordinary, the strange, and the erotic, depicted in a realistic manner.

Illustration 8.5: Bayerische Staatsoper, Munich, Peter Konwitschny's production (1995), act 1 (photo: Wilfried Hösl)

presence, although unable to see her, and they trace her motions with their hands on the ceiling. With Kundry idolized, nobody recognizes her fully as a human being. For Konwitschny, Kundry's death is completely tragic; she is consumed by a musical abyss and the knights abandon her body as they wander offstage.

Most *Parsifal* interpretations available on today's stages have shifted away from the straightforward kinds of Christian readings that flourished before the middle of the twentieth century. Skepticism continues to run high regarding the religious symbols themselves and/or Wagner's motivation for using them. It now comes as something of a shock to see unabashedly Christian images on the Wagnerian stage, especially if the designs are decidedly modern. That was precisely the path chosen by director Peter Stein and designer Gianni Dessi for their Salzburg/Edinburgh co-production (see ill. 8.6). In their second act, the garden setting for the seduction scene was richly symbolic, extending beyond the suggestion of Parsifal's Christ-like journey to conquer the evil within the maze. In designs of restrained classical purity, the drama unfolded without twists. With a hint neither of nostalgia nor of explicit critique, the Christian allusions were put forth for consideration without pre-judgment; a dazzling cross bloomed out of the final curtain. The production was poorly received at its Salzburg premiere (2002), but the reaction in Edinburgh was quite the contrary. Rare, given the more challenging recent interpretations of

Illustration 8.6: Osterfestspiele Salzburg, Peter Stein's production (2002),
Violeta Urmana shown as Kundry, Thomas Moser as Parsifal, (photo: Ruth Walz)

Parsifal, the audience was not expected to have achieved some critical distance from the original work prior to experiencing this production onstage.

Some Special Cases:
Recent Premieres and Co-Productions

Despite the great enthusiasm for Wagner in Russia before the First World War and the Soviet Revolution, only recently has there been a Wagner revival, enabling *Parsifal* to reach the professional stage. The performance of Wagner operas in the Soviet Union was irregular in the 1920s and charted an overall decline through the 1930s, when Hitler's well-known attachment to Wagner's works stimulated much skepticism. With the 1939 Nazi-Soviet pact, the notable film director Sergey Eisenstein was engaged for an avant-garde *Ring* project at the Bolshoi Theater that opened with *Die Walküre*. But the project was quickly abandoned when the Nazis invaded in June 1941. From the end of the 1940–41 season until 1991, only 18 staged performances of Wagner's operas took place in either Leningrad/St. Petersburg or Moscow.

Valery Gergiev set out to reclaim St. Petersburg's long-lost Wagner tradition when he assumed artistic directorship of the Mariinsky Theater/Kirov in 1988. His first endeavor in this regard was a production of *Parsifal* involving the British film director Tony Palmer, then already well-known for his 1982 film *Wagner*, featuring Richard Burton. Given the restricted, amateur nature of the first Russian *Parsifal* in 1913, the Palmer production that premiered at the Mariinsky in 1997 represents the country's first full-scale professional production. Somewhat modified, the production was remounted in 1998 at the Bolshoi (Palmer was the first Western director to work there) and at Savonlinna in Finland. The production is traditional by today's standards, but contains some suggestive touches. Yevgeny Lysyk's sets include an ornate backdrop with a gilt surface reminiscent of traditional Russian religious iconography. A variant of this backdrop serves for the seduction scene of act 2, evoking a more secular kind of decadence, while reminding us that Klingsor's realm and that of the Grail are closely linked on many levels. On the musical side, Gergiev and Palmer opted to use real bells for the Grail temple scenes — not a popular choice in a world of electronic alternatives, but one that offers the distinctive attack as the pitches are struck, as well as an impressive resounding envelope of sound. Palmer paid careful attention to representations of the feminine in the framing acts. In the grouping of squires who attend to Amfortas and assist in the Grail service, for instance, the female gender of the soprano was unquestionable.[86] This approach implies a gender correction, one that continues through to the opera's closing moments. As Parsifal begins to lead the Grail service, a handful of women dressed as penitents emerge, flanking the new leader and spreading flower petals about. Then, at the musical moment in which Kundry is to begin to sink, lifeless, to the ground, Palmer directs her to remain standing, steadfast and seemingly hopeful, with her hands held upwards.

Palmer incorporated excerpts of the Mariinsky production into his thought-provoking documentary entitled *Parsifal: The Search for the Holy Grail* (1998). This film, with background narrative and commentary by Plácido Domingo, includes interviews with several scholars that probe some of the issues bound up with the subject material. Robert Gutman focuses on prejudicial issues such as anti-Semitism. Towards the end of the film, however, specific interpretations of Wagner's treatment of the subject lead beyond the work itself, with Domingo and Palmer putting forth urgent questions about the relationship between life and art. The film changes directions as footage from the conclusion of the opera production is interlaced with excerpts from Ingmar Bergman's *The Seventh Seal* and Domingo's personal reflections. If, as is asserted, the opera's central message

---

[86] For the four squires, Wagner called for a soprano, an alto and two tenors; these roles are usually performed by two women and two men, although other variants are possible (for the first performance a female soprano was used together with three male singers). Wagner specifically requested that the squires be undistinguishable in their costuming and general physical appearance, and most productions today handle the female squires androgynously. This strategy reminds us of Wagner's combination of female and higher male voices in the invisible choruses, in which he wanted to avoid a strongly gendered representation.

of compassion is to have relevance to today's world, extending beyond the representation of the healing of a figure like Amfortas and the protection of a particular group of people, where should our sensibilities and compassion turn? At this juncture, contemporary singer Joan Osborne performs her 1995 song "One of Us," with lyrics that encourage tolerance and non-discrimination. This lurch into the musical future is spliced with live footage of children suffering from malnutrition and disease, and arresting glimpses of the effects of recent crimes against humanity.[87] While Palmer did not explicitly integrate such images and questions into his staged production — certainly too strong an approach given the context — his film urges us to reflect deeply upon what we experience in any performance of *Parsifal*.

Another case of a recent national premiere is the 2001 production of *Parsifal* by the State Opera of South Australia. One might expect such a premiere to take place under the auspices of Opera Australia at the Sydney Opera House, but their Wagner repertoire in recent decades has included all of the mature works except the *Ring* as a totality (a *Ring* cycle launched in the early 1980s was left incomplete) and *Parsifal*. Much earlier, Australian audiences could experience performances of the more ambitious Wagnerian repertoire by foreign touring companies. In 1913, the British Quinlan Company took their *Ring* production, complete with singers and orchestra, to Melbourne and Sydney, but further plans of a 1915 tour featuring *Parsifal* were cut short by war. A touring company organized by Benjamin Fuller, featuring British and Australian singers, announced the possibility of Australian performances of *Parsifal* in 1934 that never materialized. That same year *Parsifal* was at least, and at last, heard in full, on ABC radio.

Although Australia was respectful of the Berne copyright act in the early years of the twentieth century, she was not indifferent to the increase in English-language translations, commentaries, and adaptations of Wagner's *Parsifal* that appeared around the turn of the century. With so much attention paid to the Metropolitan production of *Parsifal*, it is hardly surprising to learn of spoken play versions (with musical interludes and other orchestral accompaniment, including some of Wagner's own music) being produced in New York within three months of the operatic premiere. By the end of 1904, the Edison Film Company released a twenty-minute film that seems indebted to one such play version, produced by Corse Payton in Brooklyn, as well as to the 1903 Metropolitan

---

[87] The version of the film initially released in the US was edited without the director's consent and does not feature some of this closing material. I am grateful to Tony Palmer for making an unedited copy of the film available to me and for providing me with information about his staged production and film.

production.[88] The Australian impresario J. C. Williamson capitalized on this heightened public interest when he contracted Hilhouse Taylor to write a drama entitled *Parsifal* that would feature the young American actress Minnie Tittell Brune as Kundry. The production premiered in Sydney in 1906, during the Christmas pantomime season, before playing in Melbourne. Taylor's *Parsifal* involved a full chorus and ballet, lavish scenery, and an orchestra that played an original score composed by Christian Helleman, prefaced by Wagner's own prelude.[89] Remarkable for its elaborate scene changes and lighting effects, particularly those involving electric light, the production remains of note in the history of Australian theater.

In contrast with the play versions produced in New York, and the Christian interpretations of Wagner's *Parsifal* that were widely maintained in the English-speaking world at this time, Taylor's adaptation was liberal and attempted to portray sexuality within a Christian perspective. Kundry, who neither dies, nor survives in obscure penitence, is the desired beloved of Amfortas throughout. At the end of the work Parsifal sends them on a soul-saving mission. Parsifal's role centers on reclaiming and returning the spear, together with Kundry. Another female character, Zana, portrays a truly unrepentant fallen woman; she is Klingsor's counterpart in an underworld that features vampire sirens and a frenzied "danse du diable." Taylor retained the religious elements of Wagner's *Parsifal* such as the Eucharist, the baptism, and Parsifal's sign of the cross after the collapse of Klingsor's garden. However, his representation of the love between Kundry and Amfortas as sexual was less a serious reinterpretation of Wagner's emphasis on asexual love than part of an agenda to offer titillating moments that would enhance controversy over the theatrical representation of religious subject matter and stimulate strong box-office sales.

Since Wagner's *Parsifal* had never been produced in Australia, there was no national production history to bear on the Australian premiere of Wagner's opera in 2001. The excitement of producing more ambitious Wagnerian repertoire began to build when Adelaide's State Opera of South Australia mounted a successful *Ring* in 1998, based on Pierre Strosser's Théâtre du Châtelet production (1994). Adelaide's production of *Parsifal*, directed by Elke Neidhardt, soon followed. Neidhardt eschewed polemics

---

[88] The film did not include any script on the screen but was sold together with a musical score for the piano. See Evan Baker's "'Parsifal' for the Stage and Screen in New York City, 1904," published together with German and French translations in the *Bayreuther Festspiele Programmheft 1996*, 144–61.

[89] Veronica Kelly, "J.C. Williamson Produces Parsifal, or the Redemption of Kundry: Wagnerism, Religion and Sexuality," *Theatre History Studies* 15 (1995), 161–81.

and also avoided an intensely Christian or solemn approach to the work, even allowing allusions to Busby Berkeley-style choreography in the seduction scene of act 2. For the most part, Carl Friedrich Oberle's sets were minimalist and austere; mirrored panels framing the stage were used for projections, such as for the dying swan, and for various lighting effects. Amfortas carried around a large unidentified book, which the Grail knights all dutifully touched, while the Grail itself was represented by a narrow cone of red light emanating from a pedestal. In the opera's final moments this light opened out to embrace the audience, as did Kundry's gaze as she stood at the front of the stage, apparently transformed.

It is easy to understand decisions to build new productions of *Parsifal* in places like St. Petersburg and Adelaide. Where *Parsifal* is less of a novelty, the rationale for supporting a production in repertory seems to be changing somewhat. Easter time still marks the performance frequency peak of the year, but fewer houses are able to maintain that tradition independently. Even if removed from the notion of a sacred Christian work outside the usual operatic sphere, *Parsifal* remains a complex, serious, and expensive work to produce. The idea of a narrowly focused interpretation — no matter how thrilling and stimulating that interpretation might seem to be at first — may diminish in appeal as a production is revived across several seasons to make the initial investment worthwhile. Such factors have surely contributed to the increase in the number of co-productions of *Parsifal* since the later 1980s. As in the early years of the twentieth century, productions of *Parsifal* are again crossing continents and oceans, not as autonomously operated tours or as rentals of pre-existing productions, but as major shared artistic and financial ventures between opera companies.

Robert Wilson's *Parsifal*, co-produced by the Hamburg State Opera and Houston Grand Opera, began its life as a production intended to premiere in Kassel in 1981. That project never reached fruition; nor did Wilson's discussions with Wolfgang Wagner concerning the centenary production at Bayreuth. Then in 1987, Wilson collaborated with writer Tankred Dorst on *Parzifal: Auf den anderen Seite des Sees* (Parzival: On the Other Side of the Lake), a play based on Eschenbach's version of the legend. By the time Wilson's production of Wagner's *Parsifal* premiered in 1991, the director/designer had been thinking about the work for quite some time. The production was unusual at the time, in that it was conceived as a trans-Atlantic co-production.[90] The North American premiere took place in Wilson's native Texas, at the Houston Grand Opera in 1992.

---

[90] An example of another trans-Atlantic *Parsifal* — a revival, not a co-production — was the 1982 La Fenice production designed and directed by Pier Luigi Pizzi, which was mounted at the Chicago Lyric Opera in 1986.

Illustration 8.7: Houston Grand Opera, Robert Wilson's production (1991),
Harry Peeters shown as Gurnemanz, Monte Pederson as Amfortas,
John Keyes as Parsifal, 1992 (photo: Jim Caldwell)

Nike Wagner regards Wilson as something of a latter-day Wieland Wagner. It has often been said that the integrated control of staging and design in Wilson's productions corresponds to Richard Wagner's concept of the *Gesamtkunstwerk*. His very distinctive production style involves elaborate lighting plans, while favoring a minimalist and not very time-specific approach to décor and costumes. Most particular is Wilson's direction of singers, whereby much that happens seems to be in slow motion. The precise and seemingly significant unnaturalistic gestures usually remain enigmatic. They are reminiscent of gestural traditions in Noh-theater but one is unable to recognize a meaning-specific code. This is perhaps the respect in which Wilson stands most apart in his approach to *Parsifal*. His unwillingness to use traditional symbols, or to use symbols in traditional ways, can leave some audiences feeling ungrounded or unguided, and smacks of self-indulgence. In act 2, for example, Wilson created intricate and barely visible maneuvers for Kundry. During the seduction scene she uses a needle to trace the outline of Parsifal's arm, and she bites this needle at the moment of the kiss; no real kiss takes place. Wilson also initially avoided representing the spear in concrete terms (although he reverted to a traditional spear on a wire when the production moved to Houston). Yet there are many images in Wilson's *Parsifal* that demand contemplation. During the act 1 Transformation scene an iceberg appears and begins moving horizontally across the lake visible in the distance. Meanwhile, a large disk of light descends slowly until it meets the iceberg when Gurnemanz declares, "Du siehst, mein Sohn, zum Raum wird hier die Zeit" (You see, my son, here time becomes space). The iceberg, which houses a black Grail box, rises up through the disk (see ill. 8.7). Amfortas appears on the disk, strongly backlit at first so that only his silhouette is seen. Instead of having the knights onstage during the act 1 Grail scene, Wilson deployed them throughout the house — an interesting acoustical experiment given Wagner's own handling of the unseen choruses. In act 3, the knights appeared onstage in tall black costumes by Frida Parmeggiani. After their non-appearance in act 1, their massive wall-like formation in act 3 has added impact. Parsifal's initial appearance in black in this act is connected to the disk, which is initially black but returns to white as Parsifal recognizes that he will take on this new role. A further transformation occurs at the very end of the opera, when a fire takes the place of the iceberg in the center of the disk.

Wilson aims at a pervasive spirituality that for some enables a revelatory performance experience. In the case of *Parsifal,* he was more inspired by Wagner's interest in Buddhism than by strictly Christian symbols.[91] Until recently, Wilson's work was far better known in Europe than in the United States. In 1998, however, he offered a new production of *Lohengrin* at the Metropolitan, which, following on the heels of Dieter Dorn's *Tristan und Isolde* (1999), marked a break from the series of conservative Wagner productions directed by Otto Schenk and designed by Günther Schneider-Siemssen. Although Houston never revived Wilson's *Parsifal,* the production will see new life in Los Angeles, starting in November, 2005.

Another current director fond of restricted motion and a calculated slowness of gesture is Klaus Michael Grüber. His production of *Parsifal* premiered in Amsterdam in 1991, where it was revived several times. In the later 1990s it resurfaced as a co-production between the Théâtre du Châtelet in Paris, the Maggio Musical Fiorentino, and the Théâtre de la Monnaie in Brussels. More recently it was seen as another co-production between the Teatro Real in Madrid and London's Covent Garden (2001). Grüber's *Parsifal* counts today as the production presented by the largest number of professional opera companies. In this the production's overriding political correctness has probably played a role. Grüber has no ideological axe to grind and seemingly no intention to provoke. He carefully sidesteps religious issues, and avoids representing the Grail as a communion cup by recourse to earlier versions of the legend. The Grail is thus a luminous crystal and the knights do not drink from their cups during the Grail

---

[91] Also in 1991, Klaus Hoffmeyer directed a production with designer Lars Juhl in Aarhus, Denmark that depicted the knights as Buddhist monks.

Illustration 8.8: The Royal Opera, Covent Garden, Klaus Michael Grüber's
production (1991), Thomas Hampson shown as Amfortas,
Stig Andersen as Parsifal, 2002 (photo: Clive Barda)

service. Historical distance is also achieved through an emphasis on
medieval elements. The chorus of knights is both threatening and haunting when they come onto the stage in the third act wheeling upright suits
of armor in front of them. Titurel, too, is suited in armor; doubling as a
coffin, it conceals his corpse from view. Throughout, Amfortas wears a
straight prosthesis that extends from his right shoulder to a wheel that rests
on the ground. This serves as a constant visual reminder that Amfortas's
actions entailed a great loss, a connection that is reinforced when Parsifal
returns the spear and heals his open wound (see ill. 8.8).

   This production features many interesting theatrical touches, although
they often lack a convincing relation to the actual work. An impressive
moment occurs in the act 1 Grail scene when a broad table in the manner
of Leonardo's *Last Supper* slides out of the wings to fill the breadth of
the stage, which in the case of Amsterdam is very wide indeed.[92] Potential
religious symbolism here is in conflict with the representation of the Grail

---

[92] The *Last Supper* image involving a broad table as opposed to the circular form
used in the original production has been a choice amongst directors and designers
since at least the 1968 Hamburg production directed by Hans Hotter and
designed by Rudolf Heinrich.

as a crystal. For the most part, the tendency of this production to strike essentially static tableaux calls too much attention to its dramaturgically loose imagery. Gilles Aillaud's sets for act 2 include a shark hanging over Klingsor's head, while the Flowermaidens scene is a confused underwater mobile-like world quoting Calder, Miró, and perhaps Klee.

Another recent co-production that develops alternate images from the Grail legend sources is the one directed by Nikolaus Lehnhoff and designed by Raimund Bauer. The opening scene of this post-apocalyptic setting shows a large meteorite lodged in the rear wall. In the Grail scenes themselves no physical object such as a chalice is present, but an unearthly yellow light glows through vertical strips in the curved back wall. The knights themselves show little joy in the Grail service, and there is an underlying uncertainty and sense of fear throughout. Another feature of this production that stems from Grail sources is the sense of tension between Christianity and a specifically Muslim realm. The production opened at the English National Opera in London in 1999, then in San Francisco in 2000, and at the Chicago Lyric Opera in 2002; as performed in Baden-Baden in 2004, the production is now available on DVD (Opus Arte). The Christian/Muslim dimension resonated in chillingly new ways after the terrorist events of the previous September. Lehnhoff's production differs substantially from Grüber's in that he opts not for picturesque tableaux but for a continuous development of the drama and characters.[93] In the seduction scene, Kundry undergoes a metamorphosis whereby she first sheds a large shell (costumes designed by Andrea Schmidt-Futterer) akin to an upside-down tulip that conceals her human body apart from her head. She continues her appeals wearing a dress that appears like a formal gown with cape but with recognizable petal-like shapes and detailing. This too she sheds, as if writhing out of a cocoon, to reveal a simple sheath that clings to her female form. Her appearance for most of the scene is explicitly contrived and lacking in conventional beauty. Several productions in recent decades have portrayed the Flowermaidens as prostitutes, emphasizing the power relation between them and Klingsor. In such cases the women are often represented not as natural beauties but in a more lurid manner. Lehnhoff's approach enables another facet of the scene to be realized, namely Kundry's lingering reluctance to fill her role together with her gradually increasing compulsion and need to seduce Parsifal, which is so carefully built up in the text and musical unfolding.

---

[93] Grüber's use of restricted gestures and fondness for slow rates of change, as well as stillness, are vulnerable when they lead to uninspired repetitions of actions seemingly casual and meaningless. Robert Wilson is especially particular about personally rehearsing the revivals of his productions, in addition to the premieres, so that the gestural level maintains dramatic tension.

Illustration 8.9: Chicago Lyric Opera, Nikolaus Lehnhoff's production (1999), Gösta Winberg shown as Parsifal, Matti Salminen as Gurnemanz, Catherine Malfitano as Kundry, 2002 (photo: Dan Rest)

The concluding scene of Lehnhoff's production involves more inter-pretation than most. Amfortas passes his crown to Parsifal before dying. Parsifal in turn places the crown on Titurel's corpse, which is represented onstage. Initially, the knights seem to form a unified group when Parsifal returns the spear (see ill. 8.9). But it turns out to be Gurnemanz, rather than Parsifal, who takes up the position of Grail leader. He is surrounded by a group of knights as Parsifal and Kundry exit the stage on a stretch of railway track that curves off into the wings into a bright beam of light. The potentially positive image of them walking towards a light is called into question by the terrible signifying power of railway tracks leading to an unknown destination. One cannot help but feel a terrible ambivalence when the knights gathered around Gurnemanz start to break away, one by one, and set out along the railway path as the music draws to a close.

As *Parsifal* moves into the twenty-first century, ever-changing historical contexts invite us back to this most complex of Wagner's operas to re-examine central issues afresh. The nature of closed societies, issues of gender, leadership, and the exercise of power — all of these remain of vital concern, as does the core notion of compassion as a redeeming quality. There is now clearly room on the world's stages for interpretive approaches of varying intensity and a plethora of concluding impressions. Having taken its place as a serious musical-dramatic piece in the operatic repertoire, and having shed some of its peculiar early performance restrictions and preconceptions, *Parsifal* has proven to be an uncommonly meaningful and enduring artwork.

Works Cited

Abbate, Carolyn. *Unsung Voices: Opera and Musical Narrative in the Nineteenth Century.* Princeton: Princeton UP, 1991.

Aberbach, Alan David. *Wagner's Religious Ideas: A Spiritual Journey.* Lewiston, NY: E. Mellen Press, 1996.

Adorno, Theodor W. *Versuch über Wagner.* Berlin: Suhrkamp, 1952.

———. "Zur Partitur des 'Parsifal.'" In vol. 4 of *Theodor W. Adorno: Musikalische Schriften.* Frankfurt: Suhrkamp, 1982. Reprinted in Csampai and Holland, *Richard Wagner: Parsifal: Texte, Materialien, Kommentare,* 191–95.

Ashman, Mike. "Producing Wagner." In Millington and Spencer, *Wagner in Performance,* 29–47.

———. "A Very Human Epic." In *Parsifal: Richard Wagner.* Opera Guide 34. London: ENO and Royal Opera, 1986.

Bailey, Robert. "The Genesis of 'Tristan und Isolde' and a Study of the Sketches and Drafts." PhD diss., Princeton University, 1969.

———. "The Method of Composition." In *The Wagner Companion,* edited by Peter Burbidge and Richard Sutton, 308–27. London: Faber & Faber, 1979.

———. *Prelude and Transfiguration from 'Tristan und Isolde.'* Norton Critical Score. New York: Norton, 1985.

———. "The Structure of the *Ring* and Its Evolution." *19th-Century Music* 1 (1977): 48–61.

Baker, Evan. "'Parsifal' for the Stage and Screen in New York City, 1904." In *Bayreuther Festspiele Programmheft 1996,* 144–61.

———. "Wagner and the Ideal Theatrical Space." In *Opera in Context: Essays in Historical Staging from the Late Renaissance to the Time of Puccini,* edited by Mark A. Radice, 241–78. Portland: Amadeus, 1998.

Barber, Richard. *The Holy Grail: Imagination and Belief.* Cambridge, Mass.: Harvard UP, 2004.

Barone, Anthony. "Richard Wagner's *Parsifal* and the Theory of Late Style." *Cambridge Opera Journal* 7 (1995): 37–54.

Barth, Herbert, Dietrich Mack, and Egon Voss, eds. *Wagner: A Documentary Study.* Translated by P. R. J. Ford and Mary Whittall. London: Thames and Hudson, 1975.

Bartlett, Rosamund. *Wagner and Russia.* Cambridge: Cambridge UP, 1995.

Bauer, Georg Oswald. "Prüfstein 'Parsifal.'" In *Bayreuther Festspiele Programmheft 1998*, 50–77.

———. *Richard Wagner: Die Bühnenwerke von der Uraufführung bis heute.* Frankfurt am Main: Propyläen, 1982.

Bauer, Hans-Joachim. *Wagners Parsifal: Kriterien der Kompositionstechnik.* Munich: Musikverlag E. Katzbichler, 1977.

Baumann, Carl-Friedrich. *Bühnentechnik im Festspielhaus Bayreuth.* Munich: Prestel, 1980.

Beckett, Lucy. *Richard Wagner: Parsifal.* Cambridge Opera Handbook. Cambridge: Cambridge UP, 1981.

Bergfeld, Joachim, ed. *Richard Wagner: Das braune Buch; Tagebuchaufzeichnungen 1865 bis 1882.* Zurich: Atlantis, 1975.

Bermbach, Udo. *Der Wahn des Gesamtkunstwerks: Richard Wagners politisch-ästhetische Utopie.* Frankfurt am Main: Fischer, 1994.

Bloomfield, Arthur. *The San Francisco Opera: 1922–1978.* Sausalito, CA: Comstock Editions, 1978.

Blumenberg, Hans. *Arbeit am Mythos.* Frankfurt am Main: Suhrkamp, 1979.

Bokina, John. *Opera and Politics: From Monteverdi to Henze.* New Haven and London: Yale UP, 1997.

Boor, Helmut de. *Die höfische Literatur: Vorbereitung, Blüte, Ausklang, 1170–1250.* Munich: Beck, 1953. 63–67; 90–114. Vol. 2 of *Geschichte der deutschen Literatur von den Anfängen bis zur Gegenwart,* ed. Helmut de Boor and Richard Newald. Munich: Beck, 1949–.

Borchmeyer, Dieter. *Drama and the World of Richard Wagner.* Princeton: Princeton UP, 2003.

———. "Erlösung und Apokatastasis: *Parsifal* und die Religion des späten Wagner." In *Richard Wagner: Ahasvers Wandlungen.* Frankfurt am Main: Insel, 2002.

———. *Das Theater Richard Wagners: Idee — Dichtung — Wirkung.* Stuttgart: Reclam, 1982.

Brinkmann, Reinhold. "Musikforschung und Musikliteratur: Eine Niederschrift von Improvisationen über ein so nicht gegebenes Thema." In *Wagnerliteratur, Wagnerforschung: Bericht über das Wagner-Symposium, München 1983,* edited by Carl Dahlhaus and Egon Voss, 150–55. Mainz: Schott, 1985.

Bujić, Bojan, ed. *Music in European Thought, 1851–1912.* Cambridge: Cambridge UP, 1988.

Bumke, Joachim. *Wolfram von Eschenbach.* 7th rev. ed. Sammlung Metzler 36. Stuttgart: Metzler, 1997.

Burnouf, Eugene. *Introduction à la histoire du Buddhisme indien.* Paris: Imprimerie royale, 1844.

Campbell, Joseph. *The Hero With a Thousand Faces.* Princeton: Princeton UP, 1972.

Carnegy, Patrick. "Designing Wagner: Deeds of Music Made Visible?" In Millington and Spencer, *Wagner in Performance*, 48–74.

Chamberlain, Houston Stewart. *Das Drama Richard Wagners*. Leipzig: Breitkopf & Härtel, 1921; In English: *The Wagnerian Drama*. London: John Lane The Bodley Head, 1923.

———. *Die Grundlagen des neunzehnten Jahrhunderts*. Munich: F. Bruckmann, 1899. In English: *The Foundations of the Nineteenth Century*. Translated by John Lees. London: John Lane The Bodley Head; New York: John Lane, 1911.

———. *Kriegsaufsätze*. Munich: F. Bruckmann, 1914.

———. *Lebenswege meines Denkens*. Munich: F. Bruckmann, 1919.

———. "Notes sur '*Parsifal.*'" *Revue wagnérienne* 7 (1886): 220–26.

———. *Parsifal Märchen*. Munich: F. Bruckmann, 1900.

———. *Politische Ideale*. Munich: F. Bruckmann, 1915.

———. *Richard Wagner*. Munich: F. Bruckmann 1895. In English: *Richard Wagner*. Translated by G. Ainslie Hight. London: J. M. Dent; Philadelphia: J. B. Lippincott, 1900.

Chytry, Joseph. *The Aesthetic State: A Quest in Modern German Thought*. Berkeley and Los Angeles: U of California P, 1989.

Cicora, Mary. *Parsifal Reception in the Bayreuther Blätter*. New York: Peter Lang, 1987.

Clampitt, David. "Alternative Interpretations of Some Measures from *Parsifal*." *Journal of Music Theory* 42/2 (1998): 321–34.

Cohn, Richard. "As Wonderful as Star Clusters: Instruments for Gazing at Tonality in Schubert." *19th-Century Music* 22/3 (1999): 213–32.

———. "Introduction to Neo-Riemannian Theory: A Survey and a Historical Perspective." *Journal of Music Theory* 42/2 (1998): 167–80.

———. "Maximally Smooth Cycles, Hexatonic Systems, and the Analysis of Late-Romantic Triadic Progressions." *Music Analysis* 15/1 (1996): 9–40.

Corse, Sandra. *Operatic Subjects: The Evolution of Self in Modern Opera*. Madison and Teaneck: Fairleigh Dickinson UP, 2000.

———. "*Parsifal*: Wagner, Nietzsche, and the Modern Subject." *Theatre Journal* 46 (1994): 95–110.

Csampai, Attila, and Dietmar Holland, eds. *Richard Wagner: Parsifal; Texte, Materialen, Kommentare*. Reinbek bei Hamburg: Rowohlt, 1984.

Dahlhaus, Carl. *Richard Wagners Musikdramen*. Velber: Friedrich, 1971. In English: *Richard Wagner's Music Dramas*. Translated by Mary Whittall. Cambridge: Cambridge UP, 1979.

Danuser, Hermann. "Musical Manifestations of the End in Wagner and Post-Wagnerian *Weltanschauungsmusik*." *19th-Century Music* 18/1 (1992): 64–82.

———, and Herfried Münkler, eds. *Zukunftsbilder: Richard Wagners Revolution und ihre Folgen in der Kunst und Politik*. Schliengen: Edition Argus, 2002.

Darcy, Warren. "Bruckner's Sonata Deformations." In *Bruckner Studies*, ed. Timothy L. Jackson and Paul Hawkshaw, 256–77. Cambridge: Cambridge UP, 1997.

———. "The Metaphysics of Annihilation: Wagner, Schopenhauer, and the Ending of the *Ring*." *Music Theory Spectrum* 16/1 (1994): 1–40.

———. "Rotational Form, Teleological Genesis, and Fantasy-Projection in the Slow Movement of Mahler's Sixth Symphony." *19th-Century Music* 25/1 (2001): 49–74.

———. *Wagner's 'Das Rheingold.'* Oxford: Clarendon, 1993.

Daverio, John. *Nineteenth-Century Music and the German Romantic Ideology.* New York: Schirmer, 1993.

Davis, Robert A. "The Truth Ineffably Divine: The Loss and Recovery of the Sacred in Richard Wagner's *Parsifal*." In *Voicing the Ineffable: Musical Representations of Religious Experience*, edited by Siglind Bruhn, 97–129. Hillsdate, NY: Pendragon, 2002.

Davis, Ronald L. *Opera in Chicago.* New York: Appleton Century, 1966.

Deathridge, John. "A Brief History of Wagner Research." In Müller and Wapnewski, *The Wagner Handbook*, 202–26.

———. "The Nomenclature of Wagner's Sketches." *Proceedings of the Royal Musical Association* 51 (1974–75): 75–83.

Deathridge, John, Martin Geck, and Egon Voss. *Wagner Werk-Verzeichnis (WWV): Verzeichnis der musikalischen Werke Richard Wagners und ihrer Quellen.* Mainz: Schott, 1986.

Dreyfus, Laurence. "Hermann Levi's Shame and *Parsifal's* Guilt: A Critique of Essentialism in Biography and Criticism." *Cambridge Opera Journal* 6/2 (1994): 125–45.

Eckhard, Meister. *Die deutschen Werke.* Vol. 1. Edited by Josef Quint. Stuttgart: Kohlhammer, 1936–76.

Eckert, Nora. *Parsifal 1914.* Hamburg: Europäische Verlagsanstalt, 2003.

Eschenbach, Wolfram von. *Parzival.* Edited by Walter Haug. Bibliothek des Mittelalters: Texte und Übersetzungen, vol. 8, nos. 1–2. Frankfurt am Main: Deutscher Klassiker Verlag, 1994.

Everett, Derrick. Monsalvat Index [on-line]. http://home.c2i.net/monsalvat/inxcommon.htm.

———. "Parsifal under the Bodhi Tree." In *Wagner* 22 (2001): 67–92.

Faerber, Uwe. "Über die musikalische Thematik des 'Parsifal.'" *Richard Wagner Blätter* 6 (1982): 17–31.

Fauche, Hippolyte, trans. *Ramayana, poeme sanscrit de Valmiki.* 9 vols. Paris: A. Frank, 1854–58.

Feuerbach, Ludwig. *Das Wesen des Christentums.* Leipzig: O. Wigand, 1841.

Field, Geoffrey G. *Evangelist of Race: The Germanic Vision of Houston Stewart Chamberlain.* New York: Columbia UP, 1981.

Friedrich, Sven. *Richard Wagner — Deutung und Wirkung.* Würzburg: Königshausen & Neumann, 2004.

Gaillard, Paul-André. "Der liturgische 'Schutt' im *Parsifal.*" In *Programmhefte der Bayreuther Festspiele 1965: "Parsifal,"* 38–46.

Geck, Martin, and Egon Voss, eds. *Dokumente zur Entstehung und ersten Aufführung des Bühnenweihfestspiels Parsifal.* Vol. 30 of Richard Wagner, *Sämtliche Werke.* Mainz: Schott, 1970.

Gfrörer, August Friedrich. *Geschichte des Urchristentums.* 3 vols. Stuttgart: E. Schweizerhart, 1838.

Gibson, Robert R. "Problematic Propaganda: 'Parsifal' as Forbidden Opera." In *Wagner* 20/2 (1999): 78–87.

Golther, Wolfgang. *Parzival und der Gral in der Dichtung des Mittelalters und der Neuzeit.* Stuttgart: J. B. Metzler, 1925.

——, ed. *Richard Wagner an Mathilde Wesendonk: Tagebuchblätter und Briefe 1853–1871.* Berlin: Alexander Duncker Verlag, 1910.

Görres, Joseph von. *Die christliche Mystik.* 5 vols. Regensburg: Manz, 1836–42.

Grunsky, Hans. "Die Symbolik der Parsifalmusik." In *Bayreuther Festspiele 1955: Programmheft,* 28–40.

Gutman, Robert W. *Richard Wagner: The Man, His Mind, and His Music.* New York: Harcourt, Brace and World, 1968.

Hamann, Brigitte. *Winifred Wagner oder Hitlers Bayreuth.* Munich and Zurich: Piper Verlag, 2002.

Hamp, Anton. *Ein Blick in die Geisteswerkstatt Richard Wagners: Von einem alten geistlichen Freunde des Meisters von Bayreuth zur Erinnerung an dessen Schwanengesang — den "Parzifal."* Berlin: A. Böhler, 1904.

Hartford, Robert, ed. *Bayreuth: The Early Years.* Cambridge: Cambridge UP, 1980.

Hartwich, Wolf-Daniel. "Jüdische Theosophie in Richard Wagners *Parsifal:* Vom christlichen Antisemitismus zur ästhetischen Kabbala." In *Richard Wagner und die Juden,* edited by Dieter Borchmeyer, Ami Maayani, and Susanne Vill, 103–22. Stuttgart: Metzler, 2000.

——. "Religion und Kunst beim späten Wagner: Zum Verhältnis von Ästhetik, Theologie und Anthropologie in den 'Regenerationsschriften.'" In *Jahrbuch der deutschen Schiller-Gesellschaft* 40 (1996): 297–323.

Haslam, Joy Calico. "The Politics of Opera in the German Democratic Republic, 1945–1961." PhD diss., Duke University, 1999.

Hasty, Will. "Performances of Love: Tristan and Isolde at Court." In *A Companion to Gottfried von Strassburg's "Tristan,"* 159–81.

——, ed. *A Companion to Gottfried von Strassburg's "Tristan."* Rochester: Camden House, 2003.

——, ed. *A Companion to Wolfram's "Parzival."* Columbia, SC: Camden House, 1999.

Hegel, Georg Wilhelm Friedrich. *Ästhetik*. Vols. 12–14 of his *Sämtliche Werke*, edited by Hermann Glockner. Stuttgart: Fr. Fromanns Verlag, 1949–63. In English: *Aesthetics: Lectures on Fine Art*. 2 vols. Translated by T. M. Knox. Oxford: Oxford UP, 1975.

Hellberg-Kupfer, Geerd. *Richard Wagner als Regisseur: Untersuchungen über das Verhältnis von Werk und Regie*. Berlin: Selbstverlag der Gesellschaft für Theatergeschichte, 1942.

Hepokoski, James. "The Essence of Sibelius: Creation Myths and Rotational Cycles in *Luonnotar*." In *The Sibelius Companion*, ed. Glenda Dawn Goss, 121–46. Westport, CT: Greenwood Press, 1996.

———. "Rotations, Sketches, and [Sibelius's] Sixth Symphony." In *Sibelius Studies*, ed. Timothy L. Jackson and Veijo Murtomaki, 322–51. Cambridge: Cambridge UP, 1993.

———. *Sibelius: Symphony No. 5*. Cambridge: Cambridge UP, 1993.

Hepokoski, James, and Warren Darcy. *Elements of Sonata Theory: Norms, Types, and Deformations in the Late Eighteenth-Century Sonata*. New York and Oxford: Oxford UP, 2005.

Holtzmann, Adolf. *Indische Sagen*. 2 vols. Stuttgart: A. Krabbe, 1854.

———, trans. *Rama, ein indisches Gedicht nach Walmiki*. Karlsruhe: G. Holtzmann, 1843.

Horowitz, Joseph. *Wagner Nights*. Berkeley: U of California P, 1994.

Hübner, Kurt. *Die Wahrheit des Mythos*. Munich: C. H. Beck, 1985.

Hyer, Bryan. "Reimag(in)ing Riemann." *Journal of Music Theory* 39/1 (1995): 101–38.

———. "Tonal Intuitions in *Tristan und Isolde*." PhD diss., Yale University, 1989.

Irvine, David. *Parsifal and Wagner's Christianity*. London: H. Grevel, 1899.

Jacobs, Heiko. *Die dramaturgische Konstruktion des Parsifal von Richard Wagner: von der Architektur der Partitur zur Architektur auf der Bühne*. Frankfurt am Main: Peter Lang, 2002.

Johnson, Sidney. "Doing His Own Thing: Wolfram's Grail." In *A Companion to Wolfram's "Parzival,"* ed. Will Hasty, 77–95.

Jung, Ute. *Die Rezeption der Kunst Richard Wagners in Italien*. Regensburg: Gustav Bosse Verlag, 1974.

Kelly, Veronica. "J.C. Williamson Produces Parsifal, or the Redemption of Kundry: Wagnerism, Religion and Sexuality." *Theatre History Studies* 15 (1995): 161–81.

Kesting, Hanjo, ed. *Richard Wagner: Briefe*. Munich: Piper, 1983.

Kienzle, Ulrike. "Komponierte Weiblichkeit im *Parsifal:* Kundry." In *Das Weib der Zukunft: Frauengestalten und Frauenstimmen bei Richard Wagner*, edited by Susanne Strasser-Vill, 153–90. Stuttgart: Metzler, 2000.

Kienzle, Ulrike. "Der vertriebene Gott: Über Glaube und Zweifel in Wagner's *Lohengrin*." *Programmhefte der Bayreuther Festspiele 2001*, ed. Wolfgang Wagner, 82–108.

——. *Das Weltüberwindungswerk: Wagners "Parsifal."* Thurnauer Schriften zum Musiktheater. Vol. 12. Laaber: Laaber, 1992.

Kinderman, William. "Dramatic Recapitulation and Tonal Pairing in Wagner's *Tristan* and *Parsifal*." In *The Second Practice of Nineteenth-Century Tonality*, edited by William Kinderman and Harald Krebs, 178–214. Lincoln: U of Nebraska P, 1996.

——. "Dramatic Recapitulation in Wagner's *Götterdämmerung*." *19th-Century Music* 4 (1980): 101–12.

——. "Die Entstehung der *Parsifal*-Musik." *Archiv fur Musikwissenschaft* 52 (1995): 66–97; 145–65.

——. "Das 'Geheimnis der Form' in Wagners 'Tristan und Isolde.'" *Archiv für Musikwissenschaft* 40 (1983): 174–88.

——. Review of Warren Darcy, *Wagner's "Das Rheingold."* *Music Theory Spectrum* 19 (1997): 81–86.

——. "Wagner's *Parsifal*: Musical Form and the Drama of Redemption." *The Journal of Musicology* (Fall 1986): 431–46; (Spring 1987): 315–16.

Kirsch, Winfried. "Richard Wagners biblische Szene *Das Liebesmahl der Apostel*." In *Geistliche Musik: Studien zu ihrer Geschichte und Funktion im 18. und 19. Jahrhundert*, 157–84. Hamburger Jahrbuch für Musikwissenschaft. Vol. 8. Laaber: Laaber, 1985.

Kloss, Erich, ed. *Briefwechsel zwischen Wagner und Liszt*. Leipzig: Breitkopf und Härtel, 1910.

Köhler, Joachim. *Nietzsche and Wagner: A Lesson in Subjugation*. Translated by Ronald Taylor. New Haven and London: Yale UP, 1998.

——. *Wagner's Hitler: Der Prophet und sein Vollstrecker*. Karl Blessing Verlag, 1997; In English: *Wagner's Hitler: The Prophet and his Disciple*. Translated by Ronald Taylor. Cambridge: Polity Press, 2000.

Köppen, Carl Friedrich. "Die Religion des Buddha und ihre Entstehung." In *Die Religion des Buddha*. 2 vols. Berlin: Schneider, 1857–59.

Koppen, Erwin. "Wagnerism as Concept and Phenomenon." In Müller and Wapnewski, *Wagner Handbook*, 343–53.

Kraft, Zdenko von. "Wahnfried and the Festival Theatre." In *The Wagner Companion*, edited by Peter Burbidge and Richard Sutton, 412–32. London: Faber & Faber, 1979.

Kratz, Henry. *Wolfram von Eschenbach's "Parzival": An Attempt at a Total Evaluation*. Bern: Francke, 1973.

Kropholler, Margaret, ed. *50 Jaar Wagnervereeniging*. Gedenkboek der Wagnervereeniging. Amsterdam: Gedrukt door van Munster's drukkerijen n.v, 1934.

Küng, Hans. "Wagner's *Parsifal:* A Theology for our Time." *Michigan Quarterly Review* 23 (1984), 311–33.

———. "Was kommt nach der Götterdämmerung? Über Untergang und Erlösung im Spätwerk Richard Wagners." *Programmhefte der Bayreuther Festspiele 1989:* 1(*Parsifal*): 22 ff.

Kupfer, Peter. Sortable GDR Production List. http://www.northfieldfineart.com/peter/gdrprod.html.

Langer, Susanne. *Philosophy in a New Key: A Study in the Symbolism of Reason, Rite, and Art.* Cambridge: Harvard UP, 1942.

Large, David C. "Posthumous Reputation and Influence." In *The Wagner Compendium,* edited by Barry Millington, 384–89. London: Thames and Hudson, 1992.

Large, David, and William Weber, eds. *Wagnerism in European Culture and Politics.* Ithaca and London: Cornell UP, 1984.

Levi, Erik. *Music in the Third Reich.* London: Macmillan Press, 1994.

Lewin, David. "Amfortas's Prayer to Titurel and the Role of D in *Parsifal:* The Tonal Spaces of the Drama and the Enharmonic C♭/B." *19th-Century Music* 7/3 (1984): 336–49.

———. "Some Notes on Analyzing Wagner: The *Ring* and *Parsifal.*" *19th-Century Music* 16/1 (1992): 49–57.

Lorenz, Alfred. *Das Geheimnis der Form bei Richard Wagner.* Vol. 4, *Der musikalische Aufbau von Richard Wagners Parsifal.* Berlin: Max Hesses Verlag, 1924; Reprint, Tutzing: Verlag Hans Schneider, 1966.

Magee, Bryan. *Schopenhauer.* Oxford: Clarendon, 1997.

———. *The Tristan Chord: Wagner and Philosophy.* New York: Henry Holt, 2002.

Mahnkopf, Claus-Steffen, ed. *Richard Wagner: Konstrukteur der Moderne.* Stuttgart: Klett-Cotta, 1999.

Mann, Thomas. "Leiden und Grösse Richard Wagners." In *Wagner und unsere Zeit,* edited by Erika Mann, 63–121. Frankfurt am Main: S. Fischer, 1963. In English: *Thomas Mann: Pro and Contra Wagner,* translated by Allan Blunden, 91–148. London: Faber, 1985.

Marget, Arthur W. "Liszt and *Parsifal.*" *Music Review* 14 (1953): 107–24.

Mayer, Hans. *Richard Wagner: Mitwelt und Nachwelt.* Stuttgart: Belser, 1978.

McClatchie, Stephen. *Analysing Wagner's Operas: Alfred Lorenz and German National Ideology.* Rochester: Boydell & Brewer, 1998.

McCreless, Patrick. "Motive and Magic: A Referential Dyad in *Parsifal.*" *Music Analysis* 9/3 (1990): 227–65.

McGlathery, James M. *Wagner's Operas and Desire.* North American Studies in German Literature, 22. New York and Berne: Peter Lang, 1998.

McPherson, Jim. "The Savage Innocents, Part 2: On the Road with *Parsifal, Butterfly,* the *Widow,* and the *Girl.*" In *The Opera Quarterly* 19/1 (Winter 2003): 28–63.

Mertens, Volker. "Richard Wagner und das Mittelalter." In Müller and Wapnewski, *Richard-Wagner-Handbuch,* 19–59.

Miller, Marion S. "Wagnerism in Italy." In Large and Weber, *Wagnerism in European Culture and Politics,* 167–97.

Millington, Barry, and Stewart Spencer, eds. *Wagner in Performance.* New Haven and London: Yale UP, 1992.

Morey, Carl. "The Music of Wagner in Toronto before 1914." In *Canadian University Music Review* 18/2 (1998): 25–37.

Müller, Ulrich. "Parzival und Parsifal: Vom Roman Wolframs von Eschenbach und vom Musikdrama Richard Wagners." In *Sprache-Text-Geschichte,* edited by Peter K. Stein, Renate Hausner, Gerold Hayer, Franz V. Spechtler, and Andreas Weiss, 479–502. Göppingen Arbeiten zur Germanistik 304. Göppingen: Kümmerle, 1980.

Müller, Ulrich, and Oswald Panagl. *Ring und Gral: Texte, Kommentare und Interpretationen zu Richard Wagners "Der Ring des Nibelungen," "Tristan und Isolde," "Die Meistersinger von Nürnberg" und "Parsifal."* Würzburg: Königshausen & Neumann, 2002.

Müller, Ulrich, and Peter Wapnewski, eds. *Richard-Wagner-Handbuch.* Stuttgart: Kröner, 1986. In English: Ulrich Müller and Peter Wapnewski, eds. *The Wagner Handbook.* Translation edited by John Deathridge. Cambridge: Harvard UP, 1992.

Murray, David R. "Major Analytical Approaches to Wagner's Style: A Critique." In *Music Review* 39 (1978): 211–22.

Nattiez, Jean-Jacques. *Wagner Androgyne: A Study in Interpretation.* Translated by Stewart Spencer. Princeton: Princeton UP, 1993.

Neef, Sigrid, and Hermann Neef. *Deutsche Oper im 20. Jahrhundert: DDR, 1949–1989.* Berlin and New York: Peter Lang, 1992.

Newcomb, Anthony. "The Birth of Music out of the Spirit of Drama." *19th-Century Music* 5 (1981): 38–66.

Newman, Ernest. *The Life of Richard Wagner.* 4 Vols. London: Cassell, 1933–47; New York: Knopf, 1946.

Nietzsche, Friedrich. *Nietzsche Werke: Kritische Gesamtausgabe.* Vol. 4. Edited by Giorgio Colli and Mazzino Montinari. Berlin: Walter de Gruyter, 1967.

Oberkogler, Friedrich. *Parsifal: Der Zukunftsweg des Menschen in Richard Wagners Musikdramen.* Stuttgart: Verlag Freies Geistesleben, 1983.

Overhoff, Kurt. *Die Musikdramen Richard Wagners.* Salzburg: Verlagsbuchhandlung Anton Pustet, 1967.

———. *Richard Wagners Parsifal.* Lindau im Bodensee: Werk-Verlag KG Franz Perneder, 1949.

Panovsky, Walter. *Wieland Wagner.* Bremen: Carl Schümann Verlag, 1964.

Petzet, Detta, and Michael Petzet. *Die Richard Wagner Bühne König Ludwigs II.* Munich: Prestel, 1970.

Pretzsch, Paul, ed. *Cosima Wagner und Houston Stewart Chamberlain im Briefwechsel, 1888–1908.* Leipzig: Philipp Reclam jun. Verlag, 1934.

Ralston, Gulliver. "David Irvine: The Case of a British Wagnerian." In *Wagner* 24/1 (2003): 23–43.

Rather, L. J. *Reading Wagner.* Baton Rouge: Louisiana State UP, 1990.

Rauschning, Hermann. *Gespräche mit Hitler.* Zurich: Europa Verlag A.G., 1940.

Regier, Willis. *Book of the Sphinx.* Lincoln and London: U of Nebraska P, 2004.

Reinhardt, Hartmut. "Wagner and Schopenhauer." Translated by Erika and Martin Swales. In Müller and Wapnewski, *Wagner Handbook,* 287–96.

Reinhardt, Heinrich. *Parsifal: Studien zur Erfassung des Problemhorizonts von Richard Wagners letztem Drama.* Straubing: Donau, 1979.

Richard Wagner: Parsifal. Musik-Konzepte 25. Munich: Text + Kritik, 1982.

Roch, Eckhard. *Psychodrama: Richard Wagner im Symbol.* Stuttgart and Weimar: J. B. Metzler, 1995.

Rosenberg, Alfred. *Der Mythus des 20. Jahrhunderts.* Munich: Hoheneichen Verlag, 1939.

———. *Selected Writings.* Edited by Robert Pois. London: Jonathan Cape, 1970.

Rosenthal, Bernice Glatzer. "Wagner and Wagnerian Ideas in Russia." In Large and Weber, *Wagnerism in European Culture and Politics,* 198–245.

Rosenthal, Harold. *Two Centuries of Opera at Covent Garden.* London: Putnam, 1958.

Rupp, Heinz, ed. *Wolfram von Eschenbach.* Wege der Forschung, vol. 57. Darmstadt: Wissenschaftliche Buchgesellschaft, 1966.

Schmidt, Alfred. *Die Wahrheit im Gewande der Lüge: Schopenhauers Religionsphilosophie.* Munich: Piper, 1986.

Schopenhauer, Arthur. *Preisschrift über die Grundlage der Moral.* Hamburg: F. Meiner, 1979.

———. *Die Welt als Wille und Vorstellung.* Edited by Heinrich Schmidt. 2 vols. Leipzig: Alfred Kröner Verlag, 1911. In English: *The World as Will and Representation.* Translated by E. F. J. Payne. 2 vols. New York: Dover, 1966.

Schüler, Winfried. *Der Bayreuther Kreis von seiner Entstehung bis zum Ausgang der wilhelminischen Ära.* Münster: Aschendorff, 1971.

Schulze, Ursula. "Stationen der Parzival-Rezeption: Strukturveränderung und ihre Folgen." In *Mittelalter-Rezeption: Ein Symposium,* edited by Peter Wapnewski, 555–80. Stuttgart: Metzler, 1986.

Skelton, Geoffrey. *Wagner in Thought and Practice.* Portland, OR: Amadeus, 1992.

Spotts, Frederic. *Bayreuth: A History of the Wagner Festival.* New Haven and London: Yale UP, 1994.

Spotts, Frederic. *Hitler and the Power of Aesthetics*. Woodstock and New York: Overlook, 2002.

Stein, Leon. *The Racial Thinking of Richard Wagner*. New York: Philosophical Library, 1950.

Strauss, David Friedrich. *Das Leben Jesu*. Tübingen: C. F. Osiander, 1835–36.

Suneson, Carl. *Richard Wagner und die indische Geisteswelt*. Leiden and New York: E. J. Brill, 1989.

Syer, Katherine. *Altered States: Musical and Psychological Processes in Wagner*. PhD. diss., University of Victoria, Canada, 1999.

Tanner, Michael. *Wagner*. Princeton: Princeton UP, 1996.

Thorau, Christian. *Semantisierte Sinnlichkeit: Studien zu Rezeption und Zeichenstruktur der Leitmotivtechnik Richard Wagners*. Stuttgart: Franz Steiner Verlag, 2003.

Todd, R. Larry. "Mendelssohn." In *The Nineteenth-Century Symphony*, ed. D. Kern Holoman, 78–107. New York: Schirmer, 1997.

Treadwell, James. *Interpreting Wagner*. New Haven and London: Yale UP, 2003.

Troyes, Chrétien de. *Le roman de Perceval ou le conte du Graal*. Geneva: Librairie Droz; Lille: Librairie Giard, 1956. In English: *Perceval: The Story of the Grail*. Translated by Burton Raffel. New Haven and London: Yale UP, 1999.

Tucker, Gillian. "Wagner's Individual Sketches for *Parsifal*." *Proceedings of the Royal Musical Association* 60 (1983–84): 91–110.

Viereck, Peter. *Metapolitics: from the Romantics to Hitler*. New York: A. A. Knopf, 1941. Republished in revised and expanded form as *Metapolitics: the Roots of the Nazi Mind*. New York: Capricorn Books, 1961 and 1965. Again republished in expanded form as *Metapolitics: From Wagner and the German Romantics to Hitler*. New Brunswick, NJ: Transaction Publishers, 2004.

Vill, Susanne. "Kunstreligion und Lebenskunst: zur Aktualität von Richard Wagners Bühnenweihfestspiel." In *"Und Jedermann erwartet sich ein Fest": Fest, Theater, Festspiele; Gesammelte Vorträge des Salzburger Symposions 1995*, edited by Peter Csobádi, Gernot Gruber, and Jürgen Kühnel, 137–49. Anif/Salzburg: Verlag Müller-Speiser, 1996.

Voss, Egon. *Studien zur Instrumentation Richard Wagners*. Regensburg: G. Bosse, 1970.

———. "Wagners 'Parsifal' — das Spiel von der Macht der Schuldgefühle." In Csampai and Holland, *Richard Wagner: Parsifal; Texte, Materialien, Kommentare*, 9–18. In English: "'*Parsifal*' and the power of feelings of guilt." *Wagner* 26 (January 2005): 22–32.

Wagner, Cosima. *Cosima Wagner: Die Tagebücher*. Edited by Martin Gregor-Dellin and Dietrich Mack. 2 vols. Munich and Zurich: Piper, 1977. In English: *Cosima Wagner's Diaries*. Translated by Geoffrey Skelton. 2 vols. New York and London: Harcourt Brace Jovanovich, 1980.

Wagner, Nike. *Wagner Theater*. Frankfurt am Main and Leipzig: Insel Verlag, 1998. In English: *The Wagners: The Dramas of a Musical Dynasty*. Translated by Ewald Osers and Michael Downes. Princeton: Princeton UP, 1998.

Wagner, Richard. *Actors and Singers.* Translated by W. Ashton Ellis. Lincoln and London: U of Nebraska P, 1995.

———. *Beethoven.* Leipzig: Verlag von E. W. Fritzsch, 1870.

———. "Das Bühnenweihfestspiel in Bayreuth 1882." Vol. 10 of *Gesammelte Schriften und Dichtungen.* In English: *Religion and Art,* translated by W. Ashton Ellis. Lincoln and London: U of Nebraska P, 1994.

———. *Gesammelte Schriften und Dichtungen.* 10 vols. Leipzig: C. F. W. Siegel, 1871–83.

———. *Mein Leben.* Edited by Martin Gregor-Dellin. Munich: Paul List, 1963. In English: *My Life.* Translated by Andrew Gray. New York: Da Capo, 1992.

———. *Oper und Drama.* Edited by Klaus Kropfinger. Stuttgart: Reclam, 1984.

———. *Parsifal.* New York: Dover, 1986. (A republication of the full score issued by C. F. Peters, Leipzig, n.d.)

———. *Parsifal: Ein Bühnenweihfestspiel in drei Aufzügen.* Edited by Wilhelm Zentner. Stuttgart: Philipp Reclam, 1974.

———. *Parsifal: Klavierauszug mit Text von Felix Mottl.* Ed. Felix Mottl. Leipzig: Peters, 1914.

———. *Sämtliche Schriften und Dichtungen.* 16 vols. Leipzig: Breitkopf und Härtel, 1912–14.

———. *Sämtliche Werke.* Edited by Martin Geck and Egon Voss. 31 vols. Mainz: Schott, 1970–.

Walker, Alan. *Franz Liszt.* 3 vols. New York: Knopf, 1996.

Wapnewski, Peter. "Mittler des Mittelalters." In *Tristan der Held Richard Wagners,* 33–63. Berlin: Severin und Siedler, 1981.

———. "Die Oper Richard Wagners als Dichtung." In Müller and Wapnewski, *Richard-Wagner-Handbuch,* 331–46.

———. *Der traurige Gott: Richard Wagner in seinen Helden.* Munich: Beck, 1978; Deutscher Taschenbuch Verlag, 1982.

Weiner, Marc A. *Richard Wagner and the Anti-Semitic Imagination.* Lincoln: U of Nebraska P, 1995.

Wessling, Berndt, ed. *Bayreuth im Dritten Reich: Richard Wagners politische Erben; Eine Dokumentation.* Weinheim and Basel: Beltz Verlag, 1983.

Westernhagen, Curt von. *Richard Wagners Dresdener Bibliothek 1842 bis 1849.* Wiesbaden: F. A. Brockhaus, 1966.

———. *Wagner: A Biography.* Translated by Mary Whittall. Cambridge: Cambridge UP, 1978.

Whittall, Arnold. "The Music." In Beckett, *Richard Wagner: Parsifal,* 61–86.

———. "Wagner and Real Life." *The Musical Times* 137 (June 1996): 5–11.

Williams, Simon. *Wagner and the Romantic Hero.* Cambridge: Cambridge UP, 2004.

Woerdehoff, Berharde. "Bruder des Bleistifts." *Die Zeit* 45 (10 November 1989).

Wolzogen, Hans von. "Richard Wagner. Parzival bei Tristan." *Bayreuther Blätter* 38 (1915): 145–47.

———. *Thematischer Leitfaden durch die Musik des "Parsifal" nebst einem Vorworte über den Sagenstoff des Wagner'schen Dramas.* Leipzig: Gebrüder Senf, 1882.

Zegowitz, Bernd. *Richard Wagners unvertonte Opern.* Frankfurt am Main: Peter Lang, 2000.

Zelinsky, Hartmut. "Die 'Feuerkur' des Richard Wagner oder die 'neue Religion' der 'Erlösung' durch 'Vernichtung.'" In *Richard Wagner: Wie antisemitisch darf ein Künstler sein?* edited by Heinz-Klaus Metzger and Rainer Riehn, 79–112. Musik-Konzepte 5. Munich: Text + Kritik, 1978.

———. "Rettung ins Ungenaue: Zu Martin Gregor-Dellins Wagner-Biographie." In *Richard Wagner: Parsifal,* edited by Heinz-Klaus Metzger and Rainer Riehn, 74–113. Musik-Konzepte 25. Munich: Text + Kritik, 1982.

———. *Richard Wagner: Ein deutsches Thema; Eine Dokumentation zur Wirkungsgeschichte Richard Wagners 1876–1976.* Frankfurt am Main: Zweitausendeins, 1976.

Contributors

ROGER ALLEN is Research Fellow and Tutor in Music at St Peter's College and Lecturer at St Edmund Hall in the University of Oxford. He is editor of *Wagner,* the journal of the Wagner Society of London, and is currently completing a new translation and critical edition of Wagner's essay "Beethoven"; his analytical work includes a study of syntactical issues in later works of Wagner and Bruckner.

MARY A. CICORA has strong interests in literature and music and has written several books on Wagner, including *Parsifal Reception in the Bayreuther Blätter* (1987), *Mythology as Metaphor* (1998), *Wagner's "Ring" and German Drama* (1999), and *Modern Myths and Wagnerian Deconstructions: Hermeneutic Approaches to Wagner's Music-Dramas* (2000).

WARREN DARCY, Professor of Music Theory and former Director of the Music Theory Division at Oberlin College Conservatory, is author of several studies of Wagner, including the monograph *Wagner's "Das Rheingold,"* published by Oxford University Press (1993), which won the 1995 SMT Wallace Berry Award. He is currently working on a large study of rotational procedures in the symphonies of Mahler.

ULRIKE KIENZLE teaches at the University of Frankfurt am Main, and is the author of *Das Weltüberwindungswerk: Wagners 'Parsifal' — ein szenisch-musikalisches Gleichnis der Philosophie Arthur Schopenhauers* (Laaber, 1992). She is an editor for the journal *Wagner Spectrum,* and is currently writing a book on *Philosophy and Religion in the Music Dramas of Wagner* (Würzburg: Königshavsen & Neumann, 2005).

WILLIAM KINDERMAN is Professor of Musicology at the University of Illinois at Urbana-Champaign. He is the author of several studies of Wagner, and is writing a book on *Parsifal.* Together with Katherine Syer, he often leads a seminar in conjunction with the Wagner Festival at Bayreuth.

JAMES M. MCGLATHERY, Professor Emeritus of German and Comparative Literature at the University of Illinois, has written books on E. T. A. Hoffmann, Heinrich von Kleist, Grimm's fairy tales, and Wagner. His history of criticism on Grimm's fairy tales (1993) and an edited volume of essays on music and German literature (1992) were published by Camden House.

KATHERINE R. SYER teaches at the University of Illinois at Urbana-Champaign. She specializes in Wagner's works and in the history of opera production, and is currently completing a book entitled *Altered States: Psychological and Musical Processes in Wagner.*

Index

Mahler, Gustav, 296
Makart, Hans, 287
Mann, Thomas, 261, 309
Manthey, Axel, 325
Marget, Arthur, 22
Matačić, Lovro von, 312
Mayer, Hans, 52
McClatchie, St ephen, 4 n
McCreless, Patrick, 174 n, 201 n
Melchinger, Ulrich, 314, 321
Meleans (in Wolfram's *Parzival*), 64
Mendelssohn, Felix, 19, 113
Merrill, Nathaniel, 312 n
Mertens, Volker, 42
Miller, Jonathan, 314
Millington, Barry, 276, 318 n
Montsalvat, 31, 96, 261
Mottl, Felix, 123 n, 249
Mozart, Wolfgang Amadeus,
   Don Giovanni, 192–94
Mysterienspiel, 42
myth, 5–8, 29, 33, 81, 89, 95
Muck, Karl, 274, 288, 296, 300
Müller, Ulrich, 36, 41
Müller Godesberg, 303
Mussbach, Peter, 326

National Socialism, 4, 174 n, 246,
   270 n, 276, 300–301, 304 n, 305 n,
   306 n, 317–18, 322–23
Nattiez, Jean-Jacques, 24 n, 209 n
Naumann, Johann Gottlieb, 19
Naville, Claude, 321
Neidhardt, Elke, 332–33
Neo-Riemannian Theory, 220–24,
   234–35, 239–41
Neumann, Angelo, 278
Newcomb, Anthony, 4
Newman, Ernest, 309
Nietzsche, Friedrich, 2, 18, 255,
   272
nirvana, 89, 100, 129–30
Novalis. *See* Hardenberg, Georg
   Friedrich Philipp von

O'Hearn, Robert, 312 n
Obie (in Wolfram's *Parzival*), 64
Obilot (in Wolfram's *Parzival*), 64–65

Orgeluse (in Wolfram's *Parzival*), 13,
   38, 43–45, 48–50, 65–68, 76,
   78–79
Ortrud (in Wagner's *Lohengrin*), 9, 84
Osborne, Joan, 331
Oswald, Roberto, 312, 315 n
Overhoff, Kurt, 24 n, 308–9

Palestrina, Giovanni Pierluigi da, 113
Pallini, Tina Sestini, 312
Palmer, Tony, 295 n, 329–31
Parmeggiani, Frida, 335
Parsifal/Parzival (in Wagner's
   Parsifal), 2, 8, 11–13, 16–18,
   24–26, 31–32, 37–43, 48–51, 53,
   55, 77–79, 93–94, 100–103, 112,
   121, 123–26, 129, 167, 170, 181,
   187, 189, 203–4, 213–15, 218,
   234–40, 260, 290, 317, 321–23,
   325–26, 332–33, 335, 338
Parzival (in Wolfram's *Parzival*), 6, 7,
   10, 12, 35–44, 48–51, 68–75, 78,
   82, 101
Payton, Corse, 331
Peduzzi, Richard, 317
Perceval (in Chrétien's *Perceval*),
   55–56, 59–62
phenomenal music, 177–94
Pirchan, Emil, 304
Piscator, Erwin, 304
Pizzi, Pier Luigi, 333 n
Poettgen, Ernst, 312
polarity of diatonic and chromatic
   music, 23–24, 121, 174, 218–19
polarization (of opinions about
   Parsifal), 1–4
Ponnelle, Jean-Pierre, 326
Porges, Heinrich, 24, 25 n, 124,
   202 n, 205
Possart, Ernst von, 281, 291
Preetorius, Emil, 300–305, 308
Puccini, Giacomo, 292

Quell, Frank de, 312

racism, 246, 262–63, 266, 269, 270 n,
   272–73
Rather, L. J., 270 n